THE PICKERING MASTERS

THE WORKS OF DANIEL DEFOE

General Editors:
W. R. Owens and P. N. Furbank

WRITINGS ON TRAVEL, DISCOVERY AND HISTORY
BY DANIEL DEFOE

WRITINGS ON TRAVEL, DISCOVERY AND HISTORY BY DANIEL DEFOE

General Editors: W. R. Owens and P. N. Furbank

Volume 4:
A GENERAL HISTORY OF DISCOVERIES
AND IMPROVEMENTS (1725–6)
and
AN ESSAY UPON LITERATURE (1726)

Edited by
P. N. Furbank

Routledge
Taylor & Francis Group
LONDON AND NEW YORK

First published 2001 by Pickering & Chatto (Publishers) Limited

Published 2016 by Routledge
2 Park Square, Milton Park, Abingdon, Oxon OX14 4RN
711 Third Avenue, New York, NY 10017, USA

Routledge is an imprint of the Taylor & Francis Group, an informa business

BRITISH LIBRARY CATALOGUING IN PUBLICATION DATA
Defoe, Daniel, 1660 or 1–1731
  Writings on Travel, Discovery and History by Daniel Defoe
  Part 1 editors, W. R. Owens, P. N. Furbank. – (The Pickering Masters)
  1. Defoe, Daniel, 1660 or 1–1731 – Journeys 2. Great Britain – Description and
  travel 3. Great Britain – History – 18th century
  I. Title II. Owens, W. R. III. Furbank, P. N. (Philip Nicholas)
  914.1'071

LIBRARY OF CONGRESS CATALOGING-IN-PUBLICATION DATA
Defoe, Daniel, 1661?–1731.
  Writings on Travel, Discovery and History by Daniel Defoe / general editors, W. R.
Owens and P. N. Furbank.
  p. cm. – (The works of Daniel Defoe) (The Pickering Masters)
  Contents: v. 1. A tour thro' Great Britain, part I / edited by John McVeagh – v. 2. 1. A
tour thro' Great Britain, part II / edited by John Mc Veagh – v. 3. A tour thro' Great Britain,
part III / edited by John McVeagh – v. 4. A general history of discoveries: an essay upon
literature / edited by P. N. Furbank

  1. Great Britain–Description and Travel–Early works to 1800. I. Owens, W. R. II. Furbank, Philip Nicholas. III. McVeagh, John. Title. V. Series.

DA620 .D31 2001
941.06'9–dc21

                                                                                    2001032197

ISBN-13: 978-1-85196-718-6 (set)

Typeset by P&C

CONTENTS

INTRODUCTION

In the summer of 1713, Defoe embarked on a *General History of Trade,* to be published in four monthly parts between June and December of that year. It was essentially a eulogy of trade, arguing that party-politics were often a clog on this providential activity, which was capable of benefiting the whole of mankind. Defoe had long argued that a country might quite reasonably continue to trade with another country even when they were at war, and his *General History of Trade* was no doubt intended partly as a hit at the Whig Opposition in Parliament, who had recently defeated a plan for a Treaty of Commerce with France. By now, Defoe argues, there are few parts of the globe where Europeans have not set their foot, so that new developments in trade will depend, not so much on discovering new countries, as on 'Improvements' made in the ones already known. He continues: 'When I come to Treat of New DISCOVERIES, which I purpose to do in a Tract by itself, I shall more strictly enquire whether farther and greater Discoveries of the yet unknown Parts of the World really are, or are not, for the General Good of the Trading World'.[1] This evidently looks forward to *A General History of Discoveries and Improvements*, a work also published serially in four parts, which came twelve years later.

The two works often echo each other and were, perhaps, thought out at much the same time. They indeed are linked even more closely than they might at first sight seem. For according to Defoe's view the greatest of all 'improvements' and technical discoveries made by humankind was in the field of navigation; and since the main motive for navigation is trade, it could be said that trade has been the inspiration for, or driving force behind, all the arts and sciences.

The point is driven home rather strikingly by the fact that much of the earlier part of *A General History of Discoveries* (i.e. up to and including Chapter 11) is a history and eulogy of, and eventually a lament for the extinction

---

1 *A General History of Trade* (1713), June, p. 43.

of, the Phoenicians, a people dedicated, above all others, to trade and to exploration of the high seas.

Defoe's account of the origin of the Phoenician civilisation follows, broadly speaking, the consensus of the time: that is to say it is based squarely on the Bible story. As a result of the confusion of tongues at Babel, the survivors of the Flood dispersed, under the leadership of Noah's three sons Ham, Shem and Japhet, and Ham's party, migrating westward from the plains of Shinaar, eventually arrived at the Mediterranean. Defoe embroiders on this, their first encounter with the sea, in picturesque fashion. 'How they ask'd one another, in the greatest Surprize imaginable, *What it was?* What it look'd like? How Frightful in the Opinion of some; How Glorious in the Opinion of others'.[2] They wonder whether it is not a dreadful enemy, like the waters of the Flood; but the land is otherwise a very pleasant one, and Sidon, son of Canaan, announces that he will plant his standard there. The land is given the name of Ham's son, Canaan, and they found a city named Sidon, proceeding some time later, when Sidon has grown very populous, to create another city, Tyre, a few miles to the south.

So much for the birth-story. Many further legends accreted round the early days of the 'Canaanites' or 'Tyrians', both in later books of the Bible and among classical authors. According to Pliny, in his *Natural History*, they invented stone quarrying and the mining and smelting of gold, and they were also were credited with the invention of the sail, and Defoe, who accepts this, proposes – in his rationalising fashion – that the story of Daedalus and Icarus is really an allegorical account of this discovery. He also repeats the story of how the Sidonians invented the rudder, from observing an eagle's tail.

It was further said that the Phoenicians, in the person of Cadmus, had invented letters. Defoe contests this, holding – in company with Samuel Bochart, Theophilus Gale and other learned opinion – that writing had first been given by God to Moses. Writing, he argued, was too sublime a conception to have been invented by mere human beings. He allows, however, that it was the Phoenician Cadmus who invented the alphabet and brought the first sixteen letters to Greece.[3] The origin and development of

2 *A General History of Discoveries*, below, p. 35.

3 On this matter it may be worth quoting from Johanna Drucker's *The Alphabetic Labyrinth* (London, 1995), p. 47: 'The Greek alphabet derived directly from the Phoenician, as is evident by the comparison of letters, whose similarity leaves little doubt on this point. Early Greek inscriptions do not have a fixed direction, they can be written right to left, or left to right, or in a regularly alternating sequence known as *boustrophedon* after the pattern made by a plowing ox. This point, combined with the visual force of script comparison, suggests an early date of transmission – one closer to 1100–1050 BC than the 9th or 8th century BC date traditionally assigned.'

writing is the theme of the other item in the present volume, *An Essay upon Literature,* a work which he wrote, or at any rate published, at almost exactly the same time.

That so much legend should surround the Phoenicians is not surprising, for in many ways they remain a rather shadowy people, partly because of the extreme paucity of their own written records. It is, however, certainly no myth that, by the time of Homer (or of King Solomon), the 'Canaanite' or Phoenician civilisation had become enormously rich and powerful. Until the 8th century BC the Phoenicians had complete mastery of the commerce and fisheries of the Aegean. They circumnavigated Africa and sailed as far afield as India and Cornwall, where they traded for tin, and after the founding of Carthage they settled towns all along the northern coast of Africa as well as in Spain (the present–day Cadiz) and along the Atlantic seaboard.

For Defoe, the Phoenicians, with their industriousness, rationalism and pragmatism, which enabled them to exploit the resources which God had offered to humankind, represented a great modernising and enlightening force and a model for later ages. He makes the remark (below, p. 72) that the destruction of Tyre by Nebuchadnezzar was probably, on the whole, a benefit to the world.

> ... it scatter'd a diligent and useful People into divers parts of the World, where they settled immediately to business, some in one place, and some in another: They were as so many Instructors to the Nations wherever they came, to pursue the same Industry, and maintain themselves by Trade, which before, 'tis very likely, they knew little or nothing of.

It is true, writes Defoe, that the science of astronomy, and 'all the *Promethean Fire*, which inflamed the breasts of Men with the most early desire of Knowledge', originated with the Chaldeans and Assyrians. 'But it will appear then that the *Phœnicians* were the *Englishmen* of that Age, that is to say, if they were not the Inventors, they were the greatest improvers of what others invented'.[4] Fantasy, indeed, takes firm hold of Defoe in regard to the Carthaginians, so that in *A Plan of the English Commerce*, published two years later than *A General History of Discoveries*, he has refugees from Carthage bringing the art of linen and woollen manufacture into Flanders.[5] It means that the Flemings, having no wool themselves, are forced to buy

---

4 See *A General History of Discoveries*, below, p. 76. Cf. *A General History of Trade*, p. 13: '... in these Days the *Tyrians* and *Phenicians* might properly be called the Center of the Trading Part of the World. These were the *Turky* and *East India* Company of those Times.'

5 See *Political and Economic Writings of Daniel Defoe* (London, 2000), vol. 7, ed. John McVeagh, p. 184.

it from England; and thus the Phoenicians become the founders of England's greatest glory, its wool-trade.

Defoe, for polemical purposes, mostly turns a blind eye to the fact that the Phoenicians were idolaters and practicers of human sacrifice; indeed he goes so far as to call them 'patterns of all commendable Virtues'.[6] In the comparison with the Romans, the Phoenicians, in Defoe's view, had all the advantage. The Romans were a vainglorious people, who were obsessed with military conquest and 'left the knowledge of the Sea, much where they found it'.[7] 'The whole Estate of the *Carthaginian* and *Græcian* Empires was swallow'd up in the Conquest of the *Romans*, a Nation inspir'd with the glory of Arms, and puff'd up with their innumerable Triumphs over other Nations; but not at all addicted to the true glories of Peace'.[8]

It was thus, as Defoe saw it, a great tragedy that the Phoenician civilisation had, eventually, been crushed and extirpated by the Romans and (as he claimed) forced to emigrate to America.[9] Indeed he depicted it as a catastrophe from which the world had never altogether recovered. The fact was, for him, epitomised in the present desolation of Africa, a continent once stored with 'such exquisite Product for Trade, such rich Gums and Drugs, such numbers of Cattle, quantities of Corn, and such a docible People', and now, under Mohammedan rule, a haunt of idleness and barbarity, its inland part a desert and its seacoast a nest of thieves, pirates and 'a Generation of Drones'.[10] He devotes a whole chapter of *A General History of Discoveries* (chapter 12) to a proposal according to which the nations of Europe should join together to extirpate these 'wretched crews' the Sallee rovers and Barbary corsairs, who ruthlessly preyed upon Mediterranean shipping and held fifty thousand Christians in slavery. The scheme was meant, perhaps, more for rhetorical effect than as a practical proposal, the objection being – as Defoe never tired of saying – the incurable factiousness of the European nations, as incapable of unity in a good cause (such as the late wars against France) as in a foolish one (like the Crusades).[11]

With a characteristic twist, he then turns on himself. 'What right have we or any of the Christian Nations of *Europe*', he asks, 'to invade and disposess these People, who however they came by their Possessions, have enjoy'd them by so long a prescription, as namely, about or above a thou-

6 See *A General History of Discoveries*, below, p.77.
7 Ibid., p. 53.
8 Ibid., p. 106.
9 See 'A Note on the Phoenicians and America', below, pp. 13–16.
10 *A General History of Discoveries*, below, pp. 27, 113.
11 He returns to this theme in Part III, chapter 2 of *A Plan of the English Commerce*. See *Political and Economic Writings of Daniel Defoe*, vol. 7, pp. 289–97.

4

sand Years?' (If we looked back at our own past, we might find our right to our country no better founded.) It would be wrong to try to exterminate them. All that is needed is to drive them fifteen or twenty miles from the coast and banish them for ever from the sea. If that were done, these men, now 'drones in the great *Hive*', might then become as diligent and as productive as any of their neighbours (pp. 119–20).

* * * * * *

This disquisition on the Phoenicians is the heart, or at any rate the most original part, of what Defoe has to say in *A General History of Discoveries*, and it is worth pausing to consider the place of this work in his *oeuvre*. It was published in four instalments between October 1725 and May 1726, and the second work in the present volume, *An Essay upon Literature*, came out in April 1726. One might have supposed that, crammed with out-of-the-way information as they are, they would have been enough to keep him occupied, but this is very far from the case. He was now free from day-to-day political journalism and political pamphleteering, and the scale on which he took advantage of this is fairly staggering. We may think of this as the period of Defoe's *Tour thro' the Whole Island of Great Britain*, the three volumes of which appeared in May 1724, June 1725 and August 1726 respectively, and to the works issued during this period we must add *The Great Law of Subordination* (April 1724), *A New Voyage Round the World* (November 1724), *Everybody's Business is Nobody's Business* (June 1725), *The Complete English Tradesman*, vol. 1 (September 1725), *A Brief Case of the Distillers* (March 1726), *The Political History of the Devil* (May 1726) and *Mere Nature Delineated* (July 1726): that is to say, four more full-length books, four lengthy tracts and a novel.[12]

To put the matter another way, within this period he produced two lengthy patriotic works, the *Tour* and the *Complete English Tradesman*, celebrating the grandeur of Britain's trade and present prosperity. (The series was to be continued in *A Plan of the English Commerce* of 1728.) As he says in the Preface to the *Tour*, he could easily have written a satire on the English but he had decided to forgo that pleasure ('they are ill friends to England, who strive to write a history of her nudities').[13] But simultaneously he published the first of a group of acerbic social-reform tracts, written in the person of 'Andrew Moreton', an irritable but public-spirited old bachelor living in Highgate. Thirdly, in *A Political History of the Devil*, he produced

---

12 For details, see P. N. Furbank & W. R. Owens, *A Critical Bibliography of Daniel Defoe* (London, 1998).

13 See *Writings on Travel, Discovery and History by Daniel Defoe*, vol. 1, p. 48.

the first of three satirical, or at least mainly satirical, books on the super-natural (the others being *A System of Magick* (1726) and *An Essay on the History and Reality of Apparitions* (1727). It may help to understand the two works in the present volume if we point out their links with these other writings.

It is plain, in view of the flattering parallel drawn by Defoe between the Phoenicians and the English, that, from one point of view, *A General History of Discoveries* is meant as a tribute to, and an intended object-lesson for, Defoe's fellow-countrymen. The conflict of values he posits between the commercial-minded and 'improving' Phoenicians and the glory-seeking Romans is echoed in an eloquent passage in *The Complete English Tradesman*. Why, he asks, is it that the English tradesman stands so high in the eyes of the world and is allowed 'to rank with the best gentlemen in Europe'?

> War has not done it; no, nor so much as helped or assisted to it; it is not by any martial exploits; we have made no conquests abroad, added no new kingdoms to the British empire, reduced no neighbouring nations, or extended the possession of our monarchs into the properties of others; we have gained nothing by war and encroachment; we are butted and bounded just where we were in Queen Elizabeth's time; the Dutch, the Flemings, the French, are in view of us, just as they were then ... instead of being enriched by war and victory, on the contrary, we have been torn in pieces by civil wars and rebellions.[14]

It is true that, on pages 211–17 of *A General History of Discoveries*, Defoe puts forward a scheme for an English colony in the temperate and sparsely-populated region of southern Chile – which would be an 'encroachment', admittedly, but was as far as possible to be made without violence or bloodshed.

He outlined this scheme in some detail to Robert Harley in 1711, soon after Harley had launched a plan for a South Sea Company.[15] Under the Company's charter, by the terms of the Grand Alliance, England had the right to take possession of some part of the Spanish dominions; and Defoe responded by proposing the seizure of an area in Patagonia (largely unpopulated and not under Spanish rule) as a step towards establishing a colony on the other side of the Andes, at Valdivia,[16] in Chile. The land

---

14 *The Complete English Tradesman* (1726), vol. 1, pp. 381–2.

15 Enclosure with letter to Harley dated 23 July 1711. See *The Letters of Daniel Defoe*, ed. George Harris Healey (Oxford, 1955), pp. 345–9.

16 There was disagreement about the spelling of this name, which sometimes appears as 'Baldivia' or 'Baldavia'. According to Defoe, in his letter to Harley, the place was founded by the Spanish general Pedro Valdivia (*c*. 1500–53).

around Valdivia was, he said, very fertile; the climate was ideally suited to the English; and the region abounded in gold.

In his theories, Defoe had evidently been much influenced by the Journal of an expedition to those parts by Sir John Narborough, published in 1694.[17] Narborough gives a glowing account of the country round Valdivia.

> They have Apples, and Plums, and Pears, and Olives, Apricocks, Peaches, Quinces, Oranges, Lemmons, and many other Fruits … These Spaniards report it to be the finest Country in the whole World, and that the People live with the greatest Luxury of any on the Earth; they enjoy their Health with so much delight, and have so much Wealth and Felicity, that they compare the Land to *Paradise*.[18]

He is almost equally enthusiastic about the plains of Patagonia, and, in a passage picked up by Defoe in *A General History of Discoveries* (p. 214), he remarks that they 'might be made excellent Corn-ground, being ready to Till; 'tis very like the Land on New-market Heath'. Being a sailor and not an economist, Narborough speculates that 'the most advantageous Trade in the World might be made in these parts, if it were but follow'd, and that leave was granted by the King of *Spain* for the English to Trade freely in all their Ports'. This also is a remark which Defoe may have remembered. Finally, Narborough asserts that the Spanish in Valdivia know very little about the interior of the country and that they are greatly hated by the Indians, who speak of them as 'devils'.[19]

Defoe's purpose in suggesting this scheme was to give some definite and practical substance to the new South Sea Company's plans, though without encouraging the (to him) absurd notion that Spain could be made to allow an open trade throughout her dominions. Whatever trading relations were to spring up between the new colony and its Spanish and Indian neighbours would, as he pictured it, be unofficial; and meanwhile a valuable exchange of products might be set in train with England's colonies in New England and the Caribbean. Defoe told Harley he hoped his scheme would be no less acceptable to him for having been formerly proposed to King William.

From now on, this project became a favourite theme with Defoe. In the version of it in *A General History of Discoveries* he lays the emphasis primarily on Patagonia, but later he would construct a whole novel around it, *A New Voyage Round the World, By a Course never sailed before* (1725). It depicts a

17 *An Account of Several Late Voyages and Discoveries to the South and North* (London, 1694).
18 Ibid., p. 96.
19 Ibid., p. 102.

voyage to the South Seas and is evidently expressly designed to show that his Valdivian and Patagonian projects were a practical possibility.[20]

Another link between the present two works and the others that Defoe was writing at the time (and a link with each other also) relates to Euhemerism, or the theory that the pagan deities were ordinary flesh-and-blood mortals before being elevated to the skies.[21] This had long been a favourite theme with Defoe. It served him for comic purposes in his poem *Jure Divino*, where Aeolus is lampooned as a French dragoon and Neptune as 'an old Dutch-Skipper',[22] but also as an analogy to the process by which princes were affirmed to enjoy 'divine right'. (This 'divine right', his poem is arguing, is a form of *idolatry*.) In *A System of Magick*, however, Euhemerism is given another twist. Defoe here envisages a history of magic and magicians in three stages. The 'Magi' were, originally, simply men of rare genius and more than ordinary wisdom and, as such, were regarded with uncomprehending awe. Then, as there came to be more of them and they were correspondingly less valued, some turned to empirical studies, such as medicine, but others assumed the dignity and trappings of priests, laying claim to intimacy with the gods. Finally, when even this did not suffice, they became sorcerers and turned to the Devil, making him a servant at their beck and call. We need not take the last too literally, for Defoe never tired of mocking the idea of a personal and physical Devil. But the gist is clear. Such a legendary figure as Prometheus (to whom the inventing of crafts and the use of fire, and even the creation of humankind got ascribed) would have been in real life a Magus – which is to say an ordinary mortal, but one endowed with a genius for 'improvement'.

The supreme benefactors of mankind, in Defoe's eyes, are the 'improvers', but they are very far from always being welcomed. It is the fate of improvers to be converted into demigods or witches and warlocks. Was it not imagined that Prometheus himself was cruelly punished by Zeus? Did not people suspect at first that printing, that great 'improvement', was the work of the Devil? The 'improvements' referred to in the title of Defoe's *A*

20 For further details of Defoe's plan see P. N. Furbank & W. R. Owens, 'Defoe's "South-Sea" and "North-Sea" Schemes: A Footnote to *A New Voyage round the World*', *Eighteenth-Century Fiction*, 13 (2001), pp. 501–8.

21 It takes its name from a romance by Euhemerus of Messene (3rd century BC) in which it is related how, on the fabled island of Panchaia, the narrator found a temple of Zeus containing a golden pillar, on which Zeus, originally merely a mortal, had recorded his own deeds and those of Uranus and Kronos. The idea is a familiar one in seventeenth-century literature. Raleigh, in his *History of the World*, writes: 'Out of the taking up of Enoch by God, was borrowed [by the heathens] the conversion of their heroes (the inventors of religion and such arts as the life of man had profit by) into stars and heavenly signs'.

22 *Jure Divino* (1706), Book I, p. 11.

General History of Discoveries include astronomy, navigation, the sail and the rudder, medicine, silk and woollen manufacture, gunpowder, the compass and the printing press; whilst *An Essay upon Literature* deals with the greatest, and almost the earliest of all improvements,[23] that is to say *writing*. *An Essay upon Literature* argues that writing (or 'literature') was too sublime an invention for the human mind and came direct from God, in the form of the Mosaic tablets. (Thus the original writing, and the original language, as talked by Adam and Eve, must have been Hebrew.) It then proceeds to discuss the alphabet, or rather the many real or supposed alphabets, including antediluvian ones, and the relation of the linear alphabet to hieroglyphics; the materials of writing (clay-tablets, waxed tablets, oiled linen, wooden boards, wood-bark, papyrus, parchment, paper, etc.); the instruments of writing (reed, stylus, pen, etc.); ink; spelling and 'prolation'; shorthand, cypher and invisible writing; writing 'hands'; and printing. He gives particular attention to the so-called 'Tironian Notes', a form of ideographic shorthand invented by Cicero's freedman Tullius Tyro, and to the 'Steganography', or system of secret writing, devised by Johann Trithemius (1462–1516).

In his opening paragraph, Defoe remarks that it is strange that, among the innumerable writers in the world, none up till now has written comprehensively about writing, that is to say the use of written characters, itself – though it is through writing that we are able to stand 'upon the Shoulders of our Fore-fathers' Learning', and without it, 'experimental Knowledge' and progress in the natural sciences would be impossible. His claim to be doing something new in this way could indeed be said to be a fair one, at least as regards Britain. The seventeenth century saw the publishing of many copy-books or works on penmanship; there were works on shorthand and cryptography, on oriental alphabets and hieroglyphics, and the mystical understanding of letter-formation; and schemes for a 'universal language' employing a 'real' character. A Scottish friend of Defoe's, Sir John Clerk of Penicuik, had written a Latin treatise on the stylus; and there were, of course, various discussions and histories of printing, but there was no really comprehensive survey.

The closest parallel with Defoe's book is perhaps the *De Arte Grammatica* of Vossius (the learned Dutch scholar G. J. Voss). Vossius's treatise, first published in 1635, covers a very wide range of literary matters, including etymology and linguistics, textual emendation, metre and accents etc.; but among them are many of the topics dealt with by Defoe, and at certain

---

23 Not quite the earliest, which was wine, a discovery with unfortunate consequences for Noah, its inventor.

points he leans heavily on Vossius, as will be seen from the explanatory notes.

The climax to which Defoe's *Essay* works up is the invention and development of printing, and here Euhemerism comes to the fore again. For if printing had been invented sooner, the nonsense of Euhemerism (as he regarded it) could never have occurred. Without printing, he writes, in an admirable sentence, how few people would know what was done in the world.

> How little a way wou'd the Fame of the greatest Heroe have reach'd? The Noise of a Victory would have been scarce heard farther than the Noise of the Cannon; much less could Things have continued in Time, longer than the Memory of the Persons concern'd wou'd preserve them, or that most corrupting multiplying Usage of Tradition have convey'd them; of which already we see so many fatal Effects, and by which Things of the greatest Moment done as it were but Yesterday, that is to say, within the Compass of two or three Ages, turn into Fable and Romance; Scoundrels are made Heroes, and Heroes are made Gods; for so no doubt the Deifying the first Tyrants of the World, such as *Saturn*, *Jupiter*, *Bacchus*, and *Mercury*, and *Belus* (or *Baal*) came about.[24]

Two themes are intertwined in these two books of Defoe's about 'improvements': the pernicious potentialities of fable and myth, and the perennial and obstinate resistance to progress – the 'dulness', 'stupidity', 'sloth' and 'indolence' of unenlightened epochs, such as the Middle Ages or the era of the tower of Babel.

There is something hard for us to swallow in Defoe's contempt for, and refusal of all sympathetic understanding of, myth and fantasy (apart from satirical fantasy, which of course he practices himself). For one thing, it narrows down the literature which he can appreciate. He is thoroughly distrustful of Homer, 'who has sung the Wars of the *Greeks*, and the siege of *Troy* from a reality into a meer Fiction',[25] and, despite his protestations of admiration, what seems most to interest him in *Paradise Lost* is Milton's 'mistakes'. The only poets he seems wholeheartedly to respond to are Rochester and 'Hudibras' Butler.[26] (On the other hand, of course, his rejection of 'fable' and 'romance' has an important bearing on his own practice as a novelist.)

One is struck, too, by his eagerness for us to scorn and ridicule the ignorance of 'rude ages': 'to pity, or rather despise the rest of the World', who

24 *An Essay upon Literature*, below, pp. 301–2.
25 Ibid., p. 241.
26 See John McVeagh, 'Rochester and Defoe: a Study in Influence', *Studies in English Literature*, 14 (1974), pp. 328–41.

know nothing of our noble discoveries, 'as grossly ignorant, stupid, and uncapable'. The fable of Thule, he says, seems to 'rais'd from the very grossest of all stupidity and ignorance',[27] and in *An Essay upon Literature* one of his arguments for writing only having come in with Moses is that the planners of that absurd project, Babel, were too sunk in an 'immense Dulness'[28] to be capable of such a noble invention.

Admittedly, it allows him some telling pages, as in his diatribe against the twelfth century: 'They had *Philosophy* without Experiment. *Mathematicks* without Instruments. *Geography* without Scale. *Astronomy* without Demonstration', etc. etc.[29] Again, the same objection does not apply when he is mocking the present day for a foolish over-estimation of the past. He makes some nice hits here, as when he writes, apropos of the so-called 'mighty' voyages of the ancient Romans to India, 'I must say, and I believe I speak with Reason; that for a *Gravesend-Wherry* to go down from *Gravesend* to the *Downs*, and cross over the Sea there to *Calais*, which they frequently do, is a much more dangerous and hazardous thing than all those famous Voyages to the *Indies*'.[30] He allows Queen Semiramis of Assyria to have had a great fleet – but it was a fleet of canoes.[31]

In his deflationary attitude towards the past and assertion of the superiority of the present, Defoe, we should notice, is altogether consistent. It is clearly with conviction that he writes of 'that Prodigy of Perfection' to which 'experimental Knowledge both in Arts and in Nature' has arrived;[32] nor is it just patriotism which, in the *Tour*, leads him to speak so much of 'improvements' and to note how 'Even while the sheets are in the press, new beauties appear in several places', almost too fast to keep up with.[33] Equally he has, as you might say, an unusually strong sense of the pastness of the past; and, in the *Tour* especially, he writes of the ruins of ancient militarism and Popery with a serene irony – though never with nostalgia.

This goes together with, or perhaps it is simply one aspect of, a leading trait of his, a lack of all capacity for awe. He is habitually facetious about Biblical characters – about Adam, 'that effeminated Male Apple-Eater';[34] the 'she-tyrant' Eve;[35] and Noah, 'the first of drunkards'[36] – and for the

---

27 *A General History of Discoveries*, below, p. 55.
28 *An Essay upon Literature*, below, p. 247.
29 *A General History of Discoveries*, below, pp. 175–6.
30 Ibid., p. 142.
31 Ibid., p. 57
32 *An Essay upon Literature*, below, p. 229.
33 See *Writings on Travel, Discovery and History by Daniel Defoe*, vol. 1, p. 49.
34 *The Political History of the Devil* (1726), p. 61.
35 Ibid., p. 62.
36 *An Essay upon Literature*, below, p. 240.

same reason he is able to make excellent fun of the Devil, it being essential in his view not to hold Satan, that 'blind short-sighted' old gentleman,[37] in awe. He is even ready, and precisely in connection with 'improvement', to question the translation of the Bible, or at least the Authorised Version. Some critics, he says – and he goes along with them – think that the words in Genesis 11:1, '*And the whole earth was of one language, and of one speech*', should really read 'All the People on the Earth, were of one Mind' (i.e. as to the project of building the tower of Babel). It seems to Defoe likely that, in the absence of the all-important 'improvement' writing to impose uniformity, the people would already have developed different dialects and be finding it difficult to understand one another. In other words, the 'confusion of tongues' would already have taken place.[38]

As an 'improvement', printing is, in Defoe's eyes, the consummation of writing. (He remarks, rather neatly, that if printing had not come before the 'Itch of writing Books' had reached its present height, scribal copying would have become as vast an industry as the woollen manufacture.[39]) Thus one cannot help finding it intensely expressive that he describes the Mosaic tablets in printing-house terms. 'The Pattern was in the Mount. There the whole Art was exhibited, the Pattern set, *a Specimen work'd off*' (my italics).[40]

* * * * * *

In places, both *A General History of Discoveries* and *An Essay upon Literature*, though they draw on a very wide range of reading, show signs of rushed composition – which is not too surprising considering the rate at which Defoe was publishing at this period. The third instalment of *A General History of Discoveries* is effective, and indeed impressive, in its picture of shifting trade patterns and the rise of new industries after the fall of the Roman empire. The fourth and last instalment, on the other hand, gets distinctly repetitive. One begins to lose sight of the overall structure of the work, which was designed to end with the impact of the nautical compass. Moreover, though Boyle's experiments with the magnet have their relevance to this last, there is something rather hand-to-mouth in Defoe's borrowing his account word for word from a reference-book.

The same may be said of an oddity in *An Essay upon Literature*, that is Defoe's including, on the subject of antediluvian alphabets, a nine-page-

---

37 *Political History of the Devil*, p. 167.
38 *An Essay upon Literature*, below, p. 269.
39 Ibid., p. 308.
40 Ibid., p. 270.

long quotation in Latin. There is no complaint to make about the quotation itself, which is extremely apt; but even in Defoe's day, one feels, readers might have found so much Latin indigestible. (In the present edition, I have thought it helpful to follow the original extract with my own translation.)

But there is a further and more puzzling problem involved. For some reason, the author of the long Latin quotation, whose name is Thomas Bang (or Bangius), comes out in Defoe's text (p. [50]) as 'the learn'd *Bugi*'. It is not clear how the mistake arose, though no doubt it has to do with the genitive form of 'Bangius', i.e. 'Bangii'.

Thomas Bang (or Bangius) (1600–61) was a Danish philologist and theologian, and Defoe's quotation is from his *Coelum-Orientis et prisci mundi triade exercitationum literariarum repræsentatum* (Copenhagen, 1657) – or rather from the posthumous re-issue of this in 1691 under the title *Exercitationes philologico-philosophicæ de artu et progressu litterarum*. Bang studied in Copenhagen and then in Germany. In 1630 he became Professor of Hebrew in Copenhagen university, and subsequently Professor of Theology. Like Defoe he held that Hebrew was the original language and was much opposed to the theory, launched by the French Calvinist Isaac Peyrerius in 1655, that God had created a race of Preadamites. He was evidently extremely knowledgeable about the supposed alphabets of Adam, Seth and Noah, but is ultimately as sceptical as Defoe himself about those 'Learned Phantasms'.

A Note on the Phoenicians and America

Defoe, as will be seen from pp. 75–6 and pp. 93–6, speculates confidently that the first peopling of America was by the Phoenicians. The question how human beings came to be in America had, as he says, been much debated among the learned, some scholars taking the view that, it being impossible to imagine them arriving either across the seas or by the land route over the Arctic, there must have been a separate creation by God. His own view was that the land route was certainly impossible, those extreme northern regions always having been totally uninhabited, but that, considering the skill and adventurousness of the Phoenicians in navigation, and the fact that they had numerous towns and colonies on the west coast of Africa, it was quite reasonable to suppose that they had discovered, and eventually settled, the new continent. They most likely first made the discovery by accident, one of their ships having being carried there by the trade winds or by a storm. They would then have followed this up with a planned voyage of exploration; and finally, after the destruction of Carthage, they made a mass exodus thither, carrying with them their domestic animals, and made America their new home. Since their African colonies fell into ruin after they left, it would not be surprising if all memory of this migration should have been lost.

The evidence for Defoe's theory, in his view, was anthropological. The idolatries and human sacrifices of the Mexicans, and the governmental usages and records of the ancient Peruvians, showed very strong similarities to Phoenician practices. Also, there were certain traditions and prophecies current among the Peruvians, which, though no longer understood by the Peruvians themselves, plainly referred to the Carthaginians.

Defoe expounds his theory in confident and colourful style and it fits in with his generally adulatory attitude towards the Phoenicians. (In *A Plan of the English Commerce* he affirms, once again, that 'there is no room for doubt' that America was 'discovered if not peopled from *Africa*, by the indefatigable Carthaginians'.[41]) He was, however, by no means alone in his basic tenet. Thus it may be worth briefly sketching the debate about the peopling of America.

In the sixteenth century there were speculations that America was the Atlantis of Plato's *Timaeu*s, and therefore known of in the ancient world. It was also suggested that the Indians were the descendants of the Canaanites, who fled before Joshua; that they were Carthaginians; or that they were the Ten Lost Tribes of Israel. On the whole, commentators at this period considered the immigrants must have come by land (though by what route was left somewhat vague), the ancients being too ignorant of navigation to cross the high seas.

An important book on the subject, published early in the next century, was the *Origen de los Indios de el nuevo mundo* (Valencia, 1607) by Gregorio Garcia. Garcia rejected the idea that the Indians were Carthaginians, on the grounds that there was no resemblance between them either in customs or in language. He likewise presented the arguments for, but dismissed, the theory that they were descended from the Romans, Greeks, Phoenicians, Chinese, Egyptians, Africans, Ethiopians, French, Cambrians, Kurlanders, Frisians or Scyths. His own guess was that the Indians came not from one nation but many, and by different routes, the migrations beginning not long after the Flood.

---

41 *A Plan of the English Commerce* (1728), in *Political and Economic Writings of Daniel Defoe*, vol. 7, p. 290.

By contrast, in the *De origine gentium Americanarum* (Amsterdam, 1644) by Robertus Comtaeus Nortmannus, the theory that the Indians were the descendants of the Phoenicians received strong support. Nortmannus quoted Curtius on an unknown land discovered by the Phoenicians, and Festus Avienus on a *periplus* by the Carthaginians beyond the Pillars of Hercules, and he pointed out that the Phoenician word for *mother (anech)* was close to the Huron word *anan*. He supposed that, since the Phoenicians were the direct descendants of Ham's cursed son Canaan, the subjugation of the Indians by the Spaniards was the fulfilment of Noah's curse.[42]

There were many other books and theories on the subject in the seventeenth century. (The famous Hugo Grotius launched the theory that the North Americans were descended from the Scandinavians, the people of Yucatan were from Africa, those of Peru from China, and those south of Peru from the Moluccas.) But the most wide-ranging treatise before the Restoration was the *De originibus Americanis libri quatuor* (Hague, 1652) of Georgius Hornius. Having summarised and criticised all the main previous theories, Hornius proposed that there had been several migrations, beginning shortly after the Flood: the Phoenicians from the west, the Chinese from the east and the Scythians from the north. The invaders had all come to the north part of America but later pushed south, losing their original physical characteristics, as well as their customs and languages, though retaining traces of their religious beliefs. This is how Don Cameron Allen summarises his account of the Phoenician invasion:

> There were, Hornius supposes, three separate waves to the Phoenician migration. The first migrants sailed from Africa to the coast of America; the second group sailed through Gibraltar, as Diodorus relates, and settled Hispaniola and Brazil; the third group is the one that Solomon and Hiram visited with their fleets. Hornius admits there are no peacocks and ivory in America, but knows it is filled with gold and apes; hence, he is ready to accept the idea that America and Ophir are the same place.[43]

It should be added that the debate continued to flourish in the nineteenth and twentieth centuries. In 1872 a certain mysterious 'Joaquim Albes da Costa' reported the discovery, on his plantation near Paraiba in Brazil, of a stone bearing an inscription in the name of Sidonian Canaanites, telling how, having embarked at Ezion-geber in the Red Sea and voyaging round Africa, they had arrived at the 'Island of Iron'. The inscription was declared a forgery by Ernest Renan, but on the strength of a further copy which turned up in 1867, the distinguished archeologist

---

42 See Don Cameron Allen, *The Legend of Noah* (Urbana, 1949), pp. 124–5.
43 Ibid., p. 129.

Cyrus Gordon argued in his *Before Columbus* (1972) that it contained 'readings unknown in 1872 but which are now authenticated by inscriptions discovered during the century that has elapsed since then'.[44]

44 Cyrus Gordon, *Before Columbus* (London, 1972), p. 122. See Nigel Davies, *Voyagers to the New World: Fact or Fantasy?* (London, 1979) for a sceptical critique of Cyrus Gordon's book and of two other recent books, Constance Irwin's *Fair Gods and Stone Faces* (London, 1963) and Barry Fell's *America B.C.* (New York, 1976), which similarly argue the 'Phoenicians-in-America' case.

A GENERAL
HISTORY
OF
DISCOVERIES
AND
IMPROVEMENTS,

In useful ARTS,

Particularly in the great Branches of COMMERCE, NAVIGATION, and PLANTATION, in all Parts of the known WORLD.

A Work which may entertain the CURIOUS with the view of their present State; prompt the indolent to retrieve those Inventions that are neglected, and animate the diligent to advance and perfect what may be thought wanting.

To be continued Monthly.

NUMB. I. for OCTOBER.

LONDON:
Printed for J. ROBERTS, at the *Oxford-Arms*, in *Warwick-Lane*.
Price One-Shilling.

PREFACE
TO THE
MONTHLY UNDERTAKING.

As the most glorious Empires in the World had their beginnings in the little Adventures of single Men, or the small Undertakings of a few; so the most flourishing Arts, the most useful Discoveries, and the most advantageous Improvements, which the World now boasts of, had their Foundations in small Things, and from thence have encreased, and been brought to their present perfection by the application of private Men, whose inspired Minds have guided them to propagate useful Knowledge, for the good of Mankind.

THE same Zeal for the general improvement of the World which inspired those patrons of Wisdom to undertake great Things, prompts us to give our Age the History of their Discoveries, and Improvements; that Men of the same Genius may be encouraged from the success of former Times to pursue the like useful Discoveries for the benefit of the Ages to come.

WE have infinite advantages beyond what the Antients could pretend to, and vast helps in the search after Knowledge, which they were utterly destitute of, for we stand upon the shoulders of three thousand Years application, and have all the benefit of their Discoveries, and Experiments handed down, gratis, to improve upon, and to encourage our Enquiries.

THEY have search'd Nature to the bottom, in-side and out-side; they have as it were anatomiz'd the Globe, and given us the naked Skeleton of its most secret Parts, for us to act upon in our farther Enquiries; Neither the height of Heaven, the depth of the Sea or the breadth of the Earth have escaped them; and if they have not discovered all that is to be known, they have nobly led us by the Hand to the very Door, where what remains is to be found.

IT is a most pleasant Retrospect they afford us of what is past, and Nature adds as agreeable a Prospect of what is to come; they have open'd her Book, and read far in it, but she shows us many Leaves, not yet turn'd over; and assures us, she has reserv'd sufficient to encourage, and to reward our future Enquiries.

> What's yet discover'd only serves to show
> How little's known, to what there's yet to know.[1]

UPON *this Supposition, the present Work is founded, and we promise our selves we shall be able, not only to give a pleasing History of past Discoveries, but a profitable view of what may yet be undertaken.*

THE *Connection of past things with present, the State of the antient World, with the State of things Modern, in order to describe the growth of things from what they were to what they now are; makes it absolutely necessary to begin our Accounts at the beginning of those things which we give an account of; how else could we call our* Work *a* History, *much less* a Compleat History? *Nor could our relation of the improvement of Arts, and Science, Navigation, or Plantation, be satisfactory to the curious and enquiring Reader, if we did not give an account of those Arts and Sciences from their beginning, and tell who were the Inventors, who the Improvers, and who the Patrons of them through all the Ages of their improvement in the World.*

THUS *in showing the growing progress of that most useful part of the Mathematicks, which we call* Navigation, *and also those surprizing Improvements which we may indeed call the perfection of human Knowledge, I mean of* Astronomy, *and the Motions, Influences, and Revolutions of the heavenly Bodies; How can we profitably describe the things themselves without giving some account of their first Introduction; I mean, to whom Heaven first communicated those Beams of Light; how, and in what manner they have been improv'd, farther and farther insight into those mysteries obtain'd, and the Science it self brought to such perfection, as we see it now is?*

THE *Historical account of the advances made by every Age in those things may be as pleasing, and instructing to the enquiring Reader, as the study of the things themselves; and may stir up the curiosity of those, not yet fully inform'd, to a desire of a more perfect Knowledge.*

HOWEVER, *tho' such a Retrospect is necessary, yet we have endeavour'd to make our History of past times, (especially of those most remote) as brief as may consist with a necessary enquiry into useful things, and shall dwell no longer upon the dark beginning of those things, than to point out the Time and Persons from whence they are derived: As we come on and advance nearer our own times the nature of things will call for a fuller description, and as that description will be the more fruitful of incidents, so it will be more agreeable to our curiosity, and more instructing, and particularly as it will kindle new desires after the farther Discoveries, and Improvements, which are still behind; of which we shall not fail to give a very full, and we believe a very satisfactory Account.*

BY *this short Retrospect, we shall have the pleasure of meeting with a vast variety of useful and pleasant Discoveries, which however they had their time of being accepted, and well receiv'd in the World, seem now to be as it were forgotten, and only look'd back upon in speculation; and yet may for ought we know be profitably reviv'd as much as any thing of that kind can do, and several others, too many to mention here.*

WE *have taken notice in the beginning of the Work, how many parts of the World which have been peopled and planted, cultivated and improv'd have, by the fate of Nations been again laid wast, and have return'd to their primitive, undiscovered State, and that before the native Wealth of those Countries had been fully improv'd, or their secret Treasure exhausted; which Countries (especially as the Commerce of the World is now established) merit very well to be repossest, the parts of them to be again discovered, and search'd into, and the whole to be restored to its primitive usefulness for the good of Mankind; such are the several Countries of* Asia Minor *now in posession of the* Turks; *the rich Country of* Ethiopia *on the West border of the* Red Sea; *the North Coast of* Africa *in the* Mediterranean Sea, *and several others; of which a distinct Account will be given, not so much as to what they have been, but as to the infinite benefit they might now be to the trading part of the World, and that prodigiously more than ever they were before.*

IN *our accounts of Improvements and Discoveries, which are yet behind, and which Mankind have before them for the encouragement of their Industry, we shall not amuse our Readers with remote and suggested possibilities, or run them upon dangerous and impracticable Projects, such as mad Men cannot, and wise Men will not meddle with: This wou'd be to puzzle and perplex our Readers with dark Schemes and uninteligible Proposals, which have neither probability of success to encourage the attempt, or rational foundation, to make them entertaining to the Reader.*

ON *the contrary we shall endeavour to show the reasonableness of every undertaking on one hand, and Feizableness of it on the other; and if as a whet to the Industry of the Ages, which may make the attempt, we should show the certainty of profit to the Undertakers, every Reader will be judge of the Fact, and to every Reader, therefore we make our Appeal.*

THE *World has been long perplex'd about an intricate Affair, which some have promis'd Mankind they shall one time or other be much the better for, and that it shall be fully discover'd to them; I mean the* LONGITUDE, *or the settled distances of East and West; we shall in the process of this Work endeavour to put an end to the Importance of that Search, by setting two things in a clear light about it.*

I. THAT *it can never be fully and finally ascertain'd, and perhaps very little more than it already is, and that therefore 'tis to no purpose to spend any farther time about it.*

II. THAT *it is not so very essential to the World, as some would have us believe, and in short, that as to the great Article of human Knowledge, 'tis not one Farthing matter whether it be more fully discover'd or no.*

IN *like manner the World has been long taken up with an enquiry, whether there is not a passage to be obtained either by the* North-East, *about the North parts of* Europe *and* Asia, *or by the* North-West, *about the North parts of* America *to*

China *and* Japan; *and many fruitless Voyages have been made, and many a stout Mariner been drown'd or frozen to Death, in the search after these Discoveries.*

IN *the process of this Work we shall show the weakness of all those attempts, the real impossibility of the Discovery it self, and the impracticableness of those Seas as to its being perform'd, were a discovery of a continued Sea really made; and with all we shall show how the World may at a very small expence come to a certainty is the great Question it self, namely, whether there be really a continued Sea or no.*

OUR *Schemes of Improvement as they respect Trade will chiefly consist of these very useful parts.*

    I. THE *discovery of several parts of the World, and passage to them, which have not been yet known.*

   II. THE *farther discovery of such Parts as are yet but imperfectly known.*

  III. THE *better improving, as well the Soil as the Commerce, of those Countries which are fully known, and Discover'd.*

  IV. THE *discovering several branches of Commerce not yet known, or meddled with in the World.*

   V. THE *extending our present Commerce into several parts of the known World, where it has not yet been practis'd.*

OUR *propos'd improvements of Arts and Science will be either touch'd at in the several Heads of Discoveries as we go on, or be spoken to under particular Heads by themselves, as occasion requires.*

IT *wou'd swell this Part too big for a Preface to give a more particular account of all the other Parts of this great Undertaking; we are rather content to venture it upon the Candour of the curious Reader, and expect its success only from the merit of the Performance.*

INTRODUCTION.

WHEN the Almighty, immediately after the DELUGE, restored Man to the Possession of the *Globe*, he deliver'd it to him as an *universal Blank*: He bid him *indeed* encrease and multiply and replenish it, *that is*, people it, spread a numerous Race upon it, that should at once both keep Possession, and enjoy the Product: But he told him nothing of what it was able to do for him; leaving that to his farther Enquiry.

THE World was to him like a rough Diamond, that has its intrinsic Value in it self, but the Outside conceal'd the Inside, and it was for him to polish it, that its Lustre might appear.

THE *Sea* was fill'd with Fish, but Man had no Knowledge of what they were good for; it was capable of being made use of for Trade, and Converse of Nations; but Mankind knew nothing of Ships, or Navigation.

THE *Land* was capable of producing all the good Things which we have seen grow upon its Surface: but Man had made no Experience of its Fertility: It had in its Bowels all the Wealth which we see since drawn from it; But our Progenitors knew nothing of the means how to come at it, or the method how to manage it when they had gotten it: The Gold was no Snare; the Iron uncapable either of Offence or Defence; the usefulness of *Copper, Tin,* and *Lead* were of no benefit, for Science *was not,* and *Art was not,* and in a Word, the Men that Nature produc'd were perfectly and compleatly Ignorant of what the World was, or what might be done to bring it to be any thing, but what it appear'd by its out-side, much less to what we have since found it to be: All this was left to the Inhabitants, to find out gradually as they wanted it, and to improve as they went on in the *Discovery.*

HOW, and by *what Steps* these Discoveries were made, and as near as we can, *when,* and by *whom*; what Uses the Discoveries that have been made have been apply'd to; how the Genius of Men is improv'd by such Discoveries, and how much farther such Improvements may probably be carry'd: These will be the Subject of our future Enquiry in these Sheets.

IN this Important Search we shall necessarily Observe, how these *Discoveries* have naturally tended to the *Improvement* of Mankind in all the Parts of useful Knowledge, and the Tendency an Encrease of Knowledge has had to encreasing the Felicity of Man's Life, to the supplying him with Conveniences for living, and Instructing him to the best use of those Conveniences: *In a Word*, how much Superior every Generation has been, because Wiser than those who went before them; whether they have been Better, for all their Knowledge, or Worse, is a Question by it self.

I HAVE often observed that the gradual Improvement of the World by those early Discoveries deserves a History, and really I must acknowledge that I think, we very much want that History, and that on many Accounts.

   I. WE are not only Ignorant (in this Age) of the Reason and Nature of the most early Improvements of Mankind, but weakly contenting our selves without eager Desire of looking forward for more, we really have lost many of the most useful Branches of Knowledge, and of Art, and are without the benefit of many of the best Discoveries which these first Ages made use of; some of which were so beneficial to them, and might be still so to us, if not neglected, and as it were forgotten.

  II. SEVERAL Countries, discover'd and planted by the Antients, the Fertility and Advantage, of which were infinitely Great, are as it were deserted again, and left to wild nature; Unpeopled, and over-run with Woods and wild Beasts, and even, require a New Discovery, and a New Plantation to render them useful to the World, as they ought to be, and as they were before.

 III. WE run away now, to *India, China*, the remotest Parts of *Asia*, to *Chili, Brasil*, and the farthest Part of *America*, for the very Product and Wealth which the Countries known in these most Early *Discoveries*, are qualified fully to supply us with; and perhaps with half the Hazard, Trouble, and Experience as the other.

THESE and many other Reasons confirm what I have said above, that 'tis very necessary to preserve the Memory of the most Antient Improvements, that we may see whether we have any need to run so much after New Discoveries, till we make the utmost Advantage of the Old Ones; and whether, while we strive to possess new Countries and carry on new Commerce, we do not abandon others already known, and leave them to be forgotten, which would abundantly satisfy as well our Ambition, as our Avarice, by their Product and Capacity of farther Improvement; without putting us to the Expence of running so far off.

BUT this is not all; by looking back upon the Early Improvement of the World, we should with Pleasure see how Mankind gradually spreading over the whole Surface, dip'd into the Wealth and Product of the several Countries, by the Industry and Application of the several Ages Inhabiting those Countries; and how those gradual Improvements dropt again as the diligent Inhabitants were removed by War, Conquests, or other Accidents, and the over running Injuries of Barbarous Nations; also how easily the Fertility and Advantages of those Countries might be restor'd, and this Part of the World reap the benefit of it, if due measures were yet taken to bring it to pass.

THESE are some of the Blessings we may find by looking back into the former State of Things in the infant World, and especially in those Nations, which being once the Center of Commerce, as well as of Arts and Sciences, are since lay'd Desolate and over run with a Barbarous People, who utterly neglecting those Improvements, have turn'd the most delicious Countries, formerly *flowing with Milk and Honey*, into a Desolate Howling Wilderness, and the most fruitful Provinces of *Asia, Greece*, and *Africa*, which formerly maintained Millions of Inhabitants, to be scarce able to feed the Wild Creatures that inhabit there.

AN Impartial full History of these Things will bring us down by just gradations to our own Times. Looking into Antiquity, is a Dry, Empty, and Barren Contemplation, any farther than as it is brought down to our present Understanding, and to bear a steady Analogy of its parts, with the Things that are before us.

OUR Times are as proper, our Circumstances as suitable, and our Genius and Temper, as forward for *Discoveries* and *Improvements*, as any that have been before us, however Antient, tho' we should look back to the most early Times; and give me leave to add, we have as fair a Field for Discoveries and for Improvement, even as the old *Phœnicians* had, of whom we may say, they had the whole World before them; our Advantages also and Ability for carrying on such Discoveries are infinitely Greater.

IT is true we are fond of running into the remotest Angles of the Globe for Discoveries, as if nothing was able to satisfy us that had been known before, and to those who continue that Humour, and think no Improvement can be made nearer home, this History will be but of little use; but I am hopeful, that after a View of these Sheets, there will be but few left of that Mind. I shall in these Discourses therefore show some Schemes of *Improvement* and some *Discoveries*, well worth the undertaking of those who have the most enterprising Genius; and where there is yet room, not for Companies and Colonies only, but for whole Nations, and Generations of Nations, even as long as the World shall last, to plant on, and Time remains to undertake it in.

BUT again, to those who are dispos'd to search for Improvements where they are to be found, and who are capable of believing that there are things forgotten that may yet be re-assum'd, and things never known which may yet be discover'd, tho' nearer home, and easier to be found than by Circling the Globe: *To such*, this Work will, perhaps, be as Profitable, as Pleasant; at least, we shall give them in *Miniature*, and in Speculation, such practicable Things as they may not yet have consider'd, and as may some time or other rouse up Adventurers to undertake; that according to the undoubted design of that Providence which made the World, it may first or last be fully Improv'd, its Treasures fully Discover'd, and all that intrinsick Wealth which Heaven furnish'd the Globe with, be found out and made use of, as he certainly at first intended it shou'd be.

I cannot believe that God ever design'd the Riches *of* the World to be useless *to* the World; that the Gold, the Silver, the Diamonds, and other Species of such Immense Worth and Value, was ever created in the Bowels of the Mountains, and the most hidden Parts of the World to lye buried there, and remain unprofitable, till they come to be melted down again in the *General Conflagration*: God will stand in no Need of the Salts and Sulphur, the Minerals and Combustible Materials, which the Earth is so full of, to assist his Power in kindling the last Fire, or setting the Earth in a Flame for the Destruction of it.

THE Learned *Burnet*[2] in his Notion of the Conflagration's beginning in *Italy*, because the Soil was full of *Sulphur*, and for the more immediate ingulphing the *Whore of Babylon*, might as well have kindled it at Mount *Heckela*,[3] in *Iseland*, where the whole Island is thought to be a solid Mass of Brimstone; or about *Newcastle* in the North of *England*, where the Mass of Bitumen is as proper to set the World on Fire from a Coal Pit, as the other is from a Mine of Sulphur; as for the *Mystical Babylon*, I mean *Rome*, (whatever her distance might be) when once that Flame is begun, I believe the whole Globe will so soon become one immense *Fire-Ball*, that the *Whore of Babylon* will quickly be in the middle of the blaze, without any possibility of an Escape.

IF then the Subterranean Wealth of the World is yet to be fully trac'd to its Fountains and that some time or other, it must be all made use of, *as I firmly believe*, why shou'd not these Ages come into some of it as well as their Neighbours? and why not *now* as well as *hereafter?*

I look upon the Northern and Western Parts of *Asia*, and of *Africa* also, and the Eastern Parts of *Europe* too, to be like Mines of Gold and Silver, which being formerly found out, and as we may say enter'd upon in part, were left off before they were *half wrought*; the Reason of it we shall touch at as we go, but the Fact being prov'd, why shou'd we not enter upon these Works again, that the Inexhausted Treasure being farther search'd into, and the discovering the bottom of them re-assumed, all that Nature had hid, and the Almighty has reserv'd for us, may be found out, and the World made as Rich, and as Learned, in all necessary Knowledge, as they were intended to be at first? and that as their Maker has made a plentiful Provision for them, they may let him know how ready they are to accept of, and improve it?

WHY are all the Coasts of *Africa*, which formerly were so Populous, so well Inhabited, so Rich, so well Improv'd, and so abounding in Gold and Silver, from their own Mountains, and with Corn and Cattle from their own Plains, abandon'd now to a Generation, who as if bountiful Nature was not able to feed them, *where formerly she fed and enrich'd so many Millions at once*, are as it were driven to inhabit only the Sea-Coasts, and to seek there, by Rapin and Piracy, to subsist and support themselves?

WHY are all the Doors of Commerce stopt up between *Europe*, and the *African, Ethiopia?* a Country stor'd with such an immense Wealth, such quantities of Gold, such exquisite Product for Trade, such rich Gums and Drugs, such numbers of Cattle, quantities of Corn, and such a docible People are able, and indeed qualified, to bring ten times more Wealth into *Europe* by Trade, than all the Empires of *New Spain, at least, under their present Management*, do bring to the unimproving *Spaniards*, or are ever like to do.

WHAT blocks up this Commerce now? Nothing, but what might soon and easily be removed, namely the *Turks*; a People, who even by Maxims of their Religion, are Enemies to all Improvements of this kind, and who rather desolate the Nations, than plant or people them: These are indeed the Present, and the only, Hindrances by destroying the Navigation of the *Nile*, which comes directly from the *Ethiopian* Lake *Dombea*, to *Grand Cairo*; and which tho' there are some Obstructions of Cataracts in the Chanel, has yet other smaller Chanels, which might preserve the said Navigation, as also the Navigation of the River *Nubia*, which runs into *Nile*, and which would maintain a Communication with the Southern Limits of the Greater *Libya* and *Numidia*; of both which I shall have an Occasion to speak largely in their Course.

BUT the *Turks*, if they cannot be removed or perswaded to open the said Passages, may not be able wholly to stop the Current of such a beneficial Commerce, as might be open'd on that side of the World if the Trading Nations would join together to undertake it: That Trade may be carryed on many other Ways, as will be explain'd in its Course.

THIS is mentioned here only as a Specimen, a Field of new Discoveries and Improvements which lyes open to the Industry and Application of this Northern Part of the World; there are not less Advantages to be found in reviewing the all-ready discover'd Parts of the World, where Time, and a Succession of Barbarism, have *as it were*, taught us to forget that they were ever known.

THE reviving the Knowledge of antient Times must necessarily be very profitable to our modern Enquiries, if they might be encouraged; and to make a beginning, that where old *Improvements* being lost they may be recover'd, and where there is room for an Addition of farther *Discoveries*, they may yet be made, for the benefit both of Learning and of Commerce, this, *in short*, is the substance of the present Undertaking.

CHAP. I.

Of the first Ages after the Flood, and how Mankind liv'd for some time; what Improvement they then made; and how they spread themselves in the World for the first 300 Years.

ACCORDING to the best Accounts of those Times, *Noah* and his Sons coming out of the Ark upon the Mountains of *Armenia*, which are to this Day call'd *Ararat*, or as some will have it, of *India* (where being the same ridge of Mountains they were still call'd by the same Name) did not spread themselves very far for some Years, but descending from the Hill, extended themselves upon the beautiful plain Country, which lyes *South* and *East* of the Mountain, and there began to cultivate the Earth as Husbandmen, for *so the Scripture says of them*, and to that the Tradition of the People in those Countries agrees.

I doubt not but this Cultivating the Earth, which the Scripture expresses by *Noah*'s being an *Husbandman*, was to be understood, that he plow'd and sow'd, or dug and planted Corn for Bread for the Subsistance of his Family and Posterity; and that long before he planted Vines or a Vineyard, as it is express'd in Scripture.

THIS Planting and Sowing of Grain for Food, was indeed his first Labour, but the planting the Vineyard I call the first *Improvement*, for it certainly came after the other, a considerable time: Corn he sowed immediately, but Vines he undertook as an Improvement, and which he had none of for some considerable time.

How long it was between the Year of the Flood and this planting *a Vineyard*, or at least before the Vines were brought to Perfection, we have no certainty from History; but this we know from the Scripture, that it was not till *Canaan* the youngest Son of *Ham, Noah*'s youngest Son, was grown up to be a Man; for *Noah* gives out the heaviest part of the Curse, for exposing and ridiculing his Drunkenness, to fall upon *Canaan* the Son of *Ham*; not upon any of the rest of his Children, or of his Brother's Children, and this therefore could not be suppos'd to be less than twenty or thirty Years; for *first*, he was not born till five Years after the Flood at least, being the fourth Son of his Father; and *secondly*, he must be suppos'd to be at Man's Estate, for it is the Opinion of the most Learned Annotators that it was *Canaan*, not *Ham*,[4] that saw and expos'd the Nakedness of his Grand-father; Why else should *Noah* omit his Father *Ham*, and load the Curse all on the back of *Canaan* his Son?

UPON the whole, I note it on this Occasion, and so far it is to my present Purpose.

First, THAT Husbandry was the first Employment. And,

Secondly, PLANTING of Vines was the first Improvement after the Flood.

NOAH it seems had but ill luck with his first undertaking, *viz.* to be debauch'd with his own new Wine; But that was his own fault, not the fault of the Wine.

SOME think as the *Devil* tempted *Eve* to eat, in the shape of a Serpent, that is, as Mr. *Milton* describes it,[5] entered into the Serpent, that he might speak to her by an articulate Voice: So he enter'd here into *Canaan*, and set him to Work, to prompt the Old Patriarch to drink; alledging to him the goodness of the Liquor, its sanative Virtue for the support of his Age, *and the like*; Drinking to him, or filling to him, and perhaps, pressing him to drink, till the Old Patriarch was surpriz'd, and took too much, or in short, till, *as the Drunkards call it*, he drank him under the Table; and then, *Devil* like, made Game at him; for which, his old Grand-father most heartily cursed him.

THIS I take to be a much more rational Account of it, than that *Noah*, who was then in the Seventh Century of his Life, shou'd not understand the strength of the Grape, or know that the luscious Juices, if taken too freely, wou'd intoxicate his Brain.

THESE Vines were planted, as the *Greek* Inhabitants tell us, on the slope of the Hill *Ararat*, towards the South, and where they have very rich Wines to this Day; which they tell you are of the very same Grapes, tho' not the very same Plant or Vine that *Noah* planted; and it is not very hard to get Drunk with them, for they are very strong Wines at this time.

FROM hence to the Confusion of *Babel*,[6] we do not find the Posterity of *Noah* travel'd very far from Home; and that tho' it was 131 Years from the Flood to the end of the Building of *Babel*, and by the undertaking it self, we may suppose they were very Numerous; yet it seems they had not sepa-rated to *replenish the Earth*, as God had commanded them; but had only reach'd to the Bank of *Euphrates*, or *Tigris*, where they dwel't, as it were all together, and spread only round themselves, and thus they intended to live, it seems; or else they wou'd never have built such a whimsical Fabrick, and with such ridiculous Views, namely, that it shou'd reach up to Heaven, and save them in case of another Deluge.

Others are of Opinion that they were not so stupid as we make them; that they did not build it for a *Stair-Case* to clamber up to Heaven by, as the Text seems to intimate; but for a Mount to fly up to, in case of a Deluge, and that it contain'd innumerable Vaults and Arches on either hand of the ascent to contain supplies of Provisions and Cattle, *&c.* for their Subsistance.

BUT be it which it will, it was ridiculous enough, that's certain, and shew'd that in those first Ages, they were but very ill furnish'd with Understanding, either of the Power of God, or of the Constitution of the World; and how ill able such a Building wou'd be to bear the shock of the Waters of the Deluge, in case another shou'd happen.

THAT which is most wonderful to me in it, is this, that *Noah*, who was still alive, and his Sons, which we know were all alive at that time, shou'd not be able to convince them of their folly and madness; but that they wou'd go on with it, notwithstanding all his Cautions, and to be sure, Perswasions to the Contrary.

Besides, this Work was a Contempt of God's Blessing, *Gen.* ix. 1, 7. Verses, *Be fruitful, and multiply, and replenish the Earth*. And again, *v.* 7. *Be ye fruitful, and multiply; and bring forth abundantly in the Earth*; which evidently intimates that they shou'd separate themselves, and spread themselves over the Face of the whole Earth, as they were before the Flood, and not keep together in one place *as they were then*; all which their Maker knew wou'd be practicable when their Number came to swell, and that even the whole Earth thereabouts, and so cultivated only, wou'd not subsist and maintain them.

FOR this Reason Heaven thought fit to confound their Speech, if the Text is to be understood literally; upon which, and we may say, as soon as they found the various Dialects, or Speeches, which they now spoke, being restrained to Families and Tribes, they immediately separated, and set out, some one way, and some another, upon *New Discoveries*; and this brings on our present main Purpose.

BY this Separation of the People into Nations, and their going to seek their Fortunes, *as it may be call'd*, they might be truly said to wander, *Ubi fata vocant*,[7] as Heaven secretly directed them; for certainly in their first Journyings from *Babel*, which they had been Building, they knew nothing of whither they went, and but little of what they went about; but went some one way some another, as if their chief Care had been only to keep as far off from one another as they could.

31

As they travel'd thus, I say, some one Way, some another in search of new Discoveries, so we cannot doubt but that every Nation made *Discoveries* suitable to their Enquiries; for the World lay open before them, and where-ever they went they found the Country pleasant, the Air agreeable, and the Soil fruitful, so that every Family had room to choose in, to their full satisfaction; and accordingly fixing themselves in such places, as by situation and pleasantness, best suited them, they soon peopled all the adjacent Countries; and so as their Number encreased, they went on farther and farther, still planting and cultivating as they went.

THEIR greatest Improvements, in their first setting out, were only such as tended to settle the wandering Condition of their Families, and their Properties, in the Countries which they took Possession of; as to every thing else, they seem'd for some Ages under the mere Law of Nature; their Government was Patriarchal, the Father of every Tribe being the Sovereign, or King of all the subsequent Branches; every other Father, having Families of their own begetting, bare Rule, as so many Viceroys under the Patriarchal Monarch, as long as he liv'd; and thus they went on, till several Tribes encreasing, and growing Populous, made themselves Kings and Governours; who, as it continued for many Years after, Governed whole Cities, with the Districts belonging to them, as absolute Monarch, and whom no Man durst disobey, on the Penalty of Life: As for their Commerce, at least as far as we can come at the Knowledge of it, 'twas wholly confined to the two great Articles of *Corn* and *Cattle*; both which, as it was the first Employment of the People, and they depended upon these for their Conveniencies and Subsistance, so I do not call them part of their Management and Improvement at all.

BUT this is not my Enquiry, for I have purposely avoided all Deductions relating to the Government of Nations, only just so far as it is concern'd with our other Design, and then shall touch it but very lightly neither.

SIR *Walter Raleigh*[8] gives us an Account, very Particular as well as Authentick, of the Rout that the several Families of the Sons of *Noah* took, after the Confusion of *Babel*; which as it may be useful in the future Enquiries I am to make I shall just touch at, thus.

First, ABOUT 130 Years after the Flood, a great Body of the multiplyed Sons of *Noah* journey'd from the Place where the Ark rested, whether in *Armenia*, or the Borders of *India* and *Persia*, (is not our business), to *Shinaar*, and there they call'd a great Council, where they made that wise Resolution of building a City, and a Tower, &c. which we call *Babel*.

Secondly, THAT from thence, God having confounded their Language, or as some have it, their Councils, they separated themselves, and as the Text says,[9] *The Lord scatter'd them over the Face of all the Earth.*

Thirdly, THAT upon this Separation, the Sons of *Japhet* spread themselves to the North-West, and inhabited the Lesser *Asia,* and all *Europe,* with the Countries of *Armenia, Georgia, Tartary,* &c.

Fourthly, THE Sons of *Sem,* or *Shem,* spread themselves to the South and East, possessing all the Country, now call'd *Persia,* part of *Tartary, India,* and away to the farthest Eastern Part of the World, even to *China* and *Japan.*

Fifthly, THE Sons of *Ham,* or *Cham,* who were the first who fell upon the Improvement of Arts and Sciences, and also Adventures for Discoveries of Nations, went Westward and Southward from *Shinaar,* and planted the Countries of *Chaldaea, Syria,* and *Canaan, Arabia, Egypt, Ethiopia,* and all *Africa.*

THIS is the general Scheme only, of their Separation; as for the particular Countries, which every Tribe or Family possessed, and where they planted themselves, as it is too long to enter upon in this Work, and also is not in my main design, I omit the Description, as not much to the purpose, in this place, but may touch upon it as we go along.

CHAP. II.

Of the particular Travels of Ham *or* Cham, *the youngest Son of* Noah, *and his Posterity; and how, among them, began the first progress of Art and Science, Commerce, and the Improvement of Commerce in the World.*

THE Sons of *Ham* or *Cham*, as I have said, marching, West and South-West, from *Shinaar*,[10] we shall trace them a little more particularly than the rest, because among them we shall find the beginning of the most useful Arts, and of the sublimest Knowledge that Mankind was first blest with, of which such great Improvements have been made, as we see this Day; and this is the Reason of beginning this Discourse so far back.

AMONG these, we find the knowledge of *Astronomy*, with the Motions and Influences of the Heavenly Bodies; which began first to be studied among the *Arabians*, and by the *Egyptians* improv'd to a very great Height, tho' under the mistaken Foundation of *Ptolemy*; whose description of the Heavenly Bodies, dividing them into Constellations, and solving the difficult Phænomena of their Motions, Revolutions, Eclipses, and Conjunctions, &c. is call'd to this Day the *Ptolemaick System*.

AMONG these, we find the first knowledge of Letters, forming of Speech into Words, and these Words being by prolation[11] of Syllables, and Letters, and the giving Sounds to them made to speak, so as to be capable of conveying the meaning of one another at the greatest Distance, which we call Writing.

AMONG these, we find the first knowledge of Ships and Vessels to sail and row upon the Waters; joyning thereby the Inhabitants of distant Nations one to another; and to them we owe the Invention of Navigation, and the Improvement of it, for the benefit of Commerce, the first Merchants being found among them.

WITH these, therefore, we are first to converse in the Work before us, and I shall, in a few Words, bring them down to the Times, when these things were first attempted in the World, and then persue their several Improvements, as they lye before us.

THE eldest Son of *Canaan* was named *Sidon*. The Family pursuing their Discoveries West and South, that is to say, into *Palæstina*, and into *Arabia*, and I take the first momentous Discovery, they made as they travel'd Westward, to be that of the Sea.

AS Sir *Walter Raleigh* wisely observes, tho' they went on Progressively spreading themselves upon the Face of the Earth, as their number encreased, yet they did not ride Post, nor go on like Travellers; and I add, that they rather proceeded like Planters, who spread gradually, farther and farther, as they found the Country too strait for them, and as their Cattle wanted Pastures, or as their Plow called for more Land, by the encrease of their People.

AS then they had, at least, 460 Miles from the Land of *Shinaar*, where *Babel* stood, to the Coast of the *Mediterranean*, we may, at least, allow them to be thirty or forty Years, if not more, in spreading Colonies so far as *Sidon*, and clearing the Lands before them, for it is to be suppos'd, that the Surface of the Earth was generally made difficult to pass, by the over-growing of Woods in the upper Grounds, and the over-spreading of Waters and Rivers in the low Lands, which they had Occasion to pass over; and that this greatly retarded their Journeying; However, otherwise, they might be forward enough to go on.

BUT tho', perhaps, *Ham* the Father, much less *Noah* the Grand-father, never saw the Western Coast of *Palæstine*, yet 'tis certain *Canaan* the Grandson of *Noah* enter'd into, and took Possession of it, and the Land it self was called by his Name.

HERE allow me to fansy, for the Readers Diversion, that we could see the wandering Travellers, when from the tops of the Hills, call'd the *Libanus*, or *Anti Libanus*,[12] (for there was the place) I say, when from the tops of the Hills, they first discover'd the open Sea, the great *Mediterranean Sea*, call'd, by way of Distinction, the *Great Sea*: How they started back at the sight; How they ask'd one another, in the greatest Surprize imaginable, *What it was?* What it look'd like? How Frightful in the Opinion of some; How Glorious in the Opinion of others; none knowing by any Means, what it was: Also how much more surpriz'd, when coming nearer to it, they could perceive that it was *not Land*, but *Water*; that it put an end to their Travels; and that when they came to the Brink of it, they could see no more Land, nothing but a vast endless Ocean of Water; and that Water subject to various Disorders, Storms, Tempests, &c. Suppose their Souls fill'd with Wonder and Amazement, they stand musing at the sight of it in Disorder, and showing what it was impossible to conceal, (*viz.*) that they thought they were now at their *Ne plus*,[13] and could never expect to pass any farther.

WHEN they came to the Shore, they were again surpriz'd to see even the Sea friendly to them, and affording them a variety of Food, little inferiour to the richest Diet which God had bestowed before; in short, that it was most agreeable living in those Climates. Accordingly they resolve to prescribe themselves, as the Laws of Nature had prescrib'd them, not having the least Notion that the Water was Navigable, or what Navigation meant; much less, that these mighty Waters were appointed to be Subservient to the benefit of Mankind: They had heard indeed of the Ark, and of the Flood, which cover'd the whole Earth, but they had not seen either the one or the other.

WRAPT up in these imperfect ideas of Things, they sat down in the Land of *Canaan*; and if Occasion requir'd, that they shou'd extend themselves farther, they did it to the *South*, or the *North*, for farther Westward they could not go.

HERE they had room to look back, and consider the furious Element, and whether it was not a dreadful Enemy that they had escaped from in the *Deluge*; Here they had time to consider what was next to be done, for that a stop being there put to their travels they must alter their Course, and extend themselves some other Way.

BUT while they are considering what, indeed, they were next to do, *Sidon*, the eldest, Son, tells them in so many Words, they may do as they think meet, but that as for him, he will fix his Standard just there, and the Borders of the Sea shou'd bound his Ambition; and accordingly, taking the Lands adjacent for his Patrimony, he built a City on the Verge or Bank of the Ocean, and call'd it by his own Name, *Sidon*.

IN the mean time his Father *Canaan* taking Possession of the Inland Country of *Palæstine*, and extending Northward, into that part which was afterwards call'd *Syria*, seated himself, and his other Children, in that goodly part of the Country and there built, on the Bank of a very pleasant River, another City, calling it after the Name of his Father *Ham, Hamas*, or *Hamascus*, now *Damascus*, which City is remaining to this Day; retains its antient Name, and that with the least alteration that is to be met with in any City in the World, and is, without dispute, the most antient City in the World; for even the Scripture makes mention of it in *Abraham*'s time; *Gen.* xv. II. where *Abraham* says, *The Steward of my House, is this* Eliezer *of* DAMASCUS; which saying of *Abraham*, was according to Calculation, in the Year of the World 2030, or thereabouts; about 370 Years after the Flood.

WHILE *Canaan* thus built *Damascus*, his Son built *Sidon*, and thereby, with the rest of his Children, settled the several Nations of the *Canaanites*, and those which were after call'd *Phœnicians*; a Wise and Industrious People, as we shall see presently.

THE great Father of them all, *Ham*, the youngest Son of *Noah*, with his other Sons, *Chus* and *Mizraim*, and *Phut*, took the South-West Course, and spread themselves into *Arabia*, and into *Egypt*; where *Ham* himself erected his first Kingdom and reigned there, according to the most antient Authors, 161 Years; beginning his Kingdom 191 Years after the Flood; leaving his Grandson *Nimrod* the first, and most early Monarch, to be King indeed, but at first without a Kingdom, which he afterwards settled in *Assyria*, and *Arabia*; of whom, at present, we shall take no more Notice, tho' hereafter we shall have Occasion to speak of him again.

CHAP. III.

Of the beginning of Commerce, *and* Navigation *in the World*.

LET not our Readers imagine, from what has been said, that we shall entertain them only with the dry Subject of Antiquity, and amuse them with the History of the Worlds Planting: Tho' it be necessary to bring every thing on gradually, and from its Beginning, that the Chain of History may not be broken, yet the process of this Work will we hope not be so Barren of Entertainment to the enquiring Readers, as to tire them with the rusty Fragments of antient Times. The business of this Undertaking being then to give a true History of Discoveries and Improvements, and of them only, I shall come immediately to the point, and leave the Original of Nations, as it really ought to be, quite out of the Enquiry.

HAVING brought the *Canaanites*, or Sons of *Canaan*, whom we are, from hence forward, to call *Phœnicians*, to the Sea Coast, and built *Sidon*, as in the last Chapter; you must allow that the *Sidonians* having but a small Territory by Land, and being an Observing, Diligent, and Improving People, *if I may judge of them by what they were afterwards*, I say you must allow them to be making divers little Enterprizes upon the Water.

THEY had never seen Boat or Vessel, or heard of any, or even of any Sea, except the Ark, and the universal Flood of Water. If any of them, by the Dictates of Nature, and the frequent Bathing themselves in the Sea, had learnt to swim, it might, for ought we know, be the only Testimony they had of the boyant power of the Water, and the Reason of hollow and empty Bodies floating upon it: And this by mere natural Deduction, as a Learned Writer suggests, was the first hint to them for making hollow Vessels to float, and consequently, to bear Burthens upon the Surface of the Water.

THERE was directly opposite to the Town a small Shoal, or Sand, which at low Water, seem'd to be an Island, lay Dry, and at some Seasons, upon a lower Ebb than ordinary, the Sea wou'd be so far sunk, as that they might wade to it; which Island was, it seems, after some time, rais'd, and taken in, to make a Mole, or Haven to the Town, and so was join'd to the Main-land: But this was not (I say) till some Ages, and the first Voyage, or Adventure by Sea, that these *Sidonians*, who were yet young in their Experiments, made, was to this Island, which, at most, could not be above a Mile from the Shoar, of which presently.

To do this, the first invention of a Boat was set on Foot; and indeed it was a poor one, and does not come up to the Negroes of *Africa*, or Natives of *America*, who, before the *Europeans* came among them, had their *Canoes*, and *Periaguaes*,[14] made of the Trunk of a Tree, hollow'd in the middle by the help of Fire, and so form'd without so much as any Iron Tool to work with; in which *Canoes*, or *Troughs*, for they were no other, they yet were seen sometimes off upon the open Sea, at a very great distance from the Shoar.

BUT the first Boats that we find they made, in these Countries, and by Consequence, in the whole World, *for these were certainly the first that discovered the Sea*, was a parcel of Osyers[15] wreathed, and tyed together, then cover'd with broad Leaves of Flags,[16] which grew in the Rivers there, and were very large and thick, and these again cover'd with the Skins of Beasts dryed, which wou'd keep out the Water: They were formed into a shape, adapted for floating, or swimming on the Water, spreading them with Sticks thrust into either Side, to stretch them out, that so being kept hollow, they might swim, and be able to carry some Weight in them also.

HENCE the cross Pieces, placed in the same manner in a Boat, used now for the Rowers to set their Feet against when they Row, are at this time call'd *Stretchers*.

AS these Boats could go but a very little way upon the Water, so they did not use to venture far in them; and usually, no farther, than that in case of a Disaster, they might swim to Shoar without them. And I suppose the first Voyage that ever was made in the World, after the Division of the Nations at *Babel*, was, as above, from *Sidon* to this little Island, being about a Mile in length.

NOR had the *Egyptians*, for a long time after, any other Boats than such as those, to cross the great River *Nile*, and even the Red Sea it self, as appears by those Lines in *Lucan*.

> *Primum cana salix, madefacto vimine, parvam*
> *Texitur in puppim, cæsoque induta juvenco,*
> *Vectoris patiens, tumidum superenatat amnem.*[17]

THE principal use of these Boats, for many Years, were only to go a Fishing under Land, or along the Shoar upon any other small Occasion they had.

AFTER some time, as the acquaintance with the Sea made them bold, they made these Boats larger and stronger, till Invention still improveing, they bound larger Sticks together, and made yet larger Boats, and stronger; and then they adventur'd farther into the Sea, till as Fame tells us, some *Sidonian* Fishermen going too far out in one of these Boats, a great Fish, not a Whale I suppose, because they are not ordinarily found in those Seas, but a great Fish, over-set, and over-turn'd one of their Boats, with six Men in it, who all swam safe to the Shoar.

UPON this Disaster, necessity calling for farther Assistance, the Inhabitants laid their Heads together, and made larger Boats, covering the Sides of them with thin Boards, and strengthen'd within by small pieces of Wood put together, and those Boards again being cover'd with Pitch, or a kind of Bitumen and Oyl, mixt together, to kept out the Water.

AND as they grew more us'd to the Element of Water, so they improv'd in the Art of Building their Boats, but we are assur'd, that they never attain'd to the Skill of giving Motion to their Boats by the Wind, and by the help of Sailors, till many Years after; and till the City of *Tyre* was built, which was not founded till some Ages after *Sidon*, and was a Colony of *Sidon*, being built, according to some Authors, 240 Years before the Temple of *Solomon*, which must be in the Year of the World 2783; but according to others, in the Year 1973, about 300 Years after the Flood, and 170 Years after the Confusion of *Babel*: For the City of *Sidon* was now large, and begun to spread it self upon the Coast every way, but especially, Northward, towards *Cilicia*, where they also built, or at least peopled *Tarsus*,[18] or *Tarshih*, which was afterwards their *Arsenal*, or Magazine for building of Ships.

BEFORE the *Sidonians* built *Tyre*, they knew but little of the Sea, nor had they arriv'd to the knowledge of Sailing on the Water, tho' they had small Boats, as above, but that part was afterwards found out by the Citizens of *Tyre*.

THE *Sidonians*, indeed, were grown Rich, Populous, and consequently Powerful by Land; but it was not the *Sidonians*, but *Tyrians* that invented the use of Sails, and taking the benefit of the Wind in their Boats, as we are assur'd by the Poet *Tibullus* in the following Line.

Prima ratem ventis credere docta Tyros.[19]

Tyrus taught first how Ships might use the Wind.

FROM such small beginnings, was deriv'd that glorious piece of Knowledge, which is now so admirably improv'd, and is so deservedly rank'd among, and esteem'd the most useful part of the Mathematicks, I mean *Navigation*; to what perfection it is since arriv'd, by what degrees it came to that Perfection, and how its greatest Advancement was reserv'd for the

Honour of the present Age, will be, according to my Title, one part of the business of this Undertaking.

We are next to understand, that in a few Years after the first settling of the Sons of *Ham*, in this Country, *Sidon* encreas'd exceedingly, whether from the pleasantness of its Situation, or the benefit of the Sea for Fishing, or that they soon began to correspond with their Neighbours, is not Material; but they grew so Populous, that finding a convenient Situation, not much unlike to *Sidon* it self, and at but about 14 Miles distance to the South, they sent out Families, as Bees do a Swarm, and taking Possession there, they began to build another Town, or City, and call'd it *Tyre*, from the Word *Zor*, or *Tor*, signifying a Rock; the first Town being built on a high Cliff, or Rock, on the edge of the Shore, having a very noble Bay, or Inlet of Water just under it, most admirably beneficial for Shipping, for secureing them from all the dangerous Winds, which blow on that Coast, and which was, most certainly, directed by Heaven, who fore-knew the Occasion they would afterwards have of such a Harbour, tho' at that Time, the Builders were entirely Ignorant of the use of it, having no knowledge of Shipping, or Navigation, of any kind whatever, other than, I have already mentioned, in little sorry Boats, without Sails, without Rudders, scarce able to deserve the Name of Boats, nor had they any other, for some Years after.

This was the poor and despicable beginning of the Noble, and truly Glorious City of *Tyre*: The Beginner of Trade; the Mother of Merchants; where Commerce had its first Birth, and where all the Trade of the World center'd in a few Years after, and continued to do so many Ages.

TYRE, Whose Merchants were Princes, and whose Traffickers were the Honourable upon the Earth, *Isaiah* 27. 8.

TYRE, Whose Navigation spread its Fame into all Parts of then known Globe, and some of whose Colonies became the most famous Establishments in the World.

TYRE, Whose People planted the Coast of *Africa*, to the Straits of *Gibralter*, and built *Utica, Carthage, Leptis*, and several other Cities.

> *Urbs antiqua fuit*, Tyrij *tenuere Coloni*,
> Carthago.[20]
> > Virg. Æneid lib. I.

In *Spain*, They pass'd the *Ne Plus ultra*, as it was afterwards call'd, of *Hercules Pillars*, and entering the Ocean, built *Cales*, then call'd *Gades*,[21] and almost made a Colony of the whole Kingdom of *Spain*, for they possess'd all the Southern Parts of the Kingdom. In *Italy*, they built *Nola*, and several other great, and populous Cities in other Parts of the World: On *this Side*, They traded with the antient *Armoricans*, the *Spaniards*, and even with the

Britains; and from thence navigated all the Northern and Eastern Seas, where never Ships, or Barks, had sail'd before; and *on the South Side*, they traded with the whole Coast of *Afric*, in the *Mediterranean*, with *Arabia* and *Ethiopia*, in the Red Sea, and even afterwards to *India* it self, by the Straits of *Babelmandel*, now called the Gulph of *Mocha*, or the *Arabian* Gulph.

As here Trade and Arts began, and afterwards, being well managed, came to flourish; so in *Egypt*, where *Ham*, the Grand Patriarch of that Race, and in *Arabia*, where also his Posterity flourished, settled and became King. The Inhabitants fell to the Study of *Astronomy*, and the motions of the Heavenly Bodies, and made a great Progress in it, and in all kinds of Natural, and in some Parts of Experimental Philosophy, besides the wicked Study of *Magic, Astrology, South-Saying*,[22] &c.

FOR as the People were all swallow'd up with Idolatry; the Devil was not idle among them neither; but as they run into the Study and Knowledge of *one Art*, he taught them *another*, while they innocently apply'd themselves to *one Thing*, he debauch'd their Fancy with *another*: Thus from the Study of *Astronomy*, he led them, as above, into the blind search after an Infernal Knowledge, by *Magic*, and divers Kinds of *Witchcraft, Divinations*, and *Conjurations, Necromancy*, and telling Fortunes, *and the like*: Hence, afterward, they came to Interpreting Dreams, which from the situation of the Country, was call'd *South Saying*, the *Arabians* being Inhabitants of all the *South* Part of the Country, between the *Persian* and *Arabian* Gulphs.

FROM hence, Idolatry encreasing, they came up to the Enthusiasm of the *Aruspices*,[23] and the Priests giving Answers by the Entrails of Sacrific'd Beasts, by the flying of Birds, and other Diabolical Practices, and as the Height and Perfection of all their Idolatry, to their Oracles, giving Answers at the Temples of their Idols, &c. But this is none of our present Business, I return to the early Discovery, as well of Arts, as of the Country, which Mankind made in the first Ages after the Flood.

AS *Ham* and his numerous Offspring, discovering *Arabia, Palæstine*, and *Egypt*, were thus busy, settling themselves West, and spreading farther and farther into *Afric*; so the Great *Nimrod*,[24] Grandson of *Ham*, by his Eldest Son *Chus*, made a very particular Discovery, namely, of the Art of Tyranny, and subjecting Right and Wrong to the Determination of Power. How he drew Mankind, who were born free, to embrace a Brutal Slavery, this we have but little light into in History, unless we may deduce it from the significant important Word, used for it in Scripture, (*viz.*) *a Hunter*, with this Emphasis upon the Word, a Hunter *before the Lord*; by which, as most of the Learned Expositors, and Annotators tell us, was meant a *Hunter of Men*: and so it imports, that *Nimrod*, being of a furious, bloody, tyrannick Disposition, first subdued a few by his mighty Strength, and then subjecting them, forced them to serve him in his farther Designs, to enslave others, till having thus gotten a Number together, ready to execute his Commands, and over run others with Violence, under his Leading: He thus subdued Nations, and began Empire.

THUS he hunted down the weak helpless People, and set up a Kingdom under himself, till then unknown in the World; for he broke the Rule of Eldership, and Paternity, setting aside the Patriarchal Kingdom or Empire, which ought to have remain'd in *Noah* (for he was still living) or at least in his Grandfather *Ham*, or his Father *Chus*, But despising all these, I say, he usurp'd the Throne, or Government and setting up for himself, erected a Kingdom of his own, bringing the rest of the Tribes into subjection to himself, and here began the blessed Discovery to the World call'd *Tyranny*, but this by the way.

THIS tyrannick Government encreasing, began the *Babylonish Empire*, and by him, was all the Country between *Palæstina*, or *Syria*, and the Rivers *Euphrates* and *Tigris*, planted, or rather subjected, of which again in its Place.

SEM, or *Shem*, the younger Son of *Noah*, and so named in the Text, *Gen.* x. 21. went away into *Chaldea*, being all the Country, lying on the lower Banks of *Euphrates*, on both sides, and reaching to the Gulph of *Persia*, and where the *Assyrian* and *Persian* Empires afterwards succeeded: hence *Abraham*, who was brought from *Ur* of the *Chaldees*, which lyes on the West Side of all those great Rivers, where they empty themselves into the *Persian* Gulph, and thence the Posterity of *Sem* extended themselves Eastward, also over all *India*, even to the Empire of *China*, and the Isles of *Japan*, the *Moluccas*, &c.

N. B. *This I Observe, in Order to Note, that tho' the Language of all the Earth was divided, yet the Sons of the Posterity of* Sem, *retained their primitive antient Speech, which was the* Hebrew *which* Abraham *spoke, and his Posterity after him who were therefore call'd* Hebrews.

JAPHET, in the mean time, and his Sons, especially *Gomer* and *Magog*, and *Madai* and *Javan*, spread themselves to the North, and planted, and peopled the Lesser *Asia*, and all *Europe*; and the Discoveries and Improvements they have since made there, we shall come to Enquire of in their Course.

THUS by the three Sons of *Noah*, as the Scripture says, *were the Nations divided in the Earth, after the Flood*, Gen. x. ult.[25]

CHAP. IV.

Of the first Discovery of Shipping and Navigation, and of several Improvements made, during the most early Ages, next after the Phœnicians *settling at* Sidon.

Tyre was the Daughter of *Sidon*, and she dwelt so near her Mother, that they went on hand in hand in the Improvement of their Navigation, as well as of their Commerce: What mean and contemptible Things they began at, I have hinted in the former Chapter, and believe, I have shewn good Reason for what I have said, for it is evident that the *Tyrians* were the first of Sailors, tho' a great while after the *Sidonians* had the use of Boats. For *Tyre*, tho' a very antient City, was not Built till about 278 Years after *Sidon*: so that they had the use of Boats, possibly such as I have already Describ'd, and, perhaps, Canoes, Periaguas, and the like, above 300 Years before they found out the use of sailing with the Wind.

The first step of Improvement, other than what I have already mention'd, namely of a Boat, and Oars, that is to say *Paddles* to give her Motion or Way in the Water, was, as I find, by good Authority, the use of a *Rudder* or *Helm* to steer or guide the Boat, in her Motion from place to place.

This, they tell us, was first learn'd from an Ingenious, or rather a Curious Observer of such Things, who took notice how a great Eagle, which us'd the Shore thereabouts, soaring, and as it were sailing aloft in the Air, in a calm Evening, turn'd her Tail from a Horizontal to a perpendicular or polar Situation, as she had occasion to guide herself this way, or that in her Flight; by which turning of her Tail, the Wind which always blows Horizontal, pushing against the Feathers, whose flat Side lay then towards it, forced the Tail forward, and that again turn'd the Body of the Eagle the contrary way. For Example, If the Eagle flew North, and the Wind blew from the East, the Eagle turning the flat Side of her Tail towards the Wind, and the Wind pushing the Tail, on that occasion due West, the Head of the Bird would necessarily be turn'd to the other way East: By the same Rule a Rudder to a Boat being caus'd to lye in the same posture in the Water, as the Tail or Rudder of the Eagle in the Wind, and push'd this or that Way by the force of a Man's Hand against the Water, wou'd necessarily turn the Head of the Boat the contrary way.

THIS method of Steering was for a very considerable Time, known only to the *Sidonians*, and that Knowledge purchas'd again, *and perhaps Dear too, at first* by the *Tyrians*; and what use did they make of it? indeed little more than to guide the small Boats they had, when they shou'd help them forward on their Way, and turn them this way, or that way, as their Occasion serv'd.

THUS Navigation was founded in Reason, and the Nature of Things, and discover'd by slow degrees, the Improvement being the effect of daily Experiment, and great Application, besides Hazards, and Difficulties, ay and Loss too; for as it is said of Physic, that the experimental Knowledge of the use and virtue of Plants, Drugs, *&c.* the *Materia Medica*, of which all Physic is Compounded, has cost the World dear, by Poisoning many Thousands of its Inhabitants before the Practice arriv'd to the present Perfection. So I make no Doubt, that this *Sea-Knowledge*, as *Navigation* is rightly call'd, cost the World the Drowning many more Thousands of its People, before the Art of Building, Fitting, and Sailing, or Navigateing Ships, arriv'd to the present Perfection.

AGAIN, as this Art, or Science of Navigation, is of inexpressible advantage to Mankind, so the Knowledge of it has been deriv'd from the most certain Principles in Nature, tho' it is Conversant in the two most uncertain Elements for its Performances, *viz.* the Wind, and the Water; but I come to the History.

IT was not many Years after the building of *Tyre* before, by the exceeding Conflux of People which from all Parts of the then known World flock'd thither, the Place became very populous, and still encreas'd daily.

THIS great Conflux of People brought on that mighty, and now, most important Thing call'd TRADE; which we have Reason to believe had also its beginning here, and of which I shall speak at large in the Process of this Work; I therefore only name it here to introduce this just Note, which is to my present Purpose, namely, *That Navigation was the Parent of Trade*, as Trade has always been the support and encouragment of Navigation: Trade had never been considerable without Ships, or Ships useful and valuable without Trade; in a Word, they are the mutual Supports of one another, and may be said to be conceiv'd and born together, by a mysterious Generation, Begetting one another.

HOWEVER, let them influence one another as they will, they are, *take them as Improvements and Discoveries*, different in their Species. I am at present, to speak of the first.

THE first Voyage by Sea, which we are to suppose these new Adventurers made, was to the Island of *Cyprus*, which was an important Discovery, and the Climate being found agreeable, and the Soil rich, it became a Colony of the *Tyrians*, tho' it had been, as some think, peopled before from the Coast of *Cilicia*. Hence in return for their planting on this Island, they receiv'd the product of the Land, (*viz.*) such as the Inhabitants, by their Industry, caus'd it to produce, namely, *Wine, Oyl, Corn*, and other Goods, for the supply of the *Tyrians*, and their great City, which every Day encreas'd in People, and in Wealth.

SUPPOSE, by this Time the *Phœnicians* to be a great and mighty Nation, and the *Tyrians*, Inhabitants of this Coast, and the *Sidonians*, the first Merchants, extending their Commerce by Sea; For the doing this, they not only built Ships and Vessels, proper for their Business; but their Business encreasing, they employ'd the *Cilicians*, who inhabited the South Coast of *Asia Minor*, to built Ships for them, the *Cilicians* being better stor'd with Timber, and other Materials for Building. And this was the Rise and Beginning of the City of *Tarsus* or *Tarshish*, where the first Building Yards and Docks, as we now call them, are supposed to have been found.

IT wou'd be a Question worth Answering, if we could speak directly to it, what sort of Vessels or Ships, as they were call'd, the *Tyrians* and *Sidonians* at first made use of. But unless the Model of one of their Boats had been preserv'd, and could be referred to, no Man can speak with Authority to the Question.

IT is said, the first Builder of a Vessel for Sailing, was a *Cilician* of *Tarsus*, and that he took his draft or model from the Breast-bone of a *Swan*, which it may be observed, even now, is the exact shape of the bottom of a Ship; and that our Ships of War, or Fregates are built also after that same make; the breast or belly of a Goose or Duck is the same; which if critically observ'd has the very dimensions and proportions by which our Men of War are built.

I NAME the Men of War because they are, as our people call it, *built for Sailing*, and the Merchant Ships, or Ships of Burthen, tho' preserving the shape in the main part for floating or bearing upon the Water, have yet a greater breadth allow'd for their carrying the greater Weight or Loading: But our Fregate built Ships[26] are exactly form'd after the model of a Swan's Body: There you will find Nature working exactly for the occasion, giving that Creature all the suitable, and just proportions necessary to its condition, and to preserve it in the Element it was appointed to live in; and the Ship Builders were much in the right, they could not have a more exact patern; there you will see the plain form of the Ship's Bow or Head, the

Keel, the Rake, the Stern, and the Bearings, or Sides by which our Ships are formed, and the due proportions both of breadth and length.

DIRECTED thus by the wisdom of Nature, they had nothing to do but by the help of Art to form their work to the Model: This we may be assur'd was the work of Time, and that so much time, that even till within the reach of our Days, the Art of building Ships, as well as of navigating them in the Seas has been growing, and improving, and whether it may not still improve, I will not affirm; tho' it must be acknowledg'd, the present Age seems to have finish'd that part of Nature's work, and that it is not capable of any considerable addition; I say considerable, because the little alterations in the upper-work ornament, and conveniences of Ships, which are daily chang'd like the Fashions of our Clothes, and which I may rather call alterations than improvements, are not worth naming in the Question; being not essential to the main end of Ship Building, I mean the Sailing, the bearing the Sea, Turning, lying near the Wind, Staying, &c. which the Seamen call the working of a Ship. These are the essential Articles of a Ship's usefulness; without them she is no more than a Trough in the Sea to roul upon the Surface, to lye and drive like the Hull when the Masts and Sails are down, or like a mere luggage Boat that is of use only to carry a Burthen, and not on any dangerous occasion. As to the Building, and carv'd Work, Painting, and Glazing, they are of little importance, but are, as I said above, frequently alter'd and chang'd by the Builders, as our Clothes are by the Taylors, and are peculiar to the Countries or Ports, or Fashions and Fancies of particular Workmen where the Ships are built.

BUT to come back to the model of the Ships built in those Days by the *Tyrians*, the *Cilicians*, and others, who were the first Navigators; it is most certain that at their beginning they were very rude, and imperfect, as well as incapable for their business; especially, if they came into any distresses at Sea; and therefore we find that for many Ages, as well by the insufficiency of their Building, as defficency of the Navigators Knowledge, and want of the Compass or Magnet, the most of their Voyages were perform'd by coasting along the Shoar, the consequence of which was, that upon any threatening Storm, or any extraordinary swelling of the Sea, they always ran into the first Harbour they could come at, and in defect of such Harbour, or upon being blown off to Sea, they were often stranded on the Shoar, or swallow'd up in the Sea with all that was in them.

THE manner of their Vessels, we may make some guess at by the description we meet with in Antient Writers, and in the pictures remaining of some of their Ships, where we find that Ships for War were always row'd by the Mariners, and Soldiers; some had twenty Oars in a Bank, or on a Side, some more, and had a Prow or Beak, as the Gallies have to this Day, but stood much higher; their Merchant Ships were built round, and turning up like a *Dutch* Hoy, and were exactly alike at either end, and thus to be sure was that Ship which the Apostle St. *Paul* was shipwreck'd in, as may be judg'd by their casting four Anchors over the Stern, and afterwards making a shew of casting more Anchors out of the Foreship, *Acts* xxvii. 29, 30.

As the shape and built of the Ship was the same in the Head as in the Stern, so the uses were the same, for they sail'd with either end forward as occasion required, and rode by the Head or by the Stern, as they found most to their advantage, having Anchors at both to ride by. This necessarily implies that they steer'd the Vessel not by a Rudder hung to the Stern-post, *as we now do*, which was turn'd by a Tiller, and a Whipstaff, as the Seamen call them, and used within the Deck, or by a Tiller only, when steer'd above the Deck; but by some piece of Wood like an Oar thrust out of a Port, or held out from the Deck of the Ship; and this might be done which end soever went formost, or if it had a Rudder, then there must necessarily be two Rudders, one before, and one behind, which is not probable, or they had a Rudder which was moveable and loose, and could be taken off and on, and so be hang'd either afore or abaft, as their Course requir'd; and this latter was certainly the case of the Ship St. *Paul* was in, for in the 40th Verse of the fore-quoted Chapter, he says, that resolving to run into a certain Creek, or in short, being in great distress, but seeing Land at a distance, they resolved to run *Bump a shoar*, so our Sailors term it, to save their Lives; the Apostle's Words are thus, Cap. xxvii. v. 40. *And when they had taken up the Anchors, and committed themselves to the Sea, they loosed the Rudderbands, and hoisted up the main Sail to the Wind, and made towards the Shoar.*

THIS loosing the Rudder bands must be thus, as they rode by the Anchors, before cast out at the Stern, they had taken off the Rudder from the *Stern-post* and had now hang'd it upon the Stem, which was become the Stern for the occasion; but now taking up the Anchors, and resolving to run the Ship on Shoar, they could not run her on Shoar with a Rudder hanging on the end which was to go foremost, which was the Stem, so they loosed the Rudder bands again, that is, unty'd it, and took it off, and then they went forward towards the Shoar.

AND this was plain also from the fourth Verse, they run the Ship on Shoar, or a-Ground by the Head, which Head, or *fore part* stuck fast, but the Stern not being on Ground, *was broken in pieces*, as it must of necessity be by the violence of the Sea, the Ship having *broken her Back*, as our Sailors call it.

THESE things are so natural that they give us almost a full description of the Ship, which at the same time we must acknowledge, was a very poor, inconvenient, and clumsy thing, compar'd to what we are arriv'd to the knowledge of making in these Days.[27]

IN the next place we find that the Ship St. *Paul* was in, tho' it was a very great Vessel, for it had on Board, besides its Lading of Corn, 276 people, Seamen, Soldiers, and Passengers, yet had but one Mast, and if I guess right, had but one Sail neither, or two at most, for Verse 17, he says, *Being afraid of the Quick-Sands they stroke Sail, and so were driven,*[28] or let her drive, as our People express it; *that is*, not being able to carry their Sail they lower'd the Yard upon the Deck; and this is agreeable to the manner of their sailing in those Seas, till within a very few Years past, when they carry'd no Top Mast at all, or but very small ones, but all their Sails lower'd at once upon the Deck if the Wind blew too hard to carry them out.

THIS is the description which Reason gives of their Shipping; from the account which St. *Paul* has left us of his Voyage; and I believe you may take a just Idea from it of the manner of their building their Ships, as well as of their ignorance in Sailing *in those Days*; and yet *those* were *Days* when the Art of Navigation was wonderfully improv'd, compar'd to what it had been at the building of *Tyre*, or *Tarsus* either.

NOW tho' this gives a sorry account of the Navigation of those Days compar'd to these; yet if we go back again to the times before that, as we must do, to form just Ideas in our Minds of the first improvements of Shipping and Navigation, we shall see that even with those small beginnings great Things were done, great Enterprizes were gone about, and great Things, not undertaken only, but finished. As,

    I. THE Navy of the *Greeks*, at the Siege of *Troy*, must be exceeding Numerous which brought the Armies of the several *Grecian* Princes, and Common-wealths, from the *Morea* or *Peloponnesus*, and other parts of the *Ægean* Sea to the *Hellespont* to form the Siege, which if the Chronology of those times is true, was above 432 Years before the building of *Rome*; I say it must be exceeding great, for the *Greeks* were an hundred thousand Men at least. But then as Sir *Walter Raleigh* observes.

       The Vessels were not great, for it was not then known how to build Ships with Decks. Vid. *Raleigh*'s History of the World, lib. 2, cap. xiv. § 2. fol. 249.[29]

    II. THE Ships of King *Solomon*, which went to *Ophir* for Gold,[30] supposing that *Ophir* to be the Island of *Sumatra*, or the *Philippines* in the *East Indies*, as some think; This from *Ezion Geber* in the *Red Sea*, was a very long Voyage, tho' even that Voyage was all perform'd Coast-Wise, and within sight of the Shoar.

III. THE several Voyages of the *Phœnician* Merchants from the same *Ezion Geber* in the *Red Sea* to the Coast of *Mozambique*, thence to the Cape *de Bon Esperance* or the Cape of *Good Hope*, and round the whole Coast of *Africa*[31] to the Straights of *Gibraltar*, and so through the *Mediterranean* to the *Levant*, that is to say, to the City of *Tyre*.

IV. THE Navy of *Alexander* the Great, when he beseig'd and attack'd the City of *Tyre*, and took it, after a Seige of seven Months, which however, had he not block'd up their Harbour with his Ships he could never have perform'd.

THESE were great undertakings, considering the infancy of Navigation, and the ignorance of the most knowing Artists, for the *Phœnicians* were the best Navigators in the World without any comparison; and as they were the first, so they continued the most improv'd in the Art of Building Ships.

IT must be acknowledg'd also to their Fame, they were bold Mariners, and that considering what indifferent Ships they had, without Decks, and consequently but ill furnish'd to keep the Sea; without conveniences to secure the Men, or to defend them, either from the rage of the Water, or from the inclemencies of the Seasons, covering themselves only with oil'd Canvass, or such as we now call *Tarpaulins*, and the like, as well to preserve themselves from Heat or Cold, and Rains, and Snows, as from the break-ings of the Sea upon them, I say, all these things consider'd, they were bold Seamen to venture, tho' it were within view of the Shoars, for they were sometimes, without doubt, driven out of sight of Land, and as we may say, out of their knowledge, by Tempests, and Storms, and no question, were often foundred and lost.

AND after this, when they came to a greater perfection in the Building Art, as in the time when the *Carthaginian* Government flourish'd, they did great things. The *Carthaginians* were a Colony of the *Tyrians*, and inherited also their Spirit in propagating Trade and Navigation; they were exceed-ingly encreas'd by the multitude of the Citizens of *Tyre*, who by the help of their Shipping, fled from the *Assyrian* Monarch, as it may be said, in sight of his mighty Army, shipping themselves off with all their Families, and all their portable Riches, which was infinitely great, and transporting them-selves first to *Cyprus*, and then to *Crete* or *Candia*, and thence to *Carthage, Utica*, and other Ports, where they planted themselves out of the reach of their barbarous Enemies, and afterwards grew into powerful Nations, States, and Common-wealths; I say the Citizens fled thence upon the famous attack which *Nebuchadnezzar* made upon the *Phœnician* Govern-ment, and particularly upon the City of *Tyre*, which he took and utterly destroy'd; but as the Story says,[32] found it entirely empty, and without Inhabitants, that all the Citizens who could get away before the City was blockt up by that furious Prince, with their Wives and Children, and their best Effects, fled away by Sea to *Cyprus*, and by Land to *Sidon*, making afterwards their more effectual escape by Sea to *Carthage*, where that City being originally a *Tyrian* Colony, they were receiv'd as free Citizens, and protected, as in Reason they ought.

THO' the *Assyrians* found some plunder; yet all the Gold and Silver, and all kinds of rich Merchandize of *Africk, Europe*, and *India*, which was in the City, was carry'd away by the flying Citizens, and was all convey'd to neighbouring Places by Shipping, and afterwards to *Carthage*, the value of which was immensly great, and was the enriching of that City, and finish'd its Glory also, by adding a prodigious number of People to the Citizens.

HERE, as I observ'd, the Spirit and Mettle of the *Tyrians*, their enterprizing Genius in Trade, and their particular disposition to Improvements and Discoveries in the World, continued and spread it self among the *Carthaginians*, who tho' they mingled with it some of their *Numidian* Barbarities and Customs, yet propogated Navigation, and the planting Colonies in distant Countries with the same Vigor as the *Phœnicians* of *Sidon* and *Tyre* had done before them.

THIS made them carry on their Commerce with *Spain* to an extraordinary degree, and as they had possession of the South parts of *Spain*, which the *Tyrians* had formerly planted and peopled, and now became subject to the *Carthaginians*, they built *New Carthage*, which flourishes to this Day, and is still call'd *Carthagena*, as also *Barcelona*, and *Malaga, Cales* having been built before by the same *Phœnicians* from *Tyre*.

As the *Carthaginians* were thus establish'd, the Art of Building Ships, and the subsequent knowledge of Navigation, shifted Hands only, and removed from *Tyre* to *Carthage*; with this reserve in favour of the City of *Tyre*, that notwithstanding the utter ruine, which as before, the *Assyrian* Monarch brought her to, yet *Phœnix* like, she reviv'd out of her own Ashes, and recover'd a Lustre and Glory, yea, and a Strength too in several things, superiour to what she was before.

I. FOR Strength, it infinitely exceeded what it had been, because warned by its former disaster, the Citizens re-built not on the same spot, but remov'd to an Island opposite to the old City, and which lay about a Mile, or something more into the Sea; so that taking up the whole Island with the plain of the new City; they seem'd to be naturally surrounded with the Sea, and thereby so fortify'd and secur'd that nothing could attack them. And,

II. THE greatness and splendor of their Buildings far exceeded what was before, and the City growing too great for the Island, spread it self to the Continent again, and consequently part of the old City was actually re-built also; so that when *Alexander*, who destroy'd it a second time, came to attack it, he found two Cities to dispute with, one upon the main Land, and one as it were in the middle of the Sea, and the Scripture says, *She was seated in the midst of the Waters*.[33]

III. THE strength and riches of their Shipping infinitely exceeded what it was before, as the knowledge of Ships, and the Art of Navigation was encreas'd and improv'd.

BUT their first disaster having, *as I have observ'd*, rais'd the greatness of the *Carthaginian* Empire, and establish'd the *Phœnician* Glory in the City of *Carthage*; the recovering of the City of *Tyre* did not at all diminish the *Carthaginians*, but rather encrease them; for the *Tyrians* Trading to the East by Land to *Persia, Palæstine*, and *Assyria*, and by the *Red Sea*, to *India*, and the Eastern Coast of *Africa*, by which all the rich Silks of *Persia*, the Spices and Gold of *India*, the Gums and Drugs and precious Perfumes and Ointments of *Arabia*, and in a Word, all the Wealth of the East was brought to the Port of *Tyre*; so the Trade between *Tyre* and *Carthage* grew so great, that the Shipping between the two Ports encreas'd to a very great degree, and, perhaps, was equal to all the Shipping employ'd by other Nations in the World.

THIS made the *Carthaginians* extend their Conquests far beyond what the *Romans* could do by Sea, and gave them infinite Advantages; the improvement of their Navigation was an improvement to their Power, and extended their Empire wherever their Ships could come; and in particular they possess'd the Islands of *Sicily* and *Sardinia*, the latter being, as I may say, at the very Gates of *Rome*.

AS this greatness of the *Carthaginians* by Sea made them formidable to the *Romans*, so it put them upon setting up a Naval strength also, that they might be able to cope with this rival Common-wealth; and thus Navigation became the darling Study of the two mighty Empires: and tho' it is true that the mutual animosity propagated the Naval Knowledge no farther than as related to War, and to matching the Power of one another, in order to Fight; yet it by degrees brought the *Romans* also into a love of the Sea, to launch into Trade, and to undertake new Discoveries, plant Colonies, encourage Merchants, and encrease Shipping; by which at last they not only over-power'd the *Carthaginians* at Sea as well as on the Land, but supplanted them in their Commerce also, and especially in *Egypt*; and the City of *Tyre* having been a second time entirely destroy'd, namely by *Alexander* the Great, the *Roman* Merchants of *Alexandria* carry'd a great part of the Trade away, which was before engross'd between the *Tyrians* and the *Carthaginians*; at length *Carthage* falling under the same fate by the *Roman* Sword, as *Tyre* had done by the Sword of the *Macedonians*, the Shipping also which was very much improv'd by the *Carthaginians* fell all into the Hands of the *Romans*, as the Empire of the whole World also did.

I CAN not say that the Genius of the *Romans* lay so much for Trade, and Discoveries or Improvements, as that of the *Carthaginians*, and the *Phœnicians* did, and therefore Navigation and the building of Ships, as also the Commerce of the World, rather receiv'd a Check for some time by the ruin of *Carthage*; nor did the *Romans* encourage Trade so much in proportion to their greatness as the other had done; for *Rome* was an inland Town, and the *Romans* were not enclin'd to Merchandize as the *Phœnicians* and *Carthaginians* were, or had been; consequently they did not at all encourage, much less improve the building of Ships, nor the making discoveries in the World, at least not for some Ages after that time.

HENCE the Cities of *Alexandria, Corinth, Syracusa, Utica*, and several others, which being Sea-Port Towns, and addicted to Trade, and for some Ages more independent than most other parts of the World, began to grow *Opulent*, and what improvement the Shipping and Navigation of the World made for many Ages, was at those places; but even those Cities themselves, notwithstanding they employ'd much Shipping, cannot be said to have added any thing to the knowledge of building Ships, or to the Navigation of the World; but those things seemed to stand at a stay, and the *Romans* left the knowledge of the Sea, much where they found it.

SAILING was much the same, the best Navigators car'd not to go out of sight of Land, and if they did, their Pilots were generally the Stars and Constellations, such as the *North Star*, or the *Ursa Major, Ursa Minor*, the *Pleiades, Castor* and *Pollux*, and the like; but if they came to thick hazy Weather, that they could not see the Shoar, and to cloudy Nights, that they could not see the Moon, or Stars, they were lost, and at their Wits ends.

AND yet the building of Ships was improv'd much more in this long interval, than the knowledge of Navigating them; for after the declining and dividing the *Roman* Empire, when the Northern Nations began to spread themselves into the Maritime Countries, the *Gauls* at *Marseilles*, and the *Goths* in *Sweden* began to be strong in Shipping.

AFTER them the *Flemings*, and the *Easterlings*, as they were afterwards called, were the most powerful in Trade, and in Shipping also, of any Nation in *Europe*, or in the World: By the *Flemings* here, you must understand the whole *Belgia*, the Subjects afterwards of the Duke of *Burgundy*, containing all the Lower *Germany*, and that included the whole seventeen Provinces from the Town and Port of *Mardyke*, between *Dunkirk* and *Calais*, to the Mouth of the *Weser*, that is to say, to the City of *Bremen*.

BY the *Easterlings*, I understand the Northern Coasts of *Germany* in the *Baltick*, such as the *Dantzickers*, and the People of *Pomeren, Prussia*, and

Livonia; those Countries which afterwards came to the *Teutonick Knights*, and where the *Hans Towns*[34] principally began their Fame.

THIS part of the World being thus encreasing in Ships and Navigation, their power by Sea afterwards, shifted hands also, and came more into the People nearer the Mouth of the *Baltick*, and on the *Elb*, such as to the Cities of *Lubeck* and *Hamburgh*, the chief of the *Hans Towns*, under the powerful support of the *German* Empire, the *Teutonick Knights* being subdued: Their other chief Cities were *Bremen, Amsterdam*, and *Antwerp*, which with *Stralsund, Stetin, Koningsberg*, and *Dantzick*, in the *Baltick*, or Eastern Sea, made a very powerful Body, and being Cities of great Wealth and Opulence in Trade, became also the patrons of Shipping and Navigation, and sometimes struggled with several powerful Nations.

BRITAIN all this while had but a small concern among the navigating World; our greatest foreign Commerce consisted in exporting three Commodities, *viz.* our *Wooll*, our *Tin*, and our *Lead*; and this was carry'd no farther than to *Antverp*, where was the *Staple*, as it was call'd, for our *English Wooll*; which to our shame, and infinitely to our loss, was manufactur'd by the *Flemings*, and the Goods when wrought sold even back again to us for our Cloathing, from whom the Materials for making them were first had.

IN all this Trade, we had but small use for Ships, and wherever the Art of Building Ships, or of Sailing in them, was carry'd on, it receiv'd but small improvement here. As the *Flemings* bought our *Wooll*, so generally speaking, they fetch'd it in their own Ships, nor had the *English* any store of Shipping till after the *Norman* Conquest, and till our Kings found themselves oblig'd to build them for the transporting their numerous Armies over to *France*; nay, even for that Service they generally hir'd Ships of the *Flemings*, having few of their own till the time of *Edward* III. and then there was not a number sufficient: But upon his invasion of *France*, he hired Ships of the *Flemings*, and *Easterlings*, for the chief strength of Shipping was found at that time among the Northern Nations. 'Tis true the *Danes*, and the *Saxons* alternately in their invasion upon this Country, and upon the Coast of *France*, had very considerable Fleets of Ships, which they coasted the Island of *Britain* with, and *Ireland* also; and that in the most early times of Shipping in these Parts: and yet even the *Saxons* at the first invasion of *Britain*, however they ventur'd over dangerous Seas, had but an indifferent Navy, if the Lines following are rightly translated from *Sidonius Apollinaris* quoted by Mr. *Cambden*.

> Armorica *the* Saxon *Pirates fear'd*,
> *Who on our* British *Shoar in shoals appeared*,
> *And thro' rough Seas* in Boats of Leather *steer'd*.[35]

IT's strange what Ships these were, because we know that long before this Shipping was improv'd very much in the *Mediterranean* Sea; however, even there it was but a mean advancement neither, in our esteem, who are come to such a perfection in these Days; for tho' the *Phœnicians*, and *Egyptians*, and after them the *Romans* and *Carthaginians* had great numbers of Ships many Ages before the *Goths* and Northern Nations; yet they were not Vessels fit for the Navigation of these Northern Seas. If now and then a Vessel did come as far as *Britain*, which they did but seldom, they perform'd it with great caution and an infinite trouble, as well as hazard, creeping along the Coasts of *Spain* and *Portugal*, and even rounding the deep Bay of *Biscay* to come to the Coast of *France*; and then hardly venturing over to the Shoar of *Britain* till they came into the narrow Seas or Chanel, where they could see the Land on both Shoars when in the midst of the Chanel, that is to say, not till they came within Cape *Ushant*, and perhaps as high as the Islands of *Jersy* and *Guernsey*, from whence taking the advantage of the flood Tides, they had an easy run to the Isle of *Wight*, or with the Tide of Ebb, they had the like to *Portland*, or *TorBay*.

IT is very remarkable too, that when any of those early Navigators had made this dreadful Voyage, for such they thought it to be, I mean the length of *Britain*, they had as much to boast and bragg of when they came home, as our Sir *Francis Drake* had afterwards, when the ignorant People us'd to say of him, that he *shot the Gulph*, that is, he went into the Gulph, or Bay of *Mexico*, and that he sail'd round the World; things which are now done every Day, and made as light of as the *Phœnicians* wou'd have made then of sailing from *Tyre* to *Carthage*, or to *Alexandria*.

WHAT strange Tales did their old Sailors tell of the terrible Island of *Britain*, and of the *Ultima Thule*, a poor Island among the *Orkneys*, which they dream'd was the *Elysium*, or dwelling of the Blessed; a Fable rais'd from the very grossest of all stupidity and ignorance. *The Case was this*, Some of the *Phœnician* Navigators being surpriz'd in the *British* Chanel with a storm of Wind at South-West, or perhaps at North-West (and it may be no extraordinary Storm neither, as we call Storms now) and finding the Sea grow dreadful, and the Waves mount high, frighted to be sure with the danger, and as they were neither by the goodness of their Ships, or their Skill in working them, able to bear such a Sea; they often *turn'd tail to it*, and run away afore the Wind; being driven quite out of their knowledge, perhaps to the Coast of *Scotland*, or farther to the Islands of *Orkneys*, before they could put in for shelter. Many dreadful things (to them *at least*, and at that time too) befel them, among which, this was one, namely, that as they went farther and farther Northward, they found the Night shorten, and the Days of a surprizing length, and growing still longer the farther they went; till at length the Storm abating, and the Sea growing calmer, they put in, I say, among the Islands of the *Orkneys*, or thereabouts, and here staying for fair Weather they found that the *Solstice coming on*, there was no Night at all.

Surpriz'd with this unaccountable Phænomenon, of which their little *Astronomy* cou'd give no account, they concluded, that as by their going so far North they were come to almost *a continued Day*, if they went a little farther they shou'd come to *everlasting Day*, and that certainly the abode of the Gods lay that way, and the *Elyzium*, or heavenly Mansions, were not far off.

Big with this Notion, they nam'd one of the Isles of *Orcades*, or *Orkneys*, as we now call them, by the name of *Thule*,[36] a Word in the *Phœnician* Language, used for the place of Blessedness, or as some expound it, the utmost bound of human Life, and therefore call'd *Ultima Thule*. Had they landed upon this fine place they wou'd have had small occasion to think it any thing a-kin to the *Elyzium*; for all those Islands are miserably barren; cold, desolate, and the Coast dangerous: The last they allowed, as appear'd by this line of *Claudian*:

Ratibusque impervia Thule.[37]

And *Thule* where no Ship durst ever steer.

Seneca[38] also calls it the utmost boundary of the mortal station of Men.

Terrarum ultima Thule.

Thule, thou last brink of the spacious Globe.

Virgil, Juvenal, and almost all the Antients have Expressions of this kind, which they receiv'd from the more antient Authors of the *Phœnicians*, and they from their still more antient Mariners, who gave them the fabulous Account of these things; and they, *not for want of ignorance*, have handed them forward to us, who have by practice found it all to be empty, and foolish, nay even ridiculous; for our Ships steer not only to their *Thule*, but beyond it into the frozen Seas of *Greenland*, and *Nova Zembla*, where we see real Wonders, which they knew nothing of, and see also that their Wonders, which they made to be so terrible, have nothing in them.

The improvement then of this particular part, (*viz.*) of early Knowledge and the Art of Building of Ships, is in it self wonderfully great, and that without any considerable relation to the Art of Navigation: It is true the well moulding and the Shape of the Vessel, as well as the stability of the Building, is much concern'd in the navigating Part, that is to say in making the Ship sail well, lye near to the Wind, bear the Sea well, and the like; but adds nothing to the Pilot's skill in directing the Ship, keeping his

Accounts, taking his Observations; which are quite of a different kind from the Builders Art.

THE first Ships of Burthen[39] that we meet with any account of from History were those of *Tyre*, call'd Ships of *Tarshish*: These were coeval in those parts of the World to *Nineveh*, as appears by the Story of *Jonah*; and it may be suppos'd they were consequently improv'd in the time of King *David*; as appears by that elegant description of a Storm in *Psalm* cvii. 23, 26. *They that go down to the Sea in Ships, that do business in the great Waters. They mount up to the Heaven, they go down again to the depths, their Soul is melted because of trouble.*

KING *Solomon*, after this, built Ships at *Ezion Gaber*, and sent them to the *East Indies*, certainly to *Ophir*, whereever it was; and it cannot be suppos'd but that they were large Vessels, considering the time they were out, as well as the length of the Voyage they went; for tho' it may be true that they only coasted along the Shoar, yet in some places they might be driven out to Sea a great way, as I have mentioned before in the case of the *Phœnicians*, in our narrow Seas; and no doubt they were so driven out to Sea very often.

ON the other hand, the biggest of these Ships, we find, made use of Oars; and even in *Augustus*'s time the Ships of War were row'd with Oars; and yet not like the Gallies used now in those Seas, but very confusedly and irregularly plac'd: nor can the best Shipwright that I have consulted about it, (and I have critically enquir'd) conceive how they could make those Ships, as they call'd them, row with three or four banks of Oars, one above another, without making them most frightful in shape, and perfectly unfit for all manner of business; but the Word *Bank*[40] seems to be wrong translated.

THE next thing to be observ'd is, that we never find any difference in the kinds of the Ships, which they made use of in those Times; but promiscuously they are all call'd *Ships*, for what business, or in what places soever they were made use of; whether in the narrow Seas, or in the Ocean, whether in Seas, or in Rivers. When *Semiramis* made her famous expedition into *India*, being that part which is now call'd the *Great Mogul*'s Country, she was oppos'd by the *Indians* in the Chanel of the River *Indus*, with four thousand Ships: But as this must be even before the building of *Tyre*, or *Sidon*, or at least before the former, and consequently before any such thing as Ships were known in the World; so the most we can suppose of them is, that they were *Canoes*, or which was worse Boats made of Osiers, and Twigs, or Rafts, or some such trifling things as above.

ALL this intimates, that we are to make allowances for the times when we talk of *Ships*, and consider *where* too, as well as *when* the things mentioned were transacted; *for example*, the *Grecian* Armies went to the Siege of *Troy*, in a Navy of a thousand *Ships*; but what Ships they could be, we are left to judge, namely, large open Boats, merely made for transporting their Soldiers, in the calm Weather *Chanels* of the *Ægean* Seas, among the Islands, where they had nothing to do but to row, or sail from one Island to another, always in sight of Land till they came to the *Hellespont*, in the entrance of which the City of *Troy* stood.

THUS our Saviour[41] is said to go into *a Ship*, in the fresh Water Lake of *Genesareth*, in some places call'd the Sea of *Tiberias*; and yet in another place it is said they were tir'd with *rowing*; also the Vessels used for fishing in the Lake are frequently call'd Ships, which at best were only fishing Boats; perhaps such as we call *Peter Boats* to this Day, because they say *St. Peter* went a fishing with such, tho' I believe nothing of the Fable neither,

IN a word, *Ship* was then the common name for all Vessels, whether made use of to transport Goods, or Men upon the Water: But after a while *Ships of Burthen* were us'd to go upon the Sea, that is to say the main Sea, and those were call'd Ships of *Tarshish*, that is to say Ships of the *Sea: Tarshish* or *Tarsus* upon the Coast of *Cilicia*, and the shoar of the *Levant*, or *Mediterranean Sea*, being the first Town that built great Ships able to navigate those Seas. Thus *Solomon's* Fleet which he built at *Aison Gaber*, or *Ezion Geber*, are call'd Ships of *Tarshish*, I *Kings* ix. 26. Nevertheless the Port of *Ezion Geber* is in the *Red Sea*, or *Arabian Gulph*, which has no communication with the *Mediterranean*; and after all even these very Ships, if the particulars are examined, will appear to have been rather great burthensom, clumsy, luggage Boats, than Ships, as we now understand the Word; nor were they qualified any more than their Sailors were skillful enough to undertake long Voyages in the great Ocean; which we now sail over. They were neither able to bear the mighty Waves, or the furious Storms which the Sailors, and the Ships of this Age go thorow, or to secure the Merchandizes from damage as we do. They had at first no Sails, for a long time; no Masts, suitable to the burthen of the Vessel; nor for a long time more, any Rigging adapted to the purpose of Sailing as now it is; in a Word, their Anchors, their Rudders, their Cables, their Shrowds, were all mean and poor, to what we see now made use of.

NEITHER their standing or running Rigging were tolerable, nor had they any such thing as Top Masts, and Top Gallant Masts, till since the improvement of the Art of *Navigation* by the use of the Compass; of which in its Course.

ON the contrary their Ships, like their Mariners, were heavy, ungovernable, unable to bear the Sea, and unqualified too. How, and by what degree they came to improve in Shipping, as well as in Navigation, we shall hear farther in its place.

CHAP. V.ª

Of the first beginnings of the Art of Navigation, and its gradual Increase in the World.

IT is observable, that almost every Science, and every Art has a known Father, a Founder, an Author, or Inventor, as well as a Patron, and Encourager, at least nominally; so we name *Æsculapius*[42] for Physic, *Atlas* and *Prometheus* for Astronomical and Geographical Knowledge, and the use of the *Sphere; Cadmus*[43] the improver (I cannot allow him the inventor) of Letters; and so of many others: But of Navigation we find no Author, or Inventor named, or so much as suppos'd to be known in the World; it has been the product of mere Nature, led on by Reason and Necessity, the allow'd Parents of all new Discoveries.

THE *Tyrians*, as I have said, are call'd the Authors of the Navigation of the first Ages, and perhaps they were really so, for that part of the World, but that is giving the Honour to a Nation, not to a particular Person; and other Nations might do the like. Some indeed tell us, that the Story of *Dædalus*[44] having made himself waxen Wings, and flying with his Son *Icarus* from the *Cretan* Labyrinth, is only an allegory, and the meaning was this, (*viz.*) That *Dædalus* having contriv'd a Boat for his escape out of *Crete*, where he was condemn'd to perpetual Imprisonment, put off to Sea in his said Boat, and being discovered by the *Cretans*, he was persued by them in other Boats with Oars: That the *Cretan* Boats, having more Oars than *Dædalus*, gain'd upon him and wou'd have infallibly over-taken him, which he foreseeing had provided against, by the invention of a Mast and Sail, represented in the Fable by Wings made with Feathers fasten'd together with Wax, by which he flew over the Sea in the Air. This Mast and Sail being beforehand fitted to the Boat, he set up the Mast in the middle of his Flight, and that being fixt according to Art, he suddenly hoisted up the Sail also, fitted to the Mast; then spreading it to the Wind, the Boat went on without the help of their rowing, and that much faster than it did before, to the great surprize of his Men: They that persued him were astonish'd to find that without making use of their Oars he flew from them as it were in the Air, and that his Sails were to him as Wings, so that they could by no means overtake him, whereupon they went back and reported that *Dædalus* had made himself Wings: The other part of the Fable is made good also the same way; for it seems his Son *Icarus* taught by his Father how to make a Mast and Sail for his Boat also, in which he was to attempt the like Escape; the young Man too eager and desirous to sail the swifter, and withal not knowing so well the nature and reason of those Sails, made his too large for the Boat, and hoisted them so high, that the Wind blowing fresh brought his Mast by the Board, or if you will, holding too much Wind, over-set his Boat; and so he was drown'd in the Sea of *Crete*, which bare his Name for a great while after.

THUS, as the Birds steering their flight in the Air dictated the use of the Rudder for steering of Ships, or Boats in the Water; so *Dædalus*, by his fertile Brain, invented the flying with Canvas Wings thro' the Seas.

IT is evident that the first Sails were made of Skins of Beasts, stretch'd out upon Poles, and extended with proper fastnings to either side of the Boat, like what we call the *Clue* of a Sail; from whence by Ropes fastned to the Boat, or Vessel, they were so spread as to be made useful to give motion to the Vessel, or Boat they belong'd to. But it was all at first no more than what we call sailing afore the Wind; they knew nothing of *Hauling Close, Trimming Sharp*, and *lying near* the Wind, and such Terms *as we now practice by*; but when the Wind was contrary, or not large to go away *afore it*, they lowr'd the Sail, and took to their Oars, and when they could not go forward by the help of their Oars, all they had for it, was to row in for the Shoar, and put into Harbour wherever they they could find it, and wait there for change of Weather: nor is it to be doubted, as I have observed before, but that many Lives were lost by the common accidents of Wind and Waves before the People arriv'd to skill sufficient to manage their Boats, whether by Sails or by Oars, I say many Lives were lost in Cases where now we find no dangers; for Example, many a Boat over-set for want of knowing how to tend the Seas, *so our Seamen call it*, to handle their Oars, Steer steady, fill, or not fill, hand, or not hand their Sails; in a Word, distress, and deliverances gave them Experience, and the Experiences added always to their navigating Skill; and thus one Age building upon the Knowledge of the Generation that preceded, they grew every Day abler for the Sea than they were before.

BUT with all this improvement, and with all the encrease of Knowledge the Antients gain'd in this useful part of mathematical Knowledge; nothing ever came so heavily on, or made so dull a progress as this of

Navigation: For at the end of near two thousand. Years practice, we find the height of their Improvement amounted to so little, that the meanest of our Mariners can sit and jest with it, in these times of better skill; making themselves merry with it, as if their Ignorance was as much a wonder to us, as our Knowledge wou'd have been to them, had they been let into it in those Days.

How do we Read with a kind of astonishment, and at least with contempt, *the little*, which History gives us an account of about the Navigation of the Antients; even of those Ages, which compar'd to the antient *Phœnicians*, and *Grecians*, are to be esteem'd as improv'd, and advanc'd in the knowledge of Sea Affairs? How do our Sailors jest with these Nations? How do we call all ignorant Seamen *Paul's Mariners*, alluding to the account given in the 27th of the *Acts*, *v.* 29. of the Voyage of St. *Paul* from the Isle of *Cyprus* to *Malta*, where in their distress 'tis said they cast four Anchors over the Stern? How do we now ridicule the ignorance of the *Portuguese*, and of the *Genoese*, who yet were in those Days the skillfullest Navigators in the World, for their creeping under the Shores to reach from one Port to another, and for having no other knowledge of Navigation than the bare steering clear of Rocks and Sands, when in their view, coming to an Anchor, or running into Harbour every Night, lest they shou'd be lost in the Dark?

The truth is, the improvements of the Art of Navigation are extremely Modern, and rather more Modern than that of Building Ships; for till the knowledge of the *Magnet* or *Loadstone*, by the power of which, Men can, *as we may say*, see in the dark, and find their way by Night as well as by Day, out of sight of Land as well as in sight of Land, in Fogs and Mists, as well as out of them; I say, till then the navigating Skill was but small: and tho' Men had Ships of good bulk and burthen before, yet they knew little what to do with them when they came into these boisterous Northern Seas, and out of sight of Land. It is true, they ventur'd boldly, and perhaps more boldly than we do now; and as they grew more and more expert in the knowledge of Astronomy, they made use of the Constellations, and heavenly Bodies, to wit, Sun, Moon, Stars, for their guidance, and to shew them their way.

First, we must allow them to have had right notions of the situation of Places, even before they had measured the Globe, and divided its Colures[45] or Meridians into Degrees of Latitude and Longitude: But when they had so divided the Globe it was easy then to ascertain the distance of Places from the Equator, or from any given Meridian, so that the Latitude of Places was adjusted by the Geographers with great ease.

THEN for sailing out of sight of Land, when they did venture to do so, all the help they had was the Position of the Northern Constellations, whose circling Motions round the Pole being prescrib'd within narrower Limits than those more to the Southward, made them be as it were fixt *to them*; so that the *Ursa Major*, or the *Ursa Minor*, or the Stars near to them, were as a *Pole Star* to them, because they were always to be seen within a known and equal distance from the *Pole Star* it self.

THESE Stars were their Guides in the Night when they ventur'd into the open Sea, as the Sun was by Day; but their difficulties lay when, in thick, hazy, or dark, and cloudy Weather, they had not the blessing of Sun, Moon, or Stars, for many Nights and Days together; then they were at a loss, bewildred, and frighted; and sometimes, *I may say oftentimes* lost for want of directions, falling upon Rocks, Lee Shoars, and high Cliffs, or covered Sands, having no knowledge of Places, and no Pilots, Charts, or Plans of Shoars to warn them of the danger; or Rules to judge of the distances, and to keep account of the Ship's way, as they do now; and so to cast up where they were, and how far from this or that Shoar, and consequently keep off from danger and destruction.

BUT let us look back to the wise Navigators of former Ages, well may I say, that they ventur'd boldly; for certainly considering the small knowledge they had of the Art it self, of Sailing, the small, and few, and insufficient helps they had for their directions in Cases of difficulty, it was most wonderful that they should undertake such Voyages as they did, and yet more strange, that they should perform them with success when they were undertaken.

FOR Example; To go back to the *Phœnicians*, and *Egyptians*, as small as their skill was in Astronomy, or as few as their Geographical improvements were, and as mean as their Ships were, yet we find that they attempted the following Voyages, and Discoveries.

I. THEY coasted the whole *Mediterranean Sea*, from the bottom of the Straights, as we call it, namely, the Sea of *Phœnicia*, where their two Ports of *Tyre* and *Sidon* stood, to the Point, or Northern Head of the Straights mouth, call'd *Hercules Pillars*, and without unto the Bay where they built the City of *Gades* or *Cades*, which continues a flourishing City and Port of Trade to this Day.

II. THEY fitted out Ships in the *Red Sea*, (*viz.*) at *Ezion Geber*, and from thence sail'd to the farthest part of the *East Indies*, (*viz.*) to the *Aurea Chersonnesus*, now call'd *Malacca*, and to the *Philippins*; from whence they brought back the Spices, and Drugs, and other rich Goods of *India*, and returning to the Port, now call'd *Sues*[46] in the *Red Sea*, the

Goods were carry'd from thence over Land to *Pelusium*, or *Damiata*, or else to *Alexandria*, both of them Ports in the Mouth of the *Nile*, whence again they were carry'd to all the Northern parts of the World by Sea; which Trade continued in the Hands of the *Alexandrians*, and since that of the *Genoeses*, and since they lost it, has been taken up by the *Venetians*, till within a few Ages that the *Portuguese* found out the way by long-Sea, round the Cape of *Good Hope*.

III. THEY sail'd likewise from the same *Ezion Geber* to the Coast of the *African Ethiopia* in the same *Red Sea*, and from thence following that extended Shoar due South, along the Coast of *Zanguebar, Mosambique, Melinda, Monomotapa*, and *Natale*,[47] they doubled the Cape of *Good Hope* it self, and seeing the Sun both to the South of them, and to the North of them, and then to the South of them again, they past along the Coast of *Congo*, and *Angola*, the *Gold Coast*, and the *Grain Coast* of *Guinea*; and continuing an unwearied Progress, pass'd the *Cape Du Verd, Cape Negro*, and *Cape Blanco*, till they came to Cape *Spartel*, in the Mouth of the *Straights*, where entring they reach'd their own Colony of *Carthage*, and thence on to *Alexandria* in *Egypt*, near the place whence they first set out.

We are well assur'd from Authors of good Authority that the *Phœnicians* performed all these Voyages, and in particular the last; and indeed they were bold Fellows in doing so, considering that besides the difficulty of the Coasts in several places, it is very probable many of those remote Countries were not yet inhabited in those early Times, and so soon after the confusions of *Babel*; In particular the South, and West parts of *Africa*, might be suppos'd to be yet unknown, and the posterity of *Canaan*, who first possest *Egypt*, and spread themselves early, and chiefly along the Shoar of the *Mediterranean* into *Libya*, and that which we now call *Barbary*, and perhaps afterwards into *Abissinia*, or *Ethiopia*, shou'd be some Ages before they wandred over the scorching Sands of *Zanguebar* on the East, or the burning Coasts of *Congo*, and *Angola* on the West, so to inhabit as far as the Cape of *Good Hope*, and the Country of *Monomotapa*; and if those Countries were void of Inhabitants, by consequence they would be empty of Provisions for the relief of the *Phœnician* Seamen, when they shou'd arrive there.

BUT be that how it will, we are, I say, assur'd they did sail that way, and whatever benefit they made of it did frequently put into the Harbours, and Ports upon those Coasts for shelter, *at least*, if not for relief; nay, one relief we are assur'd they must not only often put in for, but go on Shoar to procure, and that is *fresh Water*; nor could they continue long at Sea (in *those hot Climates especially*) without a frequent supply of it. What skill they were arriv'd to, in making Casks to put and keep Water in, is hard to know; we have some Reason to think that earthen Jarrs, and Bottles, were the best reservators they had; and of those as their Ships could not stow a great many, so neither could they hold any great quantity of Water at a time, so that they must go often on Shoar, and into Ports to recruit.

THOSE who understand this coasting way of Navigation, and especially the dangerous Shoals and Rocks, which lye at the entrance into most of the great Harbours and Rivers in the World, know also, that nothing is more hazardous than to go into some of those Rivers and Harbours without the help of Pilots, and the direction of Boats to sound the depth before them, to find good Ground for Anchor hold, good Riding from Winds, and Currents, so to prevent running on Shoar, and stranding on the Beaches and Sands, or staving on the Rocks, upon any stress of Wind that might blow.

AS the dangers were not less in those times, so the advantages and skill which the Navigators had to avoid those dangers, were not more or greater than they are now, but a great deal less; particularly for want of Pilots, and of good Anchors, and of Cables, and indeed of good Ships or Vessels; so that all considered 'tis something wonderful that such long and uncertain Voyages could be perform'd at all.

AGAIN, we are assur'd that even in those Voyages, tho' they coasted *along Shoar* (as we call it) and kept as much as possible in sight of Land, yet that they had several Gulphs to pass over, and the mouths of great Rivers to cross in, which they must needs go out of sight of Land to cross them, the strength of the Currents not admitting them to go up into those Rivers; as the great River of *Congo* in the Southern *Guinea*, for Example; and the *Rio Grand*, and *Rio de Senegall*, near *Sierra Leon* in the Northern *Guinea*; in some of which the openings are twelve to sixteen Leagues over, so that they could never see over from side to side; and in such places if the Weather was thick and hazy, the hazard wou'd be greater than ordinary to those Navigators who had no Pilots to direct them, and who knew nothing what they had to expect before them, or how broad those openings might be, nay, they could not always know whether there was any Land beyond them or not.

IN like manner those Navigators who went to the East, and made that long Voyage from the *Red Sea* to *Ophir* in the *Indies*; especially if that *Ophir* be (as we understand it to be) the Island of *Sumatra*; they had many dangerous Apertures which they could not see over, and must venture hard to pass; as for Example; from the Mouth of the *Red Sea*, which we call the Straights of *Babelmandel*, or as our Seamen call it, the Gulph of *Mocha*, they steer'd away East, keeping the Shoar of *Arabia Felix* on the Larbord side, till they came to the Mouth of the Gulph of *Persia*; It can hardly be suppos'd they went into the bottom of all that Gulph, on the *Arabian* side, which is above three hundred Miles North up to *Bassora*, and then came about again South, on the *Persian* side to *Gomeron*, and *Ormus*.

BUT I will suppose they had so much knowledge of the Country as to know that great Inlet call'd the *Persian* Gulph, was no more than a Gulph or Inlet, and that they were to cross over it to the other Shoar, namely, to *Guzeratte*,[48] and then coast away South along the *Indian* Shore to the Island of *Ceylon*, and round that vast Island into the great Bay of *Bengale*; in doing this also, they wou'd have a vast opening between the Point call'd *Din Head*[49] or Point *Dant*, being over the mouth of the great River *Indus* to *Surat*, and then again between Cape *Comaroon*,[50] the utmost Point of the main Land of *Malabar*, and the Island of *Ceylon*; the passage indeed between might be passable, if their Vessels did not draw much Water, but dangerous if they did, and even unpassable as it is now. Again, they wou'd have had a long and difficult stretch from *Point Pedro*, the Northermost Land on the East side of *Ceylon* to *Callimere*, the most Southerly point of Land on the Continent of *Coremandell*;[51] from thence supposing them to have made the Shoar, they wou'd have a long stretch into the bottom of the Bay, on the East side, along the Coast of *Coremondell*, and then another opening with a deep Bay, about twenty five Leagues broad at the mouth, from *Gardeware* to *Pawrarya* in the Kingdom of *Golconda*;[52] after which coasting the Bay of *Ballasome*, and the Country of *Bengale*, at the mouth or mouths rather of the great River *Ganges*, they wou'd have the like openings to cross over, which they could understand nothing of, unless directed by Pilots of the Country, which 'tis doubtful whether they could have at all, or at least wou'd very rarely find in those early Ages of the World: the crossing the mouth or rather innumerable Mouths of the River *Ganges* taking it from the first Point North-East of *Pipley*[53] to the Coast of *Nettingham* or *Bengale Proper*, which is all the bottom of the Bay and is at least one hundred Leagues over, is what I can entertain no notion of, considering the people we are talking of.

HOW then, these Navigators could pass all those difficult places in such Vessels, as we have Reason to believe they sail'd in, and with no better skill in Navigation, than they had at that time, is very hard to judge: That it took them up a very great length of time to coast all those unknown Shoars, and to stop, and put in so often, as *no doubt* they were oblig'd to do; this we know, and have spoken to already, and this confirms me in the enquiry after the manner of their Sailing; for unless they had thus coasted about, how could they be three Years in performing the Voyage? 'Tis certain that our Ships wou'd now go the same length, that is to say from the Mouth of the *Red Sea* to the Island of *Sumatra*, and back again in less than six Months, or thereabouts, one time with another.

THIS was the State of the World in the infancy of Navigation; and so mean a thing was Navigation it self, before they got farther lights, and helps into it. Let us see how they carry'd on their Affairs in the Discoveries of those Days, and what advantageous Improvements they made for Years after this.

CHAP. VI.

Of the early Discoveries of the first Ages, and how they became acquainted with forreign Countries.

IF I must enter into an enquiry after new Discoveries from the beginning, I must trace the several Sons of *Noah* from the Ark to the Plains of *Shinaar*, and the building of *Babel*; and must then follow them into all the several Quarters of the World, and give a History of their peopling the Earth, and whether they travel'd for fixing their Habitations, because every new settlement might then be call'd a Discovery and a Plantation: But as this wou'd be a fruitless, as well as tedious Subject, and wou'd take up this whole Work, without either Diversion or Instruction to the Reader: I leave it, as it really is remote from my Design.

BUT stepping forward some Ages from the separation at *Babel*, we find in about three hundred Years, the World pretty well peopled, the Inhabitants possest of the greatest Part of it, and infinitely multiplying in People; Those People daily spreading themselves farther and farther, for new possessions. The Sons of *Cham* possess the East of *Afric*, and the Western parts of *Asia*, such as *Arabia*, and *Syria*; the Sons of *Sem* were possest of all the East of the vastly extended Country of *Asia*, even to the utmost parts of *India*, and *China*; and the Sons of *Japhet* the Northern parts of *Asia*, and all *Europe*, call'd in Scripture the *Isles of the Gentiles*.

IN this situation, the *Phænician*, [*Sidonians*] and *Cilicians*, being the first Nations situated upon the Sea-shores, as I have observed already, first contriv'd the building of Boats, and then larger Vessels to float upon the Water; then Ships and other Vessels, *which they call'd Ships*, and then Sails to make use of the Winds and Seas in those Ships, and to guide them from place to place, and this we call Navigation; after the *Phænicians*, the *Egyptians*, and after the *Egyptians*, the *Grecians* fell into the same practice, and thus the Art of Navigation was introduc'd in the World.

THE Art being thus obtain'd, or at least begun, the Uses of it are our next enquiry; and this was in short of two Kinds.

I. To make and maintain an intercourse or communication of Nations by Water, and to bring them acquainted with one another, which was the Original of Trade.

II. To seek out new Discoveries, and plant their own people in Colonies, and Settlements in remote Countries, which were yet uninhabited, and divided from them by the great Waters, so as they could no otherwise come to the knowledge of them, much less the possession; and this is the part which comes within the compass of, and indeed constitutes this Undertaking.

THE first communication for Commerce, which the *Tyrians*, a People naturally inclin'd to Merchandize, were said to make was with the *Egyptians*, who lying on the same Coast in the Gulph, or Bottom of the same Seas, were at first easily reach'd by the help of small Boats, and other Vessels, rowing along the Shore; the communication by Land being also made long before.

IN like manner the *Sidonians* went *North*, and joyn'd their Possessions to the Sons of *Japhet* in *Syria*; and by the same Seas soon reach'd the Shores of *Cilicia*, where they built *Tarshish*.

NAVIGATION, being thus begun in these three Parts of the World, to wit, *Phœnicia, Egypt*, and *Greece:* We are now to see what use they made of it; to what Improvement it guided them, and what Discoveries they made in the World by the help of it; as also, how the Art it self, and all the subsequent Branches of Sea-knowledge, which we see the World since arrive to such perfection in, grew up gradually upon the foot of this first, and fundamental part of Science.

THE first Discovery the *Phœnicians* made by virtue of their Sea-knowledge, was the Island of *Cyprus*, which tho' they found peopled from the opposite Shoar of *Cilicia*, and that there were some few Inhabitants upon it, who subsisted themselves, and did as it were but just live, and that in a wild and undirected manner, maintaining themselves by the natural product of the Soil, *which was very rich*, yet they were first civilized, and taught to live comfortably, and like Men, by the more polite and improv'd *Phœnicians*; who finding the Country fruitful in Corn, Wine, Cattle, and especially Cotton Wooll, which they soon found the value of, they came over in great Numbers, with their Families, and settled on the Eastermost part of the Island: There they built the Towns, or Cities of *Nicosia*, and *Famagusta*, as they are called now, and in a Word, peopled the whole Island; they built other Towns, no question, the Island being full of Towns, but these are the chief.

HERE the said *Phænicians*, People, *I say*, naturally Industrious, and addicted to Commerce, erected the first Woollen Manufactures which we meet with in any of those parts of the World; that is to say, a Manufacture of *Cotton Wooll*, which in those early Times, they brought to great perfection: and afterwards it spread into *Phænicia* it self; the Cotton Wooll, which was the Fund for the Manufacture being supply'd from *Cyprus*, where it was the natural growth of the place.

N. B. *This growth of* Cotton Wooll *is still preserv'd in the Island of* Cyprus; *and tho' the* Turks, *who are naturally inclin'd to discourage Industry, and encrease of People, and of Commerce, do not carry on much of this Manufacture there, yet the* Cotton Wooll *is carry'd from thence into all the Countries round, and especially into* France, Italy, *and the* Venetian *Territories; and some is brought even to* England *it self, where it is manufactur'd in an extraordinary manner; as also in* Holland, Germany, *and the* Austrian Netherlands.

ENCOURAG'D by the success of this first Discovery; we find the *Tyrians* or *Phænicians* afterwards pushing their good fortune, and planting themselves in the next place upon the Island of *Crete*, now call'd *Candia*; and here they built *Canea*, and several other Towns on the Sea-coast, and peopled them with Inhabitants from their own Country: this, besides the Concurrence of History is confirm'd, in that the *Cretans* not only spoke the Language of the *Phænicians*, but also for that their Customes, and especially their *Idols*, were for some Ages the same.

THE antient Writers of the first Ages of the Heathen World, will have *Mercury* to be the first Author of Navigation, and that the Wings which the Antients give him in his *Hat*, and his *Heels*, are Emblems of his teaching Men to fly, that is to *sail* upon the Sea: Others tell us it was invented by the *Egyptian* God *Thoyth*, which is the same as *Mercury* and who some will have to be the antient *Termegistus*;[54] others *Moses*; That *Danaus*[55] made a Voyage from *Egypt* to *Greece* in a Galley of his own inventing; others that *Edom* or *Esau, Jacob*'s elder Brother, having spread his Dominion over the Western *Arabia* first seized the Banks of the *Red Sea*, and taught his Posterity how to build Vessels, and sail upon the Sea; and that they us'd to rob the *Egyptians*, he himself commanding them in Person; so that they make *Esau* a great Pirate, even before there were any Ships or Boats to act Piracy with, much less any to act Piracy against: All these things I look upon as Fables of the old Times, and written without any sufficient Authority; as I do also the account of the *Egyptians* trading to *India*, and to the Coast of *Ethiopia*, and *Zanguebar*; in times so early, as that we know the very Country of *Egypt* it self, tho' very soon planted, or possest rather, yet could not be fully peopled at that time.

To return therefore to the most early times of Navigation, such as the first Discovery of the Islands of *Cyprus* and *Candia*, by the *Phænicians*, no doubt the possessing those two Islands, was a great accession of Power to the *Phænicians*, as they rais'd great Tribute from them, and receiv'd great supplies of Corn from them, which at that time (the Cities of *Tyre* and *Sidon* being so much encreas'd in People) was very much wanted there.

WE cannot doubt, but that both of those Islands receiv'd a great addition of People also from the *Phænicians*, who were all *Canaanites*, when *Josuah* at the Head of such a powerful Army, as that of *Israel*, invaded the Land of *Canaan*; and as we can not question but that great numbers of People fled away for their Lives upon the first Irruption of the *Israelites*, nay even before that Irruption, hearing of their approach, and of their Victorious carrying all before then, on the other side *Jordan*; and especially upon the defeat of the Kings, which first opposed him: I say we cannot doubt but such of the People as could flee away with their best Effects, did go as Nature dictates, and as is the practice in like Cases to this Day; no doubt but this flight too was with the utmost precipitation, some one way, some another; some over the Mountains of *Libanon*; into the utmost parts of *Syria*, and towards *Damascus*, some to the Sea-side to *Tyre* and *Sidon*; and not thinking themselves safe there, they took Shipping again, and went away to *Cyprus*, to *Crete*, and to *Italy*, and even any where, *Ubi fata vocant*, wherever they found they could be safe.

THIS we have a proof of by the Pillar[56] said to be set up upon the Coast of *Barbary*, not far from *Tangier*, which had this Inscription,

We are they who fled from the Face of JOSUAH *the Robber.*

NO wonder then if the Multitudes, who thus fled for their Lives, seated themselves, as I have said, *among others*, in those two large, fruitful, and pleasant Islands of *Cyprus* and *Crete*.

To confirm the probability of this, History assures us, that at such time (many Ages after this) when *Nebuchadnezzar* the Great, the same who sack'd and burnt *Jerusalem*, and the Temple there, lay'd Seige to the City of *Tyre*, and that the Citizens saw they were not able to beat him off, or to avoid falling into his Hands, they assembled all their Ships together of every sort and size, and after beating the *Babylonian Fleet*, which block'd them up by Sea, and which tho' it consisted of three score Ships, the *Tyrians* overthrew with twelve of theirs; I say, that having thus beaten, and destroy'd the Enemies Ships, they ship'd off all their Riches, and Treasure, their Goods, and Merchandizes, and every thing that was portable, and sent it over to the Isle of *Cyprus*, to their Colony there, and then (the Ships returning) they embark'd themselves also, Men, Women, and Children, and went away after them, even in sight of the *Assyrian* Army; leaving them a naked, empty, and uninhabited City; so that the *Babylonians* being disappointed, and enrag'd, turn'd their Army upon *Egypt*, of which the Scripture gives an account; and Sir *Walter Raleigh* says,[57] God Almighty seeing his Servant *Nebuchadnezzar* disappointed of his hop'd for plunder, the reward of his undertaking, and resolving he shou'd not undertake such a great Expedition for nothing, made him amends by giving *Pharoah Necho* into his Hands, and giving him the plunder of the great and rich City of *Memphis* in *Egypt*, which he took and destroy'd.

IT is a Question in matters of Commerce, whether the destruction of *Tyre*, by *Nebuchadnezzar*, did good or hurt. If I may give my opinion, I think it was rather good than harm; for tho' it is true, that the Citizens had a very great loss in the demolishing their Houses, and ruining their public Edifices; yet as it scatter'd a diligent and useful People into divers parts of the World, where they settled immediately to business, some in one place, and some in another: They were as so many Instructors to the Nations wherever they came, to pursue the same Industry, and maintain themselves by Trade, which before, 'tis very likely, they knew little or nothing of.

ON the other Hand, as the trading part of the Citizens went off with their Riches, their Merchandizes, and all their Wealth, and above all, with their Ships, they were, except the hurry of their Flight, in as good trading Circumstances as before, and so established a general Correspondence and Commerce wherever they came.

AND both these Articles, (*viz.*) their Industry and their Wealth, was such a support to them, that after setting all the People upon business wherever they came, the *Assyrian* Conqueror was no sooner gone but they return'd to *Tyre*, re-built their City, and in a few Years it became greater, richer, and more powerful than ever it was before.

CHAP. VII.

Of the encrease of Commerce *and* Navigation *under the* Carthaginian *Empire, and the check given to useful Discoveries, by the success of the* Romans *against them. Also some probable account of the first peopling of* America, *by the* Carthaginians.

THAT the *Phœnicians* were the Founders of the *Carthaginian* State, and that *Carthage* it self was originally a Colony of the *Phœnicians*; that it was encreas'd, and multitudes of People added to it, by the flight of the People from the Land of *Canaan (Phœnicia)* upon the Irruption of the *Hebrews* under *Josuah*; all this part I think I have clear'd up in the foregoing Chapters.

THAT the *Phœnicians*, and in particular the *Tyrians* and *Sidonians* communicated to those of *Carthage* (with their People) the same trading Genius, which they were so eminent for themselves, is not to be doubted: for the *Carthaginians* soon shew'd the World that they brought with them all the subtilety of Wit, and Address in matters of Commerce; all the industry and application to Business; all the eager desire to improve in Knowledge, and encrease in Power, which the *Phœnicians* themselves were so famous for, and particularly, their thirst for Improvement by new Discoveries, planting Colonies, and peopling new Worlds in parts unknown; all this has been toucht at already, and in part describ'd.

IT cannot be doubted but that all the great Cities and Towns, and especially Sea-Ports, of which many remain, and the ruins of many more are to be seen on the North Coast of *Africa*, from *Tunis*, which was near *Carthage*, if not part of it, to Cape *Spartel*, and thence on the West Coast to *Cape de Verd*, in the Latitude of fifteen Degrees, and perhaps farther, were originally

73

of *Carthaginian* foundation; and that the Commerce settled in those Towns was also very great and flourishing during the continuance and prosperity of the *Carthaginian* Government, who went on with great Success, and a high Hand, extending their possessions in *Africa* to such a length, as no succeeding Powers have thought fit to meddle with after them, and no doubt but they found an infinite advantage of Wealth from them, as may be judg'd by what still appears.

THAT the *Carthaginian Empire* was overthrown by the *Roman* in the last Punick War, and the City of *Carthage* it self destroy'd, all the reading part of Mankind very well know; and it is none of the business of this Undertaking to enter into any account of it; but thus far is necessary to our present purpose to observe, (*viz.*) That tho' the *Romans* were great encouragers of Learning, and of Arts and Science, as in particular of Eloquence, of Poetry, and many useful and civilizing parts of Knowledge; having the greatest Poets, and Orators, and Statesmen, and Generals, flourishing under the protection of their Government, that ever the World saw; yet their Genius did not lye to Trade, to discovery of foreign Countries, or settling Colonies for Commerce, in new-found and remote Places; nor did they encourage Navigation and Plantation, or erect Manufactures, for the ends of Trade, as the *Carthaginians*, and *Phœnicians* had done before them.

FROM hence it follow'd, that with the fall of the *Carthaginian* and *Phœnician* States, all the most promising and prosperous Discoveries they had made sunk back again towards their original Obscurity: The People, who had been settled in them, not receiving supplies from their Government, or from their private Correspondents in *Carthage*, as they usually had done, and as was necessary to support the Plantations they had begun, either starv'd or perish'd for want or were oblig'd to abandon the Settlements they had made; a thing we may almost remember to have been the fate of several of the first Planters in the Northern *America*, even by our own Nation, tho' no public calamity at home prevented a Supply; as particularly at *New England, Virginia, Bermudas, Darien*, and several other Plantations, in those parts of the World.

THUS the *Goths* and *Vandals*, who succeeded the *Romans* in the Government of *Africa*, and who still pursued rather a military Possession or Conquest of the Country already settled, than an extending the Commerce for the improvement of Navigation and Plantation in remote Countries; I say, these *Goths* and *Vandals* left the said discovered Countries under the same neglected, decayed condition in which they found them; or rather in which they were, for we can hardly say they found them at all.

UNDER these decays all the inland settlements of the *Numidians* and *Mauritanians*, and all the new built Cities, and planted Colonies of *Hanno*,[58] the *Carthaginian* Admiral, on the Western Coast of *Africa*, as noted before, fell into decay, and except the Kingdom of *Fez* and *Morocco*, now possest by the *Moors*, are forgotten, and lost as it were out of the World.

BUT before I leave this part I crave leave to mention one thing, which may at least be diverting, if not positive enough to claim its being instructing, in a case which has been the occasion of much dispute among the Learned Geographers and Historians, as well of the present, as of the past Ages; and which is still not less doubtful and undetermined; namely, How, and when the great Continent of *America*[59] came to be peopled with Inhabitants, and from whence? A difficulty which has been thought so great, that some, and those not among the ignorant part of Mankind neither, would have us put God Almighty to the Repetition of a particular Creation of the Species, both of Man and Beast, for the supplying that part of the World, and which they think it was impossible shou'd be done any other way.

NOW, tho' I shall in the pursuit of this undertaking shew how easy it might have been for all the kinds of living Creatures which were found in *America*, except Man, to arrive there without the help of Navigation, much more without the necessity of a Creation; so I cannot quit this part without taking notice how easily it might be, and how rational it is to believe it was peopled by the help of Navigation from the West-side of *Africa*; and how probable, that it was so done at that time, especially when the *Carthaginians* possest that Coast; a People wholly addicted to search after new Discoveries, and boldly venturing into all parts of the World for them; as also furnished with Shipping able and sufficient to perform such Voyages, tho' not so well qualified with skill to guide them; which want of skill was however not such as to render it impossible to perform the Voyage, and at least to make the Discovery whether it was sufficient to return from thence or no: Nay the very want of skill, for ought we know, might be the occasion of the Discoveries, when some of those Navigators being by the accident of Winds, or Storms driven off to Sea from *Cape de Verd*, or the Islands lying off from the *Cape*, and running away West out of their knowledge by the force of the Weather till they came in the way of the Trade Winds and the Current which sets in towards the Coast of *America*, where they wou'd in fifteen or twenty Days, supposing a strong gale of Wind, get sight of Cape St. *Augustine*, in the *Brasils*, or of some of the *West-Indian* Islands, such as *Barbadoes*, or *Nevis*, or *Tobago*, or others in the like situation: Nor was this so improbable, much less impracticable, as some wou'd insinuate. For *Example*;

THE difficulty of Communication, between *America*, and any part of the then known World, consisted only in the following particulars.

I. THE length of the Voyage.

II. THE want of Shipping.

III. THE ignorance in Navigation.

THESE three Heads, after having been very often discuss'd, and by very learned Writers, have, I acknowledge, been voted insuperable in this particular Case; and it has been from thence concluded, That *America* could not have been peopled by Sea from the then known World, (*viz*) from any part of the Coasts of *Africa*, or of *Europe*; but that the Inhabitants must have found the way over the Northermost points of Land, or in *Europe* over the Frozen Seas, from the Continent of *Asia*, which being yet undiscovered, must be suppos'd to joyn some where in the extreme parts.

BUT as this is building all upon suggested possibilities, where all that has yet been discovered appears frightfully impracticable, and that it is evident all that part of the World is, at this time, utterly uninhabited, and we have great reason to believe, that it never was otherwise; so the passage for Mankind, that way seems to me to be absurd, so much as to reason upon, and is apparently impossible.

ON the other Hand, the passage by Sea, as it has appear'd since to be very easy, so there is no room to doubt, but it was then not only practicable, but was really performed; and this I shall endeavour to make very clear, at least very reasonable, when I come to it again, which will be presently.

BUT before I run too far from home, and that I may take every thing with me as I go, that the Reader may not lose the remembrance of things, I must go back again to *Tyre* and *Sidon* where I set out, and speak of the knowledge in Arts, as well as Trade.

THE *Phœnicians* were not only the Patrons of Commerce, and set Trade first on Foot in the World; but they were, at least, encouragers, (if not the originals) of Arts and Sciences, and the first spreaders of universal Knowledge in the World.

IT is true we give the honour of Astronomical Studies, and all the *Promethean* Fire, which inflamed the breasts of Men with the most early desire of knowledge, to the *Arabians* and *Chaldæans*; these were the Wise-men called so by way of distinction from all the rest of the World: But it will appear then that the *Phœnicians* were the *Englishmen* of that Age, that is to say, if they were not the Inventors, they were the greatest improvers of what others invented, and I must add their Improvement came so in the heels of the Invention, that the Inventors being buryed in forgetfulness, time has borrow'd from oblivion, and given the Invention to the Improvement, as you shall see in our next Chapter.

CHAP. VIII.

Of the Phœnicians being early improvers of Learning, as well as of Commerce and navigation, and particularly of their Prince Cadmus *introducing the knowledge of Letters into* Greece.

To the honour of the *Phœnician* Age, it must be acknowledged, that however for righteous Ends, and with just Reasons, to us unknown, Heaven thought fit at last to overthrow them; yet while they remain'd a People, they were patterns of all commendable Virtues; particularly such as tended to the establishing Nations, encreasing the Felicity of Mankind, peopling desolate Countries, and furnishing the Nations they planted with all things both needful and pleasant for Life.

THIS Correspondence of People not only assisted in spreading Inhabitants into remote parts of the World, and so obeying the Directions their Maker gave them at first, namely, *to replenish the Earth*; but that Correspondence necessarily begat Trade, Trade begat Navigation, Navigation by making Discoveries, begat Plantation, and remote Plantations again encreas'd Correspondence: Thus every improveing quality circulated through the World, and the whole Globe seems now to be brought into a kind of general acquaintance with it self; the remotest Nations converse, the People know one another, nay, I may say, continually talk with one another, by Missives, by Messengers, and by Correspondencies of all sorts.

TRADE is certainly a Patron of Arts, as it is the Mother of Industry; Commerce is naturally an encourager of Learning, and has by its Correspondence been the greatest assistance to human Knowledge.

HOW has Trade pickt up all the most useful Drugs in every part of the World for the supply of Physic, and for the help and health of Mankind? Do we not see the *Materia Medica* fetch'd from the most remote parts of the World? Is not every *Drugist*'s or *Apothecarie*'s Shop furnish'd from both the *Indies*, and almost from both the *Poles*? It wou'd take up more room in this Work than 'tis possible to spare to discourse fully of this one Article; and yet 'twou'd be unjust to omit taking notice how every new Discovery, every

Plantation, every new branch of Trade, furnishes some new Thing, some Rarity in Nature, some Specific in Physic for the relief of a distemper'd World.

FOR Example: How many choice Plants and Drugs did the discovery of *America* furnish this part of the World with, of which they knew nothing before? What poor weak Tools had our best Physicians to work with, in case of Agues, and all intermitting periodical Fevers? How did the Ague so master the utmost skill of Physic, that for some Ages it past for a possession of the *Devil*, till *America* furnish'd the true and only Exorcist the BARK, a Sovereign, a Specific, a neverfailing Medicine.

ADD to this, That now abus'd, but in its medicinal Virtue wonderful plant, *Tobacco*, unknown also till the same discovery of the *West-Indies*; till Navigation carry'd us to *America*, and Trade brought *America* to us. 'Twould be tedious to run into all the particulars, take some of them in gross.

THE *Sugar-Cane*, was a Discovery, as to *Europe*, of the same date; for tho' 'tis thought they knew the use of it in the *East Indies* before, 'tis certain we knew nothing of it on this side the *Mediterranean Sea* till it was brought to us from *America*.

THE *Cochoneal*, vulgarly call'd *Scutchenele*, for Dying Scarlet:

THE *Cocao* or *Nut*, for making of *Chocolate*, with many others:

SO of Woods also for Dyers, as *Logwood, Brasile-Wood, Nicaragna-Wood*, &c.

As *America* has been thus fruitful of medicinal Drugs, so have the Eastern parts of *Asia*, I mean *China, Japan*, together with the *Molucca* and *Philippine* Islands, also the Islands of *Java, Borneo, Ceylon*, and *Others*.

All these Discoveries are familiariz'd to us by Trade, and that Trade made practicable to us by the assistance of Navigation, both which, as above, we owe in their Beginnings, and first Improvement, to the Industry and Application of the *Phœnicians*, and particularly the People of *Sidon* and *Tyre*, and the parts adjacent.

BUT this was not all: As they began with Commerce and Navigation, so, as Commerce is a friend to all Improvement, and the Wealth which they gain'd by their Commerce encouraging them in the search after Knowledge, they became also great Patrons of Learning; and joining to them the *Egyptians*, who taking them as Nations were but the elder Branch or Brothers by Race to the *Phœnicians*: As *Canaan* was the Son of *Ham* or *Cham*, so *Chus* was also his Son, and so were *Mizraim, Phut*, and *Lud*; and *Cham* himself set up his Kingdom in *Egypt*, and reigned there 161 Years, while *Chus* peopled *Arabia Fælix*, and his Son *Nimrod* began the *Chaldean* or *Babylonian* Monarchy.

THIS short piece of Chronology, *which I shall trouble you with no more of*, was necessary here to shew, that tho' Science had its first Introduction in the more remote parts of the World, among the *Chaldeans* and *Arabians*, and then as far back as *Atlas* and *Prometheus*, and that the *Magi* or *Wisemen*, so call'd for distinction, and the *South-Sayers* were first found in those Parts; yet that the *Phœnicians* and *Egyptians* were the most fam'd improvers of all their Knowledge. The Great *Prometheus*, they tell us, first studied Astronomy, and made his first Observations upon Mount *Caucasus* in *Media*, and the Eastern parts of *Chaldea*; from whence he is fabled to be chain'd down to that Mountain, with a Vulture eating out his Bowels; which is only an allegory or invention, signifying, that he was eaten up or consum'd with an eager desire after Knowledge, and that he tyed himself down so assiduously to his nightly Observations of the Stars, lying on his Back on the Ground, many Nights together, on the Summits of those Hills, till by the severities of the heat and cold, Vapours of the Night, and other inclemencies of the Season, he contracted a Disease which eat out his Vitals, and destroy'd him; thus *Atlas* his Brother is said to support the Globe upon his Shoulders, and is painted with that heavy load upon his Back, intimating by way of Fable, that by his great knowledge of Astronomy, and his great Wisdom, he directed all human Government, and the Affairs of greatest import in the World.

BUT if *Prometheus*, a *Chaldean*, first by his study of Astronomy communicated Wisdom to the World; *Ptolemy*, an *Egyptian*, improved upon his Studies, and gave us the first System of that Science which prevail'd in the World for above 2000 Years, till in these latter Ages of Wisdom, that Knowledge is yet father extended, and the new Philosophy has prevail'd upon it; the *Copernican* System being found more consistent with it self, and with the rest of Nature.

THIS is that *Prometheus* to whom the antient Atheists wou'd, if possible, have ascribed some of their Maker's Honour in creating Man: The Story is worth noting, to shew how much wiser the antient Heathens were than the Atheistic part of Mankind, of what Age soever; the Fiction pretends, That *Prometheus* making the figure of a Man in Clay, Stole Fire from the Sun to envigorate the lump, and so gave it motion: The meaning was honestly this, That before *Prometheus* Mankind was little better than a lump of Earth, so grosly Ignorant, Brutish, and Stupid, that he had nothing of supernatural Knowledge in him; but that he, by the study of the heavenly Bodies, inspir'd the Minds of Men with Divine Wisdom, and the knowledge of the true God. Thus far the Moral of the Fable is good, but as afterwards carried on it rose up to an Absurdity, by that sort of People, who wou'd have it that Man made himself without any Original, or first moving Cause; on which occasion take the following short reply.

> Prometheus, *thus, so antient Poets say,*
> *First made the model of a Man in Clay,*
> *Finish'd the beauteous Parts, and when he'd done,*
> *Stole vital Heat from the prolific Sun.*
>   *But not a Poet tells us to this Day,*
> *Who made* Prometheus *first, and who the Clay;*
> *Who gave the great Prolific to the Sun,*
> *And where the first productive Work begun.*[60]

BUT this is a Digression.

AS thus the *Egyptians* had their *Trismegistus*, and their *Ptolemy*, who improv'd upon *Atlas* and *Prometheus*, and encreas'd the Knowledge and Understanding of the Ages which follow'd: So the *Phœnicians*, not confining themselves to Trade and Navigation, had their *Cadmus*, to whose Wit and Invention, they to this Day, tho' wrongfully, ascribe the invention of Letters; I say wrongfully because I think it is clear that the first knowledge of Letters was from Heaven it self, and that immediately by the Finger of God writing the *Hebrew* Law, which we call the Decalogue or Ten Commandments, and putting it into the Hand of *Moses* to teach the *Hebrews*. It is easy to bring back all the knowledge of Letters, the giving Sounds to Figures, and marks, join'd by Prolation into Words, to this great Original, and to prove that both the *Egyptians* and *Phœnicians* had no other knowledge of Litterature, but what deriv'd from this solemn Beginning.

BUT not to dwell upon that here, which I may have any occasion also to mention again: I do not by this at all lessen the Honour of *Cadmus* that learned Prince; for he was both Prince and Scholar; and tho' he did not invent the *Hebrew* Alphabet, or the first way of using Letters, and impressing Letters and Words for Speech, and Writing; yet he, as above, greatly improv'd Knowledge. I will not make *Cadmus*[61] the Improver, and God the Inventor, for 'tis evident the *Hebrew* Language was so perfect in its Original, that it has suffer'd the least alteration of its Orthography of any Language in the World; nay, we are not sure that it has suffer'd any alteration at all; and the *Jews* tell you, that all the pretended Improvements, which some speak of, are only advances towards a restoring it to its heavenly and original Purity, from which the *Hebrews* in their several Captivities had suffer'd it to degenerate.

BUT, I say not this to lessen the Honour of *Cadmus*, that learned and ingenious Prince of *Tyre*, tho' he did not bring the knowledge of Letters into the World; yet this he did, he invented a new way of writing those Letters, and form'd a new Alphabet of his own; This new way differ'd from the

Hebrew in this great and significant Article, namely, (1) That as the *Hebrew*, and from the *Hebrew* all the other Languages, at that time in use, Read from the right Hand to the left; he inverted the Order, and wrote from the left Hand to the right.[62] (2) As the *Hebrew* Alphabet was assisted by a great number of Points and Marks, by which the same Letters had their differing Pronunciation and differing Signification, he form'd a new Alphabet of simple Letters, with very few Marks or Points, but with one small dash call'd *Accent* to assign the Emphasis of Pronounduncation, to this or that particular Vowel.

THESE Letters he call'd *Alphabeta* from the two first Letters *Alpha* and *Beta*, as we call our Alphabet, in our vulgar Speech, to this Day, by the Name of the *A B C*, making a Word or proper Name of those Letters, importing the rest; so we say of an ignorant Fellow, let him go learn his *A B C*, that is the Book, where the knowledge of the Letters are first learn'd, and where the Alphabet or *A B C* is placed at the beginning.

AND yet *Cadmus* invented but sixteen of the Letters neither, the others were added long afterwards by other learned *Greeks*, of which in its place: With this Cargo of Learning, *Cadmus*, the first Merchant of that kind, is said to have gone by Sea from *Tyre* into the *Archipelague*, and landing in *Bœotia*, a Province of *Achaia*, afterwards call'd *Greece*, and now part of the *Morea*, he built *Thebes*; and was deservedly made King or Lord of it, being his own City, where, as the Poets feign,[63] he sowed Teeth, and reap'd a Harvest of Men; his Story is fabled into many sorts, each of which however, may have their Moral peculiar to themselves, but are not to our purpose here.

AS the knowledge of Letters flourish'd among the *Phœnicians*, and the study of Astronomy among the *Egyptians*, so the original Wisdom and Learning of the *Chaldæans* and *Arabians* sunk into mere South-saying, interpreting Dreams, false Prophesies, Magic, and Witchcraft; and by degrees fell into gross and stupid Idolatries, in which they practis'd the most sordid and brutish things to carry on their several kinds of Sorceries till it became a proverbial Speech, that *the Egyptians convers'd with the* Gods, the *Phœnicians* with Men, and the *Arabians* with the Devil; the meaning was, the *Egyptians* convers'd with the Stars in their Astronomical Observations, the *Phœnicians* with Men by their extraordinary forreign Commerce and Navigation, which brought some of all Nations to them; and the *Arabians* and *Chaldæans* with the Devil by their skill in Magic and Witchcraft.

NOR can we suppose, for they are inseparable, that where Learning and Science thus flourish'd (for speaking of the Times so near their Originals it may justly be call'd their flourishing) I say, where Learning was thus encourag'd, Arts wou'd go Hand in Hand with it: and some Instances may be given that it was so, and that in some inimitable particulars as that Prodigy of Architecture, as well for the Magnificence of them, as the Curiosity of the Workmanship, I mean the *Pyramids* for the repositing the dead Bodies of Men, where if we may believe Tradition, the Bodies never perish.

IN the next place, the Bodies themselves, that is the manner of so preserving them, as to make them in one respect Immortal; those they call *Mummies*, the Art of Preserving of which, as it was not known to any part of the World but those particular People, so it is now lost to them as well as to the rest of the World.

NOR is this all, but they will tell us that such was the extraordinary virtue of the Spices, and Gums, and Drugs us'd in those preperations, that they are now bought and preserv'd with the dead Bodies for the use of Physic and Surgery, that is for Pills, and other medicinal Preperations, and also for Plaisters to heal, and the Flesh and Blood, Nerves and Muscles, Sinews and Tendons, and even Bones of the dead Bodies are by the length of time so incorporated with the Sear-cloths,[64] in which they were wrap't, and with those Spices and Drugs, &c. of which those Sear-cloths are full, that altogether make now a sovereign Medicine applicable in the most dangerous of all Diseases, (*viz.*) pestilential Fevers, Epilepsies and decays of Nature, and even in some Poisons.

THIS exquisite piece of Knowledge, as it was early in practice, so with the Destruction of those Nations, it seems to be lost from among Men; and if the Conquerors of those Nations obtained any part of it, they did not seem to carry it away with them; nor did the Wisest of them, no not *Alexander* himself, or his Successors, as we read of, ever preserve that Art.

SOME are of opinion that the Skill of the several Orders of Architecture came from the *Phœnicians* and *Egyptians*; and several things seem to favour that Opinion.

(1.) THE magnificent Ruins of the two most antient Cities of those Times, which were perhaps the most Magnificent in the World for those first Ages, (*viz.*) the City of *Tyre* in *Phœnicia*, and the city of *Thebes*, that is to say the *Egyptian Thebes*, the mighty Columnes and magnificent Gate-ways, Arches, and other things of that kind which belong'd to them, being yet to be seen in the Ruins of those places.

(2.) THE Testimony of King *Solomon* to the *Tyrian* King *Hiram*, that his Subjects were skillfull in such Works as were necessary in so nice a Service, as the building the Temple of *Jerusalem*. There is scarce room to question but that *Solomon* who resolved to erect the most glorious Fabric in the World, and who even to profusion spent so prodigious a Wealth in the Building, wou'd likewise spare no cost to get the most exquisite Workmen for the finishing it; and yet we find he sent no farther than to *Hiram* King of *Tyre*, not to *Egypt*, nor to the King of *Syria*, or *Assyria*, but to *Tyre* his Neighbour King; and he gives Testimony to the Subjects of the King of *Tyre*, 2 *Chron.* ii. 7, 14. *Send me now therefore a Man cunning to work in Gold, and in Silver, and in Brass, and in Iron, and in Purple, and Crimson, and Blue, and that can skill to Grave with the cunning Men that are with me in* Judah *and* Jerusalem, *whom* David *my Father did provide.* And verse 14. *The Son of a Woman of* Dan, *and his Father was a Man of* Tyre, *skillful to work in Gold, and in Silver, in Brass, in Iron, in Stone, and in Timber, in Purple, in Blue, and in fine Linnen, and in Crimson: And also to grave any manner of Graving, and to find out every Device, which shall be put to him with thy cunning Men, and with the cunning Men of my Lord* David *thy Father.*

HERE is a compleat Testimonial that the *Tyrians* were great encouragers of Art, and had made great improvements in the most exquisite parts of Handy-craft, especially Architecture; *Thy Servants can skill (or have skill) to hew* Timber *in* Lebanon; 'tis not to be suppos'd that their skill lay only in felling the Trees, very little Art being wanted for that kind of Work; but the meaning must be, they were extraordinary skillful in framing the Work, for all the Temple was built at a distance; not the noise of an Ax, or a Hammer, was heard in the House, not so much as the cutting the Stones, but it was all done in the Mountains.

THEN for other Works. The next was the *Foundary*, which as it was in it self, an extraordinary piece of skill; so if you consider the several Works perform'd, we have Reason to believe, the like could not be done, at this time, by the greatest Masters in the World; namely, the SEA of Brass, which stood without the Temple, for the Priests to wash in; and the two Pillars or Columns of Brass which stood in the Porch: the Dimensions of both were prodigious, and such as, if the Scripture were not our Author, (and that will go but a little way with some neither) we shou'd never believe practicable. As for the *Sea* of Brass,[65] it might well be call'd a Sea indeed, for it held above 125 Ton of Water, in one solid Vessel of Brass: Then the two Columns of Brass, which the same Artist cast, being solid Brass, forty Cubits, that is, threescore Foot high, and with the Flowers, and Chain-work round them, were twelve Cubits, that is, three Fathom about.

THE same Workmen was, it seems, by the same Text, an admirable Artist at Engraving, and a worker in Gold, and Silver, and Purple, and Blue; by which I understand, either an extraordinary Embroiderer, or a Weaver of flower'd Silks, mixt with Gold and Silver; all which Arts, it seems, he had been brought up and was arriv'd to a perfection in at *Tyre.* So that the encouragement given to Arts, by the occasion of their Trade was apparently very great; nor do we read of any thing done among the *Romans* that

83

comes near it, tho' Arts might be said to flourish very much too in their Time.

FROM hence I must take the liberty to note, that upon the Destruction of this diligent People, and afterwards of their Posterity the *Carthaginians*, (who were alike industrious) their skill in those things dyed with them; the knowledge in those more exquisite Arts perish'd with them; the *Romans* that succeeded the *Carthaginians* made nothing of it; they civiliz'd the Manners indeed of some of the Nations, whom they conquer'd; but they did not encourage Arts and Sciences like the *Tyrians*, or propagate Trade and Navigation like the *Carthaginians*: and therefore we find no such Artists among the *Romans*, as those of *Tyre* appear to have been, or indeed as the *Egyptians*, and as the *Carthaginians*. The *Romans* indeed were good Architects, but it was in the latter part of their Empire, and besides they had all their orders of Building from the *Grecians*, as the *Dorick*, the *Corinthian*, the *Attick*, all *Grecian*. The most famous Masters of Sculpture and Painting, were *Grecians*; the Gladiators indeed, and the Fencers, the Great Generals, and Officers, were *Romans*; in the Fighting part they out-did the whole World; but the Arts of Peace were not their Province.

THE great Image of *Nebuchadnezzar* the King of *Babylon*, the great Coloss[66] at *Rhodes*; these were all perform'd in latter Times, tho' by the same Race of Artists; but we see nothing of it among the Artists of our Age.

SOME have said that *Nebuchadnezzar's* Image[67] of Gold, was Cast by a *Tyrian* Engineer, whom he took Prisoner at the time he besieg'd *Tyre*, of which I have spoken before; and the Gold, which must be of an immense Value, was made up out of the plunder of the Cities of *Egypt*, which he conquer'd after his disappointment at the Seige of *Tyre*; for there, tho he took the City, he got no plunder, since the Inhabitants ship'd themselves off, while he lay under their Walls, and left him to take what he could find, as you have heard.

BUT as God gave him *Egypt*[68] for his Wages, as the Text says, there he made himself full amends, and got an infinite Treasure; with which, if that part of the Story be true, and perhaps with the plunder of God's Temple and City also, he cast this monstrous Image, which he set up in the Plains of *Dura*, without the City; the height of it was sixty Cubits, that is, ninety Foot, which is within eleven Foot, half as high as the Monument; the breadth only nine Foot; how thick is not set down; and this Image was of Massy Gold.

IT is not very hard to cast up the weight of the Gold, reckoning every inch Square and Solid to be four Ounces, as no doubt it wou'd, and every five Ounces to be worth twenty Pounds Sterling, according to the present Standard of Gold, which is four Pounds per Ounce.

IF the Artist, which Cast this Image, was an Inhabitant of *Tyre*, as is not improbable; this is the use I make of it, namely, that the *Phœnicians* were (even then) great improvers of Art, and great encouragers of it also; and I with great certainty venture to say, that it was all a consequence of their being great improvers of Commerce; for Trade thriving, Arts always flourish; Commerce is a friend to Learning; Trade makes the People rich, and their Wealth puts them upon improvement of Arts and Sciences; Riches reward Application, and encourage Ingenuity; Money, where there is a Genius, inspires the Mind and gives pleasing Representations of an encrease of Gain, and especially where Wealth is gotten by Trade, it pushes on the Mind for more Trade.

NOTHING makes Arts and Sciences thrive more than their working on a public Purse; no private Man can reward as the public can; and Kings therefore are applauded as the encouragers of Learning, because they can, and very often do, bountifully reward Learned Men, Men of Genius, and of Application.

LET us then take the *Tyrians*, and the *Egyptians*, for they were contemporary: I say, let us take them in the early times of the World before the Conquests of *Nebuchadnezzar*; and while they were flourishing in Wealth by Commerce, as they both were at that time; you will also find that they were famous for Wisdom and Learning, for Knowledge and Understanding; and that they had always very great Men flourishing among them; I mean great for Learning, and for encouraging of Learning of every kind, and especially in Astronomy, in Philosophy, and in all the other parts of useful Knowledge.

IT is true, Learning was not[a] then understood to mean the same thing which we understand by it now; the Study in their Schools was not Books, but their School-Masters read them the Precepts of Antient and Wise-men, and deliver'd them in Philosophic and Wise Discourses, not in Writings or historical Narrations of their own.

AMONG these, they had the Precepts of *Noab*,[69] which contained, as the Learned say, twelve Sentences for the Government of Life; and for the guiding themselves in the various Scenes Men were ordinarily suppos'd to pass through: These Precepts, like the Ten Commandments, were said to contain, first, Directions for God's Worship; and next, The Laws of Right and Wrong, or Rules of Morality; but we never find they were committed to Writing.

THE teachings in the Schools contained Wise Comments upon that great Text, which however the Teachers themselves did not stick close to, as to Religion; the Polytheism of the Nations presently breaking in, yet the Moral Duties took place, and the Philosophers obtain'd that Name for being Lovers of Wisdom, and Teachers of Knowledge, instructing the Youth of the World, as in Wisdom and Knowledge, so also in Virtue and Piety.

FROM that first or great Class, in which, I say, the Precepts of Virtue were instill'd into the Minds of their Scholars, they proceeded to instruct them in the principles of Philosophy, as well Natural as Experimental; but how far they went at that time, we can make no judgment; some are of the opinion, that they went beyond us all, that they had a greater knowledge in many things than ever we arriv'd to since. A *French* Writer, whose Name I cannot now recollect, tells us, That above 2000 Years ago, and long before *Hippocrates*, or even *Æsculapius* himself, they had a way, with safety, to cut for the Stone in the Kidneys, which the greatest Artists in Surgery, and the greatest Anatomists tell us now, is impracticable; as also, that they had several Medicines which wou'd break or dissolve the Stone in the Bladder; that they perfectly understood the Circulation of the Blood (as indeed 'tis evident *Solomon* did) *Eccles.* xii. 6. where the Wheel at the Cistern, and the Buckets at the Well, are clear References to the stop of the Circulation.

IF these things are true, as I must confess is more than probable, what a blow to the learned World was the growing Conquest of the *Romans*? Nay rather, what injury to the general Improvement of Mankind, has Pride, and the Ambition of Men, as well States and Governments, as Kings and Princes, been in the World? who by introducing Wars and Devastations, and by inhuman bloody Measures brought Desolation upon flourishing Nations; and have as at one blow, overthrown all the learned Improvements, all the wisdom and knowledge of Arts, and of useful Inventions in the Countries they have Conquered?

HOW many Masters of Science, how many Teachers and Instructors in useful Arts did *Alexander* the Great, notwithstanding his being a lover of learned Men, bury in the Ruins of that great City *Tyre*; and in the bloody Revenge which he took of the Citizens? of whom he put 26000 to Death, by way of cold Blood Massacre? How many flourishing Merchants, their Wealth being plundered, their Wives and Children murther'd, and their Ships burnt and destroy'd, did he hang upon the Sea-shore[70] on Gibbets, in a line of six Miles in Length; and as the famous Mathematician *Archimedes* was kill'd in the sacking of the City of *Syracuse*, in the middle of all his Schemes? So how many Philosophers, Astronomers, and Men of Genius for all sorts of virtuous Improvements did *Alexander* destroy in the Ruin of that one City? Whose Wisdom died with them, and whose Knowledge could no more be convey'd to Posterity, than their Lives could be restor'd; and what amends did he, or could he make to the World for all this? What signify'd his building one sorry Port at the Mouth of the *Nile*, I mean *Alexandria*; as if he, when he had destroy'd the Merchants, who were the life of the Commerce at *Tyre*, could remove the Course of the Trade too, whither he pleas'd; whereas the forreign Correspondence, which was the life of Merchandizing, depended upon the very Men that he had destroy'd. Nor did the end answer his expectation at all; for tho' *Alexandria* did flourish, and grew a very considerable place, yet it was after a long Series of time, and upon quite a new Foot of Correspondences; namely, between *Egypt* and *Greece*, and between *Egypt* and *Italy*; whereas the *Tyrian* Merchants had establish'd a Commerce thro' the whole *Mediterranean*, up to the Mouth of the Straights; had planted Colonies at *Carthage*, at *Cadiz*, at *Palermo*, and several other places, which *Alexander* never had any Interest in, or Influence over; nor did the knowledge and study of Arts and Sciences ever come to any extraordinary height at *Alexandria* as it had done at *Tyre*. But to go from thence to the next Desolation, which the trading World suffer'd, I mean *Carthage*: How much does the trading World to this Day lament the ruin of the City and Government of *Carthage*, for the loss of which, all the Wisdom of the *Romans*, as a State, and all their encouraging of Arts and Learning, never made Mankind any amends to this Day? particularly, *Rome* never could recompense the great loss it was to the World in the ruin of that extensive Trade of *Afric* and *Egypt*, which the *Carthaginians* had establish'd; and which never to this Day has been recover'd; as you shall see in its place.

WHAT a noble Trade might we in these Islands have by this time carry'd on with the Coast of *Afric*, if there were 3000 populous Cities upon the Coast of it, as was the case in those Days? whereof one, namely, *Carthage* had 700,000 People in it, and were Masters of an immense Wealth, when the *Barbary* Coast was populous like *France*, and carry'd on a prodigious Trade with all the known World?

LET us but imagine *Africa* peopled now as it was in those Times, when the *Numidians* and *Mauritanians* were a People suppos'd to have each two Millions in Number, and inhabited all the Plains of *Barca*, the fruitful Fields of *Zagaon*, and *Tebesca*, and of *Temesna* in the Kingdom of *Fez*, places now left desolated, and almost uninhabited; when besides *Carthage*, which was the Emporium, the City of *Utica* contain'd 100,000 People; the Cities of *Tingis*, of *Portus Magnus*, and of *Taamsiga*, each as many, when the Lands were cultivated; the Corn, Cattle, Wines, Olives, and other product of the Earth consum'd upon good Terms at home; and the Copper and Brass, Iron, Allom, Almonds, Raisins, Silver, Gold, Wax, Honey, Leather, Skins of Beasts, Horses, Gums, and Drugs, which were produc'd by the Country, all along the Coast, supply'd all the rest of the known World as Merchandize for Exportation, and brought the Merchants in return the Product and Manufactures of all the Countries to which they traded.

ADD to all this, That the People of this vast Empire were not as the *Moors* and *Turks*, who succeeded them, are now; an indolent rapacious Crew of Vagrants and Thieves, who neither have Trade, or seek any; who cultivate no Lands, but for immediate Food; who have neither Numbers to consume the Product of a fruitful Soil, Merchants to export it to other Countries, or People to raise a product for the Consumption which might be demanded.

THE *Moors* of *Fez* and *Morocco*; What are they, for encouraging Nations to trade with them? What but a merciless People, with whom no Christians care to deal, much less to live among them? The *Turks* of *Algier*, *Tunis*, and *Tripoli*, what are they, but so many Dens of wild Beasts, worse indeed than the Tygers and Lyons of the Desarts behind them? Being a People accustomed to Cruelty and Robbery. They keep Faith neither with God or the Devil; they range the Seas for Plunder, and live upon the Spoil of Mankind, and of whom it may be said, 'tis the shame of Mankind that they are suffer'd to live at all.

ALL these Cities, and a number more which in the *Carthaginian* Times were inhabited, were spread, I might say indeed throng'd with diligent, numerous, wealthy, and virtuous Nations, populous beyond measure; the inland Towns rich, and made so by their own Industry; the Sea-coast Towns addicted to Commerce, and made rich by Merchandize and foreign Discoveries.

THEY did not go cloath'd like the naked *Moors* whose best Garment is a Blanket or a course woollen Mantle thrown over their Shoulders; with hardly other Clothes to cover their Nakedness, and the Women little more than a Veil to hide them. But in those Days the *Carthaginians* were gay and delicate, dress'd well, and valued themselves upon it; and as they Imported the Product and Manufactures of other Countries, wou'd no doubt by this time have carry'd on a most noble, and to us, beneficial Commerce for our *British* Manufactures, which even as it is now, are very valuable among them; and which wou'd have been a Trade by this time equal to that of *Spain* and *Portugal*, only perhaps fifteen times as much. But of this hereafter at large when I come to speak of the advantage it wou'd be to *Europe* to recover, by Conquest, those glorious Cities and Countries, and re-plant those Nations, the loss of which is now so fatal to the World.

IN the mean time, to bring the thing back to what I began it for, What amends did the *Romans* make to the tradeing part of the World, and to the improving part of Mankind by the Conquests they made? What have they done, but rooted out an industrious People, and planted in their room a Crew of strouling Vagabonds; who as they brought nothing but Brutality and Cruelty with them, so they have left the Country to a Succession of People infinitely worse than themselves; and, as to the common benefit of Mankind not at all more valuable than the Beasts of Prey which over-run the Country with them.

IT is true, the *Romans*, while their State remained flourishing, did in some measure maintain their *African* Conquests; but notwithstanding this the havock of People which they made in the last Punick War, in which 'tis said, above a *Million* of People lost their Lives, was such, that when the *Roman* Power decay'd, and the barbarous Nations broke in upon their Empire; *Africa* was able to do little; the numerous Nations, which the *Romans* subdued, were left weak, thin of People, and those few subjected and impoverish'd: and so they were unable to resist the inundations of the *Goths*, and after them of the *Saracens* and *Mahometans, Moors*, and Others; who over-run them, and by their several Conquests, brought the Country to the abandon'd Condition in which we now see it.

BY all this Series of Disasters, *Africa* is now no more a place of Trade; all the Commerce of the whole Country, from the Borders of *Egypt* to Cape *Spartel*, and from thence South to *Cape de Verd*, is not equal, put it all together, to the Trade of the single Port of *Cadiz* in *Spain*; no, nor to a half part of it, tho' you were to leave the Article of *New Spain*,[71] and the *Galleons* out of the Account.

WHAT a loss then to the Commerce of *Europe* have those two Actions been, which Men in those Days call'd Glorious; and how have we Reason to blast the Memory of *Alexander* the Great, and *Scipio Africanus* with a mark of Infamy never to be wip'd out, for destroying the only two Governments in the World, which were qualified to make all the rest of Mankind great and happy?

CHAP. IX.

Of the flourishing condition of Commerce when the Carthaginian *Government was overthrown by the* Romans: *What a blow that Conquest was to Trade; and how the knowledge of* America, *discover'd by the* Carthaginians, *was lost to the World by their Disaster.*

HAVING observ'd, in the last Chapter, what a loss to the trading World the destroying of the Cities of *Tyre* and *Carthage* severally were in the respective Ages that follow'd; and how little the *Roman* Government did, after the said Conquests, to recover Trade, and encourage useful Discoveries in the World; it comes of course to look back upon the progress of the *Carthaginians* in the time of their Prosperity, what they did towards the improvement of Trade, which future Ages, *had not their Ruin interven'd*, might have improv'd upon, and encreas'd in the World; and by which, the great encrease of Commerce, which the World has since that arriv'd to, might have been yet much more enlarg'd.

THIS enquiry is not merely to look back into Antiquity; That, as I have said, being not the business of this Undertaking; but to show us what may be, by what has been, and how evident it is, that this part of the World call'd *Africa*, which at present seems to be given up to Barreness and to wild Beasts, once was, and still might be rendred useful to the trading World, wou'd the Christian Nations apply themselves first to the Conquest of it; and then to the planting and cultivating it for the multiplying its Inhabitants, and bringing Trade and Arts to flourish in it, as once they did.

IN order then to this enquiry, and to bring it home to the proposal I am to make: Let us first see what *Africa* was in the height of the *Carthaginian* Prosperity, or, if you please, in the time of the second Punick War: That War, which being carry'd on by *Hannibal*, and transfer'd from *Spain* into *Italy*, was carry'd even to the Gates of *Rome*, and once, namely, after the Battle of *Canna*,[72] bid fair, had *Hannibal* improv'd his Victory; I say, bid fair for the ruin of the *Roman* Empire; but which, *Hannibal*'s prudence failing him, ended in the total ruin of *Carthage*.

The State of Africa *at that Time, was this.*

CARTHAGE, a noble flourishing City and Common-wealth, fat as Queen of the *South*; the City seated for Commerce, as well as for Empire, near the Port of *Golletta*, commanded the Land by her victorious Armies, and the Sea by her powerful Fleets.

SHE was possest of all *Africa*, from *Barca*, bordering on *Egypt*, to *Tangis* or *Tangier* at the Straights Mouth, and from thence *South* to *Santa Cruz* to *Cape Blanco*, and even to *Cape de Verd*.

THE *Numidians*, a powerful, and infinitely populous Nation, with their King *Jugurtha*, and the *Mauritanians*, (a Nation as populous, tho' not so fam'd in the Field, their Cavalry not being so good as the *Numidians*) were also with their King *Juba* Tributaries to the *Carthaginians*. Thus stood their Force by Land upon the Continent of *Africa*.

BEYOND, or upon the *Sea*, their Power was very great; they had conquer'd, and entirely possest the two Island Kingdoms of *Sardinia* and *Sicily*, the latter being at that time very strong, for the City of *Syracusa* was said to contain six hundred thousand People.

IN *Europe*, they possest all *Spain*, except that part we now call the *Asturias*, and the Kingdom of *Navarr*; and in *Italy*, their victorious Army was possest of all *Calabria*; great part of that we now call *Tuscany*, the City of *Capua*; and in a Word were a Terror to *Rome* it self.

AT the same time that their Power was thus extended, you are to allow them to be the most addicted to, and the greatest encouragers of Trade in the whole World. As they had a Genius for Commerce, so the Country they possest was fruitful in abundance of the Materials of Trade; that is to say, the most extraordinary product of the Earth for Exportation, and the most extraordinary product of a diligent industrious People in the most ingenious Manufacture, for their Consumption; being the Employment of the Poor, as well in the Nations about them, as of their own Subjects; also these was exported, by them, to other Countries.

THEY had then, by the advantage of Numbers at home, a great Consumption of the product of other Countries, which they brought back in return for what they exported, so that they had both the ends of Commerce in their own Hands.

THEIR Export is the chief thing to be spoken of here; for this certainly remains, may be recover'd and restor'd, and is, or wou'd be, the same as before: As for their home Consumptions of foreign Goods, that was ruin'd by the *Romans*, in destroying the People; and can never be restor'd till the

Country is re-peopled, and the Inhabitants made rich and numerous as before.

THE product of *Africa* consisted in four capital Articles of Life; and which, as being most necessary for the Sustenance or Subsistance of Mankind, was acceptable in all parts of the World: These were *Corn, Wine, Oil,* and *Salt*; of these they had not plenty only, but a profusion, not only sufficient to supply the great City of *Carthage*, and the other populous Cities which they had built, and possest upon the Coast of *Africa*,[73] such as *Utica, Tingis, Adrumetum, Aphrodisium, Tacape, Syrtes, Portus Magnus, Porta Deorum,* and many more, but they had enough to supply their foreign Colonies, as well on the Western Coasts of *Spain*, where they had several large Settlements, and which grew populous by the thronging in of the *Spaniards* and *Lusitanians*, the *Celteberians*, and other Nations to them, for the sake of the Liberty and the Protection they enjoy'd from the *Carthaginians*; but also to all their more Southern Colonies on the Western Coasts of *Africa*; where they had Cities and Sea-Ports, settled for the carrying on the Trade of those Countries, which was chiefly in Gold, and Slaves, Elephants Teeth, Drugs, Civet, and such like rich Goods, which those Countries produce to this Day.

IF any Man question how the product of those parts of *Africa* was found out in those early Times; the answer is very easy; namely, there was little or no difficulty in it, for the Ivory is found in the Desarts,[74] where the Elephants, who after several Years, cast their Teeth, dropt, and left them; and in the same manner they are found at this Day, and no otherwise; that they kill Elephants, for the sake of their Teeth, is a delusion, and a mistake; nor cou'd the *Negros* kill them, or durst come near them, except the *Numidians*, who by Stratagems took them young, and bred them up for the Wars, which the *Negroes*, to this Day, understand nothing of.

THEN, as to the Gold, which was fetch'd from those Countries, it was then, as it still chiefly is, in the Sands and Shoals of the principal Rivers, so that the Gold and the Ivory was with great Facility produced in those Countries, at that time, and consequently the Cities and Colonies of the *Carthaginians* on the Coast of *Africa* had great encouragement, being able to make such rich returns; on the other Hand, those hot Climates, being within ten to fifteen Degrees of the Line, producing little or no Corn, or other Fruits, for the subsistance of the People, were oblig'd to fetch their supplies from *Carthage*, or the Countries about it.

AND here two things are very remarkable, with relation to Trade.

    I. That, had the *Carthaginian* Government remain'd we have Reason to believe that we had found many noble Settlements and populous Cities, and perhaps Nations, upon all the Western Coasts of *Africa*, from Cape *Spartel*, quite away to the Cape of *Good Hope*; and which had still been more considerable, we had found a civiliz'd, industrious, trading People, every where planted, prepar'd for Commerce, and furnish'd with a Product fit for making their Returns for all the Manufactures, and Merchandizes of *Europe*, when we had come to trade with them.

II. As this did not happen, but that the *Carthaginian* State was overthrown and destroy'd, all these Settlements died in their infancy for want of those supplies; and when we, in so many Ages of Time, came to discover those Coasts, we found them either Desolate and Barren, and almost without Inhabitants; or those Inhabitants untaught, wild, and naked Savages, the remembrance of former People being quite lost and sunk out of their Minds, nor so much as any civilized remains left among them.

IT seems to be a Question, naturally coming in our way here, (*viz.*) Why shou'd the *Carthaginian* Settlements, on this side of *Africa*, perish and die upon the conquering the *Carthaginians*, whereas the like Settlements on the Coast of *Andalusia, Lusitania*, &c. remained flourishing, and encreasing, and have continued to this Day.

BUT the Answer to this is ready, (*viz.*) That after the Conquest of *Carthage*, the *Romans* pursued their Victory, subduing all the Countries, where the former had settled their Colonies, in *Spain* and *Portugal*, and even into the Bay of *Biscay*; where tho' they did not propagate Merchandizing, and foreign Commerce, they did not supplant the Nations or Cities, only subdued them, and left Detachments of Soldiers to keep and maintain their Possession. But the case differ'd extreamly in the South, for as there were no Nations on that side worth subduing, or any Countries worth keeping possession of, only Settlements and Colonies, which being lately made, required an expensive Supply, yearly, for their support: These the *Romans*, having but little Genius to Trade, and but few Merchants among them, had little or no regard to, and took no care about; and so they perish'd for mere want of being supported.

AND this I take to be the Reason also, why, tho' I am clear, that the discovery and first planting of the Continent of *America* was from thence, yet that Discovery was no farther proceeded on, after it was first made, or the Memory of it preserv'd, but that as the Colonies in *Africa*, from whence the first Voyage was made to *America*, was abandon'd, their Patrons at *Carthage*, being destroy'd; so with them died the very Memory of such a Discovery, and all Knowledge, that ever such a place had been found out in the World.

FOR as by the fall of *Carthage*, all the depending Colonies, which the *Carthaginians* had planted, fell to ruin, and to an irrecoverable decay, even into perfect oblivion, so it follow'd, by a natural Consequence, that all their farther Discoveries, made by way of Adventure, or otherwise, by private Persons, from those decay'd Colonies, died with them; for if these Colonies, tho' very considerable, died with the fall of their Patrons the *Carthaginians*, well might those Subsequent, or as we may call them second hand Discoveries and Improvements, fall with the destruction of their first undertakers.

NOR is it at all improbable, but that the People, who had, by Shipping, been brought to settle on the Western Coast of *Africa*, by the care, and at the expence of the *Carthaginian* Merchants, or at the expence of the Public; suppose by the Hands of that great pursuer of new Discoveries, *Hanno*, who I take to be the *Carthaginian* Sir *Walter Raleigh*, as afterwards Sir *Walter Raleigh* was call'd the *English Hanno*; I say it is not improbable, but that when *Hanno*, their Protector, was slain, the *Carthaginian* Republick overthrown, and the City of *Carthage* it self destroy'd, the Inhabitants of some or other of these Settlements, being made desperate by their Calamities, might embark at all hazards for fear of their cruel Enemies the *Romans*, and following the People, who they had before happily landed in *America*, might arrive there themselves, and make as effectual escape from the *Romans*, as their Ancestors the *Tingitanian Canaanites* did formerly from the Face of *Joshua* the Robber,[75] when they settled at *Tangier*, and began the *Mauritanian* Kingdoms of *Afric*.

AND this may be the more probable, from the Similitude of Manners and Customs, between the *Carthaginians* and the *Americans*; many of the *Carthaginian* Customs, and some say many of their very Words, being retain'd among the *Americans*, even to the time that the *Spaniards*, under the Great *Cortez* arriv'd there; particularly, many of their idolatrous Customs, Sacrificings, Conjurings, and other barberous usages in the Worship of their Gods.

IT is too large a Work to enter upon here, but those who are curious enough to search into those things, may observe, that the Heathen Temples, erected at *Mexico*, and at *Cusco*, with the manner of their Sacrifices, had a great resemblance of, and affinity to the same Rites among the *Numidians* and *Carthaginians*.

ABOVE all, the antient Forms of Government by the *Inca*'s of *Peru*, the Customs and Usages of *Attahalipa*, the *Peruvian* King; their Registers, Archives, and Laws, were so strangely Simular, and such strong Resemblance to the Courts and Governments of the *Numidian*, and *Mauritanian* Courts, that it Legitimates their descent from them, as much as any thing of that kind, and so remote in time can be suppos'd to do.

BUT besides all this, the *Peruveans* especially, and the *Mexicans* also, but especially the former, had many antient Traditions, and traditional Prophecies among them, which plainly related to the *Carthaginian* Nation, tho' the vast distance of Time, Ignorance of the People, and entire want of the use of Letters, obliterated these remains, so as to make them not legible to themselves, and but very little to the *European* Nations, which came so long after them.

THERE are some difficulties started about their Transportation from *Africa* to *America*, the carrying over with them Women and Children, the carrying living Creatures, Beasts of Prey, and the like, the length of the Voyage, the Ignorance in Navigation, and the want of Ships, all which are easily answer'd, as follows, and with that I shall dismiss the Subject.

THE Shipping of the *Carthaginians* was at that time so very considerable that we find them fitting out large Navies for the War, in which, for a great while they were Superior to the *Romans*; and we find them trading with large Ships to all the Coasts of the *Mediterranean*, and on the West-side of *Africa* and *Europe*, from the Latitude of fifteen to fifty Degrees in the Ocean, and how much farther we are not certain; but the inference I draw from it, is this. Why might not the same Ships, which cou'd cross the Bay of *Biscay*, the Bay of *Cadiz*, and the *Mediterranean* Sea, from *Carthage* to *Sardinia*, and *Marseilles*, which are all turbulent, outragious, and dangerous Seas, as well pass those so much more pacifick Seas, from the *Cape de Verd* Islands to the *Caribbees*, or to the *Cape St. Augustine* on the Coast of *Brasil*, where most of the way they have a Trade Wind, or a strong Current, or both, to favour them, with a quick Passage, as well as a safe? Why not as well as it has been possible for Men to go from *Barbadoes* to *Jamaica*; nay, from *Jamaica* to the *Honduras* in a Ship's long Boat, nay even in a Pinnace, without any Deck or Shelter; or room to stow Provisions or Water, more than for two or three Days.

IF then the Passage, which we know was practicable, might be thus perform'd, why shou'd it be impracticable for them to carry with them Women, Children, Fowles, or any other Creatures, at least any such as were found in *America*, when it was last discover'd.

IN order, however, to make these things easy to the Understanding, I desire my Reader to take notice, that I am not supposing, that this Discovery was merely accidental, by some Ship being driven off to Sea in a Tempest, and hurry'd away to the Coast of *America* by the stress of Weather, without any previous design; tho' even that part is far from impossible.

BUT I suppose the Voyage to be perform'd upon a settled design of searching after new Discoveries; That the Vessel, so fitted out for such a design, might be set out at some of the *Carthaginian* Settlements on the Coast of *Afric*, suppose about the River *Senegal*, that is to say, the Mouth of the River *Niger*, or from the *Cape de Verd* Islands.

YOU may allow, if you please, that some other Ship, bound from the Shore of *Afric*, to those Islands, had first been driven so far to the Westward, as to have discovered some of the Mountains of *America* at a great distance; but not thinking fit to venture any farther, had made the best of their way back as soon as Wind and Weather wou'd admit, but brought the News with them that there was Land to be seen that way, that there was a new World, and that whoever pleas'd to make the Adventure might find new Countries for Commerce.

THAT this News shou'd fire the Minds of a Nation, naturally enclin'd to Adventures, and new Discoveries, wou'd be much less matter of Wonder, than it wou'd be that they shou'd hear of it without any motion, or any stirring up of their Curiosity for the attempt; but that the attempt was feizible, I see nothing of room for an Objection; they whose Ships were able to keep the Sea in such Voyages; which they really did perform; and on such occasions as they were oblig'd to do when driven out of their knowledge, as above; might certainly be able to perform such a Voyage as this, in a fair Weather Sea, a Trade Wind, and a Leeward Current; so that in a Word the difficulty was nothing; nor can I make any doubt, that the *Carthaginian* Merchants did perform the Voyage, and settled themselves in *America*, when *Carthage* being destroy'd by the *Romans*, they were abandon'd to Want and Despair; than I make a doubt whether *Carthage* was destroy'd or no. As for their carrying over wild Beasts, or the manner how wild Beasts might come into *America*, I think as easy to explain as all the rest; but shall not enter into it here, being foreign to our present purpose.

I SHALL conclude this Chapter with going back to what I was upon, at the beginning of it; namely, the Product of *Africa* when under the *Carthaginian* Government; by which the Merchants of *Carthage* were supply'd for Exportation to foreign Countries, and in return for which they brought back the growth and Manufactures of those Countries to which they were Exported.

I HAVE mention'd already four very material Articles (*viz.*) Corn, Wine, Salt, and Oil; these they had in great quantity, especially *Corn*, and *Oil*, and were able to supply all the Northern parts of the World with them; but especially the Islands of the Lesser *Asia*, and the *Archipelagoe*, the Provinces of *Greece*, and in times of Peace *Italy* it self.

BUT this was not all; They had in the next place Iron and Copper; the last was not only the best of its kind in the World, but if I mistake not, the only place in the World where fine Copper was found. This Copper was carry'd, in particular, to *Corinth*, where the *Lapis Calaminaris*[76] being found, they melted the Copper, and produc'd the Brass, which in those Days was of so much Value, as to be equal to Gold. Hence, no doubt, *Solomon* supplyed himself with Brass for the famous Utensils of the Temple; where it is said the Brass was without weight; that is to say, the quantity was so great it could not be cast up: And hence the *Corinthian* Brass was esteem'd the most precious of any other kind. As to the Iron, it was found in *Numidia*, and Exported to *Italy*, to *Greece*, and to *Spain*; and was in those Days very valuable and useful.

BESIDES these, they had a very great quantity of Figs, Almonds, Raisins, Limons, Pomegranates, and other Fruit, all which they exported in Merchandize, besides the quantities which they consumed at home.

THEY had also a great Trade in Horses, which in times of Peace they sent over to *Sicily, Sardinia*, and *Italy*; also into *Greece*, and into *Spain*, and the fine breed of *Spanish* Jennets, which are to this Day so valuable in *Spain*, are said to be produc'd first from the Race of the *Numidians* Horses, which were at that time esteem'd the finest and swiftest in the World.

NEXT to this, They had great quantities of Honey, and Wax; the first, of which, was at that time an extraordinary Article of Merchandize, there being no such thing as Sugar then known in the World.

WE have some Reason to think they had also Rice, a sort of Product, which we do not read much of in those times, tho' since it is become very valuable.

THESE particular Merchandizes were the product of the inland Countries in general; but besides these they had several other things, which they fetch'd from the remoter Coasts, and were to be had in this or that particular Country only; as Civet, Emeralds, and Balm, from *Ethiopia*; Gold and Elephants Teeth, from the Coast of the West towards the *Cape de Verd*; Lyons, Leopards, Tygers, and Ostriches, from the Desarts of *Mauritania*.

NOW to look back upon all these things, 'tis evident they not only were at that time the product of *Africa*, but they are so still, and may be recover'd; were numbers of People to be found at home to propagate them, they wou'd, I say, be recover'd to as great a degree as ever; for to this Day the *French*, the *Genoese*, and the *Spaniards*, fetch great quantities of Corn, Oil, Salt, Wax, and Honey from *Barbary*; nor wou'd the Wine, the Almonds, Figs, Limons, &c. be less valuable, but that *Spain, France*, and *Italy*, abound in all those things themselves.

AS to the *Copper*, the *Gold*, the *Iron*, the *Civet*, the *Emeralds*, and the *Wax*, they are all to this Day as valuable there as ever; and are the only, or chief Articles of Trade which they have among them. But all together shew us, how great an Improvement of Trade it might be to the World to have the

Continent of *Africa* put into the possession of the diligent industrious Nations of *Europe*, who were able, and had a Genius apt to cultivate the Soil, and raise the Product to the same height, which it may be, and has been at. But of that by it self.

CHAP. X.

Of the state of Trade and Discovery, after the ruin of Tyre and Carthage; and how Commerce went back to its Original, and began again only as Nature and the Laws of Necessity directed.

TYRE being destroy'd by *Alexander the Great*, as has been distinctly accounted for, one effect was, that the Trade between *Persia, Armenia*, and *India*, on the one Hand; The Merchants of *Tyre*, and by their means *Europe* and *Africa* on the other; was entirely interrupted, and put to an end; that is to say, the Commerce of the *Indies* with *Europe* and *Africa*, was put to an end.

THE Commerce of the *Indies*, and of *Persia*, was from the beginning a Trade in Silks, and fine Works in embroidery of Gold and Silver; as also in Spices and choice Gums, Ointments, Drugs, &c. Hence the *Babylonish* Garment, stolen by *Achan*,[77] was suppos'd to be a Robe of Silk Embroidered with Gold. Hence the fetching Gold from *Ophir*, said to be the Island of *Sumatra*, was a Trade, tho' enter'd into by King *Solomon*, practis'd long before by the *Tyrians*: And from this beginning, the Trade both of *India*, and *Persia*, is to this Day carry'd on, and is still a Trade in raw and wrought Silks, Spices, Drugs, Perfumes, &c.

THIS Commerce, as I have said, was certainly began by the Merchants of *Tyre*, and may be suppos'd to be carry'd on thus, before *Solomons* Days long enough. (1) The *Tyrians* had a Trade with *Persia* and consequently with *Bactria* and *Kathay*, which is *Tartary* and *India*; which Trade was carry'd on by Land, whether by Caravans from *Babylon*, (as is now the practice, from *Bagdat*, from *Tauris*, and from *Bassora*) to *Aleppo*, or whether, by ordinary Carriage, the Desarts perhaps being at that time better inhabited; that part we cannot with any certainty be assured of.

BY this Land conveyance they receiv'd all the rich Manufactures of *Asia*, the Product of those various Countries, of which, the Silk was the special peculiar growth. The Scripture is elegant in describing the Correspondences of *Tyre* with these Nations, thereby to magnify the terror of her downfall, when the Prophet *Ezekiel* foretold her ruin by *Nebuchadnezzar, Ezek,* xxvii. 6,

I. IN her Shipping; her very Oars or Benches, or Banks for Oars, according to *Bochart, Pool,*[78] and others, were so curious and costly, that they were made of the finest Wood, to wit, *Box* and *Pine*; it was fetch'd from the Isles of *Chittim,* that is to say, from the *Ægean Sea,* and inlay'd with Ivory when it came to be wrought.

II. THEIR Sails, or as it is well expounded, the Auning or Tilts which they us'd to cover their Vessels with, like as Tarpaulins are us'd now; because, in those Days, their Ships, as they call'd them, had no Decks, so extravagantly proud and vain were they, that these were made of fine Embroidery and Needle-work, and of the finest Colours, dyed with costly Ingredients, which fine work'd Linen, 'tis said expresly, came from *Egypt, v.* 7.[79]

III. THEIR Merchandizes were fetch'd from all the remotest parts of the World, as it is most emphatically describ'd in the same Prophecy. Silver, Iron, Tin, and Lead, were brought by *Tarshish,* that is, by the Sea; and this is understood by the Learned to be from their Colonies of *Cadiz* in *Spain, Carthage* in *Afric,* and even from *Britain* it self: From whence it is known, and our own Histories confirm it, that the *Phœnicians* fetch'd Tin, Lead, and Coal; and as for Silver and Iron they had it from *Spain* and *Africa,* where they had rich Mines of both.

BRASS, is represented as coming from *Greece,* [*verse* 13.] from *Javan, Tubal,* and *Meshech*; which is particularly the Country of *Greece,* where, as I noted before, they melted down the *African* Copper, and made it into Brass, by the mixture of the *Lapis Calaminaris,* which they found in *Peleponnesus,* and other parts of the Country, call'd now the *Morea.* Then they were supply'd with Slaves, as well Men, as Women and Children, from *Meshech* and *Tubal,* (viz.) from the Countries of *Mingrelia, Colchus, Cappadocia,* on the *Euxine,* and the Shores of *Georgia,* on the *Caspian* Sea, &c.

THEY of the House of *Togarmah,* that is *Armenia,* brought them fine Horses and Mules, with Horsemen, *that is* Grooms, who had skill to break and to manage them, and Horse breeders Men enur'd to Horses, *verse* 14.

[*Verse* 15.] THE Men of *Dedan* brought them Ivory, and Ebony; This was the Country of *Arabia Felix,* where, tho' they had no *Elephants* of their own, they had the Ivory from the *Mogul's* Country on the East; or the *Ethiopian* Country on the West; where both Ivory and Ebony abounds to this Day.

[*Verse* 16.] SYRIA *was thy Merchant by reason of the multitude of the Wares of thy making*; This intimates plainly, that the Merchants of *Tyre* employ'd the People of the Countries round them in Manufactures; such as Weaving fine Linens, Dying Blue, and Purple, and Scarlet, working with the Needle, fine Embroideries, &c. also carving and cutting in Wood, in Ivory, in Metals, in Stone, and in Jewels, such as Emeralds, in particular, brought out of *Ethiopia*, Agate and Coral brought from *Spain, Carthage*, &c.

[*Verse* 17.] THEY had their finest Wheat, and Honey, and Oil, and *Balm*, from the *Israelites*, whose Country *flow'd with Milk and Honey*, and whom, God himself says he fed with the *finest of the Wheat, Psalm* lxxxi. 16.

[*Verse* 22. *to the* 24.] THE Merchants of *Sheba*, and *Raamah* {*Arabia*} and all the Princes of *Kedar, Haran, Canneh*, and *Eden, Asser*, and *Chilmad*: These Countries include *Assyria* and *Persia*, and the Trade which the *Arabians* had with *India*: These all traded in the Fairs of *Tyre*, with their rich Silks, blue Cloths, rich Apparel, and broidered Work (*Babylonish Garments, as above*) Spices, and precious Stones, of all sorts, and Gold.

HERE is the whole Trade of *Persia* and *India* describ'd with the greatest Elegance imaginable; and tho' it is so long ago, we find the same Trade remains still, and is carry'd on still from the same Countries, tho' not at the City of *Tyre*, and her Fairs and Markets, yet by the same Places and Countries, as *Persia, Armenia, India* and *Arabia*, whence, to this Day, the Merchants of *Europe* fetch the same Goods, (*viz.*) rich Silks, fine embroidered Works, painted Chints, &c. also Diamonds, Pearl, and Emralds, Spices, Balm, and rich Drugs, Perfumes, and Gums and many other Goods, perhaps then not fully discovered.

I SHALL trouble my Reader with no more Scripture Digression; tho', I think, this cannot be call'd a Digression; but I come back to the Case in Hand. All these things, were at first, brought by Land to the City of *Tyre*, or at least, being brought by Sea to the Gulph of *Persia*, were afterwards brought over Land by Caravans; and that I understand to be meant by the Merchants of *Sheba* and *Dedan*, who were certainly *Arabians* bordering on the South Coast, and who fetch'd those Goods, by Water, from the Coast of *India*; nay from the River *Indus*, the same Country which we now call *Guzurratte* and *Suratte, Bombay*, and the Coast of *Malabar*; and which were brought down to these Coasts and Rivers by Land, from *Agra, Termed, Lahore*, and other Towns and Countries bordering on the great Rivers *Oxus* and *Ganges*; from whence they receiv'd the Riches of the farther *India*, namely, the Diamonds of *Golconda*, the Gold of *Achim, Sumatra*, (the same as *Ophir*) and the Spices of *Java*, and the *Moluccas*.

NOW all these, I say, came to *Tyre* by Land, that is to say, by Caravans; and 'tis evident they did so for many Ages, and even to the time of the

101

Siege and taking of their City by the *Assyrian* Monarch: But yet many Years before that, the adventuring Merchants of *Tyre* had made attempts to go directly to those Countries by Sea; and accordingly, by permission of the King of *Egypt*, had fitted out Ships in the *Red Sea*, who, *as I have said already*, coasted the whole Southern part of the World, till then unknown.

THAT this was so is evident, in that, when *Solomon* had a mind to dip into that Trade, he hir'd Ships of *Hiram* the King of *Tyre*; and they are call'd *Hiram's* Ships, I *Kings* X. 11. *The Navy* also of *Hiram* the King of *Tyre* brought *Almug*[80] *Trees*, and *precious Stones*, as well as Gold *from* Ophir. It is indeed said, in the Chapter preceding, *verse 26. Solomon* made a Navy of Ships in *Ezion Geber*, and *Hiram* sent in that Navy his Servants, *Shipmen that had knowledge of the Sea*; the matter was this, (*viz.*) that *Solomon* being possest of *Ezion Geber*, which was a good Sea port, on the side of the *Red Sea*, in the Country of *Idumea* or *Edom*, he gave *Hiram* leave to build Ships of Burthen there, and then hir'd them of him to go to the *East Indies*.

AND this he did because he found the *Tyrians* had us'd that Trade before, and that it was very much to their advantage; and now, the Port belonging to him (King *Solomon*) *Hiram* could not do it without his leave.

BUT yet, after this Trade was found out, the Goods brought back were to be carryed a great way by Land-carriage, even thro' all the Wilderness, the same which the *Israelites* had long wandered in before they came to the Land of *Canaan*; thro' all this Country, I say, the Goods were to be brought over Land before they came to *Solomon*: And we find *Solomon* establish'd a rate of Carriage afterwards, to perform this, I *Kings* x. 29. a Chariot for six hundred Shekels, and a Horse for one hundred and fifty; and thus the Trade was carryed on for some time; for tho' *Solomon* was a wise King he was but a young Merchant.

THIS laid the foundation of what afterwards was considerably improv'd, namely, of fetching all the Spices and Jewels, Silks and Drugs, &c. (the product of *India*) by Sea to *Sues*, a Sea-port, on the utmost point Northward of the *Red Sea*; from whence they were carry'd, by Land, to *Damiata*, and afterwards to *Alexandria*, and thence again, by Sea, to all the known Ports or trading Towns of *Europe*; and this had been *Solomon*'s best way then. But since *Solomon* was so wise a Man, so great a Prince, so inspir'd a Genius, how came it, that he did not understand the frame and figure of the Globe, the situation of Places; how the Sea and the Land were extended, how the former was, every where, joyn'd; and that consequently the communication of Water was to be found out to all parts of the Earth, inland Lakes excepted? Had he known this, he might have built his Ships at *Tyre*, and sailed about as we do now.

THIS important Question brings me to the Subject, which is the main motive of this Work. This Wisdom was hid from those Ages, even from *Solomon*, himself; and this makes me say, tho' he was a wise Man, he was but a young Merchant. *No, no*, this Knowledge was left for Discovery; it was to be a whet to the Industry of future Times; it was to be search'd out at infinite Hazard by an Art [Navigation] which they knew little of, I mean, a Mathematical Navigation, which the World, at that time, understood nothing of; for the Mathematicks were not concern'd in the Navigation for many Ages after. But to return to the Trade, as it then was.

Thus stood the Trade of the World when *Tyre* was first destroy'd, (*viz.*) by *Nebuchadnezzar*; nor, as I have said, did his taking that City give any great blow to the Commerce itself, for the Merchants and wealthy Citizens, having transported themselves, and their Goods, to *Cyprus, Sicily, Crete*, to *Carthage*, and other places, which were their own Colonies, as has been noted before, they found means to carry on their business; till the rage of the War was over, and the *Assyrian* Tyrant was dead; and then they came back, rebuilt their City and Port, and became infinitely greater, richer, and stronger than they were before, and this second greatness continued several hundred Years, till the last fatal Attack, made upon them by *Alexander the Great*, which put a final end, not to the City only, but even to the name of a *Phœnician*, or of a Merchant, among them.

THIS indeed was not a stop to their Trade, but an utter ruin to it; for *Alexander* took the City by Storm, murther'd 20000 of the Citizens in the heat of Blood; hang'd 2000 of the most wealthy Merchants, upon Gibbets or Crosses, all on a row, for six Miles in length, on the Seashore; in a Word, he resolved, in his tyrannic Rage, to make himself a Terror to the rest of the World, and to make *Tyre* an Example of it, to terrify any other City that shou'd dare to stand out against him; and as to them, he did every thing he could to blot out the remembrance of the City of *Tyre* from under Heaven, and not to leave the name of a *Tyrian* Merchant remaining in the World; and all in revenge for their refusing to let him peaceably into their City; which if they had done, it was said, he resolved to have done the same, having vow'd the City a Sacrifice to his Fury, upon some former resentments not made public.

BUT when the heat, or fire, of his Anger was thus quench'd; by the Blood of such a multitude of innocent People, and the ruin of the most flourishing City in the World, the seat of Trade, and the center of all foreign Negotiation, he soon relented when it was too late; he was convinc'd what a blow he had strook to the general Correspondence of Mankind, and how he had, *as it were*, put a stop to the Trade of the World; and finding it absolutely necessary to restore things, as near as might be, to their proper and natural Chanel, especially for preserving the important Trade of *Egypt*, and the *Indies*; he resolves to erect a new *Tyre*, for an Emporium of Commerce, in the mouth of the great River *Nile*, which he did, and call'd it after his own Name *Alexandria*.

NOW tho' he could never, by all the invitations he made to the Merchants of all Nations, to come and settle there, and the privileges he gave them, and promises of greater, which he made them, bring the Trade of *Tyre* to center at *Alexandria*, as he expected; yet the Port of *Sues*, in the *Red Sea*, call'd at that time *Suz* or *Elim*, and being likewise enlarg'd by him, standing well to receive the Trade from the *East-Indies*; and there being no other Port in the World for it, these Merchandizes being of course now brought over Land to the *Nile*, and so by the *Nile* to his new City of *Alexandria*, the Trade came in time, by the same course of things, to center naturally at *Alexandria*, and made it a place of very great Business, tho' nothing like the antient City of *Tyre* which he had destroyed; the destruction of which was so mortal a blow to the Trade of the World, at that time, that it never recovered itself; that is to say, it never came to fix in one place afterwards; but divided, and ran confused into several Chanels: In all which several Chanels I shall trace it as we find it in History; now fixt and flourishing here, and then there; now unfixt and remov'd by the Wars, and by the cruelty of conquering Princes, and States; till at last the Northern Nations, namely, the *Portuguese*, then the *Dutch*, and now the *English*, finding out and pursuing the Trade to *India*, by a passage round the Sea-coast of *Africa*, all that branch of Trade from *India* to the *Red Sea* is forgotten and dropt out of the World; whether it has been the worse or the better for *Europe* remains to be spoken of by itself.

THE ruin of *Tyre*, I mean this last and fatal Destruction of it, as a trading City happen'd in the Year of the World 3618, about 330 Years before Christ. The City was rebuilt indeed afterwards, and became considerable, but not for Trade, so that I shall never have occasion to name it any more on that account. I say, its final ruin was *Ann. Mundi* 3618, after which the Trade, which was carry'd on there, as the center of the World's Commerce, divided itself, and run in different Chanels as follows.

The *East-India* Trade, as I have said, was carry'd on by the *Egyptians* and *Arabians*; whose Ships, bringing the *East-India* Goods, such as wrought Silks, Spices, Drugs, Diamonds, Pearl, Callicoes, dying Stuffs, Salt Peter, Indigo, red Earth, &c. being brought to *Sues*, and thence to *Alexandria*, the *Venetians* got into that port, and carry'd these Goods from thence all over the Northern World.

That part of the Trade of *India* Goods, which came from the *Ganges*, and the Kingdom of *Bengal*, into *Persia*, was brought to *Samarcand*, *Persepolis*, and other Cities and Countries near the *Caspian* Sea; and from thence were landed again in *Georgia*, and carry'd over Land to *Erzirum*, and to *Trapezond*, on the Banks of the *Euxine* Sea; and from thence again were brought into the *Mediterranean*; and thus the City of *Corinth* became a mighty center for Commerce, many of the *Tyrian* Merchants, who fled from their City, before *Alexander* had invested it, having settled at *Corinth*, and by their Correspondence with their old Friends in *Persia*, drawing a large Chanel of Trade that way made *Corinth* a great, populous, trading, and consequently a wealthy City.

ON the other hand, The Western branch of Commerce, which the Merchants of *Tyre* carry'd on, and by which they both exported and dispers'd that excessive quantity of Goods which they imported from *India* and *Persia*, as above; and brought back in return the product of *Europe* and *Africa*: This, which I say, was properly the Western branch of their Trade was establish'd chiefly at *Carthage* in *Africa*, *Cadiz* in *Spain*, and at *Syracusa* and *Palermo* in *Sicily*, all of them *Phœnician* Colonies; and these receiv'd no great shock in the ruin of *Tyre*, only a stop of their Commerce for the present.

BUT it's worth observing here, and it is one of the Reasons why I have enter'd so far into this particular; *I say*, 'tis worth observing how War, Tyranny, and Ambition, those Enemies to all peaceable Dispositions, have continual persecuted Trade; and how often the industrous trading part of the World has been beggar'd and impoverish'd by the violence and fury of Arms.

As Trade enriches the World, and Industry settles and establishes People and Nations, so War, Victory, and Conquest, have been the destroyers of every good thing; the Soldier has always been the plunderer of the industrous Merchant. How vainly do Men boast of their valour and gallantry in Arms, crown themselves with Laurel, and assume the name of Great, for Actions which instead of recommending their Fame to Posterity, and immortalizing their Memory, ought to make their very Names stink in the Nostrils of all great and wise Men, and shou'd make it odious so much as to read of them?

THIS is exemplified, not in the case of *Alexandria* and the City of *Tyre* only, but in all places of note, that I have now been nameing; and especially in this, That all these flourishing places, to wit, *Corinth*, *Alexandria*, and even *Carthage* itself, have been pursued by the rage and fury of the Wars, and by the cruelty and ambition of Princes, not to loss and disaster only, but, in a word, to final ruin and destruction: So that now, not the Inhabitants only, but the very places where some of the greatest Cities of Commerce stood, are not to be found, and the Names of them, are in a manner, perish'd from the Earth.

105

THIS was the fate of *Carthage*, and almost all the Cities on the North and West Coast of *Africa*, and with this ruin of Cities Trade felt the very pangs of Death, and especially with that of *Carthage*; and likewise *Corinth* seem'd to have receiv'd so mortal a blow, as that for some Ages, we find very few remains of the antient Commerce, which was so large, so flourishing, and made the World so rich, even from that one City.

THE whole Estate of the *Carthaginian* and *Græcian* Empires was swallow'd up in the Conquest of the *Romans*; a Nation inspir'd with the glory of Arms, and puff'd up with their innumerable Triumphs over other Nations; but not at all addicted to the true glories of Peace, the improvement of the industrious, the employment of the Poor, the encrease of Navigation and Commerce, or the making new Discoveries, in order to the better cultivating abandon'd Countries, or planting unpeopled Kingdoms in the World.

WITH the ruin of *Carthage*, all the Commerce of the World seem'd to be at a stand. Navigation stood stock still; the Ships were every where burnt and destroy'd, the experienc'd Seamen either kill'd in the several engagements at Sea against the *Romans*, or made Slaves, and sold for drudgery to the Conquerors, without any regard to their being at that time the usefullest part of Mankind.

THE Seamen which the *Romans* had, were few, unexperienc'd, and unapt to apply to Trade; nor had they any considerable Trade to employ them in; the adventurous Temper, the genius for Discovery, the Application to improvement, and planting, and cultivating, which was so particular to, and so much the glory of the *Carthaginians* died with them; the search after new Coasts, and Countries, and building new Cities, and Sea-ports for Traffic: The earnest thirst after a trading, navigating Glory, fell with the famous *Hanno*, who I justly call, the Sir *Walter Raleigh* of the *Carthaginian* Empire.

ALL the young Settlements, newly begun; the Plantations, and new built Cities; the Colonies and People sunk into ruin, like Infants thrown out to the Wolf, and which die for want of the Breast to suckle and nourish them, their Mother *Carthage* being cut off and destroy'd.

THE *India* and *Persian* Trade felt the blow. The Merchants of *Persia* brought their Goods to the usual Places; but the Factors had no Commissions, their employers were gone, consumed in the fire of War: The Ships came to *Sues*, in the *Red-Sea*, and the Goods, perhaps, might be landed in safety; but no buyers appear'd; the Ships which us'd to throng the noble Haven of *Alexandria* came not, for they were sacrific'd to the *Roman* Fury, in the destruction of *Carthage*.

THE returns, which usually came back in *European* Merchandizes, such as are mention'd before, the Silver, Tin, Iron, Lead, and Brass; the Corn, and

Fruit, the Wine, the Oil, these came not; the Chanel, by which they flow'd, being dam'd up by the desolation of the War; in a word, *Alexander the Great*, and *Scipio*, were the two Furies of the World, that overwhelm'd Commerce in the rubbish of their Conquests; and never concern'd themselves with the loss which all the World felt by their Folly and Rage; nay, which we may say, some of the World feels to this Day.

How Commerce, by the mere guidance of Nature, reviv'd out of all these Desolations; by what Methods, by what Degrees, and particularly, by what People it began to rise again *Phœnix like*, out of its own Ashes; what several changes and fates it has undergone, and how at length it has, together with its Sister Navigation, risen up to the glorious Magnitude which we now see it arriv'd to; what assistance it has had; what Enemies; what Dangers it has escap'd; what Difficulties it run thro', and what Dangers are yet in the way of its future Prosperity, will be farther enquir'd into in the following part of this great Undertaking.

CHAP. XI.

Of the Blow given to Trade by the ruin of Corinth *and* Carthage. *The new turn Trade took in the succeeding Ages; and by what slow degrees it began to revive in the World, and in what Places.*

As the *Roman* Conquest had checkt, and almost supprest Commerce, so it greatly discourag'd Navigation. As I said before, the Trade being ruin'd, and the Sailors destroy'd, the Ships, had they been left, were generally useless or unemploy'd. As for the *Carthaginians*, the very Name was sunk; they were no more a City, much less a Government; their Ships of War were all burnt; their Ships for Trade had neither Merchant to employ them, or Sailors to navigate them: In a word, Trade and Navigation seem'd to be both struck as with a dead Palsy both at once; and we ought to look at them both as in a worse condition for Improvements than they were in 1000 Years before, I mean when *Tyrus* was taken by the *Assyrian* King: Like a Man running a Race, who by some unhappy dissaster, or mistake, has his Ground to run all over again, and with disadvantage too; so that now there was no prospect of Recovery, Trade had no view of a Restoration.

When *Nebuchadnezzar* took *Tyre*, the dispers'd Citizens had a retreat, from whence to recover their Trade again. When *Alexander the Great* ruin'd it, he himself, as noted above, took care of the Commerce, by erecting *Alexandria* as a Staple of Trade to restore it to the World. But when *Carthage* was destroy'd, the Victors, thoughtless of the public good of Mankind, and unconcern'd for Trade, left her utterly abandon'd and forsaken; no Patron left to restore her flourishing Government; they took neither any care for it themselves, or left any one else to do it; but in short, all things were left to mere Nature, and Trade was to return only as the consequence of Mens finding it needful to correspond with one another.

The first appearance of any thing that deserv'd the name of Commerce, after the Destruction of the *Carthaginians*, was the necessary supplies of Corn which were wanted for the support of the City of *Rome*: This employ'd some Shipping to the Coast of *Africa*, and to *Egypt*, and *Syria*, according as the Consuls, who had the care of those things, directed; in which Case, the Corn was not so much an Article of Trade, as a payment of Tribute to the State from the Countries whence it came. The Consuls sending Orders to the Proconsuls, and Governours of Provinces, to send such and such supplies of Corn for the use of the Senate of *Rome*, as was required; and to pay for the same out of the ordinary Tribute. This frequently oblig'd the said Proconsuls to hire Ships for that Service, and kept up in some small measure the employment of Ships and Seamen.

THIS was the Case of St. *Paul*, when on his Voyage to *Rome* he first embark'd in a Ship belonging to *Adramyttium*,[81] which was a City near the *Hellespont*, in the antient *Greece*; and afterwards to embark in another Ship loaden with Corn, in the Island of *Crete*, or *Candia*. But this went but a little way towards reviving of that vast Commerce which was destroy'd by the ruin of the *Carthaginians*.

THE next discovery of Trade, or any thing which look'd like it, was the necessity which the Merchants of *India* and *Persia* found themselves in, of selling or venting their Goods, which they or the *Egyptians* for them brought constantly up the *Red Sea* to *Egypt*; and which from thence, being carry'd to *Alexandria*, were before that time bought up there by the *Carthaginian* Merchants, and carry'd in their own Ships to *Carthage*, and from thence sold and exported by them to all the parts of the World that were known at that time: But these *Carthaginian* Merchants now failing to come to Market, their City being burnt and destroy'd, and their Shipping also, the *Indian* and *Persian* Merchandizes were left unsold, and perhaps the Merchants who brought them ruin'd and undone; being not able to find any Market wherein to dispose of the Goods they brought, or to make returns in such Goods as they had occasion for in their own Country.

THIS caused the Merchants of *Alexandria*, by degrees, to seek and find out a Market for their Goods wherever they could have it; and particularly the Cities on the Coasts of *Italy*, and *Gaul*, [*France*] the Islands of the Lesser *Asia*, and the Shores of *Greece*, by little and little became acquainted with the Trade, and dealt in *Alexandria*, with the Merchants of *India*, or rather with the *Arabians* and *Persians*; for they were indeed the Persons who brought the Goods to *Egypt*.

N. B. *Here it is to be noted, that even then, and ever since then to this Day, the* Indian *and* Arabian *Merchants, who have brought their Goods this way for a Market, have been unconcern'd in the Wars, and Overturnings, which the ambition of Men have embroil'd the* European *World with; on the contrary, they have been a peaceable trading People, who have only sought to push on*

*their business in a quiet manner, selling their Goods, and taking back either
such Money as they could get, or such Goods as were vendible in their own
Country. And thus the* Armenians *and* Georgians, (*who are the same kind
of People*) *act to this Day; coming with their Bales of Silk, their Drugs and
Galls,*[82] *Grograms, Camel's Hair, and other Goods, to* Aleppo, *to* Scandaroon, *or Little* Alexandria; *and others of them, to the Gulph of* Persia, *to the
famous City of* Ormus, *and thence into* Egypt, *and to* Alexandria *itself.*

These Merchants, no doubt, were for a while under great Disappointments when they miss'd their old Correspondents, the *Carthaginians*, who
at certain Seasons fail'd not to meet them at *Alexandria* to buy their Goods.
What courses they took to sell their Wares, at first, we cannot, at this distance, give a particular Account of; but, this we find Reason to conclude
from some circumstances of Trade, which follow'd; namely, that after this
the *Persian* Merchants were found at *Corinth*, whither they came from
Trapesund, and from *Tripoli*, in *Cappadocia*, on the *Euxine* Sea, bringing their
Merchandizes down among the *Græcians*; and which they did, with such
good success, that in a few Years *Corinth* reviv'd and became a populous,
rich, and trading City, especially in that part, which might then be call'd
the *Indian* Trade, as we now call it the *Turkey* Trade.

In the mean time there sprung up a small infant Correspondence
between the Citizens of *Marseilles*, and those of *Alexandria*. *Marseilles* was a
City then under the *Roman* Government, and so was not liable to the Dev-
astation which *Corinth* and *Carthage* had already suffer'd; and therefore the
Citizens and Merchants of *Marseilles* were most likely to keep and carry on
the Commerce they had begun, and both the City of *Alexandria* itself, as
well as *Marseilles*, grew rich, and advanc'd both in Wealth and People by it,
and which was more than all, in Shipping; for the *Marseillians* encourag'd
by the Trade in Spices, which was the chief of the *Alexandrian* branch of the
Indian Commerce; I say, the *Marseillian* Merchants, by being possessed of
the Spice Trade, became, in a few Years, the principal Merchants of the
Roman Empire, as the Merchants of *Corinth* had been for the Silks and fine
Manufactures of *Persia* and *Armenia*; with this difference afterwards, that
the City of *Corinth* having been destroy'd by the Consul *Lucius Mummius*,[83]
in the Year of *Rome* 607, was poor, and held it but a little while. But *Marseilles* held it, and flourish'd in the Trade even till the decay of the *Roman*
Empire itself. When the *Lombards* and other *Italians*, flying to the Islands of
the *Adriatick* Sea, from the fury of the Northern Nations, who broke in
upon *Italy*, and defending themselves there during all the inundations,
whether of the *Goths*, *Vandals*, or other Barbarians, built a kind of Marine
City, and call'd it *Venice*. The Citizens of this new City and State, forming

themselves into a Government, after the manner of antient *Rome*, (*viz.*) Senate and People, the latter divided into the Nobility and common People, as *Rome* was into the *Plebeij* and *Patricij*, fell unanimously into Trade.

HAVING by their Wisdom and Courage thus establish'd themselves, and being by the situation of their Town oblig'd to carry on all their Correspondence, as well as Commerce by *Sea*, they grew Merchants of Course, and not only put in for a share of this happy Trade, but in time the whole *Roman* Empire themselves feeling the shock of the barbarous Nations, these *Venetians* engross'd it all to themselves, and the *Marseillians* were also finally excluded; the Spice Trade, and as we may say, the whole *East India* Trade, as to *Europe*, falling into the Hands of the *Venetians*, and remain'd with them till a few Ages ago, when the *Portuguese* found the way to the *Indies* by the Cape of *Good Hope*, of which in its place.

THUS I have brought down the Commerce of that part of the World almost to the present Times; by which it may be seen, how the wisest Nations, *for such the* Romans *were suppos'd to be*, have been sometimes mistaken in their Conduct; and how by neglecting to promote and encourage Trade, they have in the event impoverish'd and weaken'd themselves, and at least put from them the only Wealth in the World, and the means, by which, had Trade been supported and nourish'd among them as it ought to have been, they had probably been better able to have defended themselves against the barbarous Nations, which afterwards over-whelm'd them.

How evident was it, That the Cities of *Tyre*, of *Corinth*, of *Carthage*, and many others acquired their Wealth and Opulence by the growth of their Commerce; and tho' they were indeed overpowered by the Arms of the *Grecian* and *Roman* Emperors, yet it was not but by such a Strength as the World was not able, at that time, to resist; and yet even what a glorious Struggle did they all make with those very Powers, who at the same time were Conquerors of the whole World.

ON the other Hand; How have we seen many small Cities, Governments, and States, support themselves on this Foot? The two States of *Genoa* and *Venice*, which were singly and separately rais'd by Commerce, supporting themselves by their Wealth and naval Power, (both which they acquired by Trade) when the whole *Roman* Empire, of which they were a part, sunk in the Inundations of the barbarous Nations: These *I say* stood firm, resisted the Torrent of the *Goths*, the *Franks*, the *Vandals*, the *Heruli*, the *Gauls*, and all those furious Nations, and remain flourishing, by the help of Commerce, to this Day.

CHAP. XII.

An Argument from what has been said for engaging the Christian Powers of Europe *to root out the Barbarians, and Pirates, and restore the Peace and Commerce of* Africa, *so profitable to* Europe.

HAVING thus mention'd that the *Carthaginian* Empire in those Days was the seat of Trade; and that *Africa*, which was their peculiar Dominion, was in particular a Country enrich'd, peopled, and made powerful by Commerce, it comes in my way of Course to enquire what was its Condition afterwards, what it is now, and what is the Reason, that in a World so inclin'd to Commerce, and so encourag'd to carry it on as this is, and is like to be, this Country of *Africa*, once so great, so furnish'd for and improv'd in Business, is not restor'd to its former Glory and Wealth; and this I shall couch in a very few Words.

AFTER the destruction of *Carthage* the *Romans* kept the possession of the Country, and govern'd it under their Proconsuls for many Ages: Trade receiving no encouragement from them, as I have observ'd already, took a new turn and ran in several Chanels, (*viz.*) from *Egypt*, by way of *Alexandria* to *Marseilles*, and afterwards to *Venice* and *Genoa*, and from the *Caspian Sea*, coming thither, by way of the River *Oxus* to *Erzirum*, and so to *Taprezond*, and thence by the *Euxine* and *Ægean* Seas to *Corinth*; which thereupon reviv'd a little, till that part too was swallow'd up by the *Geneoses*, and the *Venetians*, and with them it remain'd.

As for *Africa*, Tho' *Carthage* was rebuilt, and the Country continu'd extreamly rich, populous, and powerful, to the time of *Justinian*,[84] and later; yet *Africa* never fell into Trade other than, as I have said, the exporting Corn and Copper, Wax and Salt, which was in itself no great matter.

BUT when the *Roman* Empire declin'd, the *Vandals*, the *Goths*, and at length the *Saracens*, over-run this whole Country; and as the *Mahometans* wherever they came rather laid the World waste than cultivated and improv'd it; so here from a peopled, improved, rich, cultivated Soil, a

112

populous, well planted Country, full of large Cities and Towns, and of a rich and thriving People, they brought it to be a wild uninhabited Desart, the Inland part left to mere Nature, and the Sea-coast possest by Barbarians, and a Generation of Drones, who declining the honest Industry, which makes the World rich, and encourages Arts and Peace, chose to live by Rapine and Violence; and from this principle turn'd Pirates and High-Sea Robbers: And thus from a beginning upwards of 500 Years old ever since their being expel'd out of *Spain*, they have continued in several Tribes and Nations, and under several Denominations to this Day; such as the *Moors* of *Sallee*, Subjects to the King or Emperors of *Fez* and *Morocco*; the *Turks* of *Algiers* and *Tunis*, and the *Arabians*, for such they were, of *Tripoli* and *Barca*.

THESE wretched crews of Thieves, from low and small beginnings, but encourag'd by Success, have gradually encreas'd at the expence of the trading Christian Nations of *Europe*, whom they have always prey'd upon, till they are grown up to the height of power and strength which we see them arriv'd to at this Time, when they are call'd a Government, nay are treated with as Nations, Common-wealths, and States, Regencies, or what else they please to call themselves, to the reproach of Christendom, and to the infinite loss and discouragement of the Merchants and Navigators of all the Nations about them.

HERE therefore, craving leave to make a Transition from the success of Trade, and the advancing of discovery and improvement in Commerce, of which I have hitherto spoken historically; I say, I shall make a brief Transition to the ruinous condition of this flourishing part of the World call'd *Africa*, how 'tis abandon'd and forsaken of its old and industrious Inhabitants, and is become a Den, not of Lions and Tigers only, the ordinary Inhabitants of the inland Mountains, but of Pirates and Thieves, a kind of wild Beasts infinitely more destructive to the World, and worse Enemies to its prosperity than the most ravenous Beasts of Prey in *Nubia*, or *Libya*, or the banks of the River *Niger*, which runs thro' the most desolate Country in the World.

HOW the *Africans* at this time live, how they grow every Day more savage and more untractable than before, and how at last they may, if not prevented, become more dangerous than when they possest all the Kingdom of *Spain*, wou'd take up too much time and is also beside my purpose.

BUT how they might be reduc'd, how either brought to the exercise of Arts and Industry, and be made a Blessing to the World; or how conquer'd, extirpated, and the Country clear'd of them, and the Country restor'd to the flourishing, thriving, and trading Figure which it formerly made in the World, or perhaps a greater, to the advantage, not of the Inhabitants only, but of all the Christian Nations near them: This, as it belongs to future

113

improvement in Trade, and future discovery, is exactly within the bounds of my Undertaking.

I HAVE done therefore with dull Antiquity, as to Trade; and tho' it is true I could not call this Work a History; if in discoursing of these great periods in Commerce, (*viz.*) the ruin of *Tyre* and *Carthage*, after which, Trade receiv'd such Shocks, that after them it ran always in other Chanels; I say, tho' I could not call it a History unless I had gone back to the beginning of things; and that I hope it has not been an unprofitable Work: So now I shall enter according to my Title into a short account of the Reason and Measures for recovering this lost part of the World, and restoring it to its antient Glory, I mean, as to Trade only, to the infinite advantage of its self, and of *Europe* also.

IF the Trade of *Africa* was once so very advantagious, if the Country was once so fruitful; the Nations in it so powerful and populous; the Product of it so rich and valuable, Why shou'd it not be restored to its former Condition, that we in these Parts of the World might reap at least our share of the benefit of it? This is the Question I am next to speak to.

IF the present Inhabitants are not only indolent, negligent, and discouragers of all diligence, and improvements; but Thieves, Robbers, and the worst of Robbers, (*viz.*) Pirates; if they are not only Enemies to God, and to the Christian Religion, but Enemies to Mankind, living like Beasts of Prey upon the Spoil of their innocent and industrious Neighbours; if they are not only Robbers and Pirates, but barbarous Oppressors and Tyrants; murthering, by hard and villainous Usage, the unhappy People [Christians] who fall into their Hands; why shou'd not the trading World rescue their distress'd Brethren from such miserable Captivity, and root those Barbarians off from the Face of the Earth, to restore the Commerce of that Country to the rest of the trading World?

To the reasonableness of this I shall also say something of the practicableness and easiness of bringing it to pass, and leave the rest to Posterity; who, I doubt not, however the shame of neglecting it may be ours, will one time or other have the profit as well as the glory of bringing it to pass.

THE whole force of the Barbarians mustered up together, and that in the most formidable manner that they themselves can represent it, and taken from the best Authors, stands thus.

THE Kings of *Fez* and *Morocco* are able, bringing Tag and Rag together, to draw out into the Field a very great Army; they tell us, if they join Forces, they may bring together 120000 Men; and this I am to grant, for Argument sake, whether I believe it or no, and the rather because when the Marquiss *de Lede*,[85] the late *Spanish* General, landed at *Ceuta*, with an Army, in the Year 1722, the *Moors* appear'd with a great Army, and attack'd him in his Entrenchments with such obstinacy and fury, that notwithstanding they were repuls'd with great Slaughter, yet the *Spaniards* thought fit to give over the Enterprize, and return to old *Spain*.

BUT those People who make this an Objection shou'd not forget at the same time, that the *Spaniards* were but 12000 Men; that the Season of the Year was advanc'd, and they wanted Provisions; that they had at that time Misunderstandings with the *French*, the King of *Great Britain*, and the Emperor; and that the *French*, who it was expected shou'd have join'd them with 12000 Men more declin'd it, envying perhaps the apparent advantage, and the honour of it also to the *Spaniards*.

HAD not these and other Incidents prevented; and on the other Hand, had the Powers of *Europe* joyn'd to form an Army of 50 or 60000 Men to have pursued the glorious Design, how easily wou'd the Barbarians have been overthrown, their Government been extinguish'd, and the very name of *Mahomet* and *Moors* have been driven out of *Barbary*? How easily wou'd the Cities of *Fez*, of *Mequines, Morocco, Sallee*, and *Santa Cruz*, which are the chief Places the *Moors* hold in that Country have been reduc'd, and the *Negro* Nations, who now make the flower of their Cavalry, been separated from them, and secur'd to the interest of the Invaders? How easily wou'd the Forces of the Country have been broken, and the *Moors* have been as effectually driven out of *Africa* as they were before out of *Spain*, which was done after an Establishment and Settlement there, for above 700 Years?

THIS being done, and the Coasts on the West and North of *Africa* subdued, what could the small States, or popular Governments of *Algier, Tunis*, and *Tripoli* signify, to oppose the Conquerors? How apparent was this in the enterprize of the Emperor, *Charles* V. who in a few Days took the whole Kingdom of *Tunis*,[86] but was so just or so weak as to restore it to the King to whom it belong'd before.

WITH the same ease might all those Barbarian Kingdoms be removed, and their People transplanted. A sober, religious, christian, and gallant People from all the Nations of *Europe*, I mean the Nations which we call Marine Powers; I say, how easily might such a People be planted in their room? A People diligent, industrious, enclin'd to Commerce, enclin'd to improvements, and to cultivate the Earth; then the Soil answering by its fertility, and plentifully rewarding their Labour, how soon wou'd *Africa* become the same noble, rich, and powerful Country, as it was before? Populous, well inhabited; strong, rich, fitted for Trade, exporting to all the Southern parts of *Europe*, Corn, Wine, Oil, Salt, Copper, Iron, Rice, Wax, Honey, Cotton Wool, Sheeps Wooll, *such as the Spanish*; Horses, Drugs, Gums, Balm, wild Beasts, Ostrich Feathers, Furs, and abundance of other Commodities; from the North part only; besides Gold Dust, Elephants

Teeth, Slaves, Civet, *Guinea* Grains,[87] and other things, as are now brought from the South; and besides Sugar, Indico, Ginger, Pimento, and all the growth of our *West India* Colonies, which (as has been proved) will not only grow and thrive, but be as easily and plentifully produc'd on the Continent of *Africa*, as they are now in *Brasil*, or in *Barbadoes* and *Jamaica*? The advantage of which, and the consequences of it, I shall enlarge upon hereafter.

How then, is all this beautiful, rich, and wealthy Continent of *Africa*, to the shame, as well as to the infinite loss of the *European* Christian Powers, not only suffer'd to lye uncultivated, and as it were uninhabited, but to be over-run by the Barbarians, who defy Christ, trample underfoot Religion, and exercise continual Robberies and Piracies upon our Trade; and at this time keeping fifty thousand Christians in miserable, and indeed insupportable Slavery?

NAY, let us look back and consider what is to be said of the Years past; is it possible so much as to think, without inexpressible regret, that there lye the Bones of 500,000 poor abandon'd Christian Captives, who have perish'd in the utmost Misery under horrible Cruelties and Oppressions in the tyrannick Hands of those Barbarians; and who, not being able to support the hardship and extremities of their Slavery, have died under it, as a Horse over-wrought, and not able to exert himself to the satisfaction of his cruel Driver, sinks down and dies under his load? I do not say all that Blood cryes against us, I mean, by us the Christian Nations who have suffer'd this Calamity to fall upon them; but I say, it calls loudly upon us to revenge the iniquity of the Fathers upon the Children, because they practise the same Cruelty every Day, and above all, to take a just care, for prevention, that no more Christian Slaves, no more of our Brethren and fellow Christians may fall into their Hands.

HERE may occur indeed some material Objections against the practicableness of this; but I am sure none can lye against the reasonableness.

I. HOW will you prevent the Christian Nations quarrelling about the division of the Conquest, when made, and how will you share it between them?

II. WHAT shall the Country be applyed to, when reduced, and how will it appear to be worth the Reduction?

As to the first, it is true, thro' the avarice of Christians, and the degeneracy of humane Nature, there is such an inclination in the People of all Nations and Professions to be jealous of one another, there is such a jarring and clashing of their suppos'd or real Interests, that it is the hardest thing in the World to bring them to unite in the best and most glorious Actions, or in any public Undertaking, how good, how practicable, how feazible soever; nay, and tho' it be for the universal advantage of them all.

THUS it was, that when even Religion, tho' extreamly mistaken, was the motive of those famous Expeditions to the *Holy Land*; yet jarring Interests and clashing Parties among the Christians ruin'd many a well prepar'd Army, and in the end baffled the whole Undertaking; leaving all their Conquests to fall into the Hands of the *Saracens*, even after one hundred and twenty Years Possession.

HOW often did the treachery of the *French* take the advantage of the *English* Kings being absent in the *Holy Land*, and under some frivolous pretence or other, fall upon his Territories at home.

HOW dear did *Richard* the First pay for his *Santa Terring* [*Anglice*] *Sauntering* in the *Holy Land*,[88] when after an inglorious Expedition into *Palestine*, he was trepan'd in his return by one of his fellow Christians, and made a Prisoner, by the Arch-Duke of *Austria*, on a frivolous pretence; but really, and as the event shew'd, to get Money out of him, let the cause of God and the Holy Sepulchre go which way it would?

SUCH, I say, is the power of Envy and Avarice that it is very hard to bring the Christian Nations to any concert of Measures for an universal Good; nay if this were not even now the Case, what shou'd hinder, or what did hinder Prince *Eugene* and the Imperial Armies, after the last great Victory,[89] or the Dukes of *Lorrain* and *Bavaria*, after the first taking of *Belgrade*[90] when Prince *Lewis* of *Baden*, with part of the Army, had taken *Sophia*, and had not a long march to *Adrianople*? I say, what has hinder'd them driving the *Turks* out of *Constantinople*, and consequently out of *Europe*? Was it not the same envy and division of the Christian Powers, which was really the first occasion of letting the *Turks* into *Europe*? Did not the *French* at one time, and the *Spaniards* at the other time, give Umbrage of a Rupture to the Imperial Court, and so make it necessary to end the War, rather by a Peace with the Infidels, than by a Conquest?

I COULD carry it farther; How near did the differing Councils and jarring Interests of *Europe* go, to putting the victorious Hands of the late King of *France* in possession of an universal Monarchy over the Christian World; and what difficulty, and under how many disappointments and miscarriages, and at what expence of time as well as Money was a Confederacy at last form'd, strong enough to prevent it? But this is an Article, which however valuable, and which wou'd be delightful as well as useful to enter largely upon, is yet wide of my present design, and therefore I restrain my Pen, and tho' with reluctance leave it to a fitter Occasion.

BUT to return to the Case: It may be true that it wou'd be difficult to bring the jarring Interests of the *European* Princes to joyn in the clearing the Coasts of *Africa* from this bloody Race of Infidels which now possess it: But it does not follow, that it is at all the less needful to be done, or that it wou'd be at all the less advantageous for *Europe* if it were done; and grant-ing me that, 'tis then the business of the Princes and Powers concern'd to consider of Measures for the doing it, and to answer for the omission if it is not done.

IT is none of my business to fall upon the Avarice and Envy of this or that particular Government or State, as the Cause; it is not for me to enquire, why the King of *Spain* was not seconded, thirded, encourag'd and assisted when he made an attempt for so glorious a Work, a few Years ago; and in which, had *France* alone but joyn'd with him, as they might well have done, he wou'd certainly have succeeded; for it is not the design of this Work to write Satyrs; but I may say, that all the trading part of *Europe* will have leisure to lament the loss of so glorious an Occasion, and many thousands of miserable Wretches who shall yet fall into the Hands of those Barbarians will have reason to curse the Disappointment.

I KNOW, that when the attempt was made many People look'd cooly on upon the Miscarriage, and not for want of Ignorance, seem'd pleas'd that the *Spaniards* did not succeed, pretended it wou'd encrease their Naval Power; and that they were strong enough already; that they were a Popish Crew, bloody and cruel as the *Moors*, or *Algerines* themselves; that they were Papists, and the most cruel of all Papists, and therefore we had no occasion to wish them good Speed, and the like.

BUT my Answers to all these Arguments are ready.

I. TRADE knows no Parties, no Politic, no religious Interests; Com-merce is a certain Communication of Nations occasion'd by the necessities, and for the good of Mankind; the Enemies of Trade are Enemies to all Men; Pirates and High-Sea Robbers are wild Beasts that shou'd have no Law, and whom all Men should joyn to destroy, without enquiring what or who they are: If a Bear or a Wolf set upon a Traveller you do not enquire whether he be Papist or Protes-tant in delivering him, 'tis enough, the one is a Man the other a Beast.

II. LET the *Spaniards* be who or what they will the *Algerines* are worse, the *Moors* of *Sallee* and *Morocco* are worse; the *Spaniards* do not make Prize of Merchants who peacably pursue their Business, or of Ships honestly pursuing their Voyages; when Papists are at War, and take the Ships of their Enemies, they do not sell the Prisoners for Slaves, keep them on Shoar in Vaults and Caves, and at Sea chain them down to the Oar; as to Religion it is quite beside the Question; the Inquisition meddles with no Man for buying and selling, or for sail-ing upon the Sea to this or that ports; there are no excommunicated Harbours or Bays that a Protestant Ship may not Anchor in; no dedicated Harbours that a Heretic Vessel must not take shelter in; Trade is neither Popish or Protestant; we deal with Infidels in *Turkey*, and Pagans in *China*, without exception; the Pirates of *Barbary* are not Enemies of the *Europeans*, as Catholics or Heretics, but as Merchants, and for their Money, and as Men, for their Bodies to sell them as Cattle in the Markets.

III. LET then the *Moors* or *Algerines* be treated as they are Enemies of Christians as Men, and Theives for their Goods, for the sake of Robbery and Plunder; and as such, the Christian Powers ought to Arm against them as common Enemies, laying all national or religious Animosities aside; Why shou'd not all the Nations of *Europe* joyn in so necessary a Work? Whether they can or will be prevail'd with to do it; that is another Question.

CHARLES the Fifth, justly call'd the Great, saw into the reason, justice, and necessity of this; and as he was a most magnanimous as well as a politic and understanding Prince, he apply'd himself very seriously to the Work, and made two powerful Expeditions on purpose; the first succeeded gloriously, and he took the City of *Tunis*, with the Castle of *Goletto*, and in effect the whole Kingdom of *Tunis*;[91] the second, against *Algier*, miscarried, by reason of a terrible Tempest which scatter'd and destroy'd great part of his Fleet, and he return'd with loss; but this was unavoidable, and the like might easily be prevented. But even this shews, that great and generous Princes have formerly thought this Work worthy their undertaking; that it is not done, if it is from Heaven, is a Judgment upon the Christian World for the Omission; and if it is not attempted they will always, like the *Canaanites* in the Land, be left there for Goads in our Sides; only let us remember the *Israelites* were always blam'd for not destroying the said *Canaanites*,[92] and for leaving one of them alive; and this is a Summons to me to speak to another Objection, tho' not mention'd before; namely, What right have we or any of the Christian Nations of *Europe* to invade and disposess these People, who however they came by their Possessions, have enjoy'd them by so long a prescription, as namely, about or above a thousand Years; that if we look back so many Ages into any of the Christian Nations we speak of, we may find our right to the Country we live in, as ill founded perhaps as these; that it is not sufficient to say they are *Mahometans*, and not Christians; for then we have a right to make War upon and destroy all the Heathen Nations of the World, which I do not take to be just?

To this I answer, That there is something specious in the Objection, yet there is as clear and undeniable an Argument to be used for the justice of the attempt as can be desir'd in the World; and it is form'd in a just distinction between the People as they are Men, and the People as they practise and behave. We do not execute a Murderer because he was a Man, and had ability or courage to commit the Murder, but as he was a Criminal, a Manslayer, and had shed innocent Blood.

So let the *Moors* and *Turks* of *Salee*, *Algier*, and *Tunis*, and *Tripoli*, apply themselves in a peacable manner by honest Labour, or Commerce, to cultivate the Earth, and live on the honest Fruits of their Labour, I had nothing to say; a-God's-Name let them enjoy and peacably dwell in the Land, and we might trade with them, as well as we do with their fellow Infidels at *Constantinople*, *Smyrna*, *Aleppo*, and other places; for this Quarrel does not lye against them as Men, nor as *Turks* and *Mahometans*.

But the Quarrel at them is, as they are Thieves, Robbers, and Murderers, and as such they both may and ought to be suppress'd, and 'tis the reproach of Christendom that they are not.

To make this evident, it wou'd be sufficient to advance, that the Christian Nations shou'd in case of such a War, only drive them off fifteen or twenty Miles from the Sea-coasts; there is Country enough for them all, to spread themselves as far as they please; but I think they have done enough to *Europe* for so many hundred Years together to deserve to be banish'd from the Sea for ever; let them then but be extinguish'd as Pirates, the rest will come of course, and they may be as Potent in Numbers as they will or can, the Trade wou'd soon revive; nay those very Men who are now drones in the great *Hive*, and devour the labour of the industrious World, wou'd then become laborious and diligent as other Nations are, and be a Blessing not a Judgement to the World.

This I think takes away all pretence of objection against the justice and lawfulness of attacking those People; for let them live honestly and industriously by Labour or Commerce, or any how, so as not to oppress or wrong the rest of the World, and we have nothing to say.

But as they will never do that, as long as they have Ships, and Guns, and Men to go a-robbing; I think it is but just they shou'd be at least remov'd from the Sea-shore, and be suffer'd no more to set a Sail or row with an Oar upon the Sea: Nor can this be unjust on this account, 1. They have done sufficient to forfeit the Seas, that is, the privilege of sailing upon the Water, as long as they have a Name on the Earth, or at least as Nations. And *Secondly*, They are able to give no other sufficient security for their Behaviour than that of entirely quitting the Coast, giving up their Ships, and being allow'd to have no more Ships or Boats to make use of.

How easy wou'd this be, if the *European* Powers were but once resolv'd to unite their Forces for the attempt; nor wou'd it be an Expedition that wou'd call for all their Forces, no nor for the twentieth part of their Forces, if they thought fit to make an Experiment; and how gloriously wou'd it reward their Labour?

LET us but consider the Blessing and Satisfaction which it wou'd be in Trade to have no Enemy to fear; to have Ships sail single, and as it were unarm'd, into all parts of the *Mediterranean*; to have all the Ports of *Africa* free and friendly; no danger or apprehension of danger any where: Whereas now,

NOT a Sailor goes to Sea in a Merchant Ship, but he feels some secret Tremor, that it may one time or other be his lot to be taken by the *Turks*; it is impossible for a Seaman to sail by the Coast of *Algier*, or *Tunis*, without having a kind of horrour at the place, and a little panick fear upon his Spirits about it, that sometime or other it may be his lot to be carry'd in there and sold for a Slave.

NOT an Inhabitant on the Coast of *Spain* or *Italy*, no not from *Gibraltar* to the City of *Venice*, the fortify'd places excepted, but they are in constant apprehensions of being surpriz'd in their Beds, Men, Women, and Children, and hurry'd naked, and spoil'd of all they have on board some Pirate Sloop or Bark, that has made a descent upon the Coast on purpose to carry off such a booty; and this has been practis'd all along upon that Coast.

AGAIN, from *Apes-hill*, at the mouth of the Straights, just below *Ceuta*, to the very Gates of *Alexandria*: You have not now a friendly Port, not a Town, a few the *Spaniards* have possessed only excepted, where you shall not be in danger of a surprise on what condition soever, or in what distress soever you are driven in.

ENQUIRE into Trade itself, the awe and dread of this hellish Crew puts the Merchants to a daily expence in their Business; every Voyage they lay in double store of Ammunition, and double Man every Ship; Victuals and Wages encrease the charge of the Voyage, the Ensurers advance the Premium upon every Cargo, because of the possibility only of this danger; great Guns and small Arms are added in proportion; and after all, how much Blood is shed in gallantly defending themselves when attackt, even in those Ships which are not taken.

HOW much needless expence has this been to the Trade of *Europe* in so many hundred Years as this mischief has reign'd? Nay, how much more than it wou'd have cost the Nations concern'd to have sent a hundred thousand Men at once to have reduc'd those Desperadoes, and have blow'd them all out of the World?

BESIDES this vast expence which the Merchants have suffer'd; and the public expences in the several fitting out Squadrons of Men of War to fight them, sending others to convoy their Merchants Ships, and at last sending

Envoys to treat of Peace, and make Terms with these despicable Rogues, for such they are, and in a moment upon every Caprice the Peace is broken, and our Ships surpriz'd again.

HOW have the States General been oblig'd now four Years to send Squadrons of Ships of War every Year to the *Mediterranean* to fight the *Algerines*? And at the same time, What a vast value have they lost in Ships and Goods taken by those Rovers? And how many Lives lost? How many poor Men carry'd into miserable Captivity? And so successful have they been, that they despise all the offers of Peace the *Dutch* can make; nay, the intercession of the Grand Seignior himself for the *Dutch* is refused, unless such insolent Conditions should be accepted by the States, as the very King of *Sardinia* wou'd despise: nay, the Republic of *Lucca* wou'd scorn them; amounting, in short, to little less than making the States General of the United *Netherlands* tributary to, and Subjects of the *Turks* at *Algier*?

HOW much cheaper, as well as more honourable, and indeed reasonable, wou'd it be to have all the Merchandizing part of the Christian World join together, and by sending a formidable Fleet and Army, fall upon them at once; and in one hearty attempt put an end to their Depredation, and clear the Seas of them for ever.

THEN the Trade of *Africa* wou'd be reviv'd; the Towns upon the Seacoasts wou'd be restor'd, As they wou'd be under a Christian Government, so they wou'd be inhabited by Christians; and in a few Ages the Numbers wou'd encrease, and the Country perhaps be as well inhabited as *Europe* is now, and a Trade establish'd with them in proportion; for Numbers of People encrease Trade; Manufactures wou'd be call'd for there as well as in other Countries; and as they have a plentiful Product for the supply of Returns, the advantage must be mutual.

BUT all this you will say does not reach the Case; the Objection is laid from another Difficulty; namely, Whether it wou'd be possible that the Nations cou'd agree about the division of their Conquests when they were made? that they wou'd fall together by the Ears about Shares, and by envyings and jarring Interests ruin the Undertaking, and leave the *Turks* Victorious, and more Insolent than they were before.

IF this were really true it wou'd be very sad, and the miscarriage wou'd lye heavy; but I do not see that this must necessarily follow; for if by a Treaty enter'd upon before, it shou'd be adjusted what particular part each Nation shou'd attack, and so go on in separate Bodies, tho' all shou'd fall on together, it might be easy to allot every Nation what part they shou'd possess, by appointing each Nation to conquer for themselves.

OR if it was found reasonable to join the Forces of two or more Nations together, yet they might enter into mutual Guarantee with one another to set a-part the design'd Countries to the use of those to whom they were so allotted by agreement; and to give them up peaceably, all the Confederates joining to enforce the execution of such a Treaty, when the War was over; or to declare War against the particular Nation or Power that shou'd refuse it.

CURIOSITY now might lead the Reader to desire me to enter into particulars, and to lay down a Scheme how I wou'd have them share this *Bearskin;*[93] but I think, tho' 'tis easy in itself, it wou'd be too assuming and arrogant in an Undertaking of this kind; then as here is a vastly extended Coast, such as wou'd be sufficient for all Pretenders to it, I may turn it all into a Supposition, and let the Reader digest it for himself.

SUPPOSE then, That each Nation in the *Mediterranean* had allotted them all and as much of the Coast of *Africa* as lay right against themselves; the *Spaniards*, what is over against *Spain*, which by the way wou'd be the largest part; the *French*, what is over-against *France*; the King of *Sardinia*, the part opposite to *Sicily*, the *Malteses* joining with him; and the *Sicilians*, the *Venetians*, and *Neapolitans*, all the East part from *Tripoli* to *Alexandria*, with all they could separately seize upon and support; then I give the *English* the South side of the Straights Mouth, from *Ceuta*, inclusive, to *Tangier*, and about to the Southward, as far as *Santa Cruz*; the *Dutch* in Conjunction with the *English* to enter into the Kingdom or Empire of *Fez* and *Morocco*, and driving all before them, these Infidels wou'd soon be push'd away, and our two Nations settled infallibly and equally upon the Spot.

IF any will question here, whether they will be able to conquer the Black Kings and reduce them to Reason, or not to do it, I must answer them distinctly, that it is as easy to do it, as for me to write it; but these being Speculations, I sum them all up thus, *Africa* is so large in its extent, and the Country on the Coast every where so good that there is enough to satisfy every Pretender, and let every one keep what they conquer: as for *England* give her but a free Trade with them all, she seeks no Possessions; her Factories and Settlements on the Gold Coast, in *Guinea*, excepted, of which hereafter.

CHAP. XIII.

Of the stop of Trade at the destruction of Carthage. *How Silk Worms came first to be known in* Italy; *and how the Woollen Manufactures were first Invented and set on Foot in the World.*

WE have now brought Trade to a full stop in the World; Commerce, like a Boat a Drift, was lost, and left as it were rolling upon the Water without a *Rudder*, an *Oar*, or a *Sail*; all its parts were dislocated, and scarce the name of Commerce was left in the World. The Merchants which were left, were destitute of Correspondencies; the buying part of the World destitute of Manufactures; Natures produce, which is the principle of all Manufacturing, was destitute of a Market; Goods made could not be sold, Goods wanted could not be found, Necessity was brought to put Invention upon the Rack, in order to form (as the Doctors call it) some new *Materia Medica*, a new System of Trade, and new substance of Materials, to set the World to work upon.

THE Original of all Manufacture, and (in those times, which I have been treating of) the only Materials then known, for manufacturing, were SILK and HAIR, COTTON and FLAX. This is plain from all kinds of antient Writers, and from the product of those Countries, at this time.

    I. SILK. The rich Man was cloathed in Purple, it seems he coveted to be seen in gorgeous Apparel, which could be no other than such as the *Babylonish Garment* was, that *Achan* stole, (*viz.*) Silk embroider'd with Gold and Silver, and various colours of other Silk.

II. FLAX. Fine Linen of *Egypt*, was then very well known, and the Priests Vestments were either of such fine Linen (as the Ephod[94] in particular) or of Silk.

III. COTTON. For I make no doubt, as the Women were, and wou'd be cloathed richly too as well as the Men; so, they not being able in those warm Countries, to wear heavy Clothing, contented themselves as with the rich Atlesses[95] and flower'd Silks; so with the light painted Chints, and fine *Masslapatans*, &c. of *Bengal*, and *Golconda*, and all the Callicoes of the *East-Indies*, that part between the *Ganges*, and the *Indus*; and which were brought into *Europe*, either by the *Red Sea*, to *Sues*, and *Alexandria*, or by the Caravans to *Aleppo* and *Smyrna*.

BUT *Corinth* being ruin'd on one hand, and *Carthage* the Year after on the other, by which two Cities the whole Wealth of the *Indies* circulated, there was a full stop of that Trade; nor did it ever see itself fully restor'd. For,

I. *EUROPE*, (by which I mean the Inhabitants of *Europe*) applying themselves with great vigor to Trade, it was not many Years before (especially in *Italy*) they found the method of getting the Silk unwrought from the Coast of the *Caspian Sea*, and learned to manufacture it in their own Countries; and within a few Ages more, they found means to bring over the very species, (*viz.*) the Worms, which produced those Silks, and the Mulberry Trees which fed them, and which together was the very Blood of the Commerce, and so made it appear they cou'd naturalize both to these *European* Climates; and that in time they wou'd have no more need to go to *India* and *Persia* for Clothing their People, but would be able in a few Years to make the Trade subsist at home, and cloath themselves by the product of their own Climate, and the labour of their own Hands.

THE effect of this was, That *Italy* (that is the South part of *Italy* and *Sicily*), supplying Silk, and the adjacent Country of *Lombardy*, namely, the Duchies of *Milan* and *Mantua*, furnishing innumerable Hands to manufacture those Silks, the Trade between *Europe* and *Asia*, (that is, *Persia*, *Georgia*, and *India*) died away as far as related to wrought Silks, and Manufactures of Cotton and Hair, &c. and in a few Years more was wholy confin'd to the Trade of Spices, Gums, and Drugs, which continued to be brought to *Sues*, in the *Red Sea*, and from thence to *Alexandria*; which Trade the *Venetians* and the *Genoese* shar'd between them, as shall be seen in its place; and as for the Silks, they were so far from wanting them,[96] that the *Italians*, for many Ages, out-did the *Persians* and *Indians*, and abundantly supplied themselves, and all *Europe*, with wrought Silks, without so much as thinking any more of *Persia*, or *India*.

THUS stood the Commerce of *Europe*, for some Ages, after the first decay of the *East India* Trade, by the destruction of *Corinth* and *Carthage*. The *Romans* troubled themselves not, as a State, and in their politic Capacity, with matters of Commerce; nor do I find, except what related to supplying the City of *Rome*, and the Country adjacent with Corn, any one Act of the Senate, or Edict of any Emperor, for the directing, regulating, or encouraging Commerce, or Manufactures, under the whole *Roman* Government, from the time of the destruction of *Carthage*, to the time of *Justinian* the *Great*, that is to say, for above 900 Years.

TRADE was left, as I have said, to its own Fate; Merchandizing went forward, as the Merchants of those times thought fit to act, every one in the narrow Circle, or Sphere of his own views, traded this way or that way, as they pleas'd.

I KNOW they tell us of Fleets of Ships, in the *Romans* time, which went to the *Indies*, and return'd again into the *Red Sea*; that is to say, to the Gulph of *Sues*, upon the Northern Store, or point of that Sea; but we read little of what they brought. 'Tis certain, that after *Augustus's* time, when as I said, the Citizens of *Naples* fetching only the Silk from *Persia*, began to manufacture their own Goods; I say, from that time the *East India* Ships brought home little but the Spices and Callicoes of *India*, leaving the wrought Silks of *Persia* behind, as what the *Romans* were well enough furnish'd with at home.

THUS continued the Affairs of Trade during the time of the *Roman* Grandeur; for then, *Rome* being Mistress of the World, *Italy* was the center of its Commerce; and having above six Millions and a half of People in it, the supplying them with but every one a yard of Linen, and every one a yard of Silk, was enough to have set all the Weavers in *Egypt* and *Persia* at Work.

BUT *Italy* is a warm Climate, and as it stands just where it did, it is to be suppos'd the Climate was as hot then as it is now; and this occasion'd the People, both Men and Women, to go as thin cloth'd as they could; nay it was complain'd in *Augustus's* Reign, that the Ladies Clothing, leaving the Neck and Breasts, down to the Stomach, quite bare; and the Legs, above the Knee, in part so too, the loose Robe being button'd up upon the Thigh; the rest of the Body clothed with thin Lawns and Crapes (next to a fine Muslin) lay so close to the Body that the parts were all distinguish'd thro' the covering, and it was but a civiler kind of going naked, when all the Shapes of the Body were delineated, even thro' the shade of the Habit.[97] This loose way of Dressing the *Roman Virtuosi*[98] exclaim'd at very often, as done to excite Lewdness, and *Juvenal* often Expostulates[99] with the *Roman*

Ladies about it: But that is foreign to my purpose, except thus far, namely; It proves that the Trade from *India* of fine Muslins, and fine Callicoes, and *Chints*, fully supply'd the demand of *Italy* for a long time with Clothing, especially for the Ladies. As to the Robes of the Men, the *Toga*, or loose Mantle, which the Men wore; that was supplied with a differing and remote Manufacture, namely, to those who could support the expence of it; *Persian* and *Indian* wrought Silks made the Vest, and the Robe was fine Damask; and others follow'd their example, where they could come up to the wear; for the rest several kinds of Cotton Stuffs, and Camblets[100] made of Goats and Camels Hair, such as they made use of for many Ages after, and such as they make use of in those Countries to this Day; some of which may be those we call *Turkey* Burdets,[101] and are still call'd by the Name of *Turkey* Stuffs of what kind soever.

THE Poor had their different Clothing, as the Poor have in all Nations; and by degrees, the Silk being too dear in the Materials as well as Workmanship, and Cotton being fetch'd too far to come to a reasonable price; I say, by degrees they began to make use of the Wooll from the Back of the Sheep, to make course Garments for the Poor, and to give them relief against the Inclemencies of the Seasons, as well Heat as Cold; and even in this they found themselves out-done by the *Vandals*, the *Goths*, and the other barbarous Nations; which in the several declining Years of their Empire made Excursions from their frozen Mountains into the softer and warmer Climates of *Italy*.

WHEN those wild People, especially the *Heruli*, and the *Sarmatians*, who came out of *Poland* and *Muscovy*, the Upper *Hungary* and *Austria*; and more especially the *Vandals*, who came from the frozen Shores of the *Baltick*, and the Countries about *Prussia* and *Pomerania*; I say, when these People came down, they found their Princes and Generals dress'd up in costly Furs, the Sables and Ermines, the Beavers and Foxes Skins of the Northern Climates; their Horses were cover'd, (and which ferv'd them for Saddles and Housings) with the Skins of Bears and Ounxes,[102] Buffalloes, Rain Deer, Stags, and the like.

THE Soldiers had their clothing of Skins also, but of meaner sorts; such as the Hare, the Coney, the Badger, the Otter, the Sheep, and the Lamb; of which the Fur, or Wooll, being inward, as well as outward, they were exceeding warm, and not to be endur'd when they march'd so far as *Italy*, where they soon learnt to cloath themselves with the Spoils of the Country, and often left their richest Furs behind them, especially if being beaten, as they were frequently by the *Romans*, they were oblig'd to leave their Bones behind them too, sometimes two or three hundred thousand at a time.

PROCESS of time however, mended things with those Northern People; and whereas at first they came down cloath'd with the Skins of wild and ravenous Beasts, themselves more savage, wild, and ravenous than the Beasts whose badges they wore; so in a few Ages the *Romans* perceived the Wooll of the Sheep, instead of being worn on the Backs of the poor Soldiers rough upon the Skin, and the Skin perhaps with no other dressing than being dryed in the Sun; I say, they perceiv'd the Wooll taken off from the Skin woven and manufactur'd into a different species of Garments, call'd Cloth of Wooll, or Woollen; and tho' this at first might be about as good as our Rugs, Duffels, and Blankets, or perhaps not so good; they fitted the purposes for which they were design'd, and serv'd not only to accommodate the People, but even to make them proud of the Habit. Thus we find in some of the descriptions of the antient Northern *Gauls* and *Britains*, that their Habit was a Rug, with Tags or Thrumbs[103] of Wooll hanging down on the outside, the same as we frequently find some Gentlemen affect to wear now, not for necessity, but in affectation and mimickry to look a little savage and barbarous; as if any thing that look'd wild and mountanous was a Beauty to them, and could pass for Ornaments, because they thought fit to make use of them; But the humours of a time, and of a few, is not worth a Digression; 'tis enough to tell us what was the gross beginning of that we now call the Woollen Manufacture. In all those antient Ages of the World, *Egypt* carry'd on a mighty Trade in the Linen Manufacture, and *fine Linen of Egypt* was the greatest rarity of the World of the kind; and this, with the vast plenty of Corn that always grew there, made *Egypt* Rich; for *Egypt* ever since the time of *Joseph* and his Brethren, was the Granary of the World for Corn: It is true, Corn is a Product, not a Manufacture, a Supply on Occasion to any Country, not a Commerce, but Linen was their Wealth, their main and chief Employ, a national Business, the Manufacture of the Country, and on which she chiefly depended. This we may reasonably conjecture was the Reason of the place being so infinitely and incredibly populous; insomuch that they tell us when *Nebuchadnezzar*, after his disappointment in the taking of *Tyre*, invaded and took *Egypt*, there were then twenty thousand Towns in it; some of which were great and populous Cities, and especially one, suppos'd to be the *Memphis* of the Antients, as immensly great as they say Grand *Cairo* is now, and had six or seven Millions of People in it, with the vast Wealth of which, when the *Babylonian* King plunder'd it, besides enriching his whole Army, and as some say, his whole Empire, I say, with that overplus Wealth he built or cast that monstrous Idol which he set up in the Plains of *Dura*, in the Province of *Babylon*, and which was all of Massy Gold; the dimensions of which are described, *Dan.* iii. 1. *The height sixty Cubits, and breadth six Cubits*, or, to allow a Foot and half to each Cubit, it was ninety Foot high, and nine Foot thick, being (to bring it down to vulgar Apprehension) near half as high as our Monument; all, I say, of Gold: What the shape of it was, we know the Scripture is silent in, but Authors generally agree, that like the *Collossus* at *Rhodes*, it was in the figure of a Man.

THIS infinite Number of People in *Egypt*, and the exceeding Wealth of that Country, is not at all improbable, were drawn together by Commerce; and the whole Commerce of the Country in all those early Days was in fine Linen, Purple, and Blue, Embroidery, and such nice Works of the Needle, *Ezekiel* xxvii. 7. *Fine Linen, with embroidered Work from* Egypt; and again verse 16. *Purple, and embroidered Work, and fine Linen from* Syria; and we all know that *Syria* is the next Country adjoyning to *Egypt*, and was then under *Pharaoh's* Dominion; and again verse 24. *Blue Cloths, and embroidered Works, and Chests of rich Apparel, from* Sheba *and* Ashur; these were Countries in *Arabia*, just opposite to *Egypt*, on the *Red Sea*.

THIS shews us what a place of Trade *Egypt* was, for Manufactures; and that by these Manufactures they became so prodigiously Populous; for Manufactures bring Trade, and Trade disperses, that is, consumes the Manufacture, and both bring numbers of People together; nor does it appear that any Kingdom in the World was ever extreamly Populous but by the efficiency of Trade, except *Italy* and *India*; and for those particular exceptions we may reasonably make Allowances, since their Governments are so publickly known, one happening by the immediate disposition of Heaven, and the other being occasion'd by its being the center of the great Empire of the World.

ALL the other great and populous Countries in the World, have been made so by Commerce, and by Manufactures, and by these only; as *Prussia* once the most populous spot of Ground in the World, and still continuing extreamly full of large Cities, and Towns, and People; it was then the seat of the *Teutonick Knights*, and *Hans-Men*, the great Patrons of Trade; the only, and perhaps first Merchants of *Europe*, of whom I shall speak in their turn: They were first call'd *Esterlings*, and then *Hans Towns*; and some of them retain their grandeur in Trade to this Day, as *Dantzick, Elbing, Koningsberg*, and several others.

FLANDERS, that is to say, the seventeen Provinces, which are now the most populous Country in *Europe*, if not in the World, and of which the United States[104] are but a part; how evidently did their Wealth and their exceeding multitude of People, derive from the Woollen Manufacture which thriv'd here; and which Manufacture was the effect of *England's* being so near, from whence they had their Wooll; for *England* from the most early Ages was the Store-house of the World for the best and finest

Wooll, and which indeed was to be had no where else; which same Manu-facture has since that (being restrain'd within ourselves) made *England* at this time the most wealthy and trading Country in the whole World; in proportion Populous, and growing in Numbers and Wealth every Day, so visibly, and so fast, as may in time make it, if it is not already, the most populous Nation in the World.

HOW long this Linen Manufacture reign'd in *Egypt*, History is silent in, but we may venture to say, or at least to suppose, that when the *Egyptians* submitted to *Omar* the second *Caliph* of the *Arabian* Race, *Anno*. 640. the *Arabians*, and by their example all the *Mahometan* Princes after him, living like *Arabians*, that is to say upon Rapin, Trade, which never thrives under Tyranny, forsook the Land of *Egypt*; the Merchants, plundered and robb'd by the *Saracens*, wou'd venture no more to trade to a Country where they cou'd not be protected from being ruin'd; and so the fine Linen of *Egypt*, which was the most eminent Manufacture in that part of the World, sunk so effectually out of all that Country; that in a Word, they do not (now) make Linen enough for their own use, but have it brought from *Hamburg*, from *Amsterdam*, from *Marseilles*, and other *European* Parts, where that Manufacture is since erected to the infinite profit of those Countries, and employment and support of the Poor.

HAVING thus as it were led things on to the downfall of the *Roman* Empire; Trade we find springing up in different parts of the World, as the several Governments which set themselves up after obtaining liberty from the *Roman* Yoke qualify'd themselves to give the trading World a due encouragement and protection; and the two first of these were the State of *Venice*, and the *Teutonick Order*; of both which, and the manner of their introducing Commerce into the Northern parts of *Europe*, I shall speak in their order.

CHAP. XIV.

Of the several new Discoveries and Improvements which were made in the World under the Roman *Government, after the overthrow of the* Carthaginians, *but especially after the declining state of the* Roman *Empire.*

I MUST now go back a little again to mention the other parts of my Work, and according to my Title, to speak of the Article ranged under New Discovery.

THAT Learning flourish'd under the *Roman Government* is not to be deny'd; that the *Romans* civiliz'd the World, and brought the barbarous Nations not only to submit to Government but the regularity of that Government, and the equity of their Laws made the People easy, their Persons and Properties safe; and in consequence of that Safety and Liberty the People were encourag'd to Arts, Industry, and Learning; in a Word, every thing receiv'd Encouragment under the *Roman* Administration *but Trade*.

IT is true, they did not particularly oppress Trade, or discourage the People from it, except that indeed sometimes their Taxes were heavy, and Impositions of Conquerors always discourage the Merchant; for the Sword too often reaps the Harvest of the industrious Merchant; but even in that part, the *Roman* Government was as moderate as their Circumstances wou'd admit.

BUT here lay the difference; It is not enough to the planting and establishing Commerce, that a Government shou'd not openly discourage it; but Trade and new discovery must be the nursery and darling of the Government they live under; the Merchant must receive the countenance and assistance of the Government he lives under, or Trade never rises with advantage.

COMMERCE receiv'd a mortal blow in the destruction of *Carthage*; the whole World felt the shock, as their Discoveries abroad lately begun, sunk and were destroy'd in the general dissaster, for want of Supplies; so Invention, useful Undertakings, Arts, Science, all which were flourishing and

131

encreasing at home under the *Carthaginian* Government, were likewise overwelm'd in it, and all the Manufactures sunk with it, as no doubt many were on foot, among a People whose Genius addicted them to encourage Manufacture and employ their People: All were overwhelm'd in the general Ruin; the Mines of Copper, and Iron, and even of Silver, in many Countries were left unwrought, and the Iron in particular in *Africa* was never thorowly recover'd to this Day; nor has the manufacturing the Iron, which flourish'd particularly in *Carthage*, for the making Armour, Weapons, and all the needful Utensils of War, in which the *Carthaginians* excel'd all the World, ever been restor'd to *Africa* to this Day.

IN a Word, all the trading World felt the blow; and we find nothing considerable done in Manufacture, or Inventions, relating to Trade, after the fall of *Carthage*, for many Ages: Let us see however what progress was made in other things; and how the World came gradually to the knowledge of one another.

DISCOVERIES for Trade were not made indeed, but Discoveries were made for all that, be the Reasons of them what they wou'd; for example, *Carthage* was destroy'd in the Year of the World 3804, 144 Years before our Saviour was Born. *Julius Cæsar's* progress into the North of *Europe* was not till eighty seven Years afterwards, being *Anno Mundi* 3891, fifty seven years before Christ; and tho' it was not a discovery for Commerce, or a planting for Improvement, but a mere possessing by Armies for extending Conquests and encrease of Power; yet this as well as other Conquests of *Julius Cæsar* made much about the same time, brought on the necessary discoveries of Commerce which have follow'd.

THE *Belgiæ*, by which is to be understood all the Lower *Germany*, were a potent People inhabiting the inaccessible Countries of *Westphalia, East-Friezland* and as much as was then habitable of the *Netherlands*, or *Low Countries*; for the most part of those Provinces were then rendered not habitable by the inundations of the many great Rivers, which empty themselves into the Ocean at that place; such as the *Weser*, the *Embs*; the *Rhine*, the *Maes*, and the *Scheld*, with many other lesser Rivers; which altogether pouring their Waters into this one part, as into a Common-shore[105] as either by Freshes and Floods from the Country, or North-Westerly Winds, bringing high Tides from the Sea, the Waters were rais'd above their usual height, all the lower part now call'd *Netherland*, or the *Low-Countries*, were laid under Water like a Sea, and the higher Grounds surrounded, which therefore I call Inaccessible.

THOSE People began to be better acquainted with the *Roman* Government after they found that *Great Britain* had submitted, and how well they brook'd the Conquerors, and in a few Ages afterwards, these *Belgiæ* became a Province of the *Roman* Empire; and as they liv'd among Waters became eminent for their Skill in navigating the most boisterous Seas.

BUT still those Discoveries added little to the World, in respect to Commerce, till, after some Ages, the *Belgiæ* began the great Improvement of all, namely, that of the Woollen Manufacture; which however was not, I say, for some Ages. But the first branch of Improvement, which these *Low-Countrymen* employ'd themselves in, was recovering the Land from the inundations of the Sea; and they were assisted in, if not first prompted to it, by the *Romans*; and particularly we find that *Drusus Nero*[106] the *Roman* General has the honour of cutting the great Chanel or Canal, which joins the *Rhine*, and the *Yssel*, and so upon any occasion of a Land Flood casts off a great part of the Water of the *Rhine* into the *Zuyder*, or the Southern Sea; by which means all the Country below *Arnheim* as far as *Utrecht* and *Leyden* were eas'd of that vast weight of Water which at some Seasons came down the *Rhine*, and like the *Nile*, wou'd cover the whole Country, no Dykes or Banks being able to restrain them.

THIS Chanel being thus successfully cut, and the effect of it appearing so infinitely advantageous to the Country, the example set the several Princes of the *Belgiæ* in their respective Districts or Dominions, upon that noble work, of recovering those rich Lands from the constant inundations of Water which annually overflow'd them, and render'd them useless to Mankind, and to shut them in with Banks and Walls built up with immense Labour, strengthen'd with vast quantities of Stones and solid Materials fetch'd a great way, and at a prodigious expence, buttress'd up with Piles and ranges of Piles, driven in sometimes three upon one another; and then making those Lands compleatly safe, and laying them dry, tho', as is observ'd by Travellers, the whole Surface of the Country lyes several Yards lower than the ordinary Surface of the Water; and this was done with such Art, and follow'd with such Application, tho' very gradually, and some Ages of Years in finishing, that now we see two large Governments, Kingdoms we might call them; and two most powerful and prodigiously populous Nations, namely, the *Dutch* and the *Flemings* living securely, and large Cities and Towns flourishing, which were for 4000 Years before delug'd with Water, useless and impracticable.

THIS I hope I may be allow'd to call an *Improvement*; and that this Undertaking was so antient, and the finishing it to some degree in those early times recorded, will appear by the many foundations of royal Cities laid there since the recovery of those Lands; such as that of *Rotterdam, Middleburgh, Groninghen, Ghertrugdenburgh*, and innumerable others in *Holland*; also *Bruges, Ghent, Sluyce, Ostend, Newport*, and even *Antwerp* itself, and many more on that side of *Flanders*.

THE several Improvements of the like nature in other Countries, made after the example of the *Belgiæ*, are to be mention'd in their order; as particularly the Triangle or *Delta* of *Egypt*, at the Mouth of the *Nile*, the Marish[107] of *Martigues* in the *Gallia Narbonensis* at the Mouth of the *Rhosn*; the low Land of *Prussia* drain'd by *Teutones*, thence call'd the *Teutonick Order*, at the Mouth of the great Rivers *Vistula*, and of the *Pergle*, and the *Neimen* in Poland, the same in the Fens of *Deitmarsh*, and the Lands upon the *Eyderstrom*, on the North-Bank of the *Elb*, in *Holstein* and *Sleswick*; with innumerable others sum'd up in the general Article of the Improvement of Land; which, as it is said the *Romans* first gave the example of; and to sum up all, the *Veneti* found the benefit of the like at the decay of the *Roman* State, by which alone they preserv'd themselves, retreating among the Islands of the *Adriatick* Gulph, and the drown'd Lands between the Mouths of the *Po*, and near the Influx of the *Adige*, and several other Rivers; where draining and securing those Lands from the inundation of the Rivers, they at the same time fortify'd themselves against the attacks of the *Heruli*; and afterwards of all the barbarous Nations which over-run the *Roman* Empire.

THIS is but a brief History of a long series of Time; but as a History of Improvement is a part of this Work, and this is the beginning of all Improvement in the World, in the sence of the Question; so I think it is the most considerable thing of its kind, and as it is what we see the effect of every Day before our Eyes, we cannot think it so remote as other Instances might.

HAD not this piece of Improvement been made we had known no States of the *United Provinces*; no *Austrian Netherlands*; nor had we heard of all the famous things done, and Men concern'd in the two most fatal Wars of the World, and which lasted (but with small intervals) above forty Years each; I mean the War between the *Dutch* and the King of *Spain*, when the former began to be a free State; and the late War between *France* and the Confederates, in which Liberty was effectually restor'd to all the oppress'd Nations, and *Europe* may be said to become one free People.

IT is most certain, that the Progress of *Julius Cæsar* into *Britain*, and into the Northern Provinces of the *Gauls* and *Germans*, was to the *Romans* as the planting *New-England* and *Virginia* was to the *English*, I mean a *New Discovery*; with this difference only, that they planted for Conquest, we planted for Commerce; they planted to extend their Dominion, we to extend our Trade; and as the last is the best Foundation, so it is the surest Possession, and will certainly continue longest; experience tells us so, witness the long continuance of the Colonies and Nations here in *Britain*, and in the *Low-Countries*, notwithstanding the fall of their Lords and Discoverers, the

Romans: Which have continued their Establishments in Trade, tho' the Conquerors (the *Romans*) expir'd as a Nation; and witness the *British* Colonies in *America*, which continued their trading Circumstances, when the Government of *Great Britain* receiv'd a shock, the Monarchy was overwhelm'd, and in a manner destroy'd in our own Civil Convulsions.

AND here I might make a useful Digression concerning the durable nature of Commerce; how it establishes Nations, but never destroyes them; how it renders them much more immortal than Conquest and Victory, and gives real, not imaginary Triumphs to a People; for example, The Trade in Copper which the *Carthaginians* drove with the City of *Corinth*, of which so much has been said; and of which the famous *Corinthian* Brass was made (not of the molten Gold and Copper which Fable tells us was found upon Images, among the Statues and Temples of their Gods, and which the Fire melted down in the Conflagration of the City) I say that Copper continues still a noble Product of the Country of *Africa*, notwithstanding all the Calamities, Dissolution of Governments, burning Cities, and even rooting out of People, which has happen'd in *Africa*: The *Carthaginians* went off the Stage first, the *Romans* after; the *Vandals, Goths, Saracens*, and *Moors*, have all taken their turn upon the Stage of the *African* Governments; but the Copper Mines are the same to this Day, and are like to be the same to the last Conflagration; but this is a Digression.

THE attempt of the *Romans* upon the *Britains* and the *Belgi*, as I have observ'd, were really Discoveries and Improvements; I might indeed say they were Plantations and Settlements; but those are modern Words, not in use in the *Roman* Days: Colonies indeed they were call'd, and were planted and settled as such, and such *Britain* was in general, and the several Stations of their Legionary Troops were so in particular, and altogether were more so, as their Inclinations to recover their Liberty were stronger or weaker.

BUT even *Britain*, or the *Belgi*, knew little of Trade till afterwards; for the *Romans* themselves enter'd into no measures about Trade; all that occur'd to them in planting such Colonies was to secure a Communication with them, to and from other *Roman Colonies*, or to and from Nations in subjection to, or confederacy with the *Romans*, that so the Colony might receive supplies of Provisions, and support of Troops, as occasion requir'd; and tho' this did even of itself create Commerce, and in the consequence of things did in time make Trade, by the industry and application of the People, and by their being under the *Roman* Protection; yet the *Romans* themselves never had it in their view, at least we see no room to think they had; nor do the Nations owe their Introductions to Trade to the *Romans*, any otherwise than as the *Romans* gave them Peace and Protection in the pursuit of the prospects of Improvement which the nature of things offer'd them; by that Peace and Protection the industry of the People receiv'd encouragment.

ADD to this, tho' it be but an Observation by the by, That Religion spreading itself through the World soon after these Conquests of the *Romans*, and very much by the help of those Conquests; I say Religion spreading among the Nations introduc'd (with it) principles of Morality, and civiliz'd the People.

FOR take it with you as you go, Religion (I mean the Christian Religion) did not at its first beginning to spread itself in the World, indulge, or so much as allow the Vices common now to Christians, and winked at in Christian Nations, such as Avarice, Craft, Sly and cunning Circumventing one another, Over-reaching, and fraudulently Cheating in their Dealings, and all the little nameless Cheats and Chicanries of Trade.

THE Christian Religion infus'd principles of Honesty and Plain-Dealing; it recommended a general rectitude of the Mind, a known integrity of Principle, a just and upright Conduct under the awe of an invisible Being, who inspected the minutest Actions, and wou'd call to account for the most secret conceal'd Wickedness; so that in short, where the Christians became Traders, or engaged in Arts, Manufactures, and Commerce, there, who ever dealt with them were sure to find upright Dealing, punctual performance of every Agreement; the Hand laid upon the Heart was as sacred as an Oath, and what the Mouth spoke the Hands were solemnly bound by; in a Word, a general probity and exact honest procedure govern'd all their Dealings; and this we cannot doubt encourag'd Trade, as to this Day we see that foul, unjust, and dishonest usage discourages Trade, and drives away the Merchants even from Cities, and Nations, as well as Persons.

BUT this Country and the *Belgi*, that is, the *Flemings* and *Dutch*, embraceing the Christian Religion,[108] within sixty or seventy Years after their first coming under the *Roman* Dominion, it may be said of them, with truth, that they sooner than other Pagan Nations felt the civilizing influences of Religion, by how much they with a greater willingness and forwardness embrac'd the Religion itself; for 'tis remark'd by the Writers of our Histories, in the Story of *Joseph* of *Arimathea*,[109] who was the first Apostle of the *Britains*, that the People most gladly, and with the greatest simplicity, that is honesty and integrity, receiv'd the knowledge of CHRIST.

THUS, and I think with great justice, I observe the settling Commerce in this part of the World to be the genuine, natural product of the planting Religion, and *Roman* Liberty here together; and 'tis observable to this very Day, that Trade flourishes upon the same Foundation, and declines as that Foundation sinks and decays, (*viz.*)

I. LIBERTY, for securing and preserving Property, without which Commerce cannot be safe.

II. HONESTY, for the introducing just Dealings between Man and Man, on which depends Credit, which we find by experience is the life of Trade.

NOW in these two Cases the Juncture I speak of was particularly eminent; (1) The just Government of the *Romans* establish'd Peace and Liberty; and (2) The Christian Religion coming in upon the very track or footsteps of the *Roman* Conquests, that Religion (to the immortal Honour of its very Name in the World) inspir'd its Professors with just Principles; forming their Minds by the Rules of all moral Virtues, as well as with the awe and fear of a divine Power, a righteous Judgment, and a futurity of Reward; on both these Foundations the World became more habitable than before; and Men enjoying the Tranquillity, which was the consequence of just Government, apply'd themselves to Industry and Labour; hence Arts and Learning flourish'd, and in consequence of the first,

Trade and *Navigation*.

TRADE began gradually in this part of the World by three eminent Encouragements, besides what I have already mention'd.

I. THE situation of the Country advantagious for Commerce.

II. THE diligence and application of the *Belgi*, that is to say, the *Netherlanders*, by whom I am to be understood to mean, the Inhabitants of the Country from *Picardy*, or the Mouth of the *Some*, to *Bremen*, in the Mouth of the *Weser*, or at least to *Embden*, at the Mouth of the River *Ems*.

III. BY the finding the Wooll of *England*, which was so easily adapted to Manufacture, and which we find was employ'd to that end in *Flanders*, and the rest of the *Low Countries*, even before the *Romans* quitted their footing; for we find mention made of the Wooll of *Britain* being transported to the Country of the *Belgi*: Thus the *Romans* employ'd the Ships of the *Britains*, in which they us'd to transport Wooll and Cattle to the said *Belgi*. So much for the first knowledge of Trade in these Parts of the World.

UPON the like Foundations the Commerce of the *Baltick* naturally comes to our knowledge; and Nature furnishing Materials, Trade became a Consequence: Three principle Articles of Commerce push'd natural Industry upon methods of Trade in this part of the World. Namely,

I. NAVAL Stores, by which they first supply'd themselves, and then other Nations; for the building and fitting out Ships; for these naval Stores, first came in use by supplying their own Occasions; and then became a Merchandize for supplying others: These naval Stores were,

1. TAR, from whence also Pitch, which is almost the same Species.

N.B *It is very remarkable, that Tar was long in use before Timber and Plank were known to be wanted in building Ships; the first Vessels, tho' call'd Ships, being no more than Osiers, and small pieces banded together with Withs, and after with Ropes, and cover'd with Skins, all being thicken'd, and as it were daub'd over (as the Ark was) within and without with Pitch, which is Tar.*

2. HEMP, of which, by the help of Industry, they did then as they do still, make their Cordage and Rigging for such Ships as they had.

III. COPPER and Iron. *Sweden,* and the Countries on both sides the *Bothnick* Gulph abounded in these Mettals in the most early times; and as Nature made these things necessary to Trade, and that the Merchants carry'd them by Sea almost as soon as Ships were had in the World to carry them: So we find the *Teutones,* that is to say, those *Germans* that inhabited the remotest Shores of the *Baltick,* whither the *Romans* never came, or but seldom if they came at all, and never conquer'd, nor the *Saracens* neither, were some of the first Merchants in these Northern parts of the World, and navigated the most dangerous Seas, even when their Ships were but mean little Wicker-Work Boats, cover'd with Hides and Pitch, as above.

BUT to go back to the *Romans,* as I have said, that as a State they never meddled with, much less encourag'd Trade; yet(*) a late Author[110] will have it that they establish'd a College of Merchants, and that they sent Fleets to the *East Indies;* yet even that very Writer acknowledges (†) what I have here advanc'd in these express Words, *That they sought rather to extend their Dominion than the Arts and Exercise of Commerce;* and he owns also that they had no Navigation but coasting about, very rarely hazarding themselves into the open Sea: *Strabo*[111] indeed reproaches *Eratosthenes* with Ignorance, and says, that the Antients made longer Voyages than the Moderns, and extended their Commerce to the utmost end of the World; but this Age wou'd laugh at *Strabo;* nay *Strabo* wou'd laugh at himself if he was now alive, and was to see to what an extent Trade and Navigation also, is

(*) *The History of Navigation and Commerce, page 153.*
(†) *Ibid. Sect. 9. page 159.*

now carryed, and what Ships the Merchants, as well as the Nations of this Age make use of.

BUT to return to the Trade, which it is pretended, the *Romans* carry'd on, and which the same Writer boasts of very much; 'tis plain it amounts to no more than this, *namely*, that the *Romans* (to give it you in his own Words) allur'd by the rich Merchandizes of the *Indies* sent their Fleets thither every Year.

NOW those Colleges of Merchants, which the *Romans* erected in *Rome*, were no more than what we see practis'd in several Cities in *Europe*; and in *London* in particular; I mean forming Societies of the several Trades, such as there is at this Day, and under the same title, namely, Colleges of Trades at *Brussels*: In *London* they are call'd Companies and Corporations; the several Handicrafts and Shopkeepers forming Societies among themselves, to establish *By-Laws* and Customs, for the better carrying on and the regulating the Art and Mistery of their Profession; and as the Word *Merchant* was then understood, and is so still, in almost all Countries but in *England*, it is evident it means no other then Handicrafts, &c. As to foreign Commerce and Merchandize (as we understand the Word;) the *Romans* 'tis true knew very little of it; and the little they knew was chiefly for the furnishing the great City of *Rome* with Provisions and Corn; which City was so large as indeed almost to employ all the Shipping, at that time, in the World; of which Shipping I must in the next place say a word or two.

CHAP. XV.

Of the Navigation in and for sometime *after the* Romans; *and how mean a thing their navigating Skill must be in those Ages.*

WHO ever reads the History of the Wars between the *Carthaginians* and *Romans*, which were call'd the Punick Wars, as also the Wars of *Cæsar* and *Pompey*, the Battle of *Actium*, with the other most memorable Transactions at Sea in those Days; and how big the ignorant Writers of those Times talk'd of them; wou'd think great matters were done, and mighty skill in Navigation was arriv'd to, which on the contrary, when we look back to, and compare with our Times, we see to be all grosly ignorant, and even ridiculous.

IN the Fight between the *Romans* and the *Carthaginians* off of the Coast of *Sicily*, the *Carthaginians* being worsted, lost 130 Ships; the *Romans* and *Carthaginians* often after that fitted out great Fleets of Ships; what they were I have already enquir'd, and how little they deserv'd the name of Ships; let me add to it only this, that the *Corinthians* built a great Ship which had forty *Banks* of Oars; this help'd to explain the Word *Bank*; no Man will be so stupid as to think this Ship had forty rows of Slaves or Soldiers rowing, one row above another; that wou'd have infer'd a Ship of forty Decks, one above another; but a Bank, as the Word was then us'd, intimates no more than this, (*viz.*) *a Bench*, on which sat three, four, or five Men to rule or move one great OAR; and of these, this great Ship of *Corinth* (for it was thought to be a Monster in those Days) had forty Benches or Banks of Oars; that is twenty Oars *on a side*, as Sir *Walter Raleigh*[112] thinks; but if it was meant forty of a Side, the Ship being so very large it might perhaps be so without any thing in it Miraculous.

BUT that the Antients may boast with good ground of their extraordinary knowledge in Shipping; they tell us of a vast Fleet that *Sesostris*[113] King of *Egypt* built in the *Red Sea* of 400 Sail, or 400 Ships rather; for so the Story expresses it; and I will not undertake that all or any of them had

Sails, or that the use of Masts and Sails was then known in the World: Then they tell you of another monsterous Vessel (Ship they call it) built by the same Prince, of 240 Cubits long; and another *Egyptian* Ship, which *Lucian*[114] mentions, which was 120 Cubits long, thirty in breadth, and twenty nine in depth; all which, supposing them to be true, amounts to not more, in my judgment, than long Troughs, which they us'd to carry their Luggage in upon the *Nile*; and we see every Day our Western Barges, in the River *Thames*, above 100 Foot long; and if they were four times that length, if the Navigation of the *Thames*, like that of the *Nile*, was always calm and smooth they might easily float with their Loading.

THUS we see in *Flanders* long narrow Vessels call'd *By-landers*, because they go in the narrow Canals and little deep Rivers in that Country close by the Land; some of these are longer than a Ship of 200 Tons; and thus, if we are not misinform'd, the antient *Muscovites* had Vessels on the *Wolga* which carry'd a vast Burthen down that mighty River to *Astracan*, and as I have heard, wou'd carry 1000 Men, and Weight in proportion; and had each 110 Men to manage them; and I have been told, that they built them at *Wologda*, in the Northmost part of that River; and when they had perform'd the Voyage (which was above 180 Miles) they pull'd 'em in pieces, and burnt them, using smaller Boats to come up the River against the Stream: These Boats, which I say I have been told of, they call'd *Balatoons*, and might be as big as *Sesostris*'s great Ship, and perhaps as good.

SUCH Ships as these are therefore not to be mention'd in the account of Shipping, which we are now speaking of; the *Roman* Accounts of their own Affairs will convince us that their Ships were but sorry things compar'd to what we now call Ships; young *Pompey* keeping possession of *Sardinia* ravag'd the Coast of *Italy* with his Piracies, and almost starv'd the City of *Rome* for want of Corn; but when they come to give an account of *Pompey*'s Ships: [See the formidable description,][115] they were row'd with Oars, and cover'd with Leather, and carry'd sixty Men each. At length the *Roman* Consuls to quiet the People were oblig'd to build a Fleet to fight *Pompey* and clear the Seas; and this Fleet was built and fitted out to Sea, as we see by the account of it in about six Weeks time, and *Pompey* routed: What Ships they were, may be a little guess'd at by the time they took up in building and fitting them out.

AUGUSTUS and *Anthony*, soon after this, had a great Sea Fight, call'd the Battle of *Actium*; History is not agreed about the number of the Ships they had on either side, but the lowest Accounts speak of 200 on each side; and the highest speak of three times that number.

IN the Punick War the *Carthaginians* defeated the *Romans* at Sea, because they had bigger Ships, and were more expert in managing them; that is to say they were better Seamen than the *Romans*; and that was (by the way) because they were better Merchants, and enur'd to the Sea by the consequence of the vast Commerce which they carry'd on, which the *Romans* knew little or nothing of: On this account the *Romans* were oblig'd to build larger Ships, and get *African* and *Sicilian* Seamen to match the *Carthaginians*; and then adding their own Landmen, who were better Soldiers than the *Carthaginians*, they by that means came to match the *Carthaginians* at Sea; and if they had not done, so they had never reduc'd them as they did.

BUT we are told, that all this while the *Romans* made Voyages to the *East Indies*; six Lines will explain that whole Article, *so much boasted of*: Let us see what this great Voyage to the *Indies* was. *Solomon* we allow and the old *Phœnicians* had bigger and better Ships than the *Romans*; for the knowledge of Marine Affairs receiv'd such a blow in the destruction of *Tyre* that it was never fully recover'd; and again, by that of *Carthage*; the *Romans* applying themselves (as I have said) to Conquests not to Trade, and to Victory not to Navigation.

BUT the *Romans* made Voyages to the *East Indies*. How? [See the same Author[116] mention'd before.] Following the Foot-steps of that famous Conqueror *Alexander Magnus*,[117] they made Voyages to *India* towards the Mouth of *Euphrates*: This discovers evidently the thing. The Mouth of *Euphrates* is known to all the World; that River, in conjunction with the *Tigris*, and other great Rivers, falls into the *Persian* Gulph, not into the open Sea: So that the *Roman Fleet* did this, they sail'd or row'd down the *Red Sea*, along by the Coast of *Mecca* and *Mocha*, and then passing the Straights of *Babel-Mandel*, turn'd away to the East, keeping close under Shore, by the South-Coast of *Arabia Felix*, till they came to the *Persian* Gulph, which is the Mouth of *Euphrates*; crossing which, in that part where it is so narrow, at the Island of *Ormus*, the other Shore immediately begins the *Bactrian* Country,[118] which is the true *India*, now subject to the Great *Mogul*; and coasting but a very little farther you come to the River *Indus*, from which the whole Country takes its Name; and where *Alexander* reduc'd *Porus* the *Bactrian* or *Indian* King.

THIS is the mighty Voyage to *India*, of which so much is said in honour of the *Roman* Merchants, which considering the calm Seas and warm Climate, at those Seasons, and in that Latitude, is no more than our Seamen wou'd boldly attempt at any time in a *Gravesend-Wherry*; and I must say, and I believe I speak with Reason; that for a *Gravesend-Wherry* to go down from *Gravesend* to the *Downs*, and cross over the Sea there to *Calais*, which they frequently do, is a much more dangerous and hazardous thing than all those famous Voyages to the *Indies*.

YET it is allow'd that the *Egyptians* had larger and better Ships, and so had the *Tyrians* also, and the *Carthaginians*, than any the *Romans* had or knew how to have; and it might be in those *Egyptian* Ships that the Voyages to the *Indies* were made: Hence they tell us that *Mark Anthony* when he brought up his Fleet from *Alexandria* in *Egypt*, to fight *Octavius*, when he enter'd the Mouth of the *Adria*, that is, of the Gulph of *Venice*, call'd still the *Adriatic Sea*; *Octavius*, who fitted out his Fleet at *Ravenna*, tho' he had thirty Ships more than *Anthony*, yet was doubtful of engageing till he had seventy Ships more from *Patras*; because *Anthony*'s Ships, built in *Egypt*, were larger and stronger than those of the *Romans*. This a full evidence of the Fact.

BESIDES this, 'tis evident they distinguish'd between Ships of War and Ships of Burthen; as we do (tho' with a juster Cause) to this Day. The Ships of Burthen were only carry'd by the Winds, and with the help of their Sails; whereas the Ships of War were light and nimble, and being carry'd every where by their Oars, were adapted to fight and pursue: Of these Ships of Burthen, it seems the *Romans* had none; and were oblig'd to hire them of the *Liburnians*, who were Merchants; *that is to say* they were us'd to fetch Corn from *Egypt* for the supply of the City of *Rome*, and of the Country round it, which was so prodigiously populous, that besides *Rome* itself, which had at that time several Millions of People in it, *Naples, Capua,* and many other Cities of *Italy*, which were exceeding populous, and *Italy* itself, even with the Corn of *Sicily* adjoin'd, was no way able to supply them; but they fetch'd Corn from *Egypt* in very great quantities, and from all the Coast of *Africa* besides.

HAVING thus plac'd the boasted Navigation of the Antients in a true light: Where must we look for the rise and beginning of the present knowledge of Navigation, and the skill of managing as well as building the great Ships, which we see made use of in the Commerce of the World, at this time? It is evident it must be lookt for in these Northern parts of the World; where the Seas being more dangerous, and the rapid and uncertain Tides, frightful and terrible to Sailors, as Antiquity furnishes us with many evidences to prove, requir'd stronger Ships.

> Britain, *where boisterous North Winds blow,*
> *And Tides uncertain ebb and flow,*
> *The Sailors dread* ——[119]

WE are now to suppose the *Roman* Empire declining; and if you please suppose them quite sunk, tho' it was some Ages a sinking, as such Bodies may be suppos'd to struggle long, or as we call it *to die hard*; I say suppose them sunk and gone. The barbarous Nations which over-run the *Roman*

Empire had no more view at first to Commerce and Navigation than the *Romans* had before them; so that the Conquests and Inroads made by the *Vandals, Goths, Gauls*, and *Saracens*, were all carry'd on by their Land Forces; nay, it is very remarkable that even all those barbarous Nations, which over-run the *Roman* Empire, came from such parts of the World, and by such several Routs as made the use of Shipping and Navigation entirely needless to the Conquerors. For Example:

ITALY was the center, to which they all directed their March; by the situation of their several Habitations before, we shall easily see the Rout they took to come to *Italy.*

THE *Hunns* coming out of *Pannonia*, now *Hungary, Transylvania*, and *Valachia*, march'd thro' *Croatia, Carinthia, Austria, Stiria*, &c. into *Lombardy*: There was no Sea in this way, nor any occasion for it, to bring their Stores or Provisions, which all march'd with them; and for which they had always an infinite number of Carriages.

THE *Sarmati*, which came from the confines of *Muscovy* and *Poland*, and from all the remote Countries both Southward, upon the *Borysthenes*, and Northward, upon the *Vistula*, came either into *Thrace*, and so bent their course towards *Constantinople*, which was then the Seat of the *Roman* Empire, or marching through *Moravia*, and *Austria*, came into *Lombardy* through the Country of *Trent* and *Tirol*.

THE *Saracens* were an Eastern, or rather a Southern People, and advanced from *Arabia* and *Syria*, into *Egypt* and *Africa*; or directing their march Northward fell into the Lesser *Asia, Cappadocia*, and *Bithynia*; and all this was still effected *by Land*; nor had they one Ship, or the least occasion for one.

AGAIN the *Goths* and *Vandals*, the *Cimbri*, and the *Heruli*, take them separately or together; they came from the Northern parts of *Germany*, and the Banks of the *Neckar*, the *Main*, the *Elb*, and the *Havel*; and still all of them came by Land, passing into *Italy*, by the Mountains of *Tirol.*

Lastly, THE *Gauls* did the same by the *Alps*, partly through the Duchy of *Savoy*, and the Country of the *Grisons*, or through the *Gallia Narbonnensis*, and so through the Country of *Provence* into the *Genoese* part, and by the Vallies of *Piemont.*

BUT take them all from their respective original Habitations, they had not one Ship employ'd in the whole World, towards the reduction of the *Roman* Empire, or of any of their Allies; except such as the *Saxons*, and after them the *Danes* embark'd in, for the invading of *Britain*; and these must be very poor and indifferent Things, if we reflect upon a Naval Engagement, or Sea-Fight, between the *Britains* and the *Saxons*, upon the Waters of the River *Lea*,[120] between *Waltham* and *Ware*, which is now all dry Land.

THIS brings me back to the Case in Hand; As the *Romans* made little or no improvement of Ships, or of Navigation, in raising their Empire to that pitch of greatness, which it was once arriv'd at; so the barbarous Nations, which invaded, and at length overthrew the *Roman* Empire, had no Ships, and indeed no occasion of any in the ruin and reduction of it.

WE must come on therefore farther forward than this, for all the improvements and encouragements of Navigation in the World, and of Trade also.

THREE or four Articles of Commerce, as the source of what follow'd in Navigation, may give us a light into the History of it.

I. WHEN the *Goths* and *Vandals* over-run one part of the *Roman* World, they push'd principally into *Spain*; and taking a quiet peaceable possession of all that rich Country, which was more than the *Romans* could ever do, they found principles of Commerce in the very Earth; and as they brought principles of Liberty with them (for the *Gothic* Governments,[121] which are the very same upon which the *British* Liberties are *formed*, were all such as establish'd Government on the foundation of Property) this, and the *Goths* withal receiving very early the Christian Religion, was the Reason that they became, *wherever they settled*, a most diligent and industrious People, quiet, laborious, and simply Honest; and accordingly in *Spain*, finding Materials in the very Earth, and upon it, they, sooner than any of the other Nations, began to apply both to *Commerce* and *Navigation*.

IT is true, they were, after some Ages, invaded from *Africa*, with a swarm of Locusts, call'd *Saracens*, who as the Locusts are said to eat up every green thing, so they swallow'd up and devour'd all the Industry of the *Goths*, and even the People too; in a word, they over-run the whole Country, except the two smaller Provinces of *Biscay* and *Guipuscoa*.

THESE retain'd their Liberty, and their Country being withal Mountainous, and of difficult Access, was also so well defended, that the *Biscayners* boast to this Day, that their Race is pure native *Spain*, and that they are not at all mixt with the *Moors*, either in Blood or Religion.

As these *Biscainers* retain'd their Possessions, notwithstanding the infinite swarms of the *Saracens* which came over; for I think the first attempt they made was with 600,000 Men: So the diligent People of *Biscay* finding great plenty of Iron and Steel in their Country, they apply'd themselves to the Manufacture of it; and after that, by the necessity other Nations found themselves in of a supply of things so useful to them, Ships grew necessary to encourage and push on that Commerce: Hence they tell us, that *Bilboa* and *Fuenterabia* were the first Building Ports in *Spain*; that here they not only built Ships but employ'd them also; and that by this means they began to correspond with the rest of the World, with their own Ships carrying out their own Manufactures, as also to encourage other Nations to do as they shew'd the example.

WHILE the *Biscainers* appear'd thus to be the great and first Navigators in the Northern part of the Empire; so the *Venetians* were the next, whose rise is merely owing to the necessity of Trade; I say the necessity of Trade, for they had no other way to live: First, For their Preservation from the flood of the barbarous Nations, who tore the *Roman* Empire to pieces, they were driven to the necessity, or at least saw it for their purpose to retire into such places where they might best defend themselves; and where the situation made it impracticable for their Enemies to attack them but by Sea: This retreat put them necessarily upon providing a sufficient Strength of such kind, to preserve themselves in case their Enemies should get Ships to attack them, or as the nature of their Circumstances requir'd. Thus Nature wrought in both Places, (*viz.*)

I. THE Bay of *Biscay*, a rough, tempestuous, angry Sea, and famous to this Day for exceeding great and hollow Waves, naturally drove the *Biscainers* to contrive such Vessels as might bear out against the roughest Weather; and they soon by their hardy Adventures obtain'd the credit of bold and expert Seamen: They grew famous too in Trade, for their Iron Manufacture, making all sorts of Armour, Weapons, and Habiliments of War; and for Swords the *Biscay Blades* have preserv'd the Reputation of being the best temper'd, and of the hardest Metal in the World, even to this Day.

II. THE *Veneti*, as is said above, became early Navigators in the *Adriatic Gulph*, by the very same necessity of their Circumstances; for they having retir'd from the fury of the *Heruli*, and afterwards of the *Lombards*, into the fastnesses and defences of the Islands, near the Mouth of the *Po*, and of the *Adige*; as they form'd themselves into a strong Body of People, they were soon in a condition to preserve themselves from Invasion. But how should they do to subsist? For the Islands, to which they retreated, cou'd not supply them with Corn, or any other Provisions; they were therefore oblig'd, or we may say, forc'd to go out to Sea, and look abroad for Bread: This naturally put them upon building such Boats or Ships (for Boats, as we call them now, were call'd Ships in those Days) as those Occasions call'd for.

WITH these they rang'd the Gulph for Corn, whether they sought it in the honest way of Trade, by Buying and Selling; or that, driven by necessity, they rov'd about the Seas, and made descents upon the Country, taking it where they could find it; that we cannot determine at this distance of Time: It is not improbable, but that the last was their Case; for what Merchandize could they have at that time to exchange? And for Money, it may be suppos'd, that flying, as they did, from the fury of the Barbarians, with their Wives and their Children, they could not carry any great stock with them.

HOWEVER it was, be it by Piracy and Roving, or by plain honest Buying and Selling, it is not material, but they soon became eminent for Sea Affairs; and in process of time venturing out into the *Levant*, and into the *Ægean* Sea, they found the way to *Italy*, and to the antient *Greece*, and among the rest to *Egypt*; from whence bringing back not plenty of Corn only, but the Manufactures of the *East Indies*, of which we have already said so often, that they had for some Ages been brought from *India* to *Sues*, either by Sea up the *Arabian* Gulph, or by Caravans through *Arabia* from *Cape Fartack* and *Bassora*, in the *Persian Gulph*, to *Aleppo* and *Scanderoon*: By this means the *Venetians* rais'd such a Reputation for Commerce and Navigation, and came into it so soon too, that they were for many Ages the Mart for the Silks, Drugs, and Spices of *India, Arabia, Æthiopia,* and *Persia*; and by it rais'd a general Correspondence and Commerce, with all the Nations of the World; nay, and they held it too, till within these 300 Years, as I shall shew it in its Place.

IN these thriving Circumstances we cannot wonder at the Opulence of their Merchants, the Magnificence of their City, and public Edifices, or the Power of their Navies; by which, or by their Money, they made themselves Masters of a large extended Dominion, as well in the *Levant*, as on the *Terra Firma*; for the extent of their Government was indeed exceeding great; and in a few Ages we find them Masters of all the great Islands of the *Levant*, particularly of *Cyprus*, of *Candia*, of *Scio*,[122] and *Negropont*,[123] some by Conquest, some by Purchase: They were Lords of all the Isles of the *Ægean Sea*, of all the antient *Peleponnesus*, now the *Morea*; they possess all the Coasts of *Attica, Achaia,* and *Epirus*; they commanded all the East-side of the Gulph, except *Ragusa*, and *Dulcigno*; they had the whole Coast of *Dalmatia, Istria, Croatia*, and *Friuli*, besides the Countries which they still possess in *Lombardy*, such as *Verona, Padua,* and many others.

ALL this, or the greatest part of it, was owing to the superiority of their naval Strength, which for many Ages, was the greatest, as it was certainly the first of its kind in the World; nor have they ever been overmatch'd in naval Strength by any of the Powers in that part of the World, till the *Turks* seeing a necessity of being able to give them a Check, set seriously to work to raise a Fleet superior to them: This was not till the fifteenth Century, when *Bajazet* the Second,[124] fell upon them, and took the *Morea* out of their Hands.

HOWEVER, in the several Wars they have had with the *Turks*, they have very often fought the *Turkish* Fleets, however powerful, and generally have been attended with Victory, especially in the great Battle of *Lepanto, Anno* 1457,[125] of which the World has heard so much; and where the *Turks* lost seventy Gallies, 30000 Men kill'd, and 20000 Christian Slaves set at Liberty.

THIS greatness of the *Venetian* State, as it was rais'd by Trade, and particularly by that Branch which I have mention'd, namely, the *East India* Trade, in *Silks* and *Spices*, so when the *Portuguese* found a nearer way to the *Indies*, by the Cape *de Bon Esperanza*, and thereby furnish'd *Europe* with *East India* Goods on cheaper terms, the *Venetian* Greatness felt the mortal Wound, and presently fell into a sensible decay, *Lisbon* encreasing in Wealth as *Venice* visibly declin'd.

III. HAVING thus given Instances of two sorts of People who first fell into Trade, and gave encouragement to Navigation, after the declining of the *Roman* Empire, I come now to two more Nations, who, tho' they did the same, and much about the same time, yet we cannot say it had any dependence upon, or was at all influenc'd by the rise or decay of the *Romans*; but they were rather brought into it by the consequence of things; such as the situation of their Country, the Genius and the Circumstances of their People, and above all the rest, by the necessities of Trade; and these are the *Teutonick Germans*, a sort of religious People at first, and who for Religion conquer'd the *Goths*, which inhabited the Southern Shores of the *Baltick* Seas, where they settled themselves for a long series of Ages; always encouraging the People they conquer'd to apply to Trade and Industry. Thus they grew rich and formidable in the World; and when afterwards they sunk as a Government, or Body Politic, 'tis evident, that it was not by a decay of their Commerce, for that continues still, but by the fate of the Times, and the clashing of the several neighbouring Interests which overthrew them; of which I may speak again in the next place.

I HAVE mention'd already, how those *Teutonicks* were now become the Inhabitants of *Prussia, Courland*, and *Pomerania*, from the City of *Straelsond* to that of *Dantzick, Koningsberg*, and up quite to *Riga, Revel*, and *Narva*, and were naturally brought to joyn together for Commerce: How their naval Stores grew from being a Supply for their own use, to be a Merchandize for other parts of the World. I need therefore only add, that this necessarily brought them to building of Ships, and that, such Ships as might be able to bear the shocks of those Seas, and carry the heavy Loadings of Iron, Copper, and other things of like heavy Carriage from one part to another, encouraging the World by their example to build large Ships like theirs, and to come in with them into a share of so gainful a Commerce; nor was this all, but these *Tuetonicks*, I say, came gradually to be the carryers of those Seas, by the considerable Correspondences which they held on, and the Figure they made; nay they became the most powerful as well as the richest People of all the Northern part of the World.

IN consequence of this Wealth; They possess a large and powerful Territory upon the *Vistula*; also several Provinces, as *Livonia, Courland*, the Ducal *Prussia*, with much of *Poland* and *Lithuania* in their Hands; and so powerful they were at Sea, that to whomsoever they lent their Ships, they were sure to conquer their Enemies.

I NEED not enter farther into their History: I am now talking of them as Merchants and Navigators; and as such, they were very considerable: As to their being *Teutonick Knights*,[126] or of such an Order; and how they came to obtain the Honours and Dignities they enjoy'd, and how to lose them again, that's matter of History, and no part of my present Undertaking; 'tis enough that they rose by Trade to be the chief Navigators, and the greatest Builders of Ships at that time in the World, and that they came into the last, by the consequence of the first; I mean their mighty Commerce brought them to the building larger and bigger Ships.

NOR did their extraordinary *Commerce* die, tho' they (as a natural effect) went off the Stage, when they ceas'd as an Order of Knights; their Military Order died, but their trading Power rose higher; for a Confederacy of Towns joyning together afterwards to carry on that Trade, preserv'd the trading Interest, and grew greater than ever they were before: These are those we now call *Hans-Towns*, of which the principal Places that retain that Name, and who are still a kind of Common-Wealth of Trade, are the Cities of

Hamburg,
Lubeck,
Bremen,
Dantzick, and
Koningsberg.

ALL these Towns are to this Day potent in Trade, and likewise in Shipping; and all except the last, have always, as occasion requires, Ships of War in their pay, for the protection of their Trade; and formerly have been able to fit out large Fleets, and to engage with other trading Countries in an open War; tho' now as they are too weak, so they have no occasion for that part; yet they fit out Men of War often times to convoy their Ships from the Pirates or Privateers of neighbouring Nations when they are at War with one another. But,

IV. THE fourth Article is that which I mention'd at first, (*viz.*) The *Dutch*; who, besides what I have said already, began very early to fit out Ships, and carry on a separate Business in these Northern Seas for the catching and curing of Fish.

WHAT height of Improvement this Fishing Trade has been to Navigation as well as to Trade, our present experience abundantly shows; since the *English* and *Dutch*, who have now the greatest share of the Fisheries of the Northern World, are become by consequence the most powerful Nations as well in Trade as Navigation.

ALL this while however Navigation was wrapt in its swadling Clouts; the Mathematicks, by which it is now wholly govern'd and regulated, had no concern with, or at all related to it; a very little share of Astronomy seem'd to inform the Sailors; as which was the *North Star*, which the *Ursa Major*; and these, and a few Constellations more, serv'd them so as to guide them to find Land again when they were out of their Knowledge: But all this while they had neither discover'd Guns to fight with, or Compass to sail by, but coasting, and creeping about within sight of Land was generally the utmost of their Art: How they advanc'd beyond this, and by what degrees they came to the perfection of Marine Knowledge, which is the present State of Navigation as a Science; and what infinite Advantages have been made of it in carrying Trade and Discovery up to the present height: These I shall begin to discourse of in the next Chapter.

CHAP. XVI.

How and by what degrees Trade (when set on foot in the World) spread and extended itself from one Nation to another; the Time, the Occasion, and the Consequence; and also of some New Discoveries made in the World of Trade during those Times.

THE periods of Time, in which the things mention'd in the last Chapter, shou'd be stated, and that we may preserve Chronology in our History as we go along, take in few Words thus.

THE *Roman* Empire may be said to be quite defunct when *Charlemain* King of *France* possest *Italy* and the *Roman* Emperor resided at *Constantinople*, having no power to prevent the ruin of it; and this was about the Year 800.

THE State of *Venice* was founded in the Year 453, but they did not arrive to their full Independence, and to act in Trade, and set up Liberty, till the Year 1120, or thereabouts.

THE *Teutonick Knights* began their Conquests and Progress *Anno* 1222,[127] or there abouts. Their Business was first reducing the Pagans (*Prussian* Inhabitants) by force to their Obedience, and planting the knowledge of the Christian Religion among them: Thus far their planting in *Prussia* was really *a New Discovery* to the World, at that Time: As for the *Poles*, the Country of the *Sarmatæ* had receiv'd the Gospel, and all *Poland* and *Lithuania*, as it was then prescrib'd and limited, were become Christians some Years before these Provinces of *Prussia, Courlandia, Samogitia*, and *Livonia*, heard any thing of it, or at least before they could be brought to entertain any sense of it themselves; all attempts to plant Religion among them, of which kind many it seems had been made, remain'd long ineffectual: A certain brutal Obstinacy particular to the People of those remote Countries prevail'd so far, as to make them reject all the offers that had been made for their Good, and embrace their Idols and Paganism with such an unmoveable Attachment, that nothing could at last remove them but Force and the Sword.

NAY, if we may give Credit to Historians, and those Men of Credit too, *Paganism* is not to this Day entirely rooted out of some of these very Provinces, but that the People in the mountainous part of *Samogitia*, and the *Polish Prussia*, the Desart of *Waldshont*, and even some part of *Courland*, worship the antient Idols and wooden Images of the Pagans, and keep them in their Houses: nor can they be brought to know any thing of the true God, or entertain any notion of it, or of the Christian Religion, or of Sabbath-Day, or Working-Day, nor will they hear of it, but with jest and ridicule.

BUT I am not writing of improvements in Religion, or giving a History of new Discoveries in matters of Worship, or the knowledge of God, but of improvement in Commerce and Manufactures, discoveries in Art, Science, Navigation, and Plantation; and therefore I return to my Subject from whence this is but a Digression.

THE *Teutonick Knights* were a set of Men form'd into a religious Order for the Conversion of the Barbarians, and spreading the Christian Religion in the World, in those good old Days, when Zeal ran before, and Devotion, tho', with *too much* Ignorance, rode behind. And when the Nations of *Europe* took up the Cross, as it was then call'd, that is, listed themselves at the beat of the Churches Drums to go and drive out the Heathen from God's Heritage, which it is evident he had forsaken, and given them leave to over-run, and to enclose God's Common, which he himself had laid open, as is apparent from the Circumstances.

THAT they ran before they were sent; that they neither had his help in the Undertaking, or his Blessing in the Success is evident from the confus'd manner of carrying it on as well as their being visibly abandon'd in the conclusion of it; so after some Ages spent in the Attempts, some Millions of Lives lost, and an infinite mass of Treasure, the *Saracens*, to whom God seem'd to give a more special Mission, prevail'd over them all; so their Eyes began to be open'd, and they thought fit to abandon an Enterprise which had neither human Prudence, or the ordinary success to encourage them in it.

UPON this melancholy giving up that Cause, what was to be done with the several sworn Societies of Devotees, who calling themselves Knights and Servants of Christ, had vowed their Lives and Prowess (as they call'd it) to fight for Religion, and in the Language of those devout Days, to *help the Lord against the Mighty*. The Knights *Templars*[128] and Knights *Hospitallers*;[129] for those two sorts were the chief, settled, some here, some there, as the Princes and Powers of *Europe* wou'd entertain them; till in time they became so insolent, so wicked, and so dangerous, that the Princes and Powers, who had been their Patrons, thought them unsufferable, and expel'd and rooted them out, in all Nations; the only remains of them in the World at this Day are the Knights of *Maltha*, of whom I have little or no occasion to speak in this Work.

BUT another Branch of them, wandering from *Syria*, and almost destroy'd by the *Turks* under the victorious *Saladine*, were it seems call'd Knights of *our Lady* of *Mount-Sion*. As these were instituted by *Conrade* the second Emperor of *Germany*, so they were at their first Institution restrain'd to be all of that *Nation* and were therefore call'd *Teutones*, that is to say *Germans*; and from this being call'd Knights of the *Teutones*, they soon came to be call'd *Teutonick Knights*.

AFTER they were thus, as I said, routed and driven out of the *Holy Land, Henry* Duke of *Massovia* in *Poland* invited them into his Country, and representing to them the condition of the Northern parts of his Kingdom; how all that Country, now call'd *Polish* and *Ducal Prussia, Courland, Livonia*, &c. was still in the Hands of the Pagans; and they offering themselves to the Work according to the Vows of their Order to propagate the Christian Faith, and to pull down Paganism, he gave them a grant of all the Lands they could conquer in those Countries; and thus they began the War, in which, having fought many bloody Battles with the Pagans, for they did not tamely give up their Country, any more than their Idolatry, they at last reduc'd all *Prussia, Courland*, and *Livonia*, planting themselves (as well as the Christian Religion) in their room.

HAVING thus gotten possession of the Country, they immediately began to build Cities, fortify Sea-ports, and strengthen their Possessions, finding the Country fertile and capable of Improvement. The Natives cleaving to Idolatry, were either extirpated by the War, or driven farther into the wild, waste Countries towards *Russia*, where Idolatry continued some Ages, and in the Northern parts of it, as among the *Samaoides* and *Petzoran*[130] it still remains: The *Knights* invited *Germans* of their own Nation to come and settle under them; and thus the Country became Populous; Religion flourish'd, with Religion came in Liberty of course, and with Liberty Commerce; thus in a few Ages this Country became the most flourishing place of Trade in the World; also the People were call'd *Teutones*, and their Government *Teutonick*.

HERE, the Order commanding and growing powerful, they wall'd and enlarg'd *Dantzick*, built *Elbing*, and *Mariemburgh, Koningsberg*, and *Mittan, Riga*, and *Narva*, extending their Conquests from the first to the last, and establish'd their People in the possession of all the Towns upon the *Baltic* Coast within that compass, as also upon the Banks of all the navigable Rivers.

As the Government of the *Teutonick Knights* was thus founded on Religion and Liberty, which two Heads as I have observ'd were the great encouragers of Industry and Application to Business; so the natural product of the Country led them as it were by the Hand into the several Species of Trade which they were to deal in; such as,

    I. AMBER, found first on the Shores of the *Baltic*, in these particular bounds, I mean, of *Prussia, Courland, Livonia*, &c. and perhaps (at that time) in no other part of the known World.

    II. HEMP and Flax, things infinitely useful for *Cordage* and *Canvas*, the two most necessary things requir'd for the furnishing of Ships, and for the helping on Commerce, were then very young in the World.

    III. PITCH, Tar, Rozin, all of them branches of those great and necessary things used in Shipping, or of the one general Article call'd Naval Stores, and without which the Marine Magazines could not be fully furnish'd.

    IV. WHETHER they had Iron in this Country then, or not, History is silent, but as we have good witness of its being long before that time found in *Sweden*, we need not doubt they found means to obtain it, in exchange for other Goods.

THUS began this great improvement of Trade in the *Baltic*: How this great Discovery, (as great and as usefull in its place as that of *America*, has been to *Europe* in our Days) is since encreas'd by several steps of improvement in Trade, to the magnitude which we find it in at this time, will be matter of farther History in its Course.

HOW also after the ruin of this *Teutonick* Government, and after the Order itself ceased, a trading Confederacy was fixed in that part of the World among the principal Cities, Sea-ports, and trading Towns of the *Baltic*, for the protection of their Commerce, and how other Cities, and in other parts of the World, came into that Confederacy of Trade, and were afterwards call'd the HANS, or the Union of the *Hans-Towns*, of which I have more to say hereafter; I say all this will come to be spoken of in course. I have only to add here, that this call of the *Teutonick* Knights into *Prussia* was in the thirteenth *Century*, that is to say about the Year 1232, and not before: So long was it before the Christian Religion reach'd the Shores of the *Baltic* Sea.

THIS settlement of the *Teutonicks* in *Prussia* has been the foundation of all the Commerce of the *Baltic*, which without any bluster, is at this time one of the most flourishing Articles of Trade in *Europe*; and especially attended with this particular and very valuable Circumstance, that 'tis carried on to the greatest extent with the least share of Money in Specie, of any Trade at this time known in the World.

ALL the Goods we send thither are such, as is most for our Interest to export: All the Goods we fetch from thence are such, as it is absolutely necessary for us to import.

WHEN I speak in the first Person Plural or Nationally, under the terms we, and us; I mean not, *England* or *Britain* only, but us the trading Nations of *Europe*, taken complexly. *Spain* is the only Nation that may be said to send Money in Specie into the *Baltic*; but then *Spain*, till very lately, sent no Ships thither, but contented themselves with buying all their Naval Stores at second Hand from the *Dutch*.

BUT setting *Spain* aside; *England*, or *Britain*, sends their Ships for the *Baltic* loaden with *Fish, Salt, Lead, Tin, Pewter, Sugars, Tobacco, East India* Goods, and *Woollen* and *Silk Manufactures*; being all of them, *except the East India Goods*, the growth of our own Land, or Seas, the Manufactures of our own People, or of our own Colonies, (which is all one); and all of which it is highly our own Interest to export, and which is, in one respect, clear gain to our Country.

ON the other Hand, what we fetch from thence is chiefly *Iron, Copper, Pitch, Tar, Hemp, Flax, Canvas, Linen Yarn, Pot Ashes,*[131] *Russia Leather, Hartshorn, Amber, Sturgeon, Oaken Plank, Fir, Timber, Deals,* &c., in a word, all sorts of Naval Stores, without which our Navigation, and consequently our Commerce, wou'd be dear, and be but ill carry'd on, if it could be really subsisted in the present extent of it.

THUS much for the Trade of the *Baltic*. The Trade of the *Dutch*, and of the *French*, to the *Baltic*, differs not at all from ours, but thus,

THE *Dutch* fetch a vast quantity of Corn from thence, and carry a vast quantity of Herrings thither, more than we do; also Spices, Train Oil,[132] and Whale Fin.

THE *French* fetch from thence just what we do, only they carry thither Wine and Brandy, Silks, Toys, Perfumes, Paper, and such things, instead of the Woollen Manufactures.

BUT take the Trade of all the three Nations. Here is neither Silver or Gold carry'd one way or other, but they trade infinitely to Advantage both ways without it, making good the deficiency or the balance of Trade upon one Nation, by Drafts upon another, and governing the whole by the Rates of the Exchange; which is generally negotiated upon *Hamburg*.

HAVING thus mention'd the State of *Venice*, and the trading part of the *Teutones*, or *Germans*, it follows to take notice, that about the same time the erecting the Woollen Manufacture in the *Netherlands*, and the Herring Fishing in the North came upon the Stage; and they were in their kind two great Discoveries as well as Improvements in the World: I shall speak of their beginnings with that brevity, which not our present Undertaking only, but the remote Circumstances of the things themselves (and which History gives not much light into) obliges me to.

THE coming of the Herrings annually, and in their exact Season into these Northern Seas, and not in like quantities into any other part of *Europe*, as it is surprizing and unaccountable, so it must be taken notice of here, not so much on its own particular account, as to introduce the needful Improvements in Commerce, which have been the Consequence.

THE coming of the Herrings may be a discovery in Nature, but it is not a discovery of a new Country, or Colony, and consequently does not come in within the Head of Discoveries, which I am speaking of; but the discovery of them as a foundation of Commerce merits to be spoken of here, and on all suitable Occasions.

THE first fishing for Herrings in *Europe* was certainly in *Scotland*; Nature spread the Field of Treasure before them, which, however ill they have improv'd it, has been like the *Indies*, at their Door.

ALL the *Scots* Histories mention their Fishery as well as that of the *English*, almost as far back as they mention any thing of *Britain* as a Nation; but they do not speak of it as a Trade or Merchandize. The first I meet with of this is, that the *Dutch* used to send Vessels to the Coast of *Scotland* to buy salted Fish {Herrings} of the *Scots* Fishermen, which they carry'd home to their own Country for the Subsistance of their own People; and this I think may be trac'd back to the Year 836, or thereabouts, the *Saxons* then inhabiting *Britain*, King *Alfred* then governing the Kingdom of *England*; and by this Trade the *Scots* were greatly enrich'd, the *Dutch* paying ready Money for their Fish.

BUT time and want of forecast brought the *Scots* to differ with their good Friends and Customers the *Dutch*, and putting some hardships upon the *Dutch* in buying, prompted the latter to reject the *Scots* Fish wholly, and bring Nets and Vessels of their own, and catch as well as cure the Fish upon the High-Seas themselves, to the utter ruin of the *Scots* Fishermen, and in short to the great impoverishing that whole Kingdom, and as much on the other Hand to the enriching of the *Dutch*.

UPON this new step, the *Dutch* finding the sweet of the Trade, and finding the quantity greater than they could consume at home, they began to look abroad, and carry the Herrings cur'd and pickled to other Countries, to see if they could dispose of them to advantage. And thus this great and flourishing Trade began.

IF in the process of this Work we shall trace all the other considerable branches of the Trade of *Europe* to their infancy and beginning, and bring them down from thence to their present condition, and their probable views of encrease, we flatter ourselves it will not be an unprofitable, much less an unpleasant Discovery, and be what is perfectly agreeable to our Title, and to the meaning of this Undertaking. This *beginning* of the Herring Fishery as a Commerce, was about the Year 1320, not long after the encrease of the *Teutonick* Settlements in the *Baltick*.

AND much about the same time was the first considerable greatness of the Woollen Manufacture also begun among the *Flemings*; so that the World seem'd all to launch out into Trade together. How they gradually went on we shall see in its place.

WHILE thus Navigation and foreign Negotiation began in the Bay of *Biscay*, and the Gulph of *Venice*, Exportation of Naval Stores in the *Baltick*, Fishing among the *Dutch*, and manufacturing of Wooll among the *Flemings*, we should enquire how stood things with *England, Portugal, France*, and *Spain*, which are now so considerable in Trade.

THE *Roman* Empire died, as I have said, about the latter end of the eighth Century, when the *French* or *Gallick* Kings took upon them the title of Kings of *Lombardy*.

AS the several Princes usurp'd the royalty of the Dominions which they possess'd, the *Roman* Power not being able to prevent them, *England* among the rest fell to the lot of the *Saxons*; who first driving the *Britains* out divided this Country into a Heptarchy of Kingdoms; of which in process of time the greater devour'd all the rest, as is usual in like Cases; So began the Empire of *Charlemaign*, who was King of *France*, King of *Italy*, and Emperor of *Germany*, all at once: But that is by the way.

AS the *Saxons* held the Monarchy of *England* with a short interruption from the *Danes*, till the coming of the *Normans*, we have good Reason in the Histories of those Times to observe, that *England* was all that while very little acquainted with Commerce; the Kings were taken up with continual Wars with one another, the common People being, as our antient Deeds and Charters of Lands express it, mere Slaves and Servants to the Lords. Vassalage and Villainage took up the whole mass of the People, and their whole employ seem'd to be to wait upon the Nobility, and be at their beck, as we call it, to laquy it after them to the War, which took up the *first*, or to till and plow the Land, and do the drudgery of the Husbandmen, and this took up the *last*; as for Trade little of it was known, and of Manufacture nothing at all.

YET in all this time, as far as History may be depended upon for any thing, we find the *English* Nation were mighty Gay; the Nobility gave Badges and Liveries to their Tenants and Vassals; and the Clothes they wore were very fine: Whence then did they come? 'Tis evident they came from the *Flemings*, who made all sorts of Cloth and Stuffs; that is to say all sorts that were then known, and with them they supply'd all the Countries round them; to wit, *France, Germany, Spain* and *England*, so great was the Manufacture in those Days; and this we are assur'd was so even long before that time we speak of, and even in the time when *Adrian* the *Roman* Emperor came into these parts of the World; for the Emperor *Adrian* visited in Person every part of the whole *Roman* Empire, as big as it then was; and it was then in the meridian of its Greatness.

THAT the *Flemings* then began to manufacture about the Year 260; tho' I have not positive proof, yet I see many Reasons to believe it, too long to enter upon here; and that they had their Wooll from *England* from the very beginning, I make no question; also it is very probable the Wooll of *England* was at that time an exceeding great Article; that is to say the quantity was very great for many Reasons, as I shall speak of hereafter: I say the *Flemings* in all probability began thus early to be Manufacturers; but it was some time before that Manufacture encreas'd to the degree which afterwards we find it arriv'd to.

BUT this leads me back to the Subject in Hand: Necessity introduc'd Manufacture; for the People had a necessity of Cloathing, and cloathing with Skins of Beasts began now to be left off, the *Roman* having shew'd the World a more polite way of dress; so Manufacture was the Daughter of Necessity, and Trade was the Child of Manufacture, as Navigation was the Offspring of Trade: The Genealogy is short and plain.

NECESSITY begat Manufacture, Manufacture begat Trade, and Trade begat Navigation. Let us then take the *Flemings* as they really were, the first Merchants in this part of the World, which Merchandizing began by their sending their Manufactures abroad to purchase with them necessary things for the carrying these very Manufactures On; This Merchandize necessarily imployed Ships and Sailors to fetch Wooll from *England*, Oil from *France*; also Fullers Earth, and many other Materials from *England*; and thus Trade grew up here.

IT may be wonder'd at, and indeed it is the admiration of the Age, and has been of the World, that *England*, who alone was the only Fountain, from whence the Wooll, which was, as I may call it, the Blood of the Manufacture, flowed, shou'd for so many Ages sit still, see their Neighbours grow rich, and powerful, and opulent, by their Industry and Application, and should supinely dream over it, sell the Wooll away to *Flanders*,[133] to *Antwerp*, and to *Sluice*,[134] which were in their turn the Staples for our Wooll, and see their own Women and Children idle and starving, the Poor out of Business, without Employment, flocking over to those Countries, and peopling their Towns, becoming Foreigners like themselves, and never so much as try whether they could not manufacture their own

Wooll, and not send abroad for Cloaths to wear, after those People had sent home to us for the Wooll to make them.

NOR is the ignorance and sottishness of this so wonderful, as that it should continue for so many Ages, and till within so little a while ago as the Reign of *Henry* VII. (*viz.*) in the fifteenth Century: That wise Prince was the first that look'd into the reasonableness of this Case: He saw the shameful Indolence of the Nation; and how his Neighbours grew rich by that very Manufacture, the want of which made his Subjects poor. He had liv'd abroad in Exile, and been in the Court of the Earl of *Flanders*: There he had seen the Opulence of the Court, the Industry of the People, and the Wealth of the Cities and Towns rais'd by that Industry; and in the mean time the solid Principles of the whole Trade to be found only in *England*, and no where else in the whole World; and this wrought in the Mind of that avaritious tho' politic Prince, and he presently saw when he came to the Crown, that it was his business no more to let this source of Wealth flow into the Coffers of his Neighbours, but to set his own People to Work to manufacture the Wooll at home; by which, (as he said to his Mother the Countess of *Richmond*) he shou'd not only keep the Money at home, but bring Money from all parts of the World to his own Country to buy the Manufacture here, as they did before in *Flanders*; and the event soon answer'd his End, and shewed the prudence of the Design, as we shall see in its place.

BUT to go back to this Affair of the prodigious extent of the Woollen Manufacture in *Flanders*; for People who have not read the Histories of their own Country, will hardly believe it possible, that *England* could ever be so blind, or be so ridden upon by their *Dutch* Neighbours, as to send their Wooll over to be manufactured abroad, or that if it was so, that they should continue in such a state of Indolence so long.

I SAY, lest it should be doubted, I shall only single out a *Flaming* Instance of it, in the time of one of the greatest and most glorious of our Kings, namely, *Edward* III. whose Reign is famous for its Splendor, and for the Honour of the *English* Nation; who erected the Order of the Garter; whose Court was all Magnificence, Feasting, and Tournament for the Knights, Balls and Masquerades for the Ladies; at one of which, a famous *English* Lady, in her dancing, dropt her Garter, and which the King saw and took up; from which ridiculous piece of Wantonness the Right Noble Order of the Garter took its Original or Device; yet even in this Kings Reign the Wooll of *England* was sold to the *Flemings*, to be manufactured abroad; for proof of which, to give one Instance for all the rest, and that I may not tire the Reader with so shameful and unpleasant a Story, I refer him to Mr. *Rymer's Fœdera*,[135] or *Acta Publica*, where he will find, that in the

Year 1338[136] the Laity granted to the King the one half of their Woolls throughout the whole Realm, for one Year, namely, for the next Summers Sheering; So that the King sent out his Collectors, who took the half of every Man's Wooll for the King; and of the Clergy the King took all their Wooll; so that of the Abbey of *Leicester* only the King took eighteen Sacks of Wooll, each Sack worth forty Pounds, that is to say in *Flanders*, where it seems it sold to very good profit; for in *England* the Wooll then sold for, or was rated at, but two Shillings per Stone, each Stone weighing fourteen Pounds Weight: This was in the same Year 1338.

NOW the same account says, that the King sent the Earls of *Northampton* and *Suffolk* into *Flanders*, with ten thousand Sacks of Wooll, who sold the same in *Brabant* for four hundred thousand Pounds Sterling, which is no less than forty Pounds per Pack, and which was an immense Sum in those Days.

FARTHER, we find in the next Reign to this, that the Parliament granted to the King a Tax of fifty Shillings upon every Sack of Wooll exported by our own People, and three Pounds per Sack for Wooll exported by Strangers.

THESE things are to my present purpose two ways; *First,* They shew eminently to what a great height of improvement the Manufacture was already brought in *Flanders*, and *Brabant*, and *Hainault*, that is to say all over the *Low-Countries*, in the thirteenth and fourteenth Century; and what a prodigious Consumption of Wooll was made in those Countries, that they could buy ten thousand Sacks of Wooll of the King at one Season, and pay such a prodigious price for it, at that time too.

AND *Secondly,* It is a record against us, to show the stupidity of this Nation, who to so late a time as this, and above 100 Years after it, continued to let their Wooll be carry'd out of the Land, and be manufactured abroad, to the infinite profit and encouragement of the *Flemings*; when our own People here sat begging and starving for want of Work; and for 100 Years together follow'd the Priests and Priest-ridden Princes, *ala Santa Terra*, to find Graves in the *Arabian* Desarts among the *Turks*, and all for want of Business at home.

KING *Henry* VII. a Prince of superior Genius for matters of Improvement to all that went before him, was the first that saw the folly of all this, and that open'd the Nations Eyes to see into it also: And this he did first, by inviting over several *Flemings*, who were Master Manufacturers, as we now call them, and who were thorowly skill'd in the managing, ordering, and directing the Wooll, to prepare it for working; These began with teaching our Poor in the first place to *Spin*; upon which it soon appear'd that we could both make the Yarn as good, and much cheaper than the

Flemings; so that in a little time, instead of Wooll, the *Flemings* came over hither, and bought Yarn ready Spun, just as we buy Yarn now from *Ireland*; for the Case in *Flanders* was then, just as the Case of *England* is now, the poor by a flush of Trade and constant Work were grown rich and saucy; they wou'd work indeed when they pleas'd, but they wou'd have their own price, and work how, and when, and how much they pleas'd, just as ours do at this Day; For,

The Poor of every Nation are the same.[137]

WHEREAS our Poor, that is to say the *English* Poor, were really indigent, very poor; poor and needy, glad to get any thing, and willing to do a great deal of Work for a little Money; so that when they began to fall into the Spinning, they not only did it well and handily, so as very soon to out-do their Teachers, but they wrought so cheap, and at so very low a price, that for some Years afterwards the quantity of Wooll that went abroad, was much diminish'd, and the *English* Yarn grew a valuable Merchandize in *Flanders*, and much more esteem'd than their own; at the same time the Dealers in it found the benefit by buying it so cheap in *England*; so that the Yarn Buyers and Wooll Combers in *England* grew rich, as it were on a suddain.

IN the mean time, if we may believe Tradition and Report, the *Flemings* had Wit little enough (for Nations sometimes are blind as well as Men) to take Umbrage at the great Importation of Yarn from *England*, and to make their advantage, by laying a Tax upon it, or at least to threaten the Prohibiting of it.

BUT as one Improvement generally brings on another, the King finding his People began to be acquainted with the Wooll Trade, and that the Manufacture began here and there to take footing in *England*, and being fully satisfied, that if the *Flemings* had not Wooll from *England* they could have it no where else; he resolv'd to bring them to be glad to buy their Yarn here, and give a good price for it too; and at once, strook that fatal blow that ruin'd the *Flemings* and all their Commerce, as to the Wooll itself; for he got an Act pass'd in his Parliament[138] to prohibit carrying any more Wooll out of *England*.

THIS was a mortal blow to the *Flemings*, and made such a combustion among them, that had they been able they wou'd have declar'd War against King *Henry*, and have come over and fetch'd the Wooll away by force; but he was above that, he neither fear'd them, or the whole World, as to Invasion; so they were oblig'd to be contented, and to rumage the whole World for Wooll to carry on their Business. Now tho' they had some Wooll out of *Normandy*, some from *Spain*, some from *Scotland*, and some from

161

Ireland; yet none, except the last, came up to the *English* for goodness; so that they were glad to take the *English* Yarn, which they had forbidden before, and it was but a little while that they had the liberty of the Yarn too, tho' I do not find it prohibited in King *Henry's* time neither; for tho' our People began to make several sorts of Woollen Manufactures in that Prince's Time, yet they were not immediately in a condition to work up all the Wooll of the growth of the whole Nation, and so supply themselves and other Counties too, as has been the Case since: But it was a great Improvement, and a great stroke to the support of the People, that they were able to spin it into Yarn; they did perhaps manufacture a great deal of it, and especially so much as was sufficient for the supply of their own Country, and exported abroad such Yarn only as they could not work up.

THE first Countries in *England*, who fell into the Clothing, we find to be the West-Riding of *Yorkshire*, and the Eastern parts of *Lancashire*; that is to say the great Towns of *Leeds, Wakefield*, and *Hallifax*, in the first; and *Rochdale* and *Manchester* in the last; in all the last of which the Manufacture still remains.

THEN the Western Counties of *England*, such as *Gloucester*, and *Wilts*, and *Somerset*, where also it still remains, and particularly *Berkshire*.

BUT the Woollen Manufacture never came up to its full Maturity in *England* till the time of Queen *Elizabeth*; when by the Persecution of the Duke of *Alva* in the *Netherlands*, the *Flemings* flying from the cruelty of the *Spaniards*, settled here in *England*; as at *Norwich*, at *Ipswich*, at *Colchester*, at *Canterbury*, at *Exeter*, and in several other places, and brought over with themselves the complete knowledge of the Woollen Manufactures, and People also to work them; by which the *English*, who are justly fam'd for improving Arts rather than inventing, fell into those Manufactures, and having the best of the Wooll at their Hands, soon out-wrought the *Flemings* in every particular. Thus,

THE Bays were set up at *Colchester*.

THE Says at *Sudbury*.

THE blue Cloths at *Ipswich*.

THE Womens Stuffs, and Knitting of Stockings, at *Norwich*.

THE Serges at *Exeter* and *Taunton*.

MANY of the *Dutch* Families who brought over those Arts, and settled in these Places, have left their Names and Posterities behind them, whose Families are flourishing even in the same Places to this Day; as the *De Vink's* at *Norwich*, the *Rebow's* at *Colchester*, the *Papilon's* and *Lethulier's* at *Canterbury*, and many others, who are of known *Flemish* and *Walloon* Extraction.

NAY, the Churches of Protestants erected by them, and which Queen *Elizab.* establish'd on their account, remain to this Day, as a *Dutch* Church at *Norwich*, and a *Dutch* Church at *Colchester*, and a *Walloon* Church at *Canterbury*; all which remain there to this time.

NOR is this all, but the Manufacture of Bays at *Colchester* was in the same Reign settled by Authority, and the Manufacturers encorporated, and still retain their Privileges, and are vulgarly call'd the *Dutch Bay-Hall*; for the Bays, now call'd *Colchester* Bays, were then call'd *Dutch* Bays, that is to say, being made by *Dutchmen*, or *Flemings*, who settled there from *Antwerp*.

I THOUGHT it was best to run this part thus forward to its meridian height, tho' it brings me down farther into our own times than by the course of the other Branches I am upon; that the Reader may take it all into his Knowledge together. But Navigation was not able to keep pace, for tho' by practice and improvement the Builders of Ships were even now (suppose us speaking of the Times from the eleventh to the thirteenth Century) come to some improvement; yet we find King *Edward* III. and the *French* fighting at Sea with 500 Sail of Ships on a side: And 'tis evident they had not yet the knowledge of the Loadstone to work Mathematically, or of Guns and Powder to fight Mathematically, but fought in those Ships, such as they were, by running foul of one another, and grappling together, and then come to Sword and Spears, Bows and Arrows, as on Shore: But we shall see them wiser in a few Years.

ALL this while the *East India* Trade for Spices and Callicoes, and the *Persian* Trade, for raw Silks, and wrought Silks, was carry'd on by the *Venetians*; they imported the first by the *Red Sea*, and brought them from thence by Land to *Alexandria*, and then by Sea to *Venice*, and they fetcht the raw Silk by Land from *Ispahan* to *Aleppo*, and there the *Venetian* Merchants took them, and carrying them to *Smyrna* and *Scandaroon* (just as we do now) sold them again to the *Lombards*; for much about this time we find the *Milanese*, and after them the *French*, deeply embark'd in the Silk Manufacture, which so vastly has enrich'd them; and of which I shall speak more fully in its place.

LET us now go back and enquire a little into the growth and progress of Learning and Science in the same Years, that one may go Hand in Hand with the other.

CHAP. XVII.

Of the Progress of Learning *after the downfall of the* Roman *Empire.*

IT must be acknowledged that Learning and Philosophy flourish'd in the times of the *Roman* and *Grecian* Empires; History is full of it, the Works of *Plutarch, Xenophon, Homer,* and others, among the *Greeks,* and of *Virgil, Horace, Lucan, Juvenal, Cicero, Seneca,* and several others, among the *Latines,* are standing Monuments of the soundness of their Knowledge, the beauty of their Language, their Oratory, Poetry, and other Excellencies in those polite Times.

WHEN the *Roman* Empire became Christian, their Learning exerted itself another way: The primitive Christian Bishops apply'd themselves to religious Studies. The Philosophy of the Antients consisted chiefly in Moral Precepts and Laws of Virtue, wise Sentences, and Orations in praise of their Heroes, and sometimes of their Gods: The Wisdom of *Athens* consisted in the grave old Men reading Lectures of good Manners, and good Morals; and *Seneca,* that learned and really wise *Roman,* is pictur'd to us, when bleeding to Death in a warm Bath, dictating his Morals to his Scholars. To be bred thus at the Feet of *Gamaliel*[139] was the utmost of what they call'd polite and liberal Education; for as to Languages they made no use of them. When *Strabo* and *Plutarch*[140] wrote, the World spoke *Greek;* to write in *Greek* at that time was to write to all Mankind. When *Seneca* wrote, and *Cicero* pleaded, *Latin* was the universal Character; all the *Roman* World, which in short was it, all the known World spoke then, and as a late Poem[141] well expresses it, they spoke and wrote in their Mother Tongue.

YET the *Romans* excell'd in every thing which was then call'd Learning; their Orators spoke excellently well, and charm'd the Souls of those they spoke to: *Ciceronian Latin* is a proverbial Expression to this Day, intimating how nobly *Cicero* spoke, and that the *Latin* Tongue was in its utmost perfection in his time, and he a compleat Master of it.

ALL this was under the *Græcian* and *Roman* Governments when really Pagan: But was Learning lost by the introduction of Religion? No, just the contrary; *Origen* taught Philosophy in the public School at *Antioch*; and *Cyprian* read Divinity and Philosophy also to his Pupils at *Carthage*: They not only abounded in Wisdom and Piety, but in Knowledge and Learning: After those Times, upon the declining of the *Roman* Empire, when Learning began to decay, the *Latin* Tongue was corrupted and lost, and that which once all the World spoke was sunk out of the World, only as it was to be found in the Writings of the Antients; hence it became necessary, that all those that would read the Writings of the Fathers, must be able to speak the *Latin* Tongue in its Purity.

THIS sent all the young Students to School; for the *Latin* was no where found with purity and clearness, but in the Books written by the Antients, such as those we now call the Classicks. Thus it was likewise with the *Jews*, as to the *Hebrew*; for the Children of *Israel*, or of *Judah* rather, being seventy Years in Captivity in *Babylon*, they forgot their Country so much, that they forgot their original *Hebrew*, and all spoke the *Chaldee*, [142] the Speech of the *Babylonians*, and so afterwards the *Greek*; the antient *Hebrew* was only to be found in the *Talmud*, and in the Writings of their *Rabbies*, whence it was call'd *Rabbinical Hebrew*; and those who afterwards desir'd to speak or read *Hebrew*, were sent to the Schools of their Doctors and Rabbies to learn it.

HENCE the knowledge of the Tongues, as of the *Latin, Greek*, and *Hebrew*, is call'd Learning, and he that understands, or is Master of those Tongues is call'd a Man of Learning; and in our Days if a Man understands all the other Languages spoken in *Europe*; if he is Master of Science, and understands Astronomy, Geography, and all the other Branches of the Mathematicks; if he had read all the Civil, or Ecclesiastic, Sacred, or Prophane History, were an exquisite Engineer, or a compleat Navigator; yet if he has not the *Greek* and *Latin*, he is no Scholar; which by the way is a gross Error in the common Judgment. [143]

HAVING thus mention'd the Learning of those Times, I come next to examine the Theory of Philosophy in all that time receiv'd in the World, all the knowledge of the motions of the heavenly Bodies, their Magnitude, Distances, Influences, begun among the *Chaldeans* and *Persians*, carry'd on and encreased among the Eastern *Arabians*, and consummate and compleat among the South; from whence it launch'd out into *Egypt*, and thence into all parts of the then known World; I say *Egypt* was the center of all Knowledge and Learning of that kind for many Ages, and the first System of Astronomy was read in their Schools, which was according to *Ptolemey*, and therefore call'd the *Ptolemaick* System.

IN the infant state of the World this was a great point, and Men thought themselves great proficients in Learning that could explain things by the Doctrine of *Ptolemey*; when all on a sudden, from the remotest Angle of *Europe*, a Thousand or fifteen Hundred Miles from the City of *Rome*, up starts an obscure *Polander, Nicholas Copernicus* by name, a mean Priest in the *Romist* Church; and he examining the *former System*, reflects presently that a better way, and nigher by far, to the true System was known to them, and might be reduced into practice.

COPERNICUS was accordingly, and at the first appearance of his Scheme, accepted and receiv'd, and made his Knowledge extensive to the whole World.

THIS *Copernicus* studied the thing effectually, and brought it to this perfection; that he rejected the whole *Ptolemaic System*, gave a new Scheme of the heavenly Bodies, their Motions and Distances, and gave such Demonstrations of what he said, and especially so easily solv'd several Difficulties and Inconsistencies, which were at least not solvable by the old System, that, in a word, the whole World are now come with him to reject the old *Ptolemaic System* and embrace the *New Philosophy*.

IT was indeed at first ridiculed and laugh'd at; Men could not so soon come off from the notion of the rising and setting of the Sun, which had been almost 4000 Years the received Opinion of the whole Earth, nay, was even read in the style of the Scripture; nor could they entertain any thought of the Earth rolling on upon the Poles of the Ecliptic, with the surprizing velocity of 21000 Miles[144] in twenty four Hours; and yet we who live upon the Surface of it be no way sensible of its moving, much less disturb'd with it; I say, it was look'd upon as absurd; and we find this homely Distich upon record against it;

> Copernicus *this new wild Fiction found*,
> *To make the Sun stand still, and the World go round.*[145]

BUT however they receiv'd it, the force of its Reasoning prevail'd, and in a few Ages the whole World came into it; thus the *Ptolemaic System* was rejected as impracticable and absurd; and this has been the receiv'd Philosophy ever since.

THIS *Copernicus* was born in the City of *Thorn* in the *Polish Prussia*, a City on the *Vistula*, and the first that has a Bridge over it from the Sea to that place; he was a Divine, and a Physician, as well as a Philosopher; for he was a Canon of the Cathedral Church at *Warmia* in *Prussia*; but principally delighted with the study of the heavenly Bodies, he travel'd to *Italy*, and at *Rome* set up his new Philosophy, and taught it in a kind of Mathematic Accademy, where he soon got many Followers: He was born in the Year

1473; his Hypothesis was said to be first fram'd by an antient *Greek* Astronomer *Aristarchus*;[146] and that *Copernicus* only reviv'd it; but it is evident if he did so, he much improv'd it also, and therefore it deservedly bears his Name: His Doctrine of the heavenly Bodies is as follows.

COPERNICUS makes the Sun the center of the Universe, and holds 'tis immoveable. *Mercury*, the next Planet to the Sun, compleats its Circle about it in three Months. *Venus* runs her Circle, which environs that of *Mercury*, in seven Months and a half; the Earth hers in a Circle that comprehends that of *Venus*, in a Year, but has another motion upon or round its own Axis, which is diurnal of twenty four Hours, and is that by which we explain the succession of Days and Nights. The *Moon* rolls about the Earth, and compleats hers in twenty seven Days, or thereabouts. *Mars* in a fourth Circle comes round that of the Earth, and has the Sun for the Center, the time of its Revolution being about two Years. *Jupiter* in about twelve Years. *Saturn*, the highest of all the Planets, makes its turn about the Sun in thirty Years, or thereabouts. Above *Saturn Copernicus* places the Starry Heaven, which is motionless in his Opinion. [To resume his Sentiments of the rest] the Sun is immoveable, and in the Center of the World. *Mercury, Venus*, the *Earth, Mars, Jupiter*, and *Saturn*, move in their six Circles round the Sun: But the Earth has another Motion on its own Axis, and the Moon makes its circuit round the Earth. By this System we avoid the difficulty of explaining and giving Reasons for the daily motion of the Sun in an immense space, and with an unconceivable rapidity. But tho' *Copernicus* places the Sun in the center of the World, and allows it no motion, so as not to change one place for another; yet his Followers give it a circular Motion round its Axis, and say this Revolution is compleated in twenty seven Days:[147] This they do to explain the appearances of Stains or Spots that have been discovered by Telescopes or Perspective-Glasses in its Body, but are observed to change their Situation in twenty seven Days. As for the Earth *Copernicus* gives it three Motions: *The first*, That it compleats in a Day; *The second*, The Yearly; And *the third*,[148] Which always keeps the Earth's Axis in the same Position. The *Diurnal* Revolution is that which the Earth makes in twenty four Hours upon its own Axis; so that the part that is towards the Sun is always enlighten'd, whilst the other lies dark. The Annual is, that the Earth runs through the Signs of the *Zodiack*, when between *Venus* and *Mars* it take its round about the Sun in a Years time: The third serves to give Reason for the difference of Seasons, and the inequality of Days in different Climates.

I⊤ is true that several Learned Men had made Essays of this kind; the *Primum Mobile*[149] of *Ptolemy* confounded them, it was impossible to conceive regularly of them, or to bring any Demonstrations of the Fact that were consistent; they were forced to resolve all difficulties of things into

Omnipotence. Telescopes, and more perfect Glasses than had been then found, discover'd things formerly unknown; as particularly the motion of the Sun round its own Axis in twenty seven Days, by seeing the Spots and Marks discover'd in the Body of the Sun change their situation, and come into the same place every twenty seventh Day; discovering the Satellites or Moons about the Planets, and their Revolutions and Eclipses; the Winds, Tides, and several other Phænomenas, of which the Antients had little or no knowledge, or at least could not solve the Difficulties that arose from them.

THIS has been the ground plat of vast Improvement in Science, which we may take occasion to mention hereafter in this History, and particularly of the famous *Tycho Brahe*,[150] the King of *Denmark*'s Astronomer Royal, who form'd a third System different from both these; But Death taking him off before he had brought it to perfection, the World, tho' they honour him as a great Man, yet have not receiv'd his System, or improv'd upon it. But *Copernicus* has employ'd all the Learned Men for now 200 Years to go on improving upon his System, and these having remov'd all possible Objections that were then, or have since been rais'd, this is now the receiv'd Philosophy, upon the foot of which, all the fine Experiments of the present and last age have been rais'd.

FROM hence I must pass to another perfectly new Invention or Improvement, which the World owes to the same Northern Climate, tho' not the same Country as the other; namely, the Art of Printing.[151] The other indeed is an exalted Science, but this may bear as just a Preheminence in Arts, and among the modern Improvements of Art, as that does in Science: This was the Invention of one *Koster*[152] at *Harlem*, where certainly the first Experiment that was in the World, was made. It is true that *Guttemburgh*[153] and *Faustus*, both of them Servants to this *Koster* the first Inventor, went from him, and spread the Invention, the one to the City of *Ments*[154] in *Germany*, and the other to *Paris*; and there practising it as their own, gain'd for some time the name of being the first Inventors, and *Ments* contends the point with *Harlem* to this Day; as for *Faustus*[155] he own'd himself afterwards not to be the Inventor; to which there hangs a Tale which few People perhaps have heard, and therefore may be acceptable to the Reader, since so much noise has been made of this surprizing Fellow in the World.

ALL Books being before only Manuscripts on Rolls of Parchments, Vellum, &c. and consequently both scarce and dear, and *Faustus* having printed a large Impression of the Psalter, with some Books of the New Testament, goes away with them to *Paris*, to sell them there as *Manuscripts*; and accordingly sold several of them, and had an extraordinary price for them as such: But some Learned Men of the Faculty, at *Paris* viewing these

Psalters with some admiration, were surpriz'd to observe that there was an unaccountable uniformity in the Performance.

THEY observ'd that every Line was exactly of the same length, every Word stood exactly in the same place; if any Letter was made after a particular manner, the same Letter in the same Leaf and Page in all the Books was exactly perform'd in the same manner; nay, if there was a blot, or a fault, or a mistake, it was every where the same; and this brought them to question at first soberly with *Faustus* about it; he alledg'd it was the effect of the exactness and dexterity of his Writers, imitating every thing exactly; but they were far from being satisfied with this Answer of his, and told him it was impossible.

AT length *Faustus* defending himself but indifferently, they concluded *Faustus* had practis'd some Magic Art to perform this thing in so wonderful a manner, and then began a Process of Witchcraft against him, alledging, that he dealt with the *Devil*, resolving to put him to Death; *Faustus* defended himself a long time, and a great noise it made in the World; the Books were seiz'd, and People came far and near to see Books written by a Conjurer, and by the help of the *Devil*, especially God's Word too.

IN a word, they carry'd it so that they would certainly have hang'd poor *Faustus* for a Necromancer and a Witch; so he was forced to confess how it was, and in short to show them his Art, and how to perform it. This was the whole Story of the famous Dr. *Faustus*, of which so many Books and Ballads, Tales and Harlequins have been made, and such merry doings been seen here within these two Years[156] among us.

THIS is the beginning of the use of Letters or Types for impressing or stamping the Words to be written in a Book or Roll, and which with great ease and facility is rendered practicable to the Printer.

WITH the invention of Printing came on the invention of Paper also. It had been used before, but as it was but a few Years it met with great encouragment upon the spreading of the Art of Printing: It began at *Basil* on the Frontiers of *Switzerland*, was invented there, or brought thither by two *Greeks*,[157] and was there made first in great plenty, till at last they suffer'd other Towns to see them do it also; and so the Manufacture went from them to other places in *Germany*, and so by degrees to *Genoa* in *Italy*, to *France*, and to *Holland*, and is now made in all the Nations of *Europe*, and in *Asia* also.

IT is to be observ'd, that at the same time that these things were doing, the World seem'd to rouze up to a state of Industry and Application, from a state of the greatest Indolence and Ignorance.

THE truth is, till now the Industry of the World had nothing to work upon; the lovers of Art had nothing but mere Nature to teach them;

Copernicus himself knew nothing of the true Distances and Magnitudes of the Planets, which by the help of our Telescopes (an Invention of so truly strange a nature) we are since arriv'd to: The Diameter of the Sun, the Ring and Satellites about *Saturn*, the whole Solar System, were all out of his reach; in short, tho' he made a right guess, and considering the Circumstances it was a wonderful guess too; yet all was in the dark, and the demonstrations of things are generally Modern.

EUCLID and his Elements[158] are all modern; *Archimedes* was dead, and Mathematic knowledge seem'd to have dyed with him.

BUT still the World was fir'd with a desire of knowing; Astronomy was a delightful Study. *Copernicus* no sooner set up his Astronomical Lectures at *Rome*, but all the *Virtuosi* of that Age flockt to him, till (if you will believe some People) he taught them to be Wiser than himself, and they improv'd upon his Schemes in many valuable particulars, and from which we see his Schemes are much improv'd; nor was it only this Knowledge which Men began to look into, but in the next Ages all the noble Inventions in Art, which have justly been work'd upon since that, and so much improv'd, have started into the World; such as Geography, Arithmetic, Improvements of which the Branches are full of Variety, and the mathematical Addendus, of which they are infinite.

THUS to look back a little between the Years 1400 and 1600 almost all the great and most illustrious Improvements in the sublimest parts of Knowledge, have been found out, or at least extended in these parts of the World. We are told indeed, that almost all our nicest Discoveries were found out, and in practice, in *China* before they were discover'd here: This I believe nothing of, and give less credit to what they talk of having several Arts which we have not. It is true their Japanning, or Lacquer, cannot be imitated, nor their China Ware, but it is want of the Materials, not want of the Skill or Knowledge how to perform the Operation; or 'tis want of Climate for the sudden drying and hardning their Lacquer, and so of other things.

As Printing was invented by *Koster* in 1428, or 1430,[159] Rag Paper in 1452, so Graving,[160] and Printing by the Rolling Press was brought on in 1460, and Etching a few Years after in like manner: By the like degrees Gunpowder[161] was the Invention of the same Century, and Guns follow'd it close at the Heels; it was impossible that Powder could be known, and the force of it, and Nature not direct Men to fight with it.

AND here it is worth Observation; Why did not Providence permit the first Invention of Powder to be so appropriated to one particular Prince or Nation, that they might have conceal'd the Art of making it, or the Ingredients and Materials used in the making, or the corning[162] and operation of it, or the Apparatus necessary for the purpose, so that by this means that Prince might have conquer'd all the rest of the World; for 'tis evident nothing could have stood against it, or have withstood the Army that shou'd have had the use of it exclusive of their Enemy; but either we are entirely out in in the History of it, or the discovery was immediately made so public, and improv'd in so many hands, that it appear'd in the Field in several places almost at the same time; no particular Prince or Power having any extraordinary advantage by it, at least not that I find recorded.

I MAKE no doubt, but that, when it came abroad in the World, and that it was thus particularly applicable to the use of the War, all the neighbouring Powers took care to be acquainted with the Secret, and to be furnish'd with the Species; for we do not find that it was to be had in any one particular place more than another, but that it was (as it is now) made every where, the Composition being presently known, and the Materials easy to be procur'd: So true is it, that the Ingredients for a public Mischief were easy to be had, and it seems the Monk, who made the Discovery,[163] was not at all cautious in keeping the Secret, but it took Wind presently.

NOR is it certain whether great Cannon, or smaller Pieces, were the first that were invented; if I may speak my Thoughts, it was the former, seeing we find that the smallest Gun used in fight for some time was the Harquebuss, and at first a larger sort, which they call'd Harquebuss *au croc*, because it stood upon an Iron Frame call'd a *Croc*, and fasten'd with a kind of Swivel, or Scrue, to the said Frame, being itself heavy and unwieldy, and too big for one Man to manage.

AFTER this they were made smaller, but yet too heavy for Soldiers to carry and to march with, and were carry'd on Horse-back, and the Harquebusiers, like Dragoons, when they came to fight, laid them cross the Saddle, and so fir'd them at the Enemy, standing themselves on foot by: After this they carryed Rests for them, and that continued a long time, nay, it is within the Memory of Man, that all the Musqueteers in the Armies had Rests for their Musquets, and all the Field Exercise and Words of Command were accordingly. Whether the Musquets they us'd at that time were larger and heavyer than those now in use, I know not, but I believe they were not much larger, if any thing, but it was pretended the Soldiers took the surer aim.

UPON all this, I am of opinion that the first use of Gunpowder, that is to say in the Field, was in the Artillery, and the Reason which at least guides me to this, is, that tho' they might have the use of the Gun, yet they had not of the Lock to fire it with; and it is but a very few Years (and since the Writer of this can remember) that the Firelock[164] was not known; or if it was, it was but rarely us'd, but all the Soldiers were encumber'd with

Match,[165] which had innumerable leisurly slow Inconveniences, attending it, as particularly blowing the Match, cocking the Match, trying the length, then opening the Snaphaunce, as the *Dutch* call'd it, much more properly call'd now the Pan, and besides this the Soldiers had an intollerable difficulty to keep their Match lighted, and sometimes in short after Rains, or wet misty Nights, it has been impossible the Armies cou'd engage, tho' resolv'd before to come to a Battle; and, if one Side had been more careful to keep their Matches lighted, and came on, knowing themselves in good Condition, that way, the other Side have been oblig'd to retreat and shun the Fight.

NAY, so general was the use of what we call'd Match-locks to the Musquets, that since we very well remember, and very modern in History, we find, that when honourable Conditions were given to a Garrison, who capitulated to march out in a soldierly Condition, it was always thus express'd, (*viz.*) Drums beating, Colours flying, Match lighted, Bullet in the Mouth, &c. But now the Firelock, which is the most modern Invention of all, is so universal, that instead of those Words in Capitulations, it is now only mention'd, that the Men shall have so many Charges of Powder and Ball.

I AM told by some, that the Improvements in the Art of War are such, and so considerable, that no other Improvement can come up to them; also that these Improvements ought to take a Place in the Discourse I am upon, and I grant it; but then I think the proper *Ephocha* to begin our Discourse upon warlike Improvements, shou'd begin at the Introduction of Guns and Gunpowder; for as to what was before, it is not worth notice. The *Romans* embattling in Lines and deep Bodies, the *Macedonian* Phalanx, and other the antient Methods of drawing up Armies, as also the *English* ranging their Archers and long Bows, all these wou'd require long Descriptions, but little to our Instruction: But Powder and Ball at once put a new Face, not upon the Armies only, but upon the very War; Fire and Noise were added to the Terrors of the Field, things which the Soldier had never been acquainted with before.

FIGHTING was now become a strange new Thing; When Battles were fought and Armies engag'd, they might be heard at the distance of many Miles; whereas before that, the loudest Cries and Shouts of the Troops reach'd but a small way off; But there was something stranger yet; before this Men march'd up to Battle cas'd in Steel, and made up in Greaves and Helmets, that nothing could be seen but the burnish'd Iron; nor could you come at the the Man when you were within an Inch of his Face; but now, they began to quit their retreat behind their Iron Walls, and shew the true Courage and Gallantry of a Soldier; and tho' the Bullet was much more fatal, and the Gun had much more terror in it than the Arrow, or the Bow, yet dispising Danger and scorning Armour, the Soldier now looks Death in the Face, and boldly rushes on, even in the Mouth of the Cannon and Musquet.

IT is much disputed in the World, whether Fighting is more or less Terrible, and Battles more or less Bloody, since the discovery of Powder and the use of Guns than before; some think Men rushing forward into Danger, and pushing up to the Teeth of their Enemy, they bring Things to a shorter issue now than before; formerly the Infantry endur'd Showers of Arrows for many Hours sometimes, before they could come to Swords points with their Enemies, so that they often came up wounded and out of Breath to the Fight, and left thousands of their own Side behind them dead or disabled, before the Battle could be said to be join'd; whereas now, with Fire and Thunder the Spirits of Men are immediately agitated into Fury, and they run on like enrag'd Lions, so that one Side or other must fly, or be cut in pieces very quickly. But this is not my business to enquire here, I may have occasion to speak of it again when I come to discourse of the several Improvements which have since been made subsequent to, and occasion'd by this fatal Invention; Such as,

I. THE modern Improvements of Fortifications for Encampments of Armies, and the strengthening of Towns and Fortresses, quite differing from such as were known before.

II. THE manner of approachings and attacks in Seiges and Stormings, with the numberless Improvements of the Engines of Battery, also Sapings and Counterminings, all different both in attacking and defending of strong Towns, from what were of use before.

III. THE *Tormentarij*,[166] or Artillery of several kinds, besides the mere Invention of Cannon; such as *Mortars, Patereroes, Hawitzers, Chambers, Bombs, Carkasses, Stinkpots, Hand Grenades, cum multis alijs*,[167] all perfectly new; and not possible to be otherwise.

THESE Things leading us gradually to more modern Improvements, we must adjourn them for a while, in order to bring Things more Antient up to an even Line of Time with them; and particularly to speak of the Discovery of unknown Countries, as well for Conquest as for Commerce; for it is to be observ'd, that in this same Century the knowledge of Navigation encreasing, Mens Minds were fir'd with the desire of knowing as well unknown Countries as unknown Arts; and we find the *Portuguese* and the *Genoese* pushing into new and undiscover'd Parts of the World, and after them the *Spaniards* and the *Dutch*, and as it were last of all, and out of time, the *English* and *French*; whose useful Discoveries however, have by their extraordinary Application been successfully encreas'd to a Magnitude in some degrees equal, if not superior to them all, as we shall fully make out in its place.

THE knowledge of the Magnet or Loadstone, and in Consequence of it, the Compass were among the Improvements of the fifteenth Century, the History of them I reserve for its proper place; the use I make of it here, and for which I mention it, is this, namely, that by this great and happy Discovery Mankind was infinitely encreas'd in Knowledge, and which was as much as all the rest, they were inspir'd with a desire after knowing more.

TILL then, *like* Solomon's *Fool,*[168] they seem'd to have no delight in understanding; that they seem'd to know but little but to be satisfied in their state of Ignorance, and not desire or at least not to search after an encrease of Knowledge; perhaps they believ'd, or at least fancy'd they could know no more than they did.

BUT now having open'd a Door into the vast Ocean of Mathematical knowledge, it fir'd their Souls with a happy desire of of knowing more; I say fir'd, because Mankind has ever since had an unquenchible Thirst after the compleat Discovery of Nature, and the highest degree of acquir'd Knowledge, and an indefatigable Application to farther and farther Improvements in Arts and Science; in a word, in all possible Degrees of Learning and Knowledge.

WHAT happy Success they have had, and what Progress they have made, we shall see something of in the following Chapters.

CHAP. XVIII.

Of the negative Condition of the World, as to Improvements, either in Arts, Science, or Commerce, till the thirteenth Century; and what ignorant Doings there were among the wisest and most knowing part of Mankind for want of the several Improvements made since that time, with a summary Account how those Improvements began.

As I have noted already, the World about the twelfth Century was in but a poor Condition, as to *Trade* or *Navigation*; nor indeed were they much better in all matters of useful Knowledge; Mankind seem'd to be in general stor'd with no other Knowledge than Nature and Necessity immediately dictated. In short it was a *Green-headed*[169] Age, every useful improving Thing was hid from them; they had neither look'd into Heaven or Earth, Sea or Land, as we see has been done since; they were confin'd and narrow'd in their Understandings, as they were in their Dwellings; they might be said not to know above a quarter part of the Globe, and not to understand a quarter part of that they knew; let us look a little into the particulars.

THEY had *Philosophy* without Experiment.

MATHEMATICKS without Instruments.

GEOGRAPHY without Scale.

ASTRONOMY without Demonstration.

THEY made War without Powder or Shot, Cannon or Mortars; nay, the very Mob made their Bonefires without Squibs or Crackers.

THEY went to Sea without Compass, and sailed without the Needle.

THEY view'd the Stars without Telescopes, and measured Latitudes without Observation.

LEARNING had no Printing Press, Writing no Paper, and Paper no Ink; the Lover was forced to send his Mistress a Deal Board for a Love Letter, and even a *Billet Doux* might be about the size of an ordinary Trencher.

THEY were *cloath'd* without Manufacture, and their richest Robes were the Skins of the wildest and most formidable Monsters.

THEY carry'd on *Trade* without Books, and Correspondence without Posts; their Merchants kept no Accompts, their Shopkeepers no Cash Books.

THEY had Chirurgery without Anatomy, and Physicians without the *Materia Medica*.

THEY gave *Emeticks* without *Hypecacuana*,[170] drew *Blisters* without *Cantharides*,[171] and cur'd *Agues* without the *Bark*.[172]

As for Geographic *Discoveries* they had neither seen the *North-Cape*, or the Cape of *Good-Hope*, South. All the discover'd inhabited World, and which they knew and convers'd with, was prescrib'd within very narrow Limits; that is to say, *France, Britain, Spain, Italy, Germany*, and *Greece*, the Lesser *Asia*, the West parts of *Persia, Arabia*, the North parts of *Africa*, and the Islands of the *Mediterranean Sea*; and this was the whole World to them.

NOT that any of these Countries were fully known neither, and several Parts of them not enquir'd into at all: *For Example*,

Ireland, Norway, Denmark. We have Reason to believe these Countries had never been so much as peep'd into by the *Romans*; nor for some Ages were they any otherwise known, than as the *Danes* made themselves known by their Barbarities and Piracies, and the *Irish* by their Stupidity.

GERMANY was known so far as the Banks of the *Elbe*, but very little beyond; *Poland* not beyond the *Vistula*, or *Hungary* beyond the *Danube*.

MUSCOVY or *Russia* perfectly unknown as much as *China* beyond it; and *India* also, only by a small Commerce upon the Coast; chiefly about *Suratte*, and the Coast of *Malabar*.

AFRICA had been more known, but (as has been said) by the ruin of the *Carthaginians* all the Western Coast of it was sunk out of Knowledge again, and forgotten; the Northern Part, that is to say the Coast of *Africa* in the *Mediterranean* remain'd in Knowledge, and that was all; for the *Saracens* over-running the Nations which were planted there, ruin'd all the Commerce, as well as the Religion of it.

THE *Baltick* Sea was not discover'd, or the Navigation of it known; for the *Teutones* or *Teutonic Knights* came not there till the thirteenth Century; so that Navigation was in its Swadling Cloaths, or truly in a state of *Infancy*; for as all the Naval Stores on this side of the World came from the Coasts of *Pomeren, Prussia*, and *Livonia*, little was done, or could be done, in building or fitting out Ships, till they began to furnish the Materials; except what the *Venetians* did in the *Adriatic* Gulph, who had their Naval Stores another way.

THUS far as to the Countries which might be said to be known, or half known; for no part of them could be said to be fully known, but *Italy*, and the Islands adjoyning, except the Kingdom of *France*, and the antient *Greece*.

As to modern Discoveries, how defective were those Ages, and to how narrow a compass were they confined?

AMERICA was not heard of, nor so much as a Suggestion in the Minds of Men that any part of the World lay that way.

THE Coasts of *Greenland*, or *Spitsbergen*, as the *Dutch* call it, and the Whale Fishing, was not known; the best Navigators in the World, at that time, wou'd have fled from a Whale, with much more fright and horrour, than they would have done from the Devil, in the most terrible Shapes that he ever had then appear'd in.

THE Coasts of *Angola, Congo*, the Gold and the Grain Coasts, on the West-side of *Africa*, from fifteen Degrees North to twenty five Degrees South of the Line; from whence since that time such immense Wealth has been drawn, was not discover'd, or the least enquiry made after them.

ALL the *East-India* and *China* Trade, tho' a Mine of Gold, was not only undiscover'd, but out of the reach of all Expectation. Coffee and Tea, those modern Blessings of Mankind, were never heard of; the *Indian* Ocean had never been sail'd in, other than by the coasting Barks of the *Red Sea*, and of the *Persian Gulph*, which were but small and few; all the unbounded Ocean we now call the *South Sea* was hid and unknown; all the *Atlantick* Ocean, beyond the Mouth of the *Straights*, was frightful and terrible in the distant prospect of it; nor durst any one peep into it, otherwise than as they might run a long the Coast of *Africa*, towards *Sallee* or *Santa Cruz*.

THE *North* Seas were hid in a Veil of impenetrable Winter Darkness; The *White Sea*, or *Arch-Angel*, was a very modern Discovery, not found out, till Sir *Hugh Willoughby*[173] doubled the *North Kyn*,[174] and paid dear for the Discovery, being frozen to Death, with all his Crew, on the Coasts of *Lapland*; while his Companion's Ship, with the famous Mr *Chancelor*,[175] went on to the Gulph of Russia, call'd the *White Sea*, where no Christian Nation had ever been before him.

IN these narrow Circumstances stood the frame of the World's Knowledge at the beginning of the fifteenth Century, and when Men of Genius began to look abroad, and about 'em. Now, as it was wonderful to see a World so full of People, and People so capable of Improvement, be yet so Stupid and so blind, so ignorant, and so perfectly unimprov'd; so it was as wonderful to see with what a general Alacrity they took the Alarm almost all together, preparing themselves as it were on a sudden, or by a general Possession or rather Inspiration to spread Knowledge through the Earth, and to search into every thing that it was possible to know.

How surprizing is it for us to look back so little away behind us, and see, that even in less than two hundred Years all this (now so Self-wise) part of the World did not so much as know whether there was any such Place as a *Russia*, a *Muscovy*, a *China*, a *Guinea*, a *Greenland*, or a *North-Cape*? that as to *America*, it was never suppos'd there was any such Place, neither had the World, tho' they stood upon the Shoulders of 4000 Years Experience, the least thought so much as that there was any Land that way.

As they were ignorant of Places, so of Things also. How vast are the Improvements of Science, that all our Knowledge, either of Mathematicks or of Nature, or of the brightest part of human Wisdom have their Admission among us in these two last Centuries?

What was the World before? And to what were the Heads and Hands of Mankind applyed? The Rich had no Commerce, the Poor no Employment; War and the Sword was the great Field of Honour, and the Stage of Preferment; and you have scarce a Man eminent in the World for any thing before that Time, but for a furious outragious falling upon his fellow Creatures, like *Nimrod* and his Successors of modern Fame.

Where were the Men that arriv'd to Characters, to Fame, and to Distinction, by Trade, by the Mathematicks, by the Knowledge of natural or experimental Philosophy? Where was the Sir *Walter Raleighs*, the *Verulams*,[176] the *Boyls*, or *Newtons* of those Ages? Nature being not enquir'd into, discover'd none of her Secrets to them, they neither knew, or sought to know, what now is the Fountain of all human knowledge, and the great Mistery for the Wisest Men to search into, I mean *Nature*.

As then the World are arriv'd to the height of human Knowledge, which we now see among them, and the improvements of Mankind are so infinitely greater, in these two last Centuries, than they were for so many Years before; let us go in the gradual Enquiry, and give the History of them as briefly as we can. It must be matter of wonder to this Age, and all the Ages to come, to look back and see how poorly the World went on for so many thousand Years, and even so very near the Heels of our Times; and I make no question but that after Ages, so great are the Discoveries that are still behind, will be as much astonish'd at the Dulness and Ignorance of this Age, as we are at that of the Years behind us.

How may they hereafter, when some effectual Method for ascertaining the Longitude of the Globe shall be discover'd to them, admire at our Stupidity in not being able to find it out sooner? as much as we admire at the Ignorance and Stupidity even of the great Sir *Francis Drake*, and that yet greater Sir *Walter Raleigh*, whose Geography was so weak, and so short sighted, notwithstanding they had the use of the Compass, and knew that the Earth and Sea together must be one united Globe, that they shou'd run away to the Southward as far as the *Canary* Islands, and then stand over West to the *Caribbee* Islands, then North through the Gulph of *Florida*, and so coast along the Shore of that we now call *Carolina* to find out the Coast of *Virginia*, a Voyage almost a thousand Leagues about.

In the same manner, and with no less folly, did all our well skill'd Navigators, both *English* and *Spanish*, even to this very Age, puzzle and perplex themselves, and with infinite trouble, as well as hazard, fatigue themselves in Working for one hundred Leagues through the Straights of *Magellan* to pass into the *South Seas?* which Straight 'tis very probable never Ship will pass through again, there being so fair a way, and an open Sea round Cape *Horn* without any of those Difficulties and Hazards, and very little out of the way; verifying with infinite Advantage that significant tho' homely Proverb, that *the farthest way about*, &c.

Thus the World is daily encreasing, particularly in experimental Knowledge; and let no Man flatter the Age with pretending we are arriv'd to a perfection of Discoveries. I make no question before I come to the end of this Work, to convince the Reader of what was advanc'd in the beginning of it, that,

> *What's yet discover'd, only serves to show,*
> *How little's known,* to what *there's yet* to know.

But to go back to the state of the World in the fourteenth and fifteenth Century, and to the narrow Circumstances of their Knowledge either in Trade or Navigation.

The *Portuguese* were the first considerable Adventurers that we meet with who began to look abroad for new Discoveries, and to plant new Colonies, that is to say in the Ocean. The *Genoese* have it seems made some efforts on the East-side of the *Euxine Sea*,[177] the *Palus Mæotis*,[178] and the Straights of *Cassa*,[179] where they had planted some people either at or about *Asoph*, and the Mouth of the great River *Don* or *Tanais*, and the *Borysthenes*. For Example;

The *Genoese* discover'd and planted for themselves the *Taurica Chersonesus*,[180] that is to say the Country between the great River *Borysthenes*[181] and the Straights of *Cassa*, and which is now call'd the *Crim-Tartary*; and the *Genoese* being strong at Sea possest all this Country, then very fruitful and rich; till the *Turks* spread themselves into *Europe*, and finally taking *Constantinople* shut the *Genoese* out of the *Euxine Sea*, not suffering any Christian Vessels to pass the *Bosphorus*, no not to this Day.

IN these Colonies the *Genoese* were so successful and so strong that they built many Cities, and especially Sea-ports, as *Cassa* in particular, on the great Straight or Entrance into the *Palus Mæotis*; which from that Sea is call'd the Straight of *Cassa* to this Day; and tho' the *Genoese* were shut out of the *Euxine Sea*, by the *Turks*, as above, about the Year 1450, yet they kept their footing in the *Chersonesus*, and particularly this Port of *Cassa*, till the Year 1574.

BUT the State of *Genoa* having been sunk from all their navigating Glory, and reduc'd to the small confines of their present Dominions in *Italy*; all their *Eastern* Colonies are devour'd by the *Turks*; and they are not now worth naming in the World, I mean as to Improvement and Plantation.

BUT the *Portuguese*, as I noted before, were the Nation of all the Nations in the World who first looked abroad in the World for Discoveries. *John* King of *Portugal*,[182] an aspiring and enterprizing Prince, hearing that the *Spaniards* had by the height of the *Pico Teneriffe* discover'd the *Canary* Islands, and taken Possession of them, sent out three Ships under the direction of *John Gonzales* and *Tristrian Vaz*,[183] two experienc'd Mariners, in order to find if there were any more Islands in those Seas; and these very happily discover'd and took possession of the Island of *Madera*, in the Year 1420, which has remain'd to the King of *Portugal* ever since.

IN the same fortuitous manner *Don Henry*[184] Prince of *Portugal* discover'd the *Azores*, or, as some call them the *Tercera* Islands; a *Flemish* Ship being driven to the Westward by a Storm, as they were on their way to *Lisbon*, fell in with these Islands, and runing in for shelter, and in hopes of relief, found Harbour indeed, but no relief, for the Islands were all uninhabited. After some stay, and the Wind coming about fair, the *Flemings* set sail, and coming to *Lisbon* gave an account of the Place where they had been; *Don Henry*, above nam'd, taking the hint, and desiring them as well as they could to describe the situation, went to Sea in five Ships, and happily discover'd the place, which he likewise seiz'd for the King of *Portugal*, who caused 'em to be planted and inhabited, and the *Portuguese* have been Lords of them ever since; this was in 1449.

Encourag'd by these Discoveries *John* King of *Portugal* resolv'd upon more: and having some very experienc'd Navigators in his Service; I mean experienc'd as the World then went, among whom was *Anthony Nola*[185] a *Genoese*, *Bartholomew Diaz*[186] a *Portuguese*, and several others; they put him upon making Discoveries on the Coast of *Africa*. But King *John* dying in 1433, and his Son *Edward* reigning but five Years, these Adventures were not push'd on effectually till the Reign of *Alfonso* the fifth, Grandson to King *John*, who engaged in them again.

HE began at Cape *Spartel*, the very Mouth of the Straights, and embarking a good Body of Troops in his Ships, sent them to invade *Africa*, and plant Colonies; in consequence of which Commission they took *Tangier* and *Arzilla*, and fortifying them, left strong Garrisons there. Then they proceeded upon the Western Coast forward to the South, till at length they seiz'd upon a small old *Saracen* Town, almost dwindled back into the original of Nature, and turn'd savage again; however they found a good Port, and which in all appearance had been formerly in more request, and better frequented than it was at that time; for the *Portuguese* found no Genius for Trade yet among them, or that any other Nation corresponded with them. This Port the *Portuguese* gladly seated themselves in, fortified it, and call'd it *Santa Cruz*.

IN pursuit of those important Discoveries, they took many Places, but were afterwards, by the unhappy Miscarriage of their great Expedition under *Don Sebastian*,[187] the next King of *Portugal*, driven out of them all again. This Prince, with a powerful Army, in which was the flower of all the Nobility of *Portugal*, gloriously push'd at a Conquest of the whole *Moorish* Empire, but lost the Battle, and was himself kill'd; in consequence of that Victory, *I say*, they were again driven out of all these Conquests *Anno* 1530. But to go back to their Sea Affairs. Their success at *Santa Cruz* led the fortunate *Portuguese* on to search farther South till they came to a noted Cape, which from the greeness and pleasant prospect of the Land they call'd *Cape de Verd*, or *Green-Cape*; and here (at the same time overjoy'd with their Success) stretching out into the main Sea, they found the Islands, call'd by the same Rule the *Cape de Verd Islands*.

THIS Discovery satisfy'd them for the present; and it took them up some time to plant and settle on these Islands, they being immediately valuable to the *Portuguse*; nor have they any cause to repent their possession of them at all, if it were only for the Salt they get there, which so many Ships are loaded with every Year, and of which there is yet no Diminution.

THE *Portuguese* having, as above, lost their first Colonies on the Western Coast of *Africa*, and particularly the Port of *Santa Cruz*, or *Holy-Cross*, but having in pursuit of the humour for Discoveries, which then seem'd to agitate their Nation, found out the *Cape de Verd*, and kept a long possession of that Coast; so that they were too strong there to be attackt by the *Moors*, even when they re-took their other Conquests; they from thence extended themselves all along that which we now call the Coast of *Guinea*, and seiz'd the Mouth of the great River *Niger*, which they call'd the *Rio Grande*, or the *Great River*; a Name which intimated that the World was not then much acquainted with the course of Rivers; for this was indeed but one of the several Branches, by which the truly *Grand Niger* empties itself into the Sea.

THEN they took the Coast of *Sierra Leon*, or as now vulgarly call'd *Serra-loon*, but named by them the *Hill of Lions*, from a discovery, that the Country on that Coast was very full of *Lions*; which might be so at that time, tho' it seems now to be as empty of Lions as any part of *Afric*.

HERE the *Portuguese* fortify'd: And tho' they did not build Towns and Cities, as they afterwards did farther *South*, yet they built Forts, settled Factories, and traded with the Natives for such things as the Country produc'd; namely, Elephants Teeth, Skins of Beasts, such as Lions and Leopards, for other Skins they had none; also *Tammerins*,[188] or *Guinea-Grains*, Civet and Civet Cats, but especially Bees-Wax: As for Slaves they had none, neither did the *Negroes* sell one another then, as they do now, neither had the *Portuguese* any Colonies in *America* to dispose of them to, so that the Slave Trade was not at that time begun, nor had they found any Gold at that time, or not much of it.

IMPATIENT of farther Advantages in a Country which they found fruitful and rich beyond expectation, they went on and discover'd all the Coast, running from *West* to *East*, in the Latitude of eight to four, A Climate, which by its excesive Heat, seem'd to promise neither Product or People: For in those Days, or at least till those Days, the Torrid Zone was always thought to be uninhabited; but to their surprise they found it rich in both.

THEIR first Discovery was made by *Anthony Nola*, a *Genoese*, who rang'd the whole Coasts, call'd now the *Grain Coast*, the *Gold-Coast*, and the *Slave-Coast*, and wintered at the Island of St. *Thomas*, or as they call it St. *Thoma*, an Island situate directly under the Equinoctial Line; a thing surprizing and astonishing at that time.

THIS Island being discover'd on St. *Thomas's-Day*, they call'd it by his Name St. *Thomas*: It was discover'd, I say, on St. *Thomas's-Day*, *Anno* 1471, and has been in the possession of the *Portuguese* ever since, being very useful in their Voyages from the *Cape de Verd* to the *Cape of Good-Hope*, in their way to the *Indies*, and to take in fresh Water and fresh Provisions, as our *English* Ships do at the Island of St. *Helena*, in their Voyages to the same Place.

UPON this wonderful discovery of the South Coast of *Africa*, the *Portuguese* found such a vast quantity of Gold upon all the Country, which we now call the Coast of *Guinea*, or the *Gold Coast*, that it enrich'd the whole Kingdom of *Portugal*; and it was so very remarkable, that for forty or fifty Years it was call'd the Golden Age at *Lisbon*; till about the Year 1536, when the *English* came into a share with the *Portuguese* for this beneficial Trade. And tho' at first the *Portuguese* had the possession of almost the whole Coast, yet the *English* shar'd with them a long while in great part of the profit of the Trade; and tho' they did not do so by landing and setting up Factories and Forts on the Country, as the *Portuguese* had done; yet without that charge they did it by mere trading with the Natives in such Places where they could find convenient Places to correspond with them; here they made great Advantages by the Commerce, and frequently brought home one hundred to one hundred and twenty Pounds of Gold upon a Voyage; which as Gold then bore a great Price, was a prodigious Cargo: For selling at six Pound per Ounce, the quantity of Gold amounted to seventy two Pounds per Pound; so that they frequently made from eight to ten or twelve thousand Pounds a Voyage in Gold, besides their other Goods, as mention'd before.

AMONG the rest we read of some *French* Merchants who with two Ships and a Bark went on that Coast, in the Year 1556, and brought away seven hundred Pounds weight in Gold in one Voyage, besides Tamerins, Elephants Teeth, and about fifty Slaves, (for Slaves were not bought and sold then, I say, as they are now;) and besides many other Goods, the Gold alone amounting to 50400 *l.* Sterling, an immense Sum in those Times: And our Countryman Mr. *Towerson*,[189] one of the first *Englishmen* who ever went thither on a trading account, brought away in three Voyages with two small Ships, each Voyage above four hundred and sixty Pounds weight of Gold, besides what his Men, to whom he gave certain Liberties of trading for themselves, brought off on account of private Trade.

BUT the *Portuguese* who, as I have said, first discover'd this Coast, took *Livery* and *Seisin*,[190] and settled Factories, fortify'd those Factories with strong Forts and Castles, for defending their said Commerce against, not the *Negroes* only, but against their Neighbours the *Europeans*, who with too much Reason they apprehended might attempt to supplant and remove them; and had those Forts and Castles been as well furnished with Garrisons and Cannon, and those Garrisons done their Duty, as carefully as their Masters providently built Forts to cover them, they had not been supplanted and dispossess'd, as they see themselves serv'd at this Day.

BUT so it was that the Kingdom of *Portugal* coming after into the possession of *Philip* II. K. of *Spain*, and the *Dutch* at that time, a powerful, growing, and encreasing State, having an open declar'd War with *Spain*, some of their most forward Adventurers being sensible enough of the Injury done to their said Principal, by the *Spaniards*, and resolving to see Justice done to their State, in all Places where it was possible, fell into firm Resolutions to do themselves that Justice in part upon their remote Possessions in Trade; such as their Colonies in *Africa* and *India*.

IT was a very unhappy Juncture for *Portugal* that their Country fell at that time into the possession of *Spain*, as I have said; for the *Dutch* had no War with *Portugal* till *Portugal* became *Spaniard*; and in that very interval the *Dutch* took almost all their foreign Dominions from them, as may appear in its place.

BUT I return to the first *Discoveries*, in which the *Portuguese* extended themselves upon the Gold Coast of *Africa*, as I have said, by the successful Adventures of the famous Navigator *Bartholomew Diaz*, who may justly be said to be the most skilful Navigator that the World ever had, who wrought without Instruments, and sail'd without the Compass; for he discover'd even to the *Cape of Good-Hope* before the use of the Magnet and the Needle were known in Navigation.

HE extended himself gradually from *Sierra-Leon* to *Benin*, which is a continued Coast of above 500 Leagues, between the Years 1461 and 1472, and in that time built or laid the Foundation of several considerable Fortifications; one at the Mouth of the great River or Branch of the *Niger*, call'd afterwards *Senegal*; where the *Portuguese* continue settled to this Day, and where they have several little Strengths a considerable way up the River, and some well inhabited Towns, but not much Gold; if they had, their Possessions had not perhaps been so quiet, and so long. The next Forts of Consequence were those of St. *Anthonio*, *De Elmina*, and *Sebastian*, all upon the Gold Coast, and of all which, with that whole Coast, they have been dispossess'd by the *Dutch*, or other *European* Nations; nor have they at this time any one Fort or Factory on all that Coast, except only one, till you come about the Gulph or Head of the Bay of *Benin*, which we now call the *Slave-Coast*, and where their real fix'd Possessions begin.

HOWEVER, tho' the *Portuguese* have lost all this rich Country, they did not presently do so; and tho' the *Dutch* encroach'd early upon them, yet they were not quite dispossess'd of the Gold Coast, till near 200 Years after the first discovery, namely, till the Year 1646, which as it is matter of History after the Discovery, does not so much come within the compass of this Design. But to go back therefore to the famous *Bartholomew Diaz*:

As he met with such wonderful Success in these Parts, and the *Portuguese* settled with so much Advantage, that the very Nation grew Rich, and as I have said, it was call'd the Golden Age; it may be reasonably suppos'd he was encourag'd to go on. And accordingly, being supplied with Ships and Men, he extended himself farther and farther to the *South*; and still planting and fortifying wherever he came, he in short gave the *Portuguese* a Name and a Footing at the Mouths of every River, and upon the Coasts of every Kingdom, from the *Rio Formosa* and *Benin* to the Kingdoms and Countries of *Congo* and *Angola*, and so running on South, merely for the curiosity of what might yet be discovered farther; at length he came to the *Cape de Bona Esperanza*, as he call'd it, from the good hope he immediately entertained, that seeing the Land *terminate*, as to its extent Southward, and a vast Sea open to the East, he shou'd in time find an open passage into those great *Indian Seas*, which he had heard so much of, on the South Coasts of *Asia*, and which some say he had formerly sail'd into, out of the Gulph of *Persia*: This was done in the Year 1489.

THIS Discovery immediately made a great noise in the World, and the *Portuguese* whose navigating Glory was now grown really very great fail'd not to continue to bring infinite Profits as well to the public as to the private Merchants concern'd; and this made them extend themselves upon all the Coasts, as above, in such a manner, that it was once said *Portugal* was going to remove into *Guinea* and *Angola*: But they did not end here, for some Years after they stretch'd from the Cape of *Good Hope* along to the North-East, yet still close under Shore. Thus leaving the South-point of *Africa*, and following the Coast, they began Settlements and Colonies on the East-Coast of the Main-land, as they had before done on the West; a Place never heard of before in the World. And here they took hold of the Coast of *Mozambique* and *Zanguebar*, and landing by force master'd the Natives and possess'd the Country. Here they built the Cities of St. *Sebastian*, *Port St. Esprit*, and *Melinda*; the last especially considerable, and continuing so to this Day; and of all which more may be said hereafter. This was under *Don Vasco de Gama*[191] another *Portuguese* Admiral of great fame, and was in the Year 1498 to 1500.

To this time they knew nothing of the Needle or the Compass; so that tho' they cast many a wishful Eye, as we express it, upon the vast extended *Indian* Ocean, and believ'd there were great Things, and even new Worlds to be found beyond it; yet they durst not venture out of sight of Land, especially in such remote Countries, where they found the Sun both in its elevation and declination, was continually on the North-side of them, and they must necessarily repass the Equinoctial Line, tho' they knew not exactly where it was, before they could arrive in their own Country again.

CHAP. XIX.

Of the Discovery of the Magnet or Loadstone; and how it was many Ages known without any such mathematical Improvements made upon it, as to bring it to be concern'd in our Navigation, with some account by whom it was so applyed.

THE learned Author of *Lexicon Technicum*[192] assures us that the knowledge of the Magnet is very antient, and he quotes it from *Sturmius*. By the knowledge of it he does not only say the knowledge of the mere Stone or *Fossil*, which he thinks approaches to the Species of *Iron Oar*, but that its attractive Quality was known. But even this, which we are not assured of, did not seem to answer the end for which the great Discovery was made, if that especial Application of it to the Mathematicks, and in particular to this Branch relating to Navigation had not likewise been discover'd.

NOR was this part the work of a short space of time. The Verticity or Inclination of it to the North was discover'd about the Year 1380,[193] by our Countryman *Roger Bacon*,[194] the same whom we call *Fryer Bacon*, who was a compleat Mathematician; the same which old Stories tells so many fabled Tales about, which have so little Truth to support them; yet 'tis certain this *Bacon* did strange Things by the Magic of this powerful Attractive, and for that was suppos'd to deal with the *Devil*.

BUT even this could not lead us to the use of it in the great Article, which it has since been apply'd to, but it was reserv'd for the honour of an *Italian* of *Gaæta*,[195] in the Kingdom of *Naples*; who finding its Virtue communicative to the Steel, and that all Steel would if touch'd, touch again what it impress'd: Upon this he fell to worship the Discovery, and to spread it gradually into the World; and thus by little and little it came to be of public Use, and the Discoveries which have been made by it, and the Improvements upon it are innumerable; some of them may be sum'd up out of the Learned Mr. *Boyl*[196] and others as follows.

I. THAT in every *Magnet* there are two *Poles*, one pointing *North*, the other *South*; and if a *Loadstone* be cut or broken into ever so many pieces, there are likewise two *Poles* in each piece.

II. THAT these *Poles* in divers parts of the Globe are diversely inclined towards the Earth's center.

III. THAT these *Poles*, tho' contrary to one another, do help mutually towards the *Magnetic Attraction* and to the Suspension of Iron.

IV. IF two *Magnets* are Spherical, one will turn or conform itself to the other, so as either of them would do to the Earth; and that after they have so conformed or turned themselves, they endeavour to approach and to join each other, but if placed in a contrary Position they avoid each other.

V. IF a *Magnet* be cut through the Axis, the parts or Segments of the Stone, which before were joined, will now avoid and fly each other.

VI. IF the *Magnet* be cut by a Section perpendicular to its Axis, the two points which before were conjoined will become contrary *Poles*, one in one the other in the other Segment.

VII. IRON receives Virtue from the *Magnet* by Application to it, or barely from an approach near it, tho' it doth not touch it; and the Iron receives this Virtue variously according to the parts of the Stone 'tis made to touch, or made approach to.

VIII. IF an oblong piece of Iron be any how applied to the Stone, it receives virtue from it only as to its length.

IX. THE *Magnet* loses none of its own Virtue by communicating any to the Iron; and this Virtue it can communicate to Iron very speedily, tho' the longer the Iron touches or joins the Stone, the longer will its communicated Virtue hold, and a better *Magnet* will communicate more of it, and sooner than one not so good.

X. THAT *Steel* receives Virtue from the *Magnet* better than *Iron*.

XI. A *Needle* touch'd by a *Magnet* will turn its ends the same way towards the *Poles* of the World, as the *Magnet* will do it.

XII. THAT neither *Loadstone* or *Needles* touch'd do conform their *Poles* exactly to those of the World, but have usually some variation from them; and this variation is different in divers places, and at divers times, in the same place.

XIII. THAT a *Loadstone* will take up much more Iron when arm'd or cap'd than it can alone, and that tho' an Iron Ring or Key be suspended by the *Loadstone*, yet the magnetical Particles do not hinder that Ring or Key from turning round any way, either to the right Hand or to the left.

XIV. THAT the force of a *Loadstone* may be variously increased or lessened by the various application of Iron or another *Loadstone* to it.

XV. THAT a strong *Magnet* at the least distance from a lesser or a weaker cannot draw to it a piece of Iron adhereing actually to such lesser or weaker Stone, but if it come to touch it, it can draw it from the other; but a weaker *Magnet*, or even a little piece of Iron can draw away or separate a piece of Iron contiguous to a greater or stronger *Loadstone*.

XVI. THAT in our *North* parts of the World the *South Pole* of a *Loadstone* will raise up more Iron than the *North Pole*.

XVII. THAT a plate of Iron only (but no other Body interposed) can impede the Operation of the *Loadstone* either as to its attractive or directive Quality; Mr. *Boyle* found this true in Glasses sealed hermetically; and Glass is a Body as impervious as most are to all Effluvia.

XVIII. THAT the Power or Virtue of a *Loadstone* may be impaired by lying long in a wrong posture, as also by Rust, Wet, &c. and may be quite destroyed by Fire.

XIX. MR. *Boyle* found that by heating a *Magnet* red hot, it would be speedily deprived of its attractive Quality.

XX. IF a *Loadstone* be heated red hot, and then cooled, either with its *South Pole* to the *North* in a horizontal Position, or with its *South Pole* downwards in a perpendicular one, it will change its Polarity, the *South Pole* becoming the Northern one, and *vice versa*.

XXI. BY applying the *Poles* of a very small fragment of a *Loadstone* to the opposite contiguous ones of a good large *Magnet*, Mr. *Boyle* found he could speedily change the *Poles* of the fragment, but he could not effect it in a fragment that was considerably bigger, tho' he tried many Hours.

XXII. HE observed that well tempered and hardened Iron Tools, when heated by Attrition, turning, fileing, &c. would while warm attract thin Fileings or Chips of Iron and Steel, but not when cold; yet it has been seen and tried that a large piece of a File, which was in the Hands of Mr. *Tarnwel* the *Spectacle-maker*, did retain such an attractive Quality that it would take up and keep suspended the Key of a Cabinet or Scrutoire, and needed no Attrition to excite this magnetical Virtue.

XXIII. THE Iron Bars of Windows, which have long stood in an erect Position, do grow permanently Magnetical. The lower ends of such Bars being the *North Poles*, and the upper the *Southern*; for according to the Laws of *Magnetism*, we find the lower ends of such Bars will drive away the North end of a poised *Needle*, Southerly; which shew, that by the continual passage of the subtile magnetical Particles through them, they are turned into a kind of *Magnet* themselves.

XXIV. IF a Bar of Iron that hath not stood long in an erected posture, be only held perpendicularly, its lower end will be the *North Pole*, and attract the *South Pole* of a touch'd *Needle*; but then this Virtue is transient, and will shift as you invert the Bar; for the other end when held lowermost will presently become the *North Pole*; wherefore in order to render the quality of Verticity permanent in an Iron Bar, it must remain a long time in a proper Position, but the Fire will produce this effect in a very short time; for as it will immediately deprive a *Loadstone* of its attractive Power, or change its *Poles* (as in Experiment XIX and XX) so it will as soon give a Verticity to a Bar of Iron, if, being heated red hot, it be cooled in an erect Position, or directly *North* and *South*; nay, it hath been observed often, that even Tongs and Fire-Forks, by being often heated, and then set to cool in a Position near to erect, have gained this magnetical Property; the Reason of which very different Effects of the Fire on a *Magnet*, and on Iron, Mr. *Boyle*, with his usual Modesty, suggests to be this, that the peculiar Texture or Constitution, by which a *Magnet* differs from common Iron Ore, being accurate and fine, is spoiled by the rude and violent attacks of the Fire; but this mighty Agent by working upon Iron softens and opens the Pores of the Metal (which is harder than Iron Ore) so that it becomes capable of being prevaded by the magnetical Particles, and by that means gain a vertical Quality.

XXV. MR. *Boyle* found, that by heating a piece of *English* Oker[197] red hot, and placing it to cool in a proper Posture, it plainly gain'd a magnetic Power.

XXVI. THE same noble Gentleman found that an excellent *Loadstone* of his own, having lain almost a Year in an inconvenient Posture had its Virtue so impaired, that he at first thought some Body had got at it, and spoiled it by Fire.

XXVII. IF a *Needle* be well touch'd on a good *Loadstone* 'tis known it will when duly poised point *North* and *South*; but if it have one contrary touch of the same Stone, it will immediately be deprived of that Faculty, and by another such touch, it will have its *Poles* quite changed; so that the end which before pointed North shall now point Southward.

XXVIII. DR. *Power* and Mr. *Boyle* both tryed, that after a red hot Iron had gain'd a Verticity by being well heated, and cooled *North* and *South*, and then also hammer'd at the ends, this Virtue would immediately be destroyed by two or three blows of a strong Hammer smartly given about the middle of it.

XXIX. Mr. *Boyle* found by drawing the back of a Knife, or long piece of Steel Wire, &c. over the *Poles* of a *Loadstone* leisurely, once or divers times, beginning the Motion from the middle or Equator of the Stone, towards the *Pole*, the Knife or Wire will accordingly attract one end of a poised magnetical *Needle*; but if you take another Knife or Wire, and thrust it leisurely over the *Pole*, from the *Pole* towards the Equator or middle of the Equator, this Knife shall drive or expel away the same end of the *Needle* which the former Knife would attract, which Experiment makes it very probable that the Operation of the *Magnet* depends upon the flux of some fine Particles, which go out at one *Pole*, then round about, and in again at the other.

XXX. BECAUSE it is one of the universal Laws of Nature; that Action and Re-action are always equal; therefore it is plain, the Iron must attract the *Magnet* as much as that doth the Iron, and so you may easily experiment it to be in Fact if you place a *Magnet* or piece of Iron on a piece of Cork, so as that it may swim freely in the Water, for then you will see that which soever you hold in your Hand will draw the other towards it. From all which Experiments 'tis plain (as Mr. *Boyle* concludes) that *Magnetism* doth much depend upon mechanical Principles, as also that there is such a thing as the *Magnetism* of the Earth, or that there are magnetical Particles which continually are passing from *Pole* to *Pole*; but Sir *Isaac Newton* demonstrates that Gravity is a very different thing from *Magnetism*, since the former is always as the quantity of Matter attracted, but *Magnetism* by no means so.

SEBASTIAN *Cabot*,[198] the famous and first discoverer of *America*, is said to have found out the Variation of the *Magnetism*[199] in different Positions; others have improv'd since upon the Variation, and form'd several Experiments upon that Arch which they call the *Azimuth* or magnetical *Azimuth*; which is an Arch of the Horizon contain'd between the Sun's *Azimuth Circle* and the *magnetical Meridian*; or to put it into as intelligible Terms as I can, the distance of the Sun in any particular place from the North or South Pole, and this is found by an Observation; for which they have now a particular Instrument call'd an *Azimuth Compass*, the description of which is not to the present purpose.

UPON this Magnetic Tendency to the Poles, which being communicated to the Iron or Steel, gave the Iron or Steel the same Tendency, have been form'd all the subsequent Improvements of Art useful in Navigation and in Geography. By this the Globe has been regularly measur'd, the imaginary Arch of the Heavens, and the Position and Motion of Things regularly understood.

BY this the Compass was form'd, and several Points before divided more exactly ascertained, and the Analogy form'd between space and time, the Degrees and Miles in space being made to answer exactly to the Hours and Minutes in the measure of Time.

IT wou'd be too voluminous a Task here to describe the many Improvements which take their rise in this great Discovery of the Magnetism of Nature, or rather the various Magnetisms in Nature; I chuse rather to speak of the great Improvements in *Navigation* which attended it; and by which all the great Discoveries of distant and remote Countries, and sailing over the vast and almost boundless Seas, which were terrible before but to think of, has been perform'd.

Now the adventurous Mariner confin'd himself no more to the meanness of coasting along the Shores, standing in need of the sight of Land, or of the heavenly Bodies to guide himself in again, when he was gotten at a great distance from the Land, the Needle showing him his way, as I may say, without Eyes; for the Steel pointing always duely to the North or to the South, and thereby showing any other Point, the Mariner immediately found himself at home every where, and in the darkest Night, or the thickest Fog, when neither Sun, Moon, Stars, Land-mark, or Sea-mark, was to be seen, yet they knew exactly both where, and which way they were going.

IMMEDIATELY like young Swimmers grown expert, and who scorn any longer to keep within their depth, and in shallow Waters, but boldly swim off into the Chanels of the largest Rivers; so here the Mariners scorning any longer to coast along the Shores as before, boldly travers'd the open Seas with regard to the distances they were in from the Land, so that the widest Seas could not confine their search, or the remotest Climate be conceal'd from their Discovery. By this means in a few Ages we find they make light of stretching from the narrow Seas of *Britain* to the Cape of *Good-Hope*, without ever any sight of Land between; except sometimes the little *Island* of St. *Helena* between, which it is more a Test of their exquisit skill to find, than it is a mark of Deficiency that they do not find it.

WITH the same boldness and assurance they take a run, and make light of it, over the vast Indian Ocean, from the Cape of *Good-Hope* to *Java Head*, which is almost 2000 Leagues; and again from the *Philippin* Islands over the prodigious Ocean, which we call the *South Sea*, to *Acapulco*; and all these Places they find as directly as a Carrier's Horse does his Road, or as the Carrier himself does the Inn he is to lodge at.

To such a perfection of Art are we now arriv'd merely by the addition of this one Discovery of the Loadstone; and yet we see farther Secrets in Nature every Day, which the same happy Discovery leads into; so that we may say the magnetic Quality of the Earth is an inexhausted Mine of Wonders, in which the farther we look the more Reason we see to expect greater Discoveries than were ever made before.

As the Mariners (made bold by this great Pilot the Needle) have adventured into the vast Oceans, which they durst not launch out into before, so the nature of the Thing requiring it, the Artists and Shipwrights have been call'd upon to build larger and stronger Vessels and Ships of an amazing Magnitude compar'd to what they were before.

SHIPS were no more capable of being row'd with Oars, and moor'd with Ropes. Their Vessels were more like floating Castles than what was formerly call'd Ships; the remotest Nations, and the most antient grown Woods were searched for Timber of sufficient strength to build; the largest and tallest Trees were scarse sufficient to make Masts for them, whose height were now carry'd up to what had never been known; their Yards spread a Clue of Sail to such a breadth, that at a distance a Ship carry'd the face of a Cloud rather than a Cloth; in a Word, the Ships were now call'd Carvels[200] rather than Ships; and the *Spaniards* and *Portuguese* frequently sail'd in quest of new Discoveries, and in pursuit of the Trade Improvement in Vessels of a thousand Ton Burthen, and afterwards of much more.

As they built Ships like Castles, so Guns being also brought into use, they brought their Ships to bear great Guns like as Castles did, and several great pieces of Ordinance were mounted upon these Carvels in such a manner, that they were able to maintain terrible Fights at Sea, and to answer Batteries upon the Shore in their own kind; nay sometimes to over-power the Batteries on Shore, and to enter Harbours and Ports by force, tho' defended by strong Fortifications, and man'd by strong Garrisons.

THIS made the Marine Nations grow powerful by Sea, as well as by Land, and in a few Years the *Portuguese* and *Spaniards* fitted out large Fleets, carrying great strength of Guns, and their Shipping was able to make them terrible wherever they came.

IT was very remarkable then, and it is even still worth observing, in how short an interval of Time the World came up to this height of Improvement, from the gross Ignorance which they were in before. It was but in 1498, that the *Portuguese*, ignorant of the Compass, and not daring to venture out to Sea, discover'd the Cape of *Good-Hope*, and durst go no farther; and within less than twenty Years more we find them planted upon the *Brasils* in *America*, and Masters of every Coast in the *East-Indies*, even up to the *Spice Islands*, and almost to *China* itself, their Ships carrying vast Burthens, heavy Pieces of Ordnance, and striking a Terror into all the Countries where ever they came.

So swift was the Improvement of the Times, when once they got a tast of Knowledge, and so easily did they let themselves into the most useful part of the Discovery as soon as it was made; nor was it long before the rest of the Nations follow'd them at the Heels; and that so soon as in a few Years to over-power them, and indeed in time to supplant them in some of the most valuable Settlements and Possessions they had, especially in the *East Indies*, and on the *Gold Coast of Guinea*.

But that which is the most surprizing in this driving the *Portuguese* out of their foreign Plantations and Factories, is this; that the *Portuguese* lost not only their Possessions, the *Dutch* taking from them all their Forts and Factories, Possessions and Estates, especially in the *East-Indies*, but they lost their navigating Genius, and their Fame as Seamen, and from being esteem'd (as in the fifteenth Century they were) the best Seamen in the World, they are now sunk down in their Reputation to the very worst; so that nothing on this side the *Mediterranean* is look'd upon with more contempt, or treated with more disdain in these Things than a *Portuguese* Seaman, whether we speak of the ordinary Mariners or the Masters.

It is true they did act vigorously in one Case; and indeed if they had not they would by this time have had little or nothing left of all their foreign Acquisitions worth their keeping; and this was in recovering their great Colony[201] of the *Brasils*, which the *Dutch* once had taken entirely from them, and kept the Possession of for several Years. But when the Duke of *Braganza* assum'd the Crown of *Portugal*, taking up Arms against the *Spaniards*, and by the assistance of Duke *Schomberg*, recover'd and settled the Crown in the said House of *Braganza*;[202] as the *Portuguese* vigorously recover'd their Liberty from the *Spanish* Yoke in *Europe*, so they took Arms too in the *Brasils* against the *Dutch*; and after a faint Resistance only the *Dutch* were oblig'd to quit the whole Country to them, and they retain the Possession of it to this Day; and it is now the most powerful and wealthy Colony in the World; of the Commerce of which, and its prodigious Improvements I have much to say in its proper place.

Had not the *Portuguese* recovered this great Plantation of the *Brasils* all their Settlements on the Rivers *Benin* and *Congo*, and in *Angola*, had been useless to them; for they had no occasion for the great number of Slaves which they now get in that Country; from whence we are assur'd they carry near 60000 Slaves a Year, and which is the chief Trade of their *African* Possessions, as well on that Side as at *Melinda* and *Madagascar*, the Coast of *Mozambique* and that of *Zanguebar*. It is true they carry some Gold, and a great quantity of Ivory from these Coasts, but then the greatest part of it is carry'd farther Eastward to the Coast of *India* and *Malabar*, and to other Parts of *India*, where the *Portuguese* have yet a Trade.

CHAP. XX.

Of the several Discoveries of the Islands and Continent of America. *The early product of the knowledge of the Needle, and its Uses in Navigation. Also of the Northern Navigators in quest of the North-East and North-West Passages to* China; *and whether it is probable such Passages ever will be discovered.*

As the knowledge of the Needle, and its being apply'd to such mighty Purposes in Navigation, came forward in the World with the beginning of the sixteenth Century, it was wonderful even to astonishing, to reflect how swift its Progress was.

CRISTOPHER Columbus setting out from the *Canary Islands*, as if he was assur'd there was a new Western World to be found out, tho' he neither knew or had heard of any such thing, sail'd directly West, not knowing whither he went, and resolv'd to go on till he found something.

In this Voyage he sail'd long enough to discourage any Man in the World, and to put it out of question to him, that if he found nothing he and all his Men must inevitably perish and eat one another, for he could never hope to subsist himself in going back again. In a Word he sail'd 987 Leagues by his reckoning, from the *Pico Teneriffa*, all the way due West, and never saw any thing but Land and Sea enough as, I say, to discourage any Man alive, when happily, and to the inexpressible Joy of him and all his Men, on St. *Luke's-Day Anno* 1586,[203] they discover'd Land, which proved to be the *Bahama* Islands, by him for that Reason, call'd St. *Luke's*, and since that the *Lucaya* Islands.

From hence he went North-West and discover'd the Coast of *Florida*; but finding it a barren Country, he turn'd South, and landed upon the Islands of *Cuba* and *Hispaniola*; after which, making farther and more ample Discoveries, he return'd to *Spain* to give the King of *Spain* an account of what he had seen and done.

It must be confess'd this was putting their improv'd Knowledge, *young as it was*, upon the Tenters;[204] and I may say, stretching it to the utmost, the vast extent of Waters which they were upon, and which they yet knew not the end of, was frightful; and *Columbus* himself, tho' some say he had seen some of the Southward of the *Caribbee* Islands, where the run was shorter, (*viz.*) from *Cape de Verd* by above 1000 Miles, began to give himself over for lost.

BUT this encourag'd them, and indeed is the solid comfort of the Sailors Knowledge, by virtue of the never failing unerring Tendency of the Needle always pointing to its Pole; I say this was their dependance, and this encourag'd them, (*viz.*) that they knew they did not wander, they knew they did not drive this way and that, as the Winds or Currents wou'd have carry'd them, but that which way soever the Winds blew, or the Currents set, they still kept true to their Point, and went strait on; so that they every Day, nay every Hour went farther and farther due West, and were able (whenever they thought fit to give over the pursuit of their design) to have turn'd directly back again, and if their Provisions would hold them, to have come home to the *Canaries* from whence they set out.

IT is true they were unhappily longer than they need to have been upon this Voyage; that is to say, they had a longer run before they discover'd Land, because they kept so much to the Northward of the Line; namely, in the Latitude of twenty three to twenty four Degrees; whereas if they had steer'd two Points more to the Southward all the way, they wou'd have made Land at some of the Eastmost Islands, either at *Hispaniola* or *Porto Rico*, or some of those Places in the Latitude of twenty Degrees, or thereabouts; but this mistake they soon learn'd to rectify. With this encrease of Mathematical Knowledge came many other useful Discoveries, as well as those of Navigation, such as relate to the Shipwrights Art, and other Mechanick Trades.

FIRST of all the learned Men, as if all Nature was newly laid open to them, made daily more and more Discoveries in the Principles of Things; Mines and Minerals were also infinitely encreas'd; the People more boldly ventur'd into the Bowels of the Earth than before, and the Miners dug in the Earth as the Sailors work'd upon the Waters by the Compass. Infinite Experiments were made by the *Boyls* and *Newtons* of that Age; for all modern Knowledge seems to have builded upon their first Experiments and to stand upon their Shoulders; Chymistry, Alchimy, Refining, Separating, Purging, Sublimating, and even to that yet unknown, tho' not unsought Mistery, call'd Transmutation, all had their rise and invention in these Ages, and much of it from these beginnings.

PHYSIC felt the advantage, and daily Experiments added to the Knowledge of the Learned, as the Discovery of new Countries encreas'd the Pharmacy of those Times, and added noble Simples and innumerable invaluable Particulars to the *Materia Medica* of the Physician. The *Spanish* and *Portuguese* Missionaries sent over by the Church, that is to say by the Congregation *De propaganda fide*,[205] were many of them Men of Learning; some of them, especially the Jesuits, had studied Physic, and were really good Physicians, others studied Nature, and were curious in searching after Drugs, Plants, Gums, and other Simples, and others after Minerals and Metals; so that Nature was merely ravag'd, as I may say, wherever they came.

BY these those glorious medicinal Drugs, strange exotic Plants, and Animals, with several other valuable Things were discover'd, which the World heard nothing of before; such as the *Peruvian Bark* that sovereign and specific Medicine in all intermitting and periodical Fevers, and even in that Witchcraft (or Possession, I know not what to call it) which we name an Ague: The *Cantharides*, or as vulgarly call'd *Spanish-Flyes* of wonderful and various Operation in Physic; the *Lapis Contrayerva*[206] equal, nay superior to the famous *Gascoign Powder*; the *Indian Root* or the *Hypecocuana*, esteem'd the best Emetick in the World; *Balsam* or *Balm* of *Peru*, more valuable than that of *Gilead* or of *Mecca*; the *Snake Root*;[207] the *Tamarinds* or *Guinea Grains*, the *Civet* of *Africa*, and many others, too many to enumerate.

LIKEWISE of Drugs for Dying, or as we ordinarily call them *Dye Stuffs*; such as *Logwood, Fustic*,[208] *Nicaragua Wood, Brasiletto*,[209] *Shumack, Indico*, and *Cochineal*, the last the inimitable Drug for fixing the brightest Scarlets, Crimsons, and Purples; and which was never heard of before; and to crown all, the *Cocoa* of which we now make Chocolate, the *Sugar Cane* and *Piemento*, the *Coffee* of the *Red Sea* and the *Tea* of *China*, with the Lack or Lacquer of *Japan* and *China*, and the Earthen Ware, or *China* Ware, also of the same; not forgetting the Furs or *Peltry* of *North America*; and to close all, the *Tobacco*, a Plant never heard of in the World till the discovery of *America*.

THERE are indeed no Metals that were found out in any of the Parts thus discover'd, which were not known in *Europe*, except a kind of mixture of Tin and Lead, which we call *Teutenague*,[210] of which the *Chineses* make their Canisters for Tea, and with which they line their other Vessels of Copper or Iron, Earth or Wood, and is very good for keeping such things in, as are nice in Smell, and apt to be ting'd with the tast of the Metal or Wood which the Vessel was made of; like as we tin over our Copper Saucepans and Boylers, and all our white Iron or Latin,[211] of which we make small Vessels for Kitchen Service; but I say, as to Metals we found none new; neither Jewels, for as to Emralds, Pearl, Diamonds, and Rubies, all those the World had seen before.

I⊤ would require an Index of Curiosities and Rarities in Nature should I go about to describe all the Particulars which the discovery of the *East* and *West Indies* furnish'd us with; which are now become as familiar to us as if they belong'd to and were the product of our own Soil: Some of them are us'd in Physick, others in Food, some in Arts, as Dying, Painting, and Laquering; some in Manufacturing, some in Ornaments, and all in Trade; I say it requires an Index of Rarities too long for this Work; but many of them will come of course to be spoken of hereafter.

I⊓ the mean time it ought to be mention'd here, that not only Navigation fortify'd by the addition of the Mathematics arriv'd now to daily Improvement, and Discovery, and animated the People of these parts of the World to an extraordinary search after new Worlds, sailing in new Seas, and pursuing new Adventures; but according to my Title I ought in some measure to enter upon the History of those new Discoveries, and give at least an historical Account of the Discoveries themselves, and the time of them; that so we may at once take a view of the foreign Plantations, Colonies, and Factories, which the several trading Nations of *Europe* are at this time possess'd of in *America, Africa*, and *India*, and of the encrease of their Improvements in those Countries.

I⊓ doing this I shall come of course to the material part, and which indeed is the chief design of, and the end of this whole Undertaking; namely to seek after such farther Discoveries as are still behind.

A⊔⊔ praiseworthy Knowledge seems to have a Tendency to some thing farther to be known. The great encrease of local Discovery invites us still to something beyond itself, which is still left to be discover'd. Neither *Africa* or *America* are yet fully discover'd: There are yet infinite Treasures of Trade and Plantation, to be search'd after, innumerable Nations not convers'd with, navigable Rivers not sail'd up into, unknown Lands not travers'd, and unknown Seas not navigated.

T⊦⊧ Center of *Africa*, the Extremes of *America*, the Mountains of the *Andes*, the Rivers of *Amazones* and *Oroonoque*, and all the vast Country between them are to this Day unconquer'd by the *Spaniards*, and unenquir'd into by any other Nations. These two Rivers are navigable at least a thousand five hundred Miles, if not two thousand Miles each; they receive innumerable other Rivers which are likewise navigable many Miles, perhaps hundreds from the North to the South in their way; there are numberless Nations of People, vastly populous Cities among them, no *European* has ever visited them; yet neither does the Heat or Cold defend them, or make them inaccessible. Let us then enquire a little after what is known, and after what is still to know, and see (if we can) how much more, infinitely more, the latter is than the former, that we may whet the Industry of future Ages, and tell our Posterity a little of what is before them.

CHAP. XXI.

Of the several Countries discover'd, Colonies planted, and Factories settled by Euro-
pean Nations after the discovering the use of the Needle or Compass in Navigation,
and from thence thro' the whole fifteenth Century.

I HAVE observ'd already all the Coast of *Africa* from Cape *Spartel*, at the
Mouth of the *Mediterranean Sea*, being in the Latitude of thirty two to
thirty three Degrees North, and being the North-West Point of *Africa*, to
Cape de Bona Esperanza, in the Latitude of thirty four Degrees and half
South; being the farthest point of the Land of *Africa*, South; also about
again to the East Shore of *Africa*, and along the Coasts of *Mozambique* and
Zanguebar to the Latitude of seven to eight Degrees North; I say, these
were all discover'd and planted by those three famous Navigators for the
King of *Portugal*, *Anthony Nola* a *Genoese, Bartholomew Diaz*, and *Vasco de
Gama*, *Portuguese*, and all before the beginning of the sixteenth Century, and
before the finding out the knowledge of the Magnet, or at least before the
use of the Needle in the Compass; which I mention, because for that Reason I have nothing to do with it in this Chapter.

HITHERTO the best Navigators were mere Coasters; they never willingly
lost sight of Land, nor ever thought themselves easy if they did. If Storms
began to threaten, the Winds ruffle them, and the Seas run high, they were
sure to make in for the first Port they could reach, or to come to an Anchor
under the first Weather-Shore they could make; nor did the timerous Sailors fail upon many occasions of such Hazards, which we now call trifling,
to run on Shore for safety, haling their Ships into such Creeks and Coves as
they could get them into.

ON the contrary, in our Ages, the Seamen act upon quite other Notions.
When it blows hard, and (as the Seamen call it) a *Fret of Wind*, the bold
Mariner, having a good Ship under him, shuns the Shore as the only Terror,
and as the principal place where his Danger lyes; he desires nothing more
than *Sea-room*, good Ground Tackle, and a tight Ship; the first to preserve

him from Shoals and Rocks, and the next to ride out a Storm, when in Port; I shou'd have added indeed the last, namely, that this is always suppose him to have a tight Ship under him; for that is indeed a Seaman's main Dependance.

Now, no sooner was the knowledge of the Needle discover'd, and the Seaman had obtain'd this infallible Guide, by which he could always tell by Candlelight as well as Daylight, within Board as well as without, and as well without the help of Sun, Moon, and Stars, as with them, which way they were going, and which way they ought to go, I say, no sooner was this obtain'd, but the fear of launching out, was all over; the Business was done, narrow Seas or broad Seas, Gulphs or Straights, Bays or Oceans, were now the same thing to the Mariner; he had no more to do but to inform himself rightly of the situation of every place to which he was bound, or where he found occasion to put in, and look upon the Globe or Plane of Surface, for the Latitude and meridian Distance, and he knew the way to it directly.

O'er all the liquid Mountains of the Sea.[212]

HENCE Geography fell to work to draw Charts and Maps of the Coasts, and to place every thing in its right Position upon the plane of the Globe; that every Port, River, and Harbour, being plac'd in its true Latitude, the truly skillful Seaman might be able by the Rules of this Art to know as well where it was, as which way to go to it, and how to find it.

IN consequence of this Art, the long conceal'd World began to show itself, and be found out; nothing could easily escape the indefatigable search of the diligent Seamen. As the Great thirsted after Conquest, and the Merchant thirsted after Gain, so the skillful Mariner and expert Artist thirsted after new discover'd Countries.

No Country was without them; *Spain* had its *Columbus, Jaquez Velasco,*[213] *Ferdinand Cortez,* and its *Francis Pizarro; Portugal* had its *Nola, Gama,* and *Diaz; France,* tho' they made the meanest Discoveries, had their *Sala,*[214] *La Hontan,*[215] *La Barre,*[216] and *Hennepin;*[217] the *Dutch* had *Heemskirk,*[218] *Barents,*[219] and *La Maire;*[220] and *England,* tho' they came in late, had their *Drake, Raleigh,* and *Frobisher; Davis,*[221] *Hudson, Willoughby, Smith,*[222] *Sommers*[223] and many such; by whose Vigor and Application, *England,* tho' she came in, *I say* late, very late, yet got as great a share of new Possession as she well knows what to do with, and which are in many respects equal to the best.

BY these Adventures such mighty Things have been done, and such vast Conquests and Discoveries made, as no History can parallel; not all the rapid Conquests of *Alexander the Great,* or of *Cyrus* before him; not *Julius Cæasar* with his boasted Motto *Veni vidi vici* ever came up to the conquering

Army of *Cortez* and *Pizarro*, who with less than 600 Men in their biggest Armies, *as they call'd them*, respectively, invaded a fourth part of the World, subdued Empires, slew Millions, gave Battle to Armies of 100000 Men at a time; the Histories are known (tho' too long to repeat); besieg'd Imperial Cities, such as *Mexico* and *Cusco*, and took their Emperors in the midst of their own Palaces, and surrounded by innumerable Guards.

THE Particulars are out of my Business; the manner of their Conquests are the Subject of long Histories; I am to bring them all into one Chapter; I shall notwithstanding be as explicit as I can.

THE *Spaniards* having by the navigating Skill of *Christopher Columbus* discover'd the Isles of *Cuba* and *Hispaniola*, *St. John de Porto Rico*, and *Jamaica*, *Jaques Velasco* was sent with five Ships and 300 Soldiers; with which Force he subdued those two vast Islands, where he conquer'd, and as Fame says, cruelly destroy'd five Millions of People.

FROM hence *Ferdinand Cortez*, with at most four hundred Foot and forty Horse, landed on the great Continent of *America*, near *La Vera Cruz*, march'd up sixty Miles into the Country; fought and beat an Army of 40000 *Tsalcallans*,[224] and after that another of 100000; after which the said *Tsalcallans* suing to him for Peace, became his Allies, and furnishing him with Provisions, he undertook the most daring Attempts that the World ever heard of; namely, to march directly to the Imperial City of *Mexico*, and attack the great *Montezuma*, the mightiest Emperor of *America*, in the midst of his Armies, and in a City said to contain two Millions of People.

IN a Word, he march'd, enter'd the City, was driven out of it again, recruited his Army to the number of five hundred Foot and eighty Horse, return'd, besieg'd the City, took it, kill'd 120000 People in the Storm, slew the Emperor, overthrew the Empire, destroy'd the City, re-built it, made it the Seat of the *Spanish* Empire in *America*, and so it continues to be to this Day.

THIS handful of Men, then extending every way, carry'd on the *Spanish* Conquests for above two thousand Leagues, even from the Latitude of forty Degrees North, to fifty three Degrees South, to the Mouth of the Straights of *Magellan*, subduing infinite Nations of People, another Empire, *viz.* that of *Peru*. And process of these Conquests they now *possess Florida, Guadalajara, New* and *Old Mexico, Guaxaca, Nicaragua, Guatimala, Yucatan, Honduras, Darien, Cartagena, St. Martha, New Granada, Venezula, Caracas, New Andalusia, Peru, Chili, Cusco*, and all the Countries upon the *Rio de la Plata* down to the East-side of the Straights of *Magellan*.

THIS is the Sum of the *Spanish* Empire in *America*; an extended Dominion, which were it fully planted, as it is possess'd, wou'd be more than the whole *Roman* Empire in its utmost extent, even as it was estimated in the Days of *Trajan* himself.

NOT but that it ought to be consider'd, and it will not be amiss to mention it here, that agreeable to my Title there is but *little yet known* compar'd to what there is *yet to know*; even of *America* itself; and in order to this I lay it down as a Truth, which I am able to demonstrate, *viz.* That notwithstanding the *Spaniards* are actually possess'd of all the middle part of *America*, the whole Empires of *Mexico* and *Peru*, and the Kingdom of *Chili*, extending for two thousand Leagues in length, as has been describ'd; and notwithstanding the *Portuguese* are, as they say, Masters of both North and South *Brasil*, for above seven hundred Leagues in length, from the *Rio de Amazones* or *Orelliana*, under the Line, to the *Rio de la Plata*, in the Latitude of thirty five Degrees South; and the *Spaniards* possess the said *Rio de la Plata*, and the Navigation of it, from the Spring or Fountain Head of the said River, at the City *La Plata* in *Peru*, to the *Atlantick Ocean*; and notwithstanding the *English* and *French* possess all the Shores of the great Continent call'd *North-America*, from *Hudson's* Straights, and the *Terra di Labradore*, in the Latitude of sixty six Degrees North, to *Cape Florida*, in the Latitude of twenty three, with the Island of *Newfoundland*, the great River *Canada*, the Country of that Name, and perhaps the *Louisiana* or *Mississipi* down to the Gulph of *Mexico* with all the Islands of the *Caribbees*, as well Windward as Leeward: Notwithstanding all this, yet, I say, there is much more of *America* undiscover'd, and at least unconquer'd and unpossess'd, than all the rest put together amounts to, whether we consider the extent of the Land, or the Numbers and Strength, and as I believe Riches and Wealth of the Inhabitants.

I. IT is to be consider'd, that all the part we call *South America*, from the Straights of *Magellan* South, including *Cape Horn* and the *Terra del Fuogo*, in the Latitude of fifty eight, to the *North-Sea* or Coast of *Caracas*, in the Latitude of ten Degrees North, is so far from possess'd, that it is only the Coasts which are discover'd, whether by the *Spaniards* or the *Portuguese* in any Place. *For Example*;

ON the West-side, which we call the Kingdoms of *Chili* and *Peru*, the Mountains of the *Andes*, which run parallel with the Sea for three thousand Miles, are the confess'd Limits of the *Spanish* Dominions, and on that Side we do not find the *Spanish* Bounds reach any where one hundred Miles from the Sea, till they come the length of *Lima*, where it opens a little to the East, to the Cities of *Cusco* and *Plata*, and the Mountains of *Potosi*, and then stretches away North again to the Country of *Popayan*.

ON the North-side, which is all that Country from *Cartagena* to *Cape Dragon*, including the several Provinces under the *Spanish* Dominion, call'd

Cartagena, St. Martha, Venezuela, and *New-Andalusia,* I say, in all these it is the Coast only which the *Spaniards* may be said to possess; for they have so little else, that they are no where Masters of any thing above a hundred Miles within the Land; nor can they possess what they have so far, without daily Assaults of the Natives; who with poison'd Arrows and Launces repay the *Spanish* Cruelties so effectually, that the *Spaniards* care not how little they engage with them: And all the Country farther South, to the River *Oroonoque,* is evidently out of the Possession or Power of the *Spaniards,* who as often as they have attempted to possess it for the sake of the Wealth and Fruitfulness of it, they have found their Settlements overthrown, their People massacred, and all Hopes taken from them of planting again with security; the Natives being not only Bold and Daring, but so infinitely Numerous, that it wou'd be a kind of Desperation to attempt them, unless it were with powerful Armies regularly supplyed and duly supported to carry on a general Conquest.

It is evident these People are not Tame and Passive, as the *Spaniards* found the Inhabitants of *Cuba* and *Hispaniola,* or those of the *Honduras* and *Guatimala*; but Brave and Daring, not terrifyed with the noise of a Gun, or the glittering of the *Spaniards* Swords and Armour; but tho' they have no Guns, they boldly run up to the Teeth of the *Spaniards,* and wounding them with poisoned Launces, fly from one to another with a strange kind of Courage, next to Desperation; depending upon this, that if they can but wound a *Spaniard,* so as to make him bleed, they know he is a dead Man, and so fly to another.

But not to dwell upon their manner of Fighting, this is the Consequence which reaches to the present Case, (*viz.*) That the *Spaniards* contenting themselves with the Possession of *Cartagena,* and other Ports and Places on the Sea-Coast, to secure their Commerce and Communication with *Europe,* they study as much as possible to live in Peace and good Neighbourhood with the several *Indian* Nations behind them, who they know to be populous without Number, and therefore maintain their upland or inland Possessions and Settlements, chiefly as a Barrier against them, and to carry on a gainful Commerce with them.

As this is the Case upon the whole Coast, it demonstrates what I say above, that the Possessions of the *Spaniards* are but trifling, compar'd to the main Continent; and suppose it were two hundred Miles, which we do not find it reaches any where, except about that part call'd *New Granada* and *Popayan,* and where it may be said to joyn with *Peru*; yet what is this to the vast extended Country behind it, to the River *Oroonoque,* and from thence to the *Orelliana* or *Rio d' Amazones*; and thence again to the *Rio Parana, Paraguay,* and *La Plata?* a Country of very near two thousand Miles square, full of Wealth, and full of Millions of People, fruitful, and to a Miracle cultivated, the Savage Inhabitants consider'd; and in all which, it may be said, that never *Spaniards* set a Foot there, except a *few Priests*; and those at a Price too dear to encourage any to venture to follow, for most of them were massacred by the Natives.

II. WE are to take Notice of the Plantation of the *Portuguese* on the East, or rather North-East part of *South-America*, which we call the *Brasils*. The *Portuguese*, according to their gasconading way of Writing, talk mighty big of this Colony; and it is indeed a very great Plantation, as I shall take notice of by itself; and I must add, that had any Nation but the *Portuguese* been Masters of it, the Improvement of it had been infinitely greater than it is. But take it in the utmost extent which the vain boasting *Portuguese* can pretend to; namely, from the Mouth of the *Orelliana*, or River of *Amazones*, to the *Rio de la Plata*, which is thirty five Degrees in Latitude, and which is 2100 Miles; yet what is it but a Verge of the Country, compar'd to the vast Continent behind them? The Christians (if the *Portuguese* may be call'd so) indeed are fully possess'd of the Sea-Coast: But how far do they extend themselves within the Country? From the Mouth of the River *Amazones* to *Pernambuco*, which is near five hundred Miles, and is call'd the *North-Brasil*, they are no where Masters of the Country fifty Miles from the Coast; nor have they any Cities or fortify'd Places farther into the Country. If they correspond with the Natives higher up, it is by Compacts and mutual Agreements, and the Civilities of Neighbourhood and Commerce; but the *Brasilians* are very numerous and powerful, and especially having now learn'd the use of Fire-Arms, and obtain'd the Trust of them too from the *Portuguese*; which by the way was none of the best pieces of Policy on their Side.

THESE *Brasilians*, I say, (who are very numerous) live at large in their own Towns and Villages, close at the Heels of the *Portuguese* Settlements; where in spight of all the *Portuguese* can do, they enjoy their own Government, such as it is, live their own Way, do their own Business, reserve to themselves their own savage Customs and Manners, and which they are very Tenacious of; and more than all retain their own Idolatry, and the Barbarisms of their own Heathen Rites (I can not call it Religion.) This I instance to prove, as it effectually does, that the *Portuguese* have little or no influence upon them, and consequently are very far from any Government or Dominion beyond the Bounds which they antiently possess'd; and which indeed is no more than a narrow Verge of the Country, as I have said, even all the way from the *Equinoctial Line*; (for the *Rio d'Amazones* enters the Ocean just under the Equator) to the Latitude of thirty five Degrees South.

The farthest place where the *Portuguese* have enter'd into the Land, is said to be at St. *Salvador*, where they tell us, their Gold Mines, newly discover'd, are three hundred Miles up the Country.

AND tho' this is begging the Question for one particular Spot, and I do not grant it to be so far by above one hundred Miles; yet even this, for one place does not alter the Case; for so the *Spaniards* may be said to possess all the Country upon the *Rio de la Plata* to *Peru*, because they have of late made a kind of settled Commerce by the Navigation of that great River, between the Country of *Peru* and the *Buenos Ayres* in the Mouth of the River.

BUT even this also is carried on by a civil Usage of the Natives, of whom several Nations inhabit that great Country, tho' nothing so Populous neither as farther to the North; and this Navigation the *Spaniards* make profitable to those Natives, otherwise they could never preserve it; but I say they make it profitable to them, by buying Provisions of them, and giving them *European* Goods for them; such as Knives, Hatchets, Scissars, Beads, and other Toys, such as they like; as also Cloths, Callico, Linnen, and other Necessaries; but as to Conquests and Dominion, even the *Spaniards* themselves do not pretend to it here. Nor do the *Portuguese* in the *Brasils* attempt to exercise any Authority over the *Brasilians*; as particularly appears in this, that they employ none of them as Servants; nor will the *Brasilians* be their Servants; nay, they will hardly assist them in any laborious Work, tho' paid for it.

MUCH less do the *Portuguese* make any of them Slaves; but on the contrary they bring all their Slaves from *Africa*; and all their Drudgery is done by those *Negroes*, the *Brasilians* being free, and scorning to labour for any one but themselves.

I NEED only refer for the Truth of this to *Neuhoff's* Account of Brasil,[225] and to even the *Portuguese* themselves.

THUS it is evident all the center of this vast Continent of *South-America*, for near four thousand Miles in length, and for two thousand Miles in breadth, in some Places more, is yet entirely undiscover'd, and not in the least subdued; and tho' it may be said, that the Southmost part of this Country is not full of People, especially from the Latitude of forty Degrees to the *Magellanic* Straights, But it is answer'd;

    I. WE do not know how it may be peopled far within the Land; and as for the Coast, tho' our People have not found the Inhabitants numerous, yet they always found some People, tho' they were unconversible, and fled from the *Europeans*, when they saw them; and it is more than likely, that in the more inland Parts of the Country they might be more Populous.

II. BUT for the Northern Parts, as particularly all the Coasts of the Rivers *Parana, Paraguay*, the *Marahon*, and the *Rio Grande*, with all the inner Country of *Brasils*, as far as has been seen or heard of, they are full of People, even surprizingly so.

III. All the Country bordering on the South-side of the *Rio d' Amazones*, and all that vastly extended Country, between that River and the *Oroonoque*, reaching for two thousand Miles from West to East, and above one hundred and fifty Miles from North to South, are so exceeding full of People, so throng'd, and so continually multiplying and encreasing, that if the Country were not the most fertil and productive of all manner of Things needful for human Life, it would be impossible they should subsist; nay, some who have calculated upon the Accounts given by *Texiera, Orelliana*,[226] Sir *Walter Raleigh*, and others, tell us, that if the rest of the Country is equally Populous with that Part which they saw, and as there is Reason to believe it is, there must be more People in it than there was in all that part of *America* which the *Spaniards* subdued, and in which, according to *Los Casas*,[227] the *Spaniards* put forty Millions to Death, besides those that escap'd their Fury by flight, or were otherwise so fortunate to escape them by Favour.

IN a Word, we have Reason to believe that there is no Christian Nation in *Europe*, where the like Numbers of People are to be found in a narrower compass than on the Banks of the *Rio d' Amazones*, or of the *Oroonoque*, except just the United *Dutch* and *Flemish* Provinces; where the particular advantages of Commerce have drawn such Numbers of People together.

IT is not improper to mention here, what some Historians have, and not improperly suggested on this Occasion, that the great Ravages which the *Spaniards* made in *America*, at their first landing among those innocent People, and the Terror which their Cruelties struck into the Minds of the Inhabitants, was such, as made all those who were at distance sufficient, fly for their Lives, with their Wives and their Children, into any of the adjacent Countries that would receive them, and that could shelter them from the Fury of their Enemies.

THAT thus, from the adjacent Countries of *Peru* West; from *Nicaragua*, and *Guatimala*, North-West; from that which we call *New-Granada, Venezuela*, and St. *Martha* North; in all which Countries, the Cruelties and Butcheries of the *Spaniards* were sufficient to terrify the poor People; I say from these Parts it is suppos'd vast Multitudes, nay Millions of poor frighted People fled into these remoter Countries, among the Fastnesses of inaccessible Woods, and Mountains; for the Cordileiros or Mountains of the *Andes* begin in that part of the Country next to *Peru*. Hitherto, I say, no doubt they went; and being hunted thence by the *Spanish* Horse, fled afterwards farther into the flat Country, where the vast Confluence of Waters and Springs forms the great Rivers *Paria* or *Oroonoque*, and *Orelliana* or *Amazones*; the latter of which is no less than three Miles broad, two thousand Miles from its Influx into the Sea.

AMONG these Waters they were secured, the *Spaniards* being in no Condition for such a pursuit, and finding also a sufficient Wealth in the Palace of the Emperor of *Peru* to glut their Avarice, till they fell out about sharing the Spoil, and so fell to killing one another, and gave the *Indians* some respit.

THAT the *Peruvians* fled hither, is less doubted; for the *Spaniards* perceived, upon *Pizarro*'s murthering their King, and plundering his Palace, that the People of the Country were as it were vanish'd on a sudden, and to be seen no more; that is to say in such Multitudes as they at first appear'd in; and yet they had not massacred so many of them, as they had done in other of the Provinces before. Upon which *Pizarro* caused the Country to be penetrated Eastward and Southward to find out the Inhabitants; but the People he sent soon brought him Word, that the Mountains Eastward were unpassable; and as to the Country Southward, which was *Chili*, he soon met with such Resistance there, and so did the *Spaniards* that succeeded him, that they began to be weary of the War, and were glad to let the *Chilians* alone; and thus their Conquests received a Check for some time.

As they fled to the Mountains of the *Andes*, to the Sources of the River of *Amazones*, and the inaccessible Lands among those Rivers, from *Pizarro* and his *Spaniards* in *Peru*; so they fled in Multitudes from the same wicked and bloody Rage in the Provinces of *Popayan, New Granada, Venezeula*, and *New-Andalusia*; and these took Shelter Southward, on the Banks of the *Oroonoque*; a Country, by the like prodigious Conflux of Waters, as difficult of Access as the other. And these Nations, which were infinitely Numerous, taking Shelter in those Low Countries, which were fruitful and rich, and qualify'd fully to receive and entertain them, 'tis no Wonder, that all that part of *America* is now so exceeding Populous.

II. FROM hence take a View of the Northern Parts of *America*, such of them as are known and discover'd; for it is not with the North of *America* as it is with the South. The South is known to be every where surrounded by the Sea, except in the finall Isthmus of *Darien*; and our *European* Ships of several Nations have sail'd round it, and do so continually. But as to the North Part, we have discover'd only one Side of it, namely, the East; we neither know its extent one way or other, North or West, whether it joins West to the Land off

Jesso[228] and *Japan*, or North to *Europe*, and the Lands round and beyond the Pole.

It is discover'd indeed to *Frobisher*'s *Straights*, and the Coast of *Greenland*, as far as to eighty Degrees North Latitude. But tho' all that Land how poor and how severely Cold it may be, is yet inhabited, those Inhabitants remain unvisited, except on the first Discovery, and the Country lyes abandon'd and deserted.

We have three great Inlets into the Land of *North-America* from the Sea; that is to say at *Hudson's Straights*, and all the several Bays call'd *Davis's, Bassins's, Button's*, and *Hudson's*, but little or no Possession; and all to the Westward of those Bays, be it as far as *Asia* or not, tho' full of People, is unpossess'd by the *Europeans*, except our *English* Settlements at the bottom of *Hudson's Bay*; where at best, we have not two hundred People; so all those deep Bays are in the Hands of the Natives, of what Nation soever they may be call'd, and how Numerous soever they are.

The next Inlet the *Europeans* have into the Land is by the River of *Canada* or St. *Laurence*; and here the *French* indeed visit and discover great Tracts of Land up to the Lakes *Heuron, Illonois*, and several others. But what are all the Countries that the *French* have planted? Are they not full of the Native Inhabitants unconquer'd, unsubdued, and who live under their own Kings or *Caisicks*,[229] and govern'd by their own Laws, make Peace and War absolutely as they please? The *French* are only a handful of People here and there planting a little Ground, by the Banks of the Lakes and Rivers; and who being dispers'd into many Places, and at great Distances, are not to be nam'd with the infinite Multitudes of People which spread over all that Country to the West.

Let any one that pleases to follow this Observation read but Father *Hennepin*,[230] and the Discoveries of Monsier *De Salle*,[231] of *Ferdinand Soto*,[232] and of several others; and they will find that the undiscover'd Country is, to that planted by the *French*, more than as ten thousand to one.

Even the Colonies of the *English* in *New England, New-York, New-Jersey*, &c. What are they but a long measur'd out Plantation upon the Coast? None of those Colonies have any Possessions or cultivated Lands above 150 Miles from the Sea worth naming. Let them go up the River from *New-York* to *Albany*, which is the highest and most remote of all the Colonies, or up the *Delaware* River, where the Waters joyn almost with those of *Virginia*; nay, let us take the third great Inlet of Water, which is that we call the Bay of *Cheseapeake*; yet even here the bottom of the Bay is not above two hundred Miles from the Capes or Entrance; and as it goes away North, it is not full 150 from the Sea in a Line, the Bay running away due North, after it receives the first Rivers of *James* and *York* and *Rapahannock*.

WHAT then are these Colonies, tho' Great in themselves, and Powerful and Potent, as now encreas'd, compar'd to the vast Continent of *North-America*? Whose extent North I have describ'd a little, and whose Western Coast is not yet discover'd? Neither do we yet know whether, *as I said*, it is bounded by the Sea *yea* or *no*.

HOW little then of this newly discover'd World is yet known, compar'd to what there is yet left to know? And what room is here still for the industrious World to put themselves forth for the extending the Discoveries already made, and forming the Nations, whether by Conquests or otherwise, into Societies, both for Commerce and for Strength?

THIS Part, tho' remote from the present Argument, is not so far from the design of this Work: And tho' it may be spoken of more largely hereafter by itself, yet I may take this Notice of it here; *namely,* that this very thought opens a Door for future Ages, and for yet more enterprizing Nations, to think of enlarging the *European* Settlements in all these Parts of *America*; which as it may easily be done by making their beginning with sufficient Strength and Numbers of People; so where attempted with such sufficient Numbers, the fertility of the Soil may more than sufficiently answer for the Success. For no Plantation undertaken by sufficient Numbers of industrious People can fail of Success, if the fertility of the Soil is such, as may answer to produce, the blessing of Heaven concurring, a sufficient encrease for their Subsistence. To make this feasible in any Place, I shall in short propose it for one Place, in the Manner following.

CHAP. XXII.

A Proposal for a new Settlement in America, being wholly founded on the mere Improvement of the Land as a Plantation, without any view of Commerce till after the first Success is ascertained.

THERE is a large tract of Land in *America* unpossess'd at present by any *European* Nation; abandon'd for so long, as that, even the *Spaniards* themselves do not, and cannot, even by a long prescription of Years, lay any Claim to it.

THIS is that Country, beginning at the Plains of St. *Andrew*, above the Bay of that Name, about 120 Miles South of the *Rio de la Plata*, in the Latitude of thirty seven, and reaching to *Port St. Julien*, in the Latitude of fifty to fifty one, being in length fourteen Degrees, or 840 Miles from North-East to South-West.

THIS Country extends from East to West, from the Shore of the *Atlantick Ocean* to the East-side of the Mountains of the *Andes*, which limit the Possessions of the *Spaniards* in that part of the Kingdom of *Chili*, which extent is in the most Northern part at least 1200 Miles, narrowing gradually, as the Continent is narrow'd to the South-West, till off of *Port St. Julien*, at the Mouth of that River the breadth is about 560 Miles.

As the Climate in this Latitude must necessarily be Temperate, the coldest Winds, which in a South Latitude must blow from the South, coming over but a small tract of Land, and then blowing every way from the Sea: So Experience of Travellers assures us of another important Article for Temper of Air, (*viz.*) That the Surface is generally *Plain*, not Mountainous and Hilly; and Dry, not Boggy or Fenny; fully suited, and indeed prepar'd by Nature to produce Grass and Corn, the two great Articles of Man's Sustenance, and to make a healthy Climate both for Man and Beast.

THAT the Soil bears Grass in a great and extraordinary Manner, we have first the Testimony of several *English* who have view'd it, and have found for above 100 Miles within the Land, the whole Surface cover'd with good

Grass, fit for Pasturage of Cattle; and as far as they could see, the Plains lay extended every way, all full of excellent Grass, high in its Season as a Man's Knee; and when graz'd down by the Cattle, matted with Clover, and an excellent Turf fit for Sheep or Horses, and as good as can any where be seen.

THAT this Grass is sweet and good, qualify'd to feed and fat up the largest black Cattle,[233] is evident, past Contradiction, from this, that the black Cattle carry'd into the *Buenos Ayres*, and other Parts, by the *Spaniards* and *Portuguese*, having been suffer'd to run Wild, have so encreas'd, and spread themselves to the Southward of the River *De la Plata*, that most of this Country is over-run with them; and the Hunters from the *Buenos Ayres* make it a very great Trade to kill them for their Hides; which is the chief return of Merchandize which they now bring from that Port, the Ports South of *Peru* only excepted.

THE fertility of the Soil and temperature of the Climate thus ascertain'd, what remains then to secure a flourishing Settlement but beginning such an Undertaking with a sufficiency of two Things?

    I. A SUFFICIENT store of Corn for Bread only, for support of the Colony for one Year, till the Land being cultivated and planted might produce a Sufficiency of their own for future Supply.

    II. A SUFFICIENT Force to preserve and protect the Settlement against any assault of the *Spaniards*; as to the Natives, their Number is not considerable.

As to Flesh, the Country abounding in Deer, and Black-Cattle, there wou'd be no need to provide. But lest the Pains of Hunting shou'd be thought too great a Hindrance of the more needful Work of planting the Land, a Breed of Cattle might be taken in, either at our own Colonies of *New-England* and *Virginia*, or at the *Brasils*, where the *Portuguese* have a very great plenty of all kinds, as Cows, Horses, and Hogs.

NOW, not to enlarge on the several Excellencies of this Country for a Colony, it is particularly adapted for a Colony of *English*; by the aptness of the Climate and of the Soil for all the usual growth of *England*, such as *English* Corn for Bread, Barley for Malt, Apples and such other kinds for Cyder, &c. In short, the Country is as it were singled out for *Englishmen*; not only to live in, but to live just after the manner of *English* People's living. Not too hot to bear Wheat, or to make Malt, or to preserve Beer; not too cold to produce the tenderer Plants for Kitchen Gardening, for wearing Cloths, and dressing after the ordinary Manner; or too Cold for the Health and Safety of the Cattle, who in violent Colds, deep Snows, and continued Frosts, perish for want of Food.

NOR is the Country over-grown with Woods, so as in *New-England, Virginia*, and all the Northern Colonies, where there is no present Planting till after immense Labour and Expence to clear the Ground of Timber, and prepare it for the Corn; whereas this Country, tho' supply'd with Woods at proper Distances, lyes already plain, over-grown with good Turf, is already good Pasture, and the Plow may be immediately set into it to make it good Arable.

To these Advantages take the following Negatives.

I. HERE are no venemous Creatures; such as in the *Brasils* the Country is dangerously full of, (*viz.*) Here are no Snakes and Serpents; of which in the *Brasils*, they find some as big as a Man's Thigh, and fifteen to twenty Foot long.

II. No Lions, Tygers, Wolves, Elephants, Bears, or other ravenous and furious Beasts, at least we do not read or learn from Travellers who have been on Shore here, that any such Creatures were ever seen; no nor so much as Monkeys and Baboons; a kind of Creatures many ways mischievous and destructive to the diligent Planter.

III. No Allegators or Crocodiles in the Rivers, nor any other noxious Creatures, at least not that I have heard or read of, and I have been diligent to gain Information by both.

WITH all these Encouragements, What shou'd hinder a Colony being planted here with Success? All the Miscarriages of former Colonies wou'd be secur'd against here. It is observable, that all the Plantations which the *English* establish'd in *North-America* met with great Difficulties, and Disappointments in their Beginnings, but that all of them happen'd from some other of these Causes and Accidents.

I. THE Treachery or Falshood and Cruelty of the Natives or *Indians*. Thus in *Virginia* they suffer'd two Massacres; and in *New-England*, three very fierce Wars, all in the infancy of their Settlements, and almost to their Ruin.

II. DISSENTION among themselves, which was twice the Ruin of *Virginia* in particular.

III. NEGLECT of Friends in *Europe* not supplying them in time, till they, having no Product of their own, have been ready to starve; nay, some have perish'd, and others abandon'd the Colonies, by reason of the extreme Necessities they have been reduc'd to.

ALL these three Heads are and may be effectually guarded against in this Settlement, and that in such a manner as to be without the least Apprehensions of them, or any of them. For as to Natives, as I have said, here are no Numbers to make them formidable; and as to the *Spaniards* either they are to be treated with, or fought with, and either of them is easy enough.

As to private Dissention, an establish'd Authority and Government sent with them, may sufficiently provide against and prevent it.

And as to Supplies, a sufficient Magazine carry'd at first, puts the Colony out of Fear, the Soil being ready for the Plow as soon as they come there, which was not the Case in any of the other.

Such a Colony being settled in this manner and secured of Success, the next Enquiry wou'd be, What encrease of Commerce wou'd this be to us, and how wou'd they Trade?

Sir *John Narbrough*,[234] a well known Person for his Experience in such Things as these, being sent by King *Charles* the Second in the *Sweepstakes* Man of War for the discovery of the Straights of *Magellan*, winter'd in this Port, and went several times on Shore with twenty or thirty Men at a time, spreading themselves, sometimes one way and sometimes another, to take a view of the Land, and gives the same Account as I have had confirm'd from other Hands; and as I have here taken Notice of, (*viz.*) that the Ground is not Mountainous; he likens it to *New-Market Heath*, that it bears excellent sweet and good Grass, and wou'd bear good Corn.

He confirms also, that they found in all their stay there, nothing Venemous, nothing Ravenous, no noxious Vermin, Insects, or Serpents, nor any of those most nauseous of all Gods Creatures, Monkies or Apes; but Ostriches and Guianacoes, that is *Peruvian* Sheep, which are as large as Mules, and carry Burthens like Mules in *Peru*, as also abundance of Deer.

But to return to the Subject of Commerce, for without Commerce, say the enquiring World, of what use is a Colony? To this I answer:

I. Numbers of People make Commerce in the very consequence of their living together. And therefore the first Article wou'd be, that as they must have all their Clothes, Utensils, and Furniture, from *Europe*, there wou'd be immediately, with a new encrease of People, a new Consumption of the Woollen and Linen Manufactures of *Europe*, besides all the necessary demands of Iron, Brass, Lead, Tin, Copper, &c. in all the necessary Materials for the Conveniencies of Life.

II. The Inhabitants, who, tho' not so numerous as to be troublesome or dangerous, yet are not wanting, wou'd soon be civiliz'd, so as to wear Clothes of some sort or other, and consequently wou'd encrease the said Consumption.

III. There could be no question, but that a Correspondence wou'd be soon establish'd over the *Andes*, or by Passages which the Natives wou'd discover into *Chili*, and so to the *South Seas*; and whether the Correspondence were with the native *Chilians*, or with the *Spaniards*, or with both, the consequence wou'd certainly be a very great Market for all kinds of *European* Goods, especially our own *British* Product and Manufactures as above.

IV. AND to crown all, I cannot doubt, but such an *English* Colony, as they grew great and consequently strong, wou'd be able to extend themselves into *Chili* itself, so as to plant there, and secure to themselves some important Harbour on the Shore of the *South-Seas*; of which there are many, which the *Spaniards* have not possession of, and never had any, whatever Claim they may make to the Property of them, according to their antient Pretences, that the Pope gave them a Right to all the Kingdoms of the *American* World; which was no more the Pope's to give than it was the King of *Spain*'s before he gave it; so that the Right is undoubtedly in the *Chilians* or native Inhabitants; who as they were never conquer'd, and never conceded their Right to the *Spaniards*, or to any other Nation, so they have still a Right of Inheritance, and may concede it to the *English*, or any other Nation whatsoever.

THIS Part, and the Advantages of it to *England* above any Colony, or indeed above all the Colonies they yet possess in *America*, wou'd take up a Volume by itself to enlarge upon; it is evident at first sight, that there is in its view an Ocean of Commerce, and a Sea of Wealth, were it rightly pursued; but I cannot dwell upon it here.

HOWEVER I must not leave it abruptly neither, for in farther Answer to the Question proposed, about what benefit of Commerce wou'd come from such a Colony, it remains to say what Returns we shall find there. How shall the Ships be freighted back? And how shall they pay for the Goods they will take from us?

I MUST confess it is not likely that a Country so well situated for a Plantation, and so encouraging for People, shou'd want a Product to return to *Europe*; and tho' it may not be obvious to a Stranger at first View, give me leave to say in the General, 'tis only the best qualify'd for, and the best furnish'd with Returns, of any Country wherever the *English* are yet planted on the Continent of *America*.

NEW ENGLAND and *New-York*, and all our Northern Colonies are distress'd for Returns; and were it not for our Islands which take off their Corn and Cattle, (*viz.*) Their Flower, Peas and Malt (in Beer), their Fish, Pork, Beef, Horses, and Lumber, they wou'd not be able to pay *England* for the Clothes they wear; and instead of being an Advantage wou'd be an insupportable Burthen to us and to themselves; for they have nothing to make Returns to *England* in, but Furs and Skins of Beasts, which they call Peltry, Train-Oil, Turpentine, Rice, and Tobacco; the two last appropriate to *Carolina* and *Virginia*; the rest wou'd not in their Value load the tenth part of the Ships that go thither, or pay for one twentieth part of the Goods they consume. But here on the contrary, are several rich and valuable Articles for Returns, of which, as the Country can never be exhausted, so we can never be glutted with the Quantity.

    I. As the Mountains of the *Andes* are known to be full of Gold on the West-side, by which the *Spaniards* receive from the Country of *Chili* an immense Treasure every Year, yet are not said to have made any effectual Search, such is their Sloth, or to find any more of it than the Natives bring them from the Rills and Brooks issuing every where out of the Hills; so it cannot be reasonably doubted, but that the Rivers and Brooks issuing from the same Mountains on the Eastside, and of which there are an exceeding great Number, must partake of the same Treasure; to which Eastern-side of the Mountains this Colony wou'd immediately extend itself.

NOR do I speak this only upon the probability of it, as above, but the Experience of divers, who have travers'd the Country, even close up to those Mountains, from the *Rio de la Plata*, who confirm it, that it is really so. And Sir *John Narbrough* in his Wintering there, as above, found several small pieces of Gold, tho' at so great a Distance.

So that upon the whole there is a moral Certainty of Gold, and that even, tho' a Communication with *Chili* should not be obtain'd; and if it should be obtain'd, as it does not seem rational to question, then the having Gold in any reasonable Quantity, is no more to be doubted, than it is, that there are Rivers issuing from the Mountains and running into the *South Seas*.

   II. THERE is a Commodity infinitely valuable in *Europe*, because extreamly wanted, and in its proportion as sure a Wealth as Gold itself, and that is *Salt-Petre*. This we have likewise the Testimony of Sir *John Narbrough* for, who asserts it of his own Knowledge, both as to the *Quality* and the *Quantity*; that it is found on the Surface of the Earth, and in several Pits; so that as he gave King *Charles* an account, many Ships might be loaded with it.

  III. THE Hides of Black Cattle are to be had without Number in the North Part of this Country, towards the *Rio de la Plata*, and which we cannot doubt of getting, because we know they are at this time, the chief Return of any bulk, which is brought from the *Buenos Ayres*: And we know likewise by unquestioned Evidence, that all that part of the Country is over-run with those Cattle, whose Flesh the *Spaniards* destroy for the sake of the Hide only, and these Hides are in point of Merchandize, such a Return as *Europe* can never be over-stock'd with.

216

IV. THERE are likewise Deer Skins, Ostrich Feathers, and Seal Skins in great abundance; which may be call'd an Article for Returns, tho' the Quantity may not be great, but the other three Articles are sufficient.

WHAT Drugs, medicinal Plants, or Minerals, may be found, must be left to farther Discovery. But why shou'd this Country be wholly void of such Things, of which almost all the World produce some.

THERE are many navigable Rivers which give Inlets into the Country, and consequently make farther Discoveries easy; the Sea is full of Fish, and at least there can be no question but great Quantities of Train Oil would be made; so that in a Word there could be no want of Returns to support and establish Trade.

THE Product of Corn wou'd be great, and on Occasion they might come in for a share of selling it to the *Portuguese* in *Brasil*; who tho' they have plenty of other Grain, yet are always willing to buy *European* Flower, which this wou'd be, tho' growing in *America*. But shou'd that fail, it is not a longer Voyage, nor any way so hazardous, to *Barbadoes* and *Jamaica*, than it is from *Ireland* to those Islands; so that they might send Beef, and Pork, and Flower, and Beer, directly thither, the Voyage taking at the medium of the Colony, being 1140 Leagues, that is to say, from forty Degrees South, to thirteen or seventeen Degrees North, with very little variation of Longitude: Whereas from *England* to *Ireland*, and thence to *Barbadoes*, is thirty seven Degrees in Latitude, (*viz.*) from fifty to thirteen, besides the Westing in Longitude, and besides the danger of the Voyage.

I NEED say no more. If any Man enquires after the prospects of future Improvement promis'd in this Work, let him take this for one; and tho' I may propose several more, yet I cannot say the whole World can present one more Promising, more capable of infinite Advantages, or every way more suited to the *British* Nation, as well the Constitution of the People as of their Commerce.

N. B. *Sir* John Narbrough, *in his Voyage mention'd above, being sensible of all that I have said here about a Settlement; and in order to obviate the Pretences of any other Nation, as far as those Pretences may be grounded upon Possession, took a formal Possession of this very Country in the Name of King* Charles *the Second, his then reigning Sovereign; declar'd he found the same uninhabited by any* European *Nation, and fixing up a Cross of Wood, with an Inscription cut in Brass fixt upon it, he proclaim'd King* Charles *Sovereign of the Country: This I mention (not that I think any Body has a Right to dispossess the Natives of a Country) to intimate, that at least the* English *have as good a Title to it, as any other Nation whatsoever.*

CHAP. XXIII.

Of the several Attempts made for Discoveries of and for Planting in the unknown World, after the obtaining the knowledge and use of the Magnet, *and of the* Compass; *and particularly of the* Portuguese *beginning their Trade in the* INDIES.

I SHOULD now go back to the Discoveries made in the fifteenth and sixteenth Century, and proceed to take Notice, how, in consequence of that great Discovery of all, I mean *the Compass*, Navigation being as it were let loose, and the Seaman's Hands unty'd, which were fetter'd and manacl'd before by their Ignorance, not daring to venture far from the Shores; I say in consequence of this great Discovery, all the *European* Nations went to work, spreading the Seas with Ships, and searching every part of the Ocean for new Worlds.

GAMA and *Diaz*, who had, as above, travers'd the main Land of *Afric*, to the Cape *de Bona Esperanza*, and about to *Melinda* and *Mosambique*, now launch'd out Eastward; and passing the great Island of *Madagascar*, as a thing beneath their Ambition, and which they might secure afterwards, press'd on over the *Indian Ocean* till they happily discover'd the Coast of *India* itself: And the first Place they landed upon was at *Calicut*, where they fix'd and fortifyed; from thence they coasted the Shores of *Malabar*, and discover'd the Island of *Ceylon*, loading their Ships with Pepper, Cinamon, and other Spices; as also Callicoes and Silks, and in short a prodigious Cargo came back. Upon the same Coast they saw and set their Hearts upon the City of *Goa*, tho' not in Condition then to attack it, but from thence they steer'd West again for *Madagascar*, where they landed, gave the Name of St. *Augustine* to the Bay and Port, which still retains that Name; victualled their Ships with good Beef salted and dryed in the Sun, stor'd themselves with fresh Provisions, Wood and Water, and came safe back to *Lisbon*, making a most surprizing advantage of the Voyage, which caus'd them to fit out again three Ships the next Year: Then they seiz'd upon the City of *Goa*, but were beaten out of it again by the *Indians*, but the next

218

Year took it again, and have kept it to this Day. And making this the center of all their Acquisitions in the *Indies*, proceeded to the Eastern Part, and in three Years afterwards made themselves Masters of all the rest of the trading Parts or Coasts of *India*; such as that of *Coromondel, Golconda, Bengale, Sumatra, Java*, with all the *Spice Islands*, and even from thence North to *China* and *Japan*.

How they were afterwards wound out of all these again, either by Force or Stratagem, or both, being supplanted and driven from them all by the *Dutch*, is matter of History, not of Discoveries or Improvements, and so does not relate to the Subject I am upon.

While the *Portuguese* were busied in these successful Adventures to the East, some of their Ships by the mere Misadventure of bad Weather, and a great and continued Storm from the South-East, being driven far West in their Voyage towards the Cape of *Good Hope*, and almost in the utmost Despair, lest they shou'd perish for want of Water, or by the Fury of the Storm, happily made Land to the Westward, in the Latitude of twelve Degrees South of the Line; and running in at all Hazards discover'd that glorious Colony, such they have since made it, of the *Brasils*; which giving an account of to the King of *Portugal*, at their return, a little Squadron of five Ships were sent the next Year to take Possession of it. These entering the River of *Pernambuco*, they took Possession of the Country and built the City *Olinda*, now call'd by the Name of the River, and *Port Pernambuc* or *Pernambuco*; from hence they have spread their Possessions since, as far North as to the *Rio d' Amazones* under the Line, or in the Latitude of thirty Minutes North, to the Mouth of *Rio de la Plata*, in the Latitude of thirty five Degrees South, being no less than 2000 Miles in length; the encreasing Wealth of which Colony we all have an account of yearly from *Lisbon*, the *Portuguese* generally one Year with another bringing from thence two Millions Sterling of Gold in Specie, besides an immense Value in Sugars, *Brasil* Tobacco, Hides, and other Goods.

During these Acquisitions of the *Portuguese*, which were indeed infinitely beyond what any other Nations had made at that time, the *English* labouring as it might be said not in the Fire, but in the Extremities of Cold, made equivalent Discoveries to the North, not at that time equivalent in Wealth, but afterwards by the inimitable and unweary'd Diligence of the People, made equivalent in every thing; I mean their several Plantations of *Virginia, Newfoundland, New-England, Bermudas, Hudson's Bay*, and such other Colonies as they fix'd upon, on the Continent, or near it, of *North America*; and which we have since seen improv'd also in their Degree to an unexpected Magnitude; I say unexpected, because of the Difficulties which they met with in their first Attempts, by the Repulses from the Natives, who many times furiously supplanted them, destroying at once the Labours of many Years, and sometimes treacherously massacring and murthering the People: Notwithstanding all which, we find them now advantagiously planted; and by the force of Industry, and the help of Commerce, we see those Colonies yielding a Return of *Tobacco, Rice*, rich *Furs, Trayn Oil, Turpentine, Fish*, and sundry other Productions of the Continent; and *Sugars, Indico, Ginger, Cotton, Cocoa, Pimento*, and other Productions of the Islands, which are in their amounts, and as improv'd by our Trade, equal to the Gold of the *Brasils* and the Silver of *Potosi*.

IN the same compass of time we find the *French* making Discoveries in the Bay of St. *Laurence*, the Rivers of *Canada* and *Mississipi*, and planting the Inland part of *North America*; from whence however they have as yet found nothing to bring back, but Furs from the Land, and Fish from the Sea; which notwithstanding has made those Colonies very profitable to them. They have also a large Share of the Island Colonies, together with the *English* in the *Caribees* or *Antilles Islands*; such as St. *Martin, Guadaloup, Santa Cruz, Marygalante, Petit Guaves*, a Colony on the East-end of *Hispaniola*, also *Martinico, Granade*, and several others of smaller note, but chiefly upon *Newfoundland*, where they have improv'd the Fishery to a considerable degree.

IT is true the *Dutch* had no Share in these Improvements; however they came in afterwards by way of Spoil, upon the Improvement and Labour of the *Portuguese*, as has been said. We are to understand that the *Dutch* were at this time labouring under the Weight of a terrible War with the *Spaniards*, and were not a State, or Government, or People, till many Years after these first Discoveries, as all that know any thing of their History must needs know; it is no Wonder therefore, that the *Dutch*, however diligent a People they are, and fam'd for their Application, even to Discoveries; yet as they were Subjects to the King of *Spain*, and had no Being as a Nation, they could not be concern'd in any of the most early Improvements and Discoveries of those Times.

THUS I have in a Summary way run through the Adventures of those first Ages of navigation. The Improvements of these Discoveries will take up an agreeable as well as profitable Part of our farther Progress in this Work; and what Improvements are yet behind to make, and which will probably be made in these and other Parts of the World not yet attempted; as particularly an *Ethiopian* Commerce, which I take to be a Scene of Trade yet unopen'd, and which bids fair to out-do in Profit to us the Commerce of both the *Indies*, as I shall make appear at large: This and several others I shall leave to treat of in their Order.

The CONCLUSION.

As these four Months of this Work bring down the most early Discoveries and first Improvements of Mankind to a particular Period; I mean the time when by the discovery of the Magnet and the use of the Compass, Men were particularly qualify'd to visit remote Countries, and make both Discoveries and Improvements also in Trade and Plantation; so really it wou'd be abrupt to publish them to the World thus in one Article without summing up briefly what is past, and taking a little notice of what is to come.

It could not be, but that when we come to run over the Advances which the Men of the most early Ages made in these useful Branches of human Knowledge, such as Art, Science, and the planting foreign and new discover'd Countries abroad, our account should be a kind of an abridgment of Things, and we shou'd be able to speak but to Generals only. It was indeed impossible it shou'd be otherwise, for the improving Nations left few Accounts of their Improvements behind them; the Ages gave no Histories of the Undertaking, or of the Undertakers; we have little left to judge of their Works but by the Effects of them.

We know the *Phœnicians* planted Colonies at *Carthage* and at *Cadiz*, and we know the *Carthaginians* planted again on the Coast of *Africa*, and of *Europe*, every way; because we have seen the Colonies planted, bearing the Image and Superscription, nay the very Names of its Planters; and remaining after *Carthage* itself has been destroy'd; as at *Cartagena* in particular the Name is preserv'd, and the Memory and Idolatry, the very Customs, Rites, and Usages of the *Carthaginians* were found among the *Moors* when the *Mahometans* came upon them, and are among some of the Southern Natives to this Day.

From the scatter'd Remains of *Roman* Antiquity in all the Nations where the Eagle spread its victorious Wings much of the *Roman* History is drawn out, and the many Breaches and Intersections of the Historian's lost Labours are supplied.

From the Systems of a few of the antient *Greek* Philosophers the Wisdom of the Wisemen of the *South* is handed down to us, and by the Fragments of Astronomy, us'd by the Antients, the more perfect Experiments have been made; so that learning seems to be descended to the

221

present Ages by Inheritance, and they stand upon the Shoulders of the *Chaldeans, Persian*, and *Arabian* Astrologers; that is to say Star-gazers, for they were but little better at first.

NOR can the particular History of the gradual Improvements of the World in these superior Branches of human Knowledge be collected otherwise, than as they discover'd themselves in now and then an extraordinary Man in the World. It was a dangerous thing for a Man to be a little more than ordinarily knowing in any Mathematical or Astronomical Knowledge; the World stood at Gaze at him; they either exalted him to the Skies, and plac'd them among the Gods, as *Mercury* and *Bacchus* are said to be exalted; or plac'd them among the wonders of Nature; as *Atlas, Prometheus, Hercules*, and others; or condemn'd them as Witches, Wizards, and Dealers with the Devil; as Dr. *Faustus*, Fryer *Bacon*, and several others more Modern have been serv'd; who were honest Men, but more than ordinarily intimate Searchers into Nature, and thereby acquir'd a stock of Knowledge superior to others in the Age they liv'd in.

THE Manner being thus imperfect, by which we have at best come at the knowledge of the most antient Things; it follows, that our search into Antiquity must be likewise very imperfect, and the Gradations of the Antients in their several Improvements in Science and useful Arts, very hard to describe. It is enough therefore, and our Readers will we hope expect no more from us, that we are able to deduce Things from just Originals, and hand them down as Nature has been helped to hand them to us in the General, till we come to the Ages in which History has been more regular in recording Things worthy to be known with a due certainty.

HITHERTO we have given an account of what the World did before, and without the helps of Art; now we must enquire a little what the World did afterwards, and with such Helps, and how the Wisemen of the World manag'd themselves, after such useful Expedients, as these were introduc'd among them.

As Heaven had bless'd them with such helps to Knowledge, we see they have not been idle, at least these Northern Nations have not: And how have we by improving these noble Discoveries learn'd to pity, or rather despise the rest of the World, (who know nothing of them) as grosly ignorant, stupid, and uncapable?

IT will remain to the compleating this Work, that we should now go on to enquire into the several Steps made upon the Foundation of these great and useful Discoveries, for the encrease of the Wisdom and Understanding of Men; and for the carrying on Commerce and Conquest in the World; for it is apparent it has not been for nothing that Heaven has open'd these Treasures of Wisdom and Knowledge to the World.

WHAT Embellishments then have they been to the Creation? What Beauties have they added to the Minds of Men? What Additions have they been to their Wealth, to their well living, and to their well doing? For Wisemen will add every Day something by their Knowledge to every new thing they see and know.

THIS will be a very profitable Enquiry many Ways, and particularly as it will direct the World to the farther Improvements they are yet to make upon most, if not all the several Articles which are already improv'd.

THERE are no doubt new Countries and Lands yet to be discover'd, new Colonies to be planted, which were never discover'd, or planted before; and which is still worth our Consideration, those already planted are capable of new Improvements, and farther Planting, which I think I may call improving. For Example; I think no Man can doubt, at least I cannot be perswaded to doubt, but that COFFEE might be made to grow in Countries of the same Latitude, and to the same Perfection as at *Mocha*, and we need never be at the Trouble and Expence to send to the *Arabian Gulph*, and pay our Money in hard Species for it to the *Turks*, when it might be rais'd in the same or a more Southerly Latitude upon the Coast of *Africa*, or in the Islands of *America*; in both which we are or may be possess'd of Places of our own proper Growth for the planting it. For Example, *Mocha* is upon the Continent of *Arabia*, in the Latitude of eleven Degrees or thereabouts; we again have a Factory at the Mouth of the *Rio Grand*, or near it, and at *Sierra Leon* in *Africa*: Why might not we be able to improve a Colony there, or thereabouts, for the planting of Coffee? as the *Dutch*, for Example, have shown us the way, and done it at *Batavia* in much the same Latitude? Or if that will be suppos'd not to be practicable, tho' I know not why, we have then Islands in the *West-Indies*, which we call our own; such as *Tobago*, St. *Vincent*, and even *Jamaica* itself, which we have Reason to believe, tho' not exactly in the same Latitude, would all of them produce the Plant if it were try'd; but on the Coast of *Guinea* we have the very exact Latitude to plant it in, and therefore no Objection can lye against that.

IN the like Case, can any Man perswade us to believe, that *Nutmegs* and *Mace* will grow no where but in the Isle of *Banda*; *Cloves* no where but at *Ternate, Amboyna*, &c. and *Cinnamon* no where but at *Ceylon*; that *Tea* will not grow in any Dominions but those of *China*; or that the same Latitude and Temperature of Climate wou'd not produce the same Plants?

LET the Experiments be made and the Negative prov'd, and then indeed no Man will oppose it; for Demonstration puts an end to all Arguments; but till then we must be allow'd to judge as Reason and the nature of Things direct us.

I MIGHT go on to explain myself as to Improvements in many Cases, where some particular Plants useful in the World are kept up as a Property to such and such Nations, and no Body suffer'd to Trade in them, but such and such; as Cocheneal seems to be engross'd by the *Spaniards*; Sugars to the *American* Islands and Colonies; and so many other Things which we are not able to produce nearer home, by being possess'd of the same Climate in other Parts of the World; but this requires a farther room for Discourse.

THE INDEX

AN
ESSAY
UPON
LITERATURE:
OR,
An Enquiry into the Antiquity and Original of LETTERS;
PROVING

That the two Tables, written by the Finger of God in Mount *Sinai*, was the first Writing in the World; and that all other Alphabets derive from the *Hebrew*.

With a short View of the Methods made use of by the Antients, to supply the want of Letters before, and improve the use of them, after they were known.

LONDON;

Printed for Tho. Bowles, Printseller, next to the Chapter-House, St. *Paul*'s Church Yard; John Clark, Bookseller, under the Piazzas, *Royal-Exchange*; and John Bowles, Printseller, over-against *Stocks Market*, M.DCC.XXVI.

AN ESSAY

ON THE ORIGINAL OF

LITERATURE, &c.

It is something strange, that among the abundance of Writers in the World, and the multitude of Authors who have publish'd their Labours for the instruction of Mankind in this Age, not one has thought it worth while to give any significant Account of the Art by which all their Works are perform'd; and by which indeed all manner of Science is convey'd from Age to Age, and handed down from our Ancestors to this Day; I mean that of Writing.

Printing and the Knowledge of Types impressing their Forms on Paper by Punction, or the work of an Engine (*for such is the Printing Press*) is a Modern Invention born of Yesterday; and *however advantageous to the World*, is what the World, it seems, made shift without, and was wholly ignorant of for above 5000 Years, and it is not yet full 300 Years old; that Art being the Invention of a Soldier, as that of Gunpowder and Guns was of a Scholar,[1] the *Dutch* affirming that *Lawrentius Costerus*, of *Harlem*, was the first Author of Printing; tho' others say, that *John Faustus* of *Mentz* invented it, and from thence was taken for a Conjurer, and gave Birth to the Stories we have going under the Name of the Famous Doctor *Faustus*.[2]

But Writing is of a very ancient Date, and has been the most useful of all Arts in the World, as it has been the preserver of Knowledge, and has handed down the first Principles of Science in the World, from one Generation to another; by which we, to this Day, stand, (and all the Ages before us, for many hundreds, nay, some thousands of Years, have stood) upon the Shoulders of our Fore-fathers Learning, and have improv'd upon their Invention; carry'd on progressive Knowledge, upon the foot of their Discoveries, and brought experimental Knowledge both in Arts and in Nature, to that Prodigy of Perfection to which it is now arriv'd.

IF there was such a Time when Men had not the Knowledge of Letters, as no doubt there was, tho' some question it to this Day: I say, if there was such a Time, Knowledge and Discoveries in Philosophy, or in Mechanick Arts, with History and the Knowledge of Things past, had great Difficulties attending them, and particularly this, that they were preserv'd only in the Repositories of those undecay'd Memories when Men were living Records of a Thousand Years[3] standing; which by the way, is full as long as most Writings or standing Registers remain in the World; at least such as are of any significance to us; the sacred Records of the Scriptures, and some part of the *Roman* and *Grecian* Histories excepted; which yet (the latter especially) leave Things very uncertain and ill attested to us, and so as fills us rather with Disputes about what was, or was not Genuine, than with a true Account of things. But in the *Antediluvian* World, if they had not the use of Letters, and a written Chronology, which yet I will not assert; yet *Oral Tradition*, had so just an Authority, the Authors living so many Years to perfect their Posterity in the Particulars of what they related to them, that we have no Reason to doubt the Truth of what was handed down from Father to Son; when MOSES, the first *Historian*[4] *that we know of*, was not so remote from the last Days of *Noah*, as that the Particulars could be lost, but being convey'd from Father to Son, he might be well able even without the help of Divine Inspiration, to write the whole History of the state of things before the Flood, *Noah* having without doubt made a perfect Relation of them to his Sons.

As to *Writing*, and the knowledge of Letters, the first we meet with in Scripture, and *Scripture is the oldest as well as the truest Account of these Things in the World*, was the two *Tables of Stone*, written by the Finger of GOD himself; containing the written Law of God, the same which we call the *Decalogue*, or Ten Commandments.

I know it will be answer'd, that tho' it was written by the Finger of GOD, yet there must certainly have been some Writing among Men before that, how else could the Children of *Israel* read it? But to this it may be as reasonably objected, if there had been any such thing as *Writing*, or the use of Letters before, what need had there been for GOD himself to have written the Ten Commandments with his own Hand? And what need had *Moses* to carry two New Tables up into the Mount, to have the same Words written again? Why cou'd not *Moses* have written the same Words over again, which 'tis very likely were left legible enough, notwithstanding breaking of the Stone. It is true, neither of these Arguments are Conclusive; but I think, both of them weigh much in the Case, and import, that those Tables were the first *Writing*,[5] or written Language, that was seen in the World.

BUT further, Tho' the *Ægyptians* were esteem'd, and justly too, the *Magi* of the Earth at that time; and had made Discoveries in many useful Parts of Science, in whose Wisdom *Moses* is said to be very Learned, we yet know of no knowledge of Letters among them, but that they wrote all by a Way particular to themselves, (*viz*) by *Hieroglyphicks* or paintings of Creatures and Figures, which at best, and however Ingenious the *Egyptians* were in suiting those *Hieroglyphicks* to their own Understanding, it must be allow'd that it was but a poor Shift, compared to the present improvement of Letters, and the Writing and Printing those Letters in Books as is since practis'd in the World.

AND so ignorant has the World been of the use of Letters, even since those Times, that we find upon the Discovery of any of the Unknown Parts of the World, and particularly in *America*, they had not only no knowledge of Letters, but they had no Notion of forming Speech into any intelligible Description, but by meer Sound and speaking with the Mouth, which by Custom they learn'd from one another; and hence it was, that they had such an infinite variety of different Languages (if it be proper to call them Languages) or rather differing Dialects of the same Language, that you were no sooner pass'd from one Tribe to another, but you found they understood little or nothing of the other's Speech.

NAY, so ignorant were the *Americans* of the use or meaning of Letters, and writing Words upon Paper, which should be intelligible at a Distance, that they tell us the following Story, which happen'd at our first planting of *Virginia: Viz*. Captain *Smith*,[6] one of the first Adventurers, happening to be taken Prisoner among the *Indians*, had leave granted him to send a Message to the Governor of the *English* Fort in *James Town*, about his Ransome; the Messenger being an *Indian*, was surpriz'd, when he came to the Governor, and was for kneeling down and Worshipping him as a GOD, for that the Governor could tell him all his Errand before he spoke one Word of it to him, and that he only had given him a piece of Paper: After which, when they let him know that the Paper which he had given the Governor had told him all the Business, then he fell in a Rapture the other Way, and then Capt. *Smith* was a Deity and to be Worshipp'd, for that he had Power to make *the Paper speak*.

NOR was the rest of the World one jot wiser than these People, as to this particular of having Letters form'd to express their Speech, except that which the *Egyptians* attain'd to, who were accounted the wisest People in the Earth, and those by their utmost Wisdom arriv'd to little more than this, that they were sensible of the Defect, had a Notion of something wanting, that when they had spoken to one another Face to Face, they cou'd know nothing more: They cou'd not preserve the Memory of things but in their own Minds, or send any Intelligence from one to another in remote Places, but by express Messengers retaining the whole Message they went about in their Memories.

BUT the Knowledge of the Defect, or the Sense of the want of such a thing as a legible Character, did not at all put the *Modus*, or Manner of doing it into their Thoughts, they had no Notion of expressing Sounds by Words without Speech, or that any Character to be form'd, cou'd signify, and direct to the Repetition of the Words spoken; it wou'd have been as Easie for a Man deaf and Dumb, to entertain a Notion of what sound Meant, or of what it really was to speak, as of having any Set of Figures, to direct the Tongue to the sound of Words from them.

BUT those *Ægyptians* being cunning and studious Artists, and Receiving their Knowledge from the *Arabians*, who they say were the first Astronomers; they invented a way of Writing by *Hiroglyphicks*, that is to say, by figures of Beasts, and painting of the Creatures, which they were speaking of, so as thereby to understand the Thing they intended: For Example, if they had order'd a Person to carry a Sheep to such a Town, they would paint a Man with a Sheep on his back going into the Gates of the City, or Town, and the like if a Man would say in *English*, I saw an Ox upon a Bridge, the writing was an EYE, a SAW an OX upon a BRIDGE and the like.

IT cannot be deny'd, but that they carried this Art of speaking a great length, and abundance of Ingenious things were done that way; but all was Circumlocution, going round the Bush, and round the Bush, and indeed to very little Effect, for the World was not able to form any Method fully to Express themselves to one another at a Distance.

IT might be very well worth while to enquire here whether they had any Commerce in those Days, and how that Commerce was carry'd on? How they kept their Accounts, and what Equivalent they had for writing to maintain Correspondence, which to us in these Days would seem impossible? Nay, I do not see, I Confess, that they were able to send a Messenger of an Errand, tho' it were but into the Market, or from one part of the Town to another, for more Business, or with more particular Orders, than the Bearer could carry in his Head; as to keeping Accounts, tho' Figures indeed are a kind of universal Character in the World, and understood alike, over (at least) all the Christian World, yet we do not read that Figures were in use before Letters, or that Arithmetick, (tho' now an eminent Part of Mathematick Knowledge) was known or understood any sooner than Letters; or that the forming them, and Numbering things by them, was known before writing was known: All the ways that I meet with, by which Men cast up Numbers of things, were prescribed by pointing to their Fingers, and consequently reach'd only to the Decimal Point, to

Number Ten, which they could tell upon their Fingers; if they went any farther, they did it by telling the same Fingers over again, and so making two Tens, and three Tens, and four Tens as they had Occasion; and by this Means they cou'd cast up tho' with Difficulty as far as Ten Tens, which we call a Hundred, but which they knew no Name for, till many Ages of the World were run off.

SOME are of Opinion that this Numbering upon the Fingers was the true original of all Arithmetick, and that from thence it was that the first Invention of Numbers and Figures stop't at Number Ten, and carry'd on all Ennumeration by Repetition of Decimal Periods, from Ten to *Twenty, Thirty, Forty, Fifty*, which is no more or less than as above, Two-tens, Three-tens, Four-tens, Five-tens, and so on to a Hundred, and then as the Things to be Numbered or added encrease, Counting those Hundreds, up by Tens, as One Ten Hundred which they call a Thousand, and then by Two ten Hundreds, and Three ten Hundreds, and the like to a Hundred ten Hundreds, that is a Hundred Thousand, and still keeping to the first way of Numbering every Ten: OF these Hundred Thousands, Ten was call'd a Million, and so over and over again, *ad infinitum*, and still every Tenth of one or another Denomination or kind, had a new Denomination, so that by Doubling, and Redoubling, all kinds of Numbers may be reckon'd, at least all that are practicable to Men; there being a kind of Infinity in Arithmetick beyond human Capacity of accounting, or least of expressing; no Number of any thing being so great, but that it may be doubled, or reckon'd over again to a Tenth of those Doublings, and so on again till every Ten adds Ten-fold to what went before, 'till we come to Innumerable, and even then to ten Hundred Thousand Millions of Innumerables, if such a Term was agreeable to Sense.

WHAT Method the wise *Egyptians* had to supply this Defect of Numbers by their Hieroglyphicks, I can by no Means meet with in any Author; but what Notions they have of it themselves, and which they must entertain from the Traditional Relicks of their Fore-fathers, is this, (*viz.*) They us'd certain Bundles of Reeds, which lay open in some publick Place in every City, each Bundle consisted of ten Reeds, which Reeds, excepting those of the first Bundle, had each of them ten Knots like a Bamboo Cane, and perhaps was made of some Cane that grew in Joints, like that we call a *Bamboo*; the Reeds of the first Bundle, only stood for Units, and when reckon'd over, number'd but Ten, whereas, the other Reeds which had Knots in them, stood every one for Ten; and the Number of one of those Bundles was equivalent to our Hundred. There was a Mark placed to separate between the Reeds that were in Tale,[7] from the others, for in reckoning any Number, they removed the Reeds one by one from the Right to the

Left Side of the Mark, (counting their Knots) till they had compleated the Number their Business requir'd.

BUT with all their reckoning, it seems they had no Numeral Sounds; they had no Numerical Letters, or Words, such as One, Two, Three, Four, and so on to Ten; no Words for a Hundred or for a Thousand, much less had they any Figures to express them by.

As to their *Hieroglyphicks*, which were their Types of Expression, we have nothing considerable extant that ever I have met with; what is pretended to of that Kind I shall speak to by it self: There have been Obelisks and Monuments discover'd indeed in the antient *Thebes*, that is to say, in the Ruins of it, or in some such Remains of Antiquity, which have been found among the *Ægyptians*, on which various *Hieroglyphick* Figures have been found; but we have no Rule left, by which to interpret them, or to understand in the least what they signify'd; so that the Art of Writing by *Hieroglyphicks*, if there was ever such an Art, I mean to write intelligibly one to another at a distance, is so entirely Lost, that it remains a Question, whether ever it was really Intelligible in the same manner as our Writing is, or no; that is so Intelligible as to furnish Missives from one to another; and if not, we need not set so much by the Wisdom of those Ages, and of the People in those Countries as we have done, or think it so much a Loss to the World, that the Memory of them, and use of them is not preserv'd; seeing they were not able to find out by all their Penetration a Method to convey the Mind, without speaking, much less able to hand Words from one to another, by such an Equivalent to Speech as we do now by Pen, Ink, and Paper.

NEXT to the *Ægyptians*, the *Phenicians* are esteem'd the antientest People in the World, who were of any Fame for Wisdom, and Knowledge; and they are fam'd for two Things, in which they certainly did outdo all the rest of Mankind, at that time; these are (*first*) the Knowledge of Navigation (2.) Of Commerce: The *Syrians* and *Sydonians*, and the Inhabitants of all that Coast, which was then call'd *Phenician*, and extended from that we now call *Scandaroon*, almost to *Alexandria* in *Ægypt*, were all Merchants, and very great Merchants too, as we find in the Prophesies of the Ruin of those Cities by *Isaiah, Ezekiel, Zephania*[8] — and other Prophets, where it is said that their Merchants were Princes, *that is* very considerable Merchants, Trading to *India, Æthiopia*, and as we may suppose, to all the Coasts of the *Red* Sea, and by Land over the Deserts, to the Gulph of *Persia*; I say we may suppose this from the said Prophets, who in reckoning up the prodigious Wealth of their Merchants describe the Countries they Traded to, by the several Sorts of Merchandizes they Traded in, and which they had it seems vast Stores of always by them; such as Gold, and precious Stones, which they are suppos'd to have from *Ethiopia*, on the Western Bank of the *Red* Sea, and which came by Shipping to *Ezion Gebar*, or *Baalzephon*, and from thence by Land Carriage, or as they now call it by Caravan, to the said Ports of *Tyre, Sidon, &c.* Then the Silks, the Purple, the Scarlet, and fine twin'd Linnen; these denote their Trading into *Persia*, which as it was, and is to this Day, the Country of the World, where the best Silk is naturally produc'd; so were the *Persians* fam'd for their rich Manufactures of all kinds, the Workman-ship of which was, and is to this Day, admirably fine; and this we read of far back as the *Babylonish Garment*, which *Achan*[9] found among the plunder of the City of *Jericho* and which he thought of so much value, that next to the Wedge of Gold, he was tempted by it to run the hazard of his own Life, and of God's Curse, pronounced by *Joshua* his General.

THESE Things, I say, prove the *Phenicians* to be a kind of universal Mer-chants, and that they corresponded with the whole World in Trade; for besides their Trade to *Africa* and the *East-Indies*, and to the Islands which the Scripture speaks of, we find in our own Histories that they traded to this very Island of *Britain*, which was at that time esteem'd the utmost Bounds of the Earth.

AND yet even these expert Merchants, these skilful Navigators, knew nothing of Letters; their Money, which was found here many Ages after, had no Inscription upon it, but consisted chiefly of Rings of Copper, and Brass, and Iron, with only a Stamp of an old Tower or Castle, which, 'twas suppos'd, represented the strong Castle of *Sidon*, said by the Prophet *Isaiah* to be built in the midst of the Sea,[10] and on which her Pride of the strength of her Situation was founded.

NEXT, the *Arabians* claim to be not only a more Ancient Nation than the *Ægyptians*, or than the *Phenicians*, but to have taught them all their Knowledge, as particularly their Skill in the Art of Navigation to the *Phe-nicians*; and the motions of the Heavenly Bodies, with the knowledge of Astrology, and Judgment in hidden Causes in Nature to the *Egyptians*; whence the Wise Men were call'd *South-sayers*,[11] the People of the South, which were the *Arabians* by their Situation, being esteemed the Author's of all that kind of Knowledge; and these *Arabians* pretend to have Peopled *Egypt*, and even *Ethiopia* itself, by Collonies transported over the *Red Sea* from *Arabia*, which lies extended on the East-side, as the other do on the West-side of that Sea; for which Reason it is to this day call'd the *Arabian Gulph*.

YET these *Arabians* themselves, so far as we can learn, had not the use of Writing, or the least knowledge of Letters; nor do we find any remains of such a thing among them, or any Pretences to it, tho' their Pretences to their being Originals of all Learning in the World, run very High in the

Writings of their antient Authors, and higher by far than we have Reason to believe they have any Authority for.

YET these I say, had no knowledge of Letters, and cou'd never form to themselves an Idea of Writing, or marking a Sound of Speech down in legible Characters, or as that poor *Virginian* express'd it, to make a piece of Paper speak.

WE have indeed an Account of the Inventors of Musick and Musical Instruments in the Scripture, even much antienter than *Noah*'s Flood, but we do not know any thing of the invention of Musical Notes by that same Ante-Diluvian Artist; for as the Notes by which we prick down, *as it is call'd*, our Tunes, are a kind of Universal Character, being understood alike by all Nations, who understand Musick, so the doing it was a kind of Writing, and will undeniably be so esteem'd, *of which hereafter.*

BUT we have reason to believe, that this particular piece of Knowledge also is much more Modern, and even more Modern than *Orpheus* himself, to whom some will give the Honour of that Invention, and had it not been Modern, the same Hand who had found out the Way to make Marks upon Lines speak in the Language of Musick, and sing or say, *FA, LA, SOL, &c.* would certainly have seen it possible to have form'd other Words upon the same Foot, and have brought the World to a Method of understanding one another much sooner than they did.

THE pricking down of Tunes therefore by Marks which we call Notes, and to which we give Tones, or Sounds of Art, is certainly a Modern Invention; as indeed the Names of the Figures or Notes do evidently imply, which are Latin Originally, and mostly now *Italian*, a Speech which we know is but the Bastard-child of the Latin. *Some say the Emperor* Nero, *who as much a Tyrant as he was, is allowed to be the greatest* Master of Musick of the Age he liv'd in; was also the Inventor, or at least the Finisher, of that Part of Musical Knowledge which relates to the pricking down the Notes of Musick upon Paper; and particularly, that tho' the whole Notes might be mark'd before, and that many Ages, even back to *Apollo* himself, or to *Orpheus*, yet that the Divisions of Notes[12] in which our Modern Masters so much excell, were the Work of that Emperor; and that he brought them to the great Perfection which they remain in to this Day. I do not affirm this, nor am I enclined to Compliment such a Monster of Nature as that Emperor was, at so high a rate, as to advance the Probability beyond what it ought to be: That *Nero* was a good Fidler may be true, and he was certainly so; but that he had any thing else good about him, I never heard, except this, of improving the musical Notes.

I see no part of the World, which we can apply to, *farther than we have*, for the original of this Art of writing, except to *China* and *Japan*, whose claim to Knowledge of Letters, and to the Art not of writing only, but even to that of Printing too, is as extravagant, as that of the World's being created 11000 Years ago, and their Claim to a Chronology of their own Monarchy for 7000 Years past.

THESE People pretend to have known Letters, and have had a written Character for many thousands of Years; and perhaps before that account of Time, when according to our Register the World was created; what Authorities they have, they best know, nor is it at all worth our inquiry; we are well assur'd that we have Divine Authority for our Account of Time, from its Beginning to this Day, and that by Consequence their pretences to such Antiquity are Fictitious, and to the last degree Ridiculous, and on the same Account, their pretended Knowledge of Letters must be so too.

I know it is fabl'd of *Cadmus*[13] that he invented Letters, and others say the *Phenecians* were the Authors, but these are uncertainties, and have little more than what I justly say is fabl'd of them, for even who this *Cadmus* was, is a doubtful thing, and whether really there ever was such a Man in the World, or no; but of that hereafter.

UPON the whole, as we are sure the two Tables of Stone, were written by the Finger of God, that is to say, Divine Power impress'd, by what Method we know not, those Words on the two Tables of Stone, and at the same time no doubt instructed *Moses* in the reading of them, and in the Knowledge of their Sounds; so we have an unquestion'd Authority to assign the Knowledge of Letters, and the Art of writing them to a Divine original; that is to say, that the Knowledge was immediately dictated from Heaven, and that *Moses* was enabled to Instruct the Children of *Israel* in the Knowledge of them, by an immediate Divine inspiration.

NOW if we look upon the Face of the World for so many Ages, and how notwithstanding so many Arts were known to them, and discover'd by their own search, that yet they had no Notion, nor ever could have of Letters, and Writing; I say, if we look thus on the real difficulty of making any Discovery of that kind, we may depend upon it, that if God himself in Favour to his Creatures, and to his own People of *Israel* in the first Place, had not inspir'd them with this Knowledge, all the Power of Invention that was ever bestow'd on Man before, could not, nor would to this Day have been able to do it.

MANKIND had no Idea of such a thing among them, it was not in them to make a peice of Paper speak, and to stamp a Voice and Words, which were neither more or less than meer Sounds, to stamp them on a Paper, and empower other People to speak over again, by the help of those dumb Figures, the same Words that the first Person had uttered at a hundred or a thousand Miles distance; no Man could imagin such a Thing feasible, nor did it ever, as I have Reason to believe, enter into any Man's Thoughts to contrive any thing of such a kind.

BUT God from Heaven giving Laws to Men, gave not an oral, but a written Law, and it was from him, that Letters were cloathed with Sounds, to be convey'd to any distance, and by the sight, and upon any occasion that requir'd it, repeated Articulately as often as was requir'd, by which the Sense of things was convey'd from Man to Man, and from Age to Age. It was his own doing, and from him alone it deriv'd.

HERE I place the true Original of Writing, and indeed of all Literature; if there was any thing known before this, 'tis more than we have any Account of in History or Monument among the Antiquities of the most antient Buildings: The Ruins of the most antient Cities show no Inscriptions, the old *Babel*,[14] part of which remains to this Day, has no appearance of any thing Written; the *Ægyptian* Pyramids the next peice of Antiquity to *Babel*, at least that we know of, which are Fair, and preserv'd entire, have yet no Figures or Semblance of Letters left upon them.

THE great Men of those Ages frequently erected Columns and Pillars to preserve the Memory of their Actions, and to preserve their Names; but without any Letters to signifie whose they were. Oral Tradition preserv'd their Names from Generation to Generation. The great *Nimrod*, the mighty *Semiramis*, *Jupiter* himself, however deify'd for great Actions; I have great Reason to believe of them, what would be very scandalous to say of a great Monarch in our Days, that none of them could write their own Names.

NAY, to carry it farther, had Writing been in use, had the World known Letters, and could thereby have written down a true History of the Lives of the Great Men of the first Ages of the World, as well the Post Deluvian Heroes, as those before the Flood, their Tyrannies, the horrid Desolations, the inhuman and unnatural Lusts, the Murthers, and other Crimes they committed, would have recommended them to Posterity in other Figures, and shown them in different Colours from what the next Ages saw them in; Instead of placing them among the Stars, and worshipping them as Gods, they would have been rank'd among the blackest Devils; their Memory would have been the Abhorrence and Terror of future Ages, and not the Subject of their Admiration first, and at last of their Adoration.

What should we have understood of *Jupiter*, who is said to have made War upon, deposed, and murthered his Father *Saturn*, but as an accurs'd Paricide, justly doom'd to a Station in eternal Darkness, for one of the first Usurpers and King killers in the World? How would *Noah*'s Drunkenness,[15] of which it pleases Heaven, by the help of Writing, to give us a Part, (at least) of the truer History, been abhorr'd and detested by the Ages following, and recorded to his Shame, if a true Account of it cou'd have been written down and preserved to Posterity? Instead whereof, he is by the Miss-understandings of the People carrying the Story but from Tongue to Tongue, made the God of Wine, extoll'd as a Patriot to the World, by furnishing them with so excellent, so delicious a Liquor as the juice of the Grape; and hence he is made the Idol of all the Revels of Mankind, Father of Drunkards, and has Temples rais'd to him where the *Bacchinalia* or Feasts to this drunken good Man, are celebrated with all manner of Excesses, Lewdness, and infinite Debaucheries; and all this for want of the knowledge of Letters, and the skill of writing a true Account of the first Crime of *Noah*, which he good Man afterwards repented of. Had he known the abuse that wou'd have been put upon the World in his Name, he wou'd no question have left some Monument of his abhorrence of it, tho' he cou'd not write it down. *N. B.* He is supposed to be the *Bacchus* of the Antients.

IT is the Opinion of some, and the *Jews* had such a traditional Notion, whether True or not, that *Noah* did not stop at once drinking Wine to excess, as is signify'd in the Text; but that he grew a grievous Drunkard, a kind of habitual Sot; and that he expos'd himself by it in the vilest manner, to the Contempt of his Posterity; that especially his Son *Ham*, and his Grandson *Canaan*, made a Sport of him, and ridicul'd and expos'd him for it, which is signify'd, say they, by his being Uncover'd in his Tent, and by their seeing his Nakedness; and that he continu'd in this habitual Drunkenness a Hundred Years: But that *Shem* and *Japhet* being religious, sober good Men, left not their Father in this Excess and Extravagance, but by their Prayers and Entreaties to him, and to God for him, convinc'd him at length of his Sin, and brought him to be a most sincere Penitent: Thus they cover'd his Nakedness, concealing his Infirmity as much as possible, and restoring him by Degrees to his Senses; for which he afterwards gave them his Blessing, and on the contrary, heartily Curs'd his Son *Ham* and all his Posterity; but especially young *Canaan*,[16] who, 'tis suppos'd, had a great Hand in exposing and making Sport with his Grandfather's Infirmity and Wickedness: But this is a Digression; I shall not affirm that this Story is true in Fact, but rather adhere to the Letter of the Text, which seems to point it out as a single Offence.

EITHER Way it serves to the Purpose in hand: 'Tis most certain that the want of Letters, and the World not being able to collect and write down the true Lives, (or History of the Lives) of these first Great Men, has been the main Reason of their Names and Memories being so grosly abus'd, and the World so much more abus'd about them, as to exalt for their Adoration the vilest of Men, call the Stars by their Names, build Temples to their Honour, and Worship them as Deities, who were here on Earth the worst of Men, meer incarnate Devils, Monsters not fit to live, and who had nothing but flagrant Wickedness to recommend them; as *JUPITER*, a Paricide, King-killer and Usurper of his Father's Throne. *MARS*, a Fury and outragious Monster for Murther and Rapine, and therefore made the God of War. *MERCURY*, a Sorcerer and notorious Wizard, a Fortune-teller, and dealer with the Devil. *VENUS*, a beautiful Woman, but an everlasting Whore, an insatiate impudent Strumpet, an infamous notorious She-Devil, the vilest and worst of her Sex. *BACCHUS*, (if *Noah* really was the Man) the first of Drunkards, tho' otherwise, and afterwards, a good Man and a Penitent, which they that Worship'd him never heard of; or if they did, never plac'd that Part among the Vertues, for which they ador'd him. O! had they known the Use of Pen and Ink in those Days, and had they had a *Juvenal* to have Satyriz'd and Recorded the immortal Crimes of those Wretches, who they call'd the Immortal Gods, how would they ha' been set forth in their True Colours! and how wou'd the World have made their very Names a Curse, and an Execration to Posterity, rather than Idoliz'd them for Vertues and for Hero's? But all this mistaken Opinion of these Men, is owing, under the Disposition of Providence, to the want of the Use of Letters, and of Faithful Writers, to have recorded the Histories of those Times, free from Fable and Romance, and to have set the Actions of those Men in a true Light.

SINCE the use of Letters, since Writing came into the World, and since History has preserv'd the true Account of the Actions of Men, we have had no new Gods set up; no Statues have been nick-nam'd, nor infamous Men exalted after their Death to the Rank of Deities: Some of the *Roman* Emperors indeed aspir'd to the Title, and impiously accepted of what, in those Times, they call'd Divine Honours; even *Alexander* the Great had the Vanity to approve of it, being fond of being stil'd the Son of *Jupiter*. But History has done Heaven Justice, and the Ages when these Men liv'd having had the blessing of Pen, Ink and Paper, or the Equivalent to them, (of which I shall speak presently) have branded the Names of these Men with a just Mark of Infamy for the Attempt; and by leaving the Memory of their Deeds upon Record, have register'd their Names amongst the worst of Men; the Great Sir *Walter Raleigh*,[17] hints this, when speaking how the most Wicked among mortal Men, were made Immortal among the Heathen. He says, it is not to be wonder'd at that

'*Alexander Magnus, Tiberius, Nero, Caligula*, and others, ought to be number'd among them, being as Deform'd Monsters as any of them; and he adds, how cou'd the same Honour be deny'd to *Laurentia* and *Flora*, which was given to *Venus*, seeing they were as famous Harlots as she.'

Vid. Sir Walter Raleigh's Hist. of the World, fol. 52.

This is one of the Benefits of History; we have now no more dependance upon Tradition or the oral History of Men and Things, the Writings of the Antients are our Foundation to fly to for the Characters of Things, and of Men; and tho' it is true, that even since the use of Letters and of Writing, there has too much Fiction and Fable enter'd into the Writings of the Learned, especially their Poetical Works, as *Homer* in particular, who has sung the Wars of the *Greeks*, and the Siege of *Troy* from a Reality, into a meer Fiction; yet even among these we find Room to pick out Fragments of Truth, enough to make a Judgment both of the Times, and of the Actions of Men performed in them.

PART II.

HAVING thus advanc'd a Proposition in Honour of the Subject I am upon, namely, that Writing and the use of Letters is of divine Original, and that there was no knowledge of Letters, much more of Writing, before that of the two Tables of Stone written by the Finger of God in *Mount Sinai*: It seems needful that I should examine Antiquity a little and see what Pretences are made in the World to the original of Letters, the knowledge of Sounds in form of those Letters, and the writing or impressing them upon the Materials prepar'd for that purpose, of all which in their Order.

THE Time when *Moses* brought the Children of *Israel* out of *Egypt*, and Encamp'd them at the Foot of *Mount Sinai*, was the Year of the World 2515,[18] *Moses* being then 80 Years old, for he was born in the Year 2434.

IF we look back, we shall find this was so short a Time, even after the Flood itself, or especially after the Death of *Noah*, who died in the Year of the World 2005, that as first, it is not likely that Letters came into the World so soon, being by the general Opinion of all Writers, not above 500 Years after the Confusion of Languages. So (2.) It is more Antient, and far beyond all the famous Men, to whom History, or even Fable itself, would give the Honour of being the Authors of Learning, and of bringing the knowledge of Letters into the World.

CADMUS[19] is the most antient of these, and who, *Pliny* says, brought the knowledge of Letters into *Greece*, from whence others have ignorantly enough made him the Inventer of them: But all we have of *Cadmus* is, that he brought 16 Letters of the *Greek* Alphabet into *Peloponesus*, that is, into *Greece*, where he built the City of *Thebes*, and from whence all the Learning and learned Writings of the *Greeks* had their beginning. Some would have us believe this *Cadmus* to be a Great Grandson of *Noah*, and to have come directly from *Assyria* soon after the Confusion of Languages: But this is all Fiction, and we find by more authentick Accounts, that *Cadmus* was not born till after the Year 2600, or thereabouts, which was Eighty-six Years after the Tables of Stone were written in *Mount Sinai*, and that he was a *Phenician* born, being the Son of *Agenor*, a King of the *Phenicians*.

Now, as the *Phenicians*, who were *Canaanites*, might easily learn the use of Letters from the *Hebrews*, and make some improvement in that Knowledge in 86 Years, Forty of which was after the *Israelites* were planted in *Canaan*, before *Cadmus* was born, and Sixty Years more before he went into *Greece*: This is not improbable at all.

THIS *Cadmus*, Fame tells us, carry'd with him 16 Letters of the *Greek* Alphabet into *Greece, to-wit,* α β γ δ ε ι η χ λ ν ο ϖ ζ σ τ υ. Four more, 'tis said, were added by *Palamedes*, but not till the time of the Siege of *Troy*, which was not till 220 Years after. This *Cadmus* also lived some time in *Egypt*, at a Town call'd *Thebes*, from whence it seems his Ancestors came to *Tyre*, a City of the *Phenicians*.

Now, after the Children of *Israel* had by the Finger of God, been instructed in the knowledge of Letters, for *Moses*, inspir'd from Heaven, no doubt taught them first to Read, and then to Imitate that Heavenly Scripture the Law, otherwise it had been of no Use to them: I say, after this, and after it came to be look'd into by other Nations, who Convers'd with the *Israelites*, it is no Wonder that those Nations form'd Letters also of their own making, and gave them Sounds proper to their own speaking, after the manner of the *Hebrews*, with whom they Convers'd.

IT is also to be observ'd, that this seems confirm'd (at least to me) in that the first Nations which we read of, who had the use of Letters after the *Hebrews*, were those who were the nearest to them in their Habitations; such as the *Egyptians*, FROM WHOM they came, and who at the first Time of appearance of this Heavenly Art, liv'd not above two Days Journey from them, and the *Phenicians* TO WHOM they came, that is, when they (the *Israelites*) Conquer'd *Canaan*, and who then liv'd not *near them* only, but even *among them*, for the *Phenicians* were the very *Canaanites*, which the *Israelites* shou'd have destroy'd,[20] but did not.

THE *Phenicians* then having made a beginning, (for 'tis apparent they had then form'd but Sixteen Letters of Four-and-twenty) *Cadmus* with what Knowledge was then in the World, went into *Greece*, and there taught his Citizens of *Thebes* the use of those Sixteen Letters, which for that Reason they pretend he Invented: But 'tis evident, that he only brought them with him into *Greece*, but did not invent them in *Greece*, the *Phenicians* having the Use of them before the *Thebans*; and thus also other Writers not allowing themselves to think, *or perhaps not knowing the History* of the Transactions at Mount *Sinai*, and of *Moses* his instructing the *Israelites*, give the Honour of the first knowledge of Letters to the *Phenicians*; and others again to the *Egyptians*, both which bring it so near to the *Israelites*, as still confirms the

Probability of what I have here advanc'd, and which, I think, stands now almost beyond the reach of Contradiction.

WE ought then a little to enquire what kind of People those were, to whom all the Great and Wise Actions of those early Ages of the World are ascribed, that we may see when they liv'd, and whether they assumed to themselves any thing that may contradict our present Thesis, or entitle those Men to the Honour of introducing this Knowledge into the World.

APOLLO, a Name understood in various Manners by the Antients, in the Heaven he is call'd the *SUN*; in Hell *PLUTO*; on Earth *APOLLO*; and who was indeed but a Minstrel, or Fidler, in English a Ballad-singer, a Tumbler, or a Merry-Andrew, or Mountebank, or what you please; yet is said to be a teacher of Science, and judge of Wit, and rectifier of the Understanding among the People.

ATLAS, the Brother of *Prometheus*,[21] was rather Prior to *Moses*, tho' he liv'd in some part of the time of *Moses*, but *Prometheus* himself was King of *Armenia*, and reign'd in the time of *Moses*. This is that *Prometheus* of whom so many Fictions are made by the Poets, as of his making a Man of Clay; stealing Fire from *Jupiter*; as also of his being Chain'd on the Top of Mount *Caucasus* by the Hands and Feet, and a Vulture all the while devouring his Bowels.

ALL these Fables are Construed to signify no more than the Greatness of his Wisdom and Knowledge, as that of his Brother *Atlas* carrying the World upon his Shoulders, was, to signify that he supported the Government of the whole World, by the Wisdom and Justice of his Laws.

(a) St. *Augustine*[22] says, That *Prometheus* was feign'd to have form'd Men out of Clay; that is to say, he formed the Minds of Men, by instilling Principles of Knowledge, and of Wisdom into them, and was an excellent Instructor of Mankind. So *Theophrastus*[23] and others interpret him stealing Fire; or as it was called by some, the invention of Fire, whereby he gave Life to his Men of Clay, or of Wood, which he had made; that is, says he, that he inspir'd the Minds of Men, or fir'd their Minds with earnest Desires after Knowledge: And that whereas, before him, Men were but silly ignorant, and blind, he enlighten'd their Minds with Knowledge: And by that Vulture gnawing his Bowels on Mount *Caucasus*, is signify'd the gnawing, earnest, anxious Desire, he had to compass the System of Astronomical Knowledge, and the Motions of Heavenly Bodies, not then attained to by any of humane Race.

ALL this I mention, (tho' something remote) for this Reason, and so I bring it down to my Purpose, (*viz.*) That some have made this *Prometheus*

(a) *August*. de Civit. Dei. *lib*. 18.

the first inventor of Letters in the World. But this is evidently contradicted; for that before him, *Moses* had the written Law in the Mount, as above; so that whatever *Prometheus* had, he must, or at least might have from *Moses* many Years after.

(a) Dr. *Goodwin*,[24] in his Collection of the *Jewish* Antiquities, agrees with my proposed Article, (*viz.*) That *Moses* first taught the Use of Letters to the *Jews*; that the *Phenicians* learned them from the *Jews*, and the *Grecians* from the *Phenicians*; that *Moses* learned them by Inspiration, having the first writing of them from the Hand of God himself, this the Scripture positively asserts; and thus my deriving the knowledge of Letters from a divine Original is, I think, sufficiently supported.

THE next Persons who Authors would entitle to the Invention of Letters, are, 1. (b) *Palamedes*,[25] who the *Greeks* talk very much of; but this *Palamedes* lived no sooner than the Siege of *Troy*, 163 Years before *Homer*; whereas the written Law of GOD was given to *Moses* Sixty Years before the City of *Troy* was built, (*viz.*) *Anno Mund.* 2514, and *Troy* was built, *Ann. Mund.* 2574, and was destroy'd again by the *Grecians, Anno Mund.* 2870. 2. *Memnon*;[26] the same Author tells us, this *Memnon* brought the use of Letters into *Egypt*. But again, as above, even *Memnon* is by Others said not to be the Inventor of Letters to the *Egyptians*, only of forming a kind of Intelligence, by Figures, or *Hieroglyphicks*; and knew nothing of an Alphabet of Letters to form Words from by Prolation.[27] As for the other *Memnon* he was too Modern, being kill'd by *Achilles* at the Siege of *Troy*: And as to the *Egyptian* Figures or Hieroglyphicks, I shall speak of 'em afterwards.

THE *Arabians* are the next who claim the Invention of Letters; but they who pretend to it in their behalf, can bring no Authorities for it; nor do we meet with it in any History, but some Writings of the *Sarazens* and *Turks*, whose Credit is too low with me, to give any thing for Authentick, upon their Authority.

Antiquity then gives us no Light into any thing, at least, that I ever met with, to weaken, much less to contradict the Proposition I have advanc'd, namely, That the written Law of GOD, gave the first appearance of Letters in the World; the progression of Knowledge, and the use of Letters I shall account for afterwards; thus, (*viz.*) That from *Moses* the use of Letters were taught the *Israelites*, and by them communicated to the rest of the World, namely, to the *Phenicians* on one Hand, and by them to the *Greeks*, and on the other Hand to the *Egyptians*; and by them to the *Ethiopians*.

(a) *Goodwin*, Civil. & Eccles. Rites, *p.* 275.
(b) *Servius*, Lib. 2. *Goodwin*, pag. 275

THAT the *Egyptians* should learn it from the *Ethiopians* (for *Memnon* was an *Ethiopian*) is still more unlikely, the *Ethiopians* being never fam'd for communicating Knowledge to the World, or indeed retaining any valuable Degree of it among themselves: Besides, had *Memnon*, who liv'd in the Year of the World, 2233, been the Inventor of Letters, and had brought those Letters in Use among the *Egyptians*, How came it to pass that the *Egyptians* used the lame unintelligible ænigmatick Method of Figures and Hiero-glyphicks, &c. and that for several Hundred Years after the supposed Time of *Memnon's* Life.

THESE Hieroglyphicks had various Significations, according to the receiv'd Usage of the Country; as by a Circle was meant the *Sun*; by a Semi-circle, the *Moon*; the Image of a Hawk, being the King of Birds, signified the King of *Heaven*; by the Figure of a Man, *Wisdom*; a Horse harness'd, *Strength*; a Lyon, *Courage* and *Fortitude*; a Horse Un-bridl'd, signified *Lib-erty*; by a Crocodile, *Impudence*; by a Fish, *Hatred*, and the like. And these Figures with many other, were used till after the Children of *Israel* went out of *Goshen*.

ALL these Things concur to confirm, *as far as a Thing of this Nature, and so very Antient, can be expected to be confirmed*, that the World had not the use of Letters, till the exhibiting of the written Law of GOD at Mount *Sinai*.

I shall add but one thing more, and that is the Improbability that Let-ters could be in use in the World much sooner than that time, as the World was then stated; The Nations were not so settled as to be very well Improved, or indeed very Populous at that time: Sir *Walter Raleigh* observes,[28] That even some Ages after this, Men were advanced to the Government of Nations upon the meanest Terms of Excellence that could be imagin'd. *Atlas* was chosen King of *Mauritania*, because he had know-ledge of Heavenly Bodies. *Hercules*, because of his great Strength was Deify'd: *Mercury* for Magick and Cunning: *Pelasgus* was chosen King of *Arcadia*, because he taught the People, but how to build simple low Cot-tages, to defend them from Storms and Rain, and learned them to grind Acorns, and make Bread of them for their Nourishment, who liv'd before upon Roots and Herbs. Is it likely that these rude Ages, when Wit and Knowledge was at so low an Ebb, should invent so Noble, so sublime a Thing, as the use of Letters? Forming Sounds by the help of Characters which should speak, and be repeated from Mouth to Mouth.

HOW falsely then have the *Grecians* boasted of their antient Learning, and of the antiquity of their Knowledge, their Philosophy, and *the like*, when this was the poor Ignorant People who inhabited the *Arcadian* Plains, where afterwards all the Learning of this Part of the World sprung up.

THEN as to the time of *Moses*, let us consider that *Moses* gave this Knowledge to the *Israelites* before the planting of any of the *Grecian* Commonwealths; consequently, it must be long before the antient Learning of the *Greeks* began; for as I have observ'd, it was long before the building of the City of *Troy*, above 146 Years before the Building of *Thebes*, and still more before the first using of Letters among the *Greeks*. I say,

AGAIN, Let us go back to the time of the Flood itself, and of *Noah*, who Re-peopled the World by the Posterity of his three Ante-Diluvian Sons. The Flood was in the Year of the World, 1656, being the next Year after the Death of *Methuselah*: After the Flood, According to Sir *Walter Raleigh's* Account,[29] it was 170 Years to the beginning of the building of *Babel*; This Building having been begun upon the most ignorant Notions of things, that could be supposed to come into the Heads of rational Creatures, and shews an immense Dulness in the People of that Time, to think that a human Building could resist an universal Deluge; *but that by the way.*

THIS Building, with the digging the Foundation, which must be a prodigious Gulph for so vast a Fabrick, which was some Miles in Circumference, the preparing and bringing the Materials, and making the Bricks, &c. is supposed to take up 130 Years more, which is in all, 300 Years. Now, from the Confusion of Languages to the Birth of *Jacob*, was but 213 Years, according to his Account; and it can hardly pass for probable, that the Confusion which that division of Languages made among them was so recover'd, that they should have advanced to any Inventions in that Time; much less to so Glorious an Improvement as this of writing down their Speech by the help of Letters, and as the poor *Indian* said, making *the Paper* or the *Tables* they wrote upon, to *Speak*. From *Jacob* then to the exhibiting of the Law on *Mount Sinai*, which was about 345 Years; was indeed no extraordinary length of Time, the Confusions and Dulness of those days considered, for introducing so noble a Part of Knowledge into the World.

BUT let us go back to this Story of the *Egyptians*, having the use of Letters before the *Israelites*; where is the probability, that GOD himself, who gave the *Israelites* the written Law, and wrote it with his Own Hand, should imitate the *Egyptian* Magicians? for this *Memnon* was a famous Sooth-sayer, or Magician, a *Negro* by Nation, born in *Ethiopia*: Or whether was more probable, namely, that it should be true that the GOD of *Heaven* should write after *Memnon's* Copy; or that *Memnon* rather hearing that the discovery of such a wonderful Knowledge was brought into the World by Inspiration from Heaven, went immediately into the Wilderness among the *Israelites*, to learn the Method from them, and carry'd it back with him into *Egypt*, from whence he was to them the first Inventor, and might pass for such in the Esteem of the future Ages of the World; as *Cadmus* did, by going on the same happy Message into *Greece*.

THE only Difficulty to be started here, is the Time of this *Memnon*, when he liv'd? which they pretend, *but without any certainty*, was the 23d Century of the World's Age; so that he must probably be in his Grave, before *Moses*, or must have liv'd above 250 Years. Now, as to this, we have not, I say, the least Authority of Authors to be depended upon, for the time of *Memnon's* Life, any more than the length of it; and therefore I do not conceive that Part to be of Force enough, to contradict the Authority I have brought for the Original of Letters; and especially, because we read of no Writings extant in all that time, either there, or in any other Part of the World. The great Library of *Ptolemy*, King of *Egypt*, which had in it so many thousand Books, that is to say, Manuscripts, *if that Story be not all Fable*, yet had it not any Books, *as we find reason to believe*, that were written before *Moses*: In a word, we find no certain Notice, even in *Josephus*,[30] or any other Author, of any Writing, of Gods or Men, before this one glorious discovery of Knowledge, made by the True GOD, among his Chosen People the *Jews*: So that really all Argument from Probability seems to be against them.

ON the other Hand, there is the highest Probability, that all the other Nations, especially the *Egyptians*, deriv'd their Knowledge of Letters from the *Israelites*, as above.

AGAIN, the similitude of the Writing it self in all those Ages and Countries, intimates the same Original; the *Hebrew* Character was then, and is still, written from the Right-Hand to the Left, and the *Egyptians* in their first Language, wrote after the same manner, *as we shall see in our next Discourse*, till many Ages afterwards; Then the *Greek* Tongue was spoken in *Egypt* as the Universal Language, as it was also among the *Jews*, notwithstanding their being first taught the *Hebrew*.

THUS, I think, it is as clear as any thing can be made, whose Proofs are so remote, that the knowledge of Letters was of Divine Original, brought down from Heaven; *for so, what was brought from GOD himself, might justly be said to be, and that it was brought to the Israelites by* Moses, the Servant of GOD, who was divinely inspir'd, to instruct the People in the Use, in the Pronunciation, in the Reading, and in the Writing of them; and this made me say, that Writing is almost as antient as Letters.

THIS also brings me to speak of the Nature of *Letters* themselves, (*viz.*) That they were not only meer Figures, call'd by particular Names; for as such they were still but Hieroglyphicks, as the Images of living Creatures were before; those Images were meer Independent Marks, design'd to direct the Mind as any particular Mark might mean. *But this was quite another thing*, here was a certain strange and, *but by Divine Inspiration*, an

248

incomprehensible way of giving Diction to those Letters, which not only distinguished them from one another, but made them capable also of being joined to one another by Prolation, and Sound, by which means those Letters forming a distinct Syllable, or Syllables, had again, a distinct Compound Note, and those Syllables being farther join'd, compounded other distinct Sounds, form'd from or out of several of the compound Sounds which went before; out of that far fetch'd Variety, forming the concording Sound of whatever Word or Words the Tongue could express; These Sounds had such an infinite Variety, that as the sound of six Bells may be chang'd 720 times, so the Sounds of 24 Letters are capable of an innumerable reflux, sufficient to form Words enough, and those of differing Sounds, to express the meaning of Mankind in all Languages now in Use in the World; nor would there be need to invent any more Letters, if there were ten Thousand differing Languages more than there are.

'Tis hardly to be conceiv'd, how a Man making a certain Figure upon a Table, should frame his Mouth to make a Sound for that Letter or Figure; or how when he had fram'd his Mouth to form a Sound, he could suit a Figure to express that Sound by? *For Example*; Why must an *A* represent so many Things as we see it does, being the first beginning in Sounds, and the first Singular in Speech? Why must a Circle *O* express our Exclamations, when we cry out for Pain and the like?

THESE seem to me to be Difficulties not in the Power of Human Invention; besides the innumerable Arcana that I have not Time or Room to mention here. Three Things in Nature, seem to me to Claim an immediate Inspiration from Heaven, as being above the reach of Human Invention, I mean meerly Human; These are (1.) MUSICK. (2.) NUMBERS. (3.) LETTERS. And these I call the *Three Infinites below*.

IF these did not come immediately from *Heaven*, Whence then did they come, and who were the Authors? To say they were Antediluvian, is to agree them to be Divine, because the consummate Knowledge of that State of the World, seems also to have been all from divine Original. But in all the Account of Things, all the Histories of Time and Persons, *taking in the sacred inspir'd World and all*, we find nothing recorded of the Original of any of these mighty THREE; till this of giving a written Language from *Heaven*, by which the Tables of Stone might be said to Speak, and the *Israelites* were taught to Read and Write.

OF *Numbers* I have spoken something; of *Musick* I shall say no more than this, that we have an Account of him that invented musical Instruments,[31] and perhaps not that without divine Direction neither: But he invented only the Instrument, to improve the Knowledge, and Delight Mankind: But Harmony, and the Beauties of Sound, which are the Foundation of

Musick, these are the Daughters of God; Unaccountables, beyond the reach of Human Invention; form'd in the Air, and directed by him that made that Air, in the proper divisions and proportions of Notes, for the further improvement of Sound.

NOR are these three Heads very remote from one another; they seem to be a Chain of Things of Affinity to one another, and are all apply'd in Conjunction on many Occasions, deriving from the same Principles, and blended one with another; there is Musick in Words, and there is Harmony in Numbers; particularly Numbers run thro' and are the Measure of Sound, which make Musick: In a Word, they are equally descended from above, and were equally above the Power of Nature to invent.

SOME have been of the Opinion, *among whom I confess I am inclin'd to be one*, that all Learning, as well as all literature, as promulgated in the World, began in *Moses*; to whom all Knowledge, and Science was communicated from Heaven, either by Inspiration, or Revelation; to whom all Precept also was given, either by Tradition from the Patriarchs, or by the immediate Voice of God. Hence the History of the World was written by him, as deriv'd from *Adam*, and the Antediluvian Patriarchs to *Noah*, and from *Noah* easily transmitted to *Moses*, who was not so far remov'd from Father *Noah*, as that the Accounts transmitted from Father to Son might not easily be handed on in unalterable Truth.

UPON this Foot it was that the Scripture spake of *Moses*, that he was learn'd in all the Wisdom of the *Egyptians*; which may be understood, either *as some*, that he was learn'd above all the Wisdom of the *Egyptians*; OR, *as others*, that he had easily made himself Master of all their Traditional Knowledge, which to him was but poor trifling Stuff, *as indeed it was*; consisting chiefly in their Magick and Conjurations, things which some think they were both instructed and assisted in Personally by the *Devil*; and in Astronomical Observations of the Motions of the Stars, which last they borrow'd from the *Arabians*, and they as it was said from *Ishmael* their great Ancestor, who also was instructed by *Abraham*, and he by Divine Revelation.

OTHERS suggest that *Job* was first Astronomer, that he form'd the Stars into Constellations, and gave those Constellations their Names; whence in the Book of *Job*, when GOD speaks to *Job* out of the Whirlwind, he is said to make use of the Names of the Constellations, and of the word *Mazzaroth*,[32] which to this Day is not well understood, and leaves us doubting whether it be an unknown Constellation, and was then only call'd so, and may be known since by other Names; or the whole Zodiack including all the Signs put together.

AND this may be the Reason, why some think that *Job* was Contemporary with *Moses*, in the latter part of his Life especially; and that he wrote his own History, having receiv'd the Knowledge of Letters from the *Israelites*, by the hand of *Moses*.

WHEN I mention thus the Introduction of Letters by *Moses*, I might again Quote the Words of the learn'd *Lud. Vives*,[33] in his Commentary upon *St.* Austin, *de Civit. dei*, lib. 18. cap. 39. St. Augustine's[a] words are short, thus, *The* Hebrew *Letters began from the Law given by* Moses: To this *Lud, Vives*, adds thus, *The vulgar Opinion of us Christians*, says he, *and also of the* Hebrews *Is, that the* Hebrew *Letters had* Moses *for their Author, which* EUPOLEMUS, *as also* ARTAPANUS, *and other prophane Writers also do assert*; who deliver that *Moses was the most wise Man in the World, and the Inventer of* Letters, *which he deliver'd over to the* Jews, *from whom the* Phenicians, *who were Neighbours to the* Jews *receiv'd them, and the* Grecians *by* Cadmus *from the* Phenicians: *The same* Artapanus *suggests that* Moses *likewise gave the Knowledge of Letters, and the Letters themselves to the* Egyptians.

This so exactly agrees with what I have already advanc'd from Reason, and the Nature of things, that I think it amounts to as much Confirmation of it, as History can yeild us. The Reverend and very learn'd Dr. *Gale*,[34] mentions the same thing also, in his Treatise of the original of the *Heb.* Letters, where he saith that *Moses* was stiled *Mercury* by the *Ægyptians*, because he taught them Wisdom, and the Knowledge of Letters: *vid.* Dr. *Gales* Court of the *Gentiles*, pag. 56. The same learn'd Author tells us, that *Plato* in his *Phædrus* contends, that the first Invention of Letters was in *Egypt*, by one THEUTCH,[35] of whom it was a great doubt, whether he were a God, or a Man; and other Authors bring this THEUTCH to be the same, that the *Ægyptians* call'd *Mercury*, and that this *Mercury* was *Moses* is affirm'd, says he,

'by *Artapanus* in *Eusebius Prepar. Evang.* lib. 9. cap. 4'. *His words are these*, 'Whom the *Hebrews* call *Moses*, and the *Greeks Musæus*, the *Ægyptians* call'd *Mercury*; and hence *Mercury* was said to be the God of Learning, because he was suppos'd to be the Inventer of Letters.'

Now the same learn'd Author insists that all the Oriental Languages derive from the *Hebrew*, and that therefore all the Nations, who spoke those Languages must derive their Letters from *Moses*, who taught the *Hebrew*, and that the Similitude with the Manner of Printing and the several readings of the Letters effectually acknowledge their Original. I know Monsieur *Du Pin*[36] is of another Opinion; but as he touches it but in a Summary and suppositious Manner I shall refer what he says to another Place.

WHAT is said already, fully confirms me in the Opinion, as before, that the Exhibition of the two Tables in the *Mount*, written, as the Text affirms, by the Finger of God, was the first Specimen of Letters ever known in the World; and why else could not the Coppy be done again in the Camp, as I have observ'd already, after the first Tables of Stone were broken by *Moses*, without carrying new Tables up to have the same Hand *at that time inimitable* perform the Operation?

SOME have entertained a Notion, whether from the old *Jews*, fruitful in Fictions, or from some other Brain given to Invention, that upon the Tables of Stone before, or immediately after, the writing of the Law, was an Alphabet of the *Hebrew* Letters, as a Key to instruct the *Israelites* in the writing part for the future; but this also I give the World, as indeed it is a peice of Invention; but it intimates that the *Israelites* had occasion of such a Direction, having probably never seen any writing before. Certain it is, that we do not meet with any writing, or any Alphabet in those Ages, before the *Hebrew*; what has been advanc'd of Antidiluvian Alphabets, of *Noahs* Alphabet, and the like, I shall consider by its self.

WE are indeed told of a great variety of antient Writings, particularly *Trismegistus*[37] is said to have written 30000 Volums, and that he lived before, or was at least as antient as *Moses*; but then there is an unsurmountable Difficulty in the word Volume, how it should be understood in after times, whether a Book, as it is here Suggested, or the Leaf of a Book, as in the 40 *Psalm* v. 7th *In the Volume of the Book, is it written, Lo, I come*, where *Volume* must be understood only a Leaf; here then is a Difficulty in the word Volume, and what Translators must call it in different Languages; for we are certain there were no Books in *Moses's* time, no, not Rolls, as we find was afterwards the usuage in the times of the Prophets, *Isaiah, Jeremiah, Ezekiel*, &c. Either then it must be suppos'd that *Trismegistus* wrote 30000 Tables of Stone, or Leaves of the *Papyri*, or that the Translators mean, that he wrote as much, as was *when Coppy'd*, or Translated, made up into 30000 Rolls, or Volums. So we read of the five Writers in the *Apocryphal* Book of *Esdras*, Book II. cap. xxiv[a] v. 44. *In Forty Days they wrote Two Hundred and Four Books*; what these Books were, is perfectly described in the same Chapter, Verse the xiv, *Look thou prepare thee many* Box-Trees, *and take with thee* Sarea, Dabria, Selemia, Ecanus, and Asiel. *These five, which are ready to write swiftly.* In the Margin its said, *Box-Tables to write on*, instead of *Box-Trees*; so that those Books were only so many *Tables* of Box-wood, of which I shall say more in its Place; but as to the 30000 Volumes of *Trismegistus*, tho' if they were written, 'tis probable they were no more than so many Tables of Wood, yet I must not forget that the whole Story of the 30000 Volumes or

Tables is treated by good Authors as fabulous: and indeed I think, deserves to be so treated.

FOR this *Trismegistus*, which some call *Mercury*, and the *Egyptians Thanut*, was an *Egyptian*, and at the most is suppos'd to be but Contemporary with *Moses*, and so might have all his Knowledge of Letters from *Moses*, that is to say, from the *Hebrew* original. He is also said to be the Inventor of all the liberal *Arts* and *Sciences*; *all which might be* after he had attain'd the Knowledge of Letters, and even without it, for 'tis manifest that the *Egyptians*, and before them the *Arabians* were Astronomers, Magicians and WISE MEN, *as those Ages call'd them*, or to speak in our Modern way, *Learn'd Men*, and yet they wrote only by *Hieroglyphicks*, not by Letters; and if *Trismegistus* us'd Letters, 'tis more than probable that he had them from MOSES, *as above*; and yet of all his 30000 Volums, which 'tis said he wrote, we know of no more, than of two Dialogues, preserv'd to the World under his Name; One call'd *Pæmander*, and the other *Asclepius*,[38] that is, the Persons speaking to one another, by way of *Dialogue*, are so call'd. The first of these Dialogues, *is concerning the Will of God*, and the other the *Power of God*; and these are Quoted by (a) several of the ancient Fathers, to prove the Truth of Religion from the Authority of so antient a Writer, DU PINN *Bibliothec. Patrum, or Ecc. Hist. of the first Cent.* Vol. I. Fol. 3.

(a) By St. *Clement* in lib. i *Aromat.*[39] By St. *Augustin* in Tract de 5 *Hæres.* and in lib. 8. de *Civit. Dei.*[40] By *Cyril* of *Alexandria.*[41] Contra Julianum lib. 1. By St. *Justin.*[42] And by *Lanctantius*,[43] inst. lib. 4.

PART III.

IT seems needful that I should take a little farther Notice here, *at least enough to let the Reader know that I have considered such a thing*, that there have been some Notions started in the World of the Knowledge of Letters, and the Use of Writing before the Deluge; and some have had Assurance enough to offer at the Manner: The first I met with in our Nation, was one *Hepburn*,[44] a *Scotsman*, a Person who indeed wanted no Learning, but a little too assuming; he was a Student at *Vienna*; He insisted upon *Enoch's* being the Father of Antediluvian Literature, and has gone so far, as to pretend to give an Alphabet, which he calls *Henochi literas*, and which is to be seen in some antient Writers, who spent perhaps more time in forming, than searching, after such a thing; for there does not appear, at least I cannot find that there does appear, any just Authority for what they have advanc'd.

THE utmost Evidence, *except what seems to lye in the Invention of these learned Criticks*: I say, the utmost Evidence that I met with among them, seems to amount to no more than a probability that it might be so, which I readily grant; but can by no means allow that this is a sufficient Proof of the Affirmative: They are pleas'd to introduce their Notions of this kind, by way of Interrogation and Inquiry. Why may we not believe, *say they*,

> 'That God who inspir'd the Minds of the Patriarchs in the Antediluvian Age, with all useful Knowledge, should not be suppos'd to have given this Knowledge among the rest, since this was a thing so many ways useful to them? nay, so absolutely necessary was it, to their Conversing profitably and usefully one with another, that they could hardly be said to be able to live happily without it.'

I THINK all this might be granted without prejudice to any ones Opinion, or Belief, that notwithstanding all this, it really might not be so; and that God, who knew for how short a Continuance that World was intended, and how it was not to the length of full two Ages, for the Flood

254

was in the Year 1656[a] of the Worlds Creation, knew very well they were capable of preserving the History of every Thing which was needful for them to know, by the Assistance of their Memories; which no Question were qualified for retaining the Knowledge, and Remembrance of Things material to be remember'd, as effectually as was needful to any of the Purposes they cou'd require.

THE two principal Supports of this Opinion of Antideluvian writings, and indeed the only Arguments that seem to carry Weight in them, or that requires any Answer, are these.

> I. THE Words of St. *Jude*, receiv'd in the *New-Testament*, vers. 14, 15. *And* Enoch also, the seventh from Adam, *Prophesied of these, saying, Behold, the Lord cometh with ten Thousands of his Saints, To execute Judgment upon all, and to convince all that are ungodly among them, of all their ungodly Deeds which they have ungodly committed, and of all their hard Speeches, which ungodly Sinners have Spoken against him.*

FROM *hence*, they will have it be, that the Patriarch *Enoch*[45] wrote these Words in a Book; to which they should add, that *Noah* must also preserve that Book, or Writing, whatever it was, in the *Ark*, and so leave the same to his Posterity; which had it been true, would doubtless have been preserv'd to future Generations, as a valuable and precious piece of Antiquity; and if the use of Letters had been convey'd to the Post Diluvians by *Noah*, as the same Persons insinuate was done, we cannot doubt, but such a sacred Oracle would certainly have been Coppied many times, yea Thousands of times, and that it could not but have been preserv'd to the use of us his Posterity.

SINCE therefore they bring us Scripture for a Testimony, which however, if granted to be to their Purpose, is no Proof the Fact, only of the Suggestion or Probability. *I say*, since they bring Scripture, let us see what is the Opinion of the learn'd Commentators upon this Text: The Continuators of the Learned Mr. *Pool*,[46] say thus, *Enoch* – Prophesied. *Note*,

> 'He doth not say *Wrote*, and therefore from hence it cannot be prov'd that there was any such Book as *Enoch's* Prophesies receiv'd by the *Jews*, as Cannonical Scripture; but that rather, this was some Prophesy of *Enochs* deliver'd to them by Tradition, and handed down by the Patriarchs from one to another, and which pass'd as a certain Truth, *that is to say*, that *Enoch* did so Prophesy.' Vid. *Pool's Annotat*, upon the Epistle of St. *Jude*.

IF *Enoch* wrote this, Why was it not said, *as it is written*, in the Prophesies of *Enoch*, the Seventh from *Adam*, &c. which is the usage of Scripture: This Text militates nothing in favour of *Hepburn*, or any of those antient Writers, or of their Notion of the Knowledge of Letters in the Antediluvian World;

for *Enoch* might, and certainly did, Prophesy, as the Text here Quotes; but this was no other than the Words of *Enoch*, preach'd to that sinful World, warning them of their approaching Destruction; then handed down to *Noah*, and by him to his Posterity by *Oral Tradition*, and remember'd even to that Day, when *Jude* Quotes them, *as above*.

IT is plain from the rest of the Writings of the Apostles, and from the Words of Christ himself, that when our Saviour referr'd the *Jews*, in his Discourses to them, to any of the antient Writers, he usually introduced it with those Words, *for it is Written*; particularly in his return to the Devil, when he Tempted him to cast himself down from the Temple; and also when the Devil propos'd to him to Worship him, and also when he Tempted him to command the Stones to be made Bread, *Mat.* iv. 4, 7, 10. *But he answer'd and said, It is written, Man shall not live by Bread alone, but by every Word that proceedeth out of the Mouth of God.*

Jesus said unto him, it is written again, Thou shall not tempt the Lord thy God.

Then saith Jesus unto him, get thee hence, Satan: For it is written, Thou shalt Worship the Lord thy God, and him only shalt thou serve.

BUT seeing then, 'tis only said here, that *Enoch* Prophecied, it argues no more that *Enoch* wrote what he Prophecied, than that *Moses's* Relation of what *Adam* and *Eve* said one to another was written down for the Authority of *Moses*, or that the Serpent wrote down what he said to *Eve*, when he tempted her to break GOD's Command, forbidding her to eat. Thus without showing any dis-regard to the Testimony of Scripture, I think 'tis Evident, that what St. *Jude* says of *Enoch's* Prophesy, is as to this Case nothing at all to the Purpose.

THE Second Testimony is Quoted from *Josephus*, in his *Antiquities* of the *Jews*. lib. I. *cap*. 3. Where speaking of the Sons of *Adam*, and particularly of SETH, the only succeeding Son of *Adam*, after *Cain* and *Abel*, that the Scripture makes mention of. His Words are thus render'd in *English*, in our common Edition of *Josephus*,[47] by Sir *R. L'Strange*.

'SETH being brought up under the Tuition of his Father, prov'd a wonderful Man, and wholly given up to the Study of Vertue, and his Children were the lively Image of so excellent a Father.

'THESE were the first that made their Observations upon the Motions of the Heavens, the Courses, and Influences of the Stars; and having been foretold by *Adam* of the universal Deluge, and Conflagration to come, they erected two Pillars, one of Brick, the other of Stone, which they were sure would be of Proof against either Fire or Water. Upon those Pillars they engrav'd the Memorials of their Discoveries, and Inventions, there to remain for the Benefit of the Ages to come; and least the Tradition should be lost for want of a Record.

THIS they did, and their Foresight and Providence was not in vain, for the Stone is yet seen in *Syria* to this very Day.'

Josephus' Antiq. of the *Jews*. cap. 2. fol. 6.

Now not to Enter here into the long Chain of Argument, brought against this Opinion by the Antients, and particularly by St. *Augustin*, who rejects it entirely. *I say*, not to Enter into their Arguments, 'tis enough to Enter my Protest against this Relation, as impossible to be True by the nature of the Thing; and that it is not Rational to Conceive, that any of the Fabricks, Buildings or Monuments of the old World could remain, and be visible after the Flood; and whether we consider the Deluge as a meer flux of Water collected by a supernatural Power into such a Position, as to cover the Face of the Earth for near Eleven Months, or whether we consider the Deluge according to the Hypothesis of the Learn'd *Burnet*[48] to be an *Absorption*, or a Breaking in of the Surface of the Earth into the great Deep, or Abyss of Water, which till then was Subterraneous and unseen. *I say*, whethersoever of these were the real Fact, I take it to be inconsistent with the nature of the Thing, that any Column, or Pillar could remain after the Flood. *I mean*, such as the Hand of Man could make, whose Dependance must be on the Surface of the Earth, on which it stood. Seeing we all agree, that even *on the first Supposition*, the Surface of the Earth would be too much soften'd, and the furious Motion of the Waters would be so forcible, especially at their first flux, and towards their Ebbing off, that no human built Fabrick could stand in its way; and if it be true, on the next Hypothesis, as has been the Opinion of the Learn'd, that the Face of the whole Globe of the Earth was chang'd, and renew'd; 'tis also not likely that any Building, however firm, of the old World could remain, no, not the same Face of the Surface; but Mountains were cast up, deep Valleys made, *and the like*, and every thing overturn'd. Not so much as *Eden*, the Garden of God, was preserv'd, or the Place perfectly known where it stood, tho' describ'd so mathematically in the *Pentateuch*, as to name the Rivers,[49] their Entrance in, and thro' and Coming out of it.

IT would seem strange then, that this Column of Antediluvian Structure should remain, and not any other thing belonging to the old World; no City or Town, no Work of the antient Inhabitants; no Monument, Altar, Temple, or Castle, however strong built, if such they had; nothing remaining in any Place of the World, to intimate that there had been Inhabitants there before them; no, not so much as the Ruins of any thing, and yet that this *Column* in *Syria* should remain, and be not only visible in *Josephus's* time, but should show the Engravement, with the History of the *Time when*, and the Reason, or *Cause for which*, it was erected. These are Improbabilities, which argue strongly against the Authority of one single Writer, and I think may serve for a sufficient Answer.

FURTHER, if this Pillar was remaining, the Writing, and Engravement upon it was remaining also; otherwise, How did it testify the Meaning of it? And how did the *Jews* receive from it the History mention'd above? and if these were remaining, How comes it to pass that so glorious a Monument of Antiquity was not preserv'd, that the Words, or at least the Characters were not copyed, and taken off, and by some artful, careful Hand, preserv'd for the Use and Information of Posterity? Strange! that the Pillar should remain, and the Reason of it be told, and not a Word of the Inscription preserv'd, as the just Authority for Proof of the Facts, said to be, or intended to be preserv'd by that Column. But so it is, *Josephus* himself does not so much as intimate that any Copy of the Inscription, or Engravement, on the Pillar had been preserv'd, or does he so much as give us any of the Words, or Letters made use of in it.

WHAT then is the Authority of *Josephus*, to prove there was such a Column, or what the Column it self? If it had been really preserv'd as I am fully satisfy'd it was not, and could not? *I say*, What is all this to the proving the Knowledge of Letters in the Antediluvian World; Unless the Inscription, or any part of it, which was said to be engrav'd on the Column, had been also shown us, that we might know what Letters they used, and in what manner the Sound of Words was drawn out from them?

IT is True, the learn'd *Bugi*,[50] in his Treatise, entitl'd, *Exercitationum Literariarum*, Collects all that was advanc'd by those antient Writers, concerning these Letters, and gives us, or pretends rather to give, the several Alphabets of *Adam, Enoch*, and *Noah*, and his Authors, or Authority for this, which are principally,

Angelus Roccha[51] a Camerino, in *Bibliothecæ* Apostolicæ Vaticanæ Commentario, quem *Romæ*, Ann. 1591, edidit.

Claudius Durretius,[52] in Historia de linguis Universi, *Coloniæ*, 1613.

Theseus Ambrosius,[53] in Appendice Introductionis ad Chaldaicam linguam, Syriacam, Armenicam, atque decem alias linguas, quas Papiæ in Italia evulgavit, 1539.

Jacobus Bonaventura Hepburnus[54] Scotus, Ordinis sancti Francisci de Paula, qui Pontificis *Pauli* v. privilegio & Superiorum licentiâ confirmatus forum extruxit Romæ, 1616, & *Auream Virgam* inscripsit.

FROM these several Authors, are collected the several Alphabets call'd by them, as in the following Transcripts, from the said learn'd Author are to be seen, and to which I refer, thinking it sufficient to give the Transcript, with the Authority, from whence I bring it; without any Suggestion of the Truth of it, which indeed, I conceive is not to be found, otherwise than in the fruitful Invention of these Authors, which I leave the learn'd Reader to Judge of.

QUEST. I.

Quinam Auctores Literis Antediluvianis patrocinentur, de iis testentur, & quibus figuris illæ expressæ extent?

ORdiemur a primi-hominis, Adami, Alphabeto, *quô, Si genuinum esset, antiquius prodi aut promi nequibat, humanâ quidem industriâ & solertiâ elaboratum. Hujus* Adamæi Characteris *originem quod spectat, non heri aut hodiè nata, ante seculum viguit, diuq; in animis credulis sedem fixit. Veluti vero hæc* Literarum *prima stirps, ut putatur, à publicis Monumentis & nitidis Sculptorum cœlis gratiam, ita ab illustri* Adami *nomine splendorem, a diuturnitate vero temporis, quo intacta & severioris examinis secura floruit, robur ac duramentum nacta est.*

Ingrediamur modò atque contemplemur spaciosum Literarum *Forum, quod* Jacobus Bonaventura Hepburnus Scotus, Ordinis Francisci de Paula, *Pontificis* Pauli V. *privilegiô & superiorum licentiâ confirmatus extruxit Romæ* 1616, & Auream Virgam *inscripsit: mox velut in acta publica relatum testimonium de* Literis Protoplasti *intuentium oculis obversabitur. Nam inter Sexaginta octo differentes Literarum formas magnô quidem studio conquisitas, sed majori impendio in æs incisas, spectatur talis typus*

ADAMÆI ALPHABETI.

Sic vidimus Hepburni *testimonium* Literarum Adamæarum *monumentis confignatum. Sed tantum vidimus. Quare à nuda* Characterum Adami *indice tabula obiter inspecta, quam* Hepburnus *Pontifici* Paulo V. *dicavit, rectà progrediemur ad lustranda* monumenta Italiæ à Laurentio Schradero Halberstadiense Saxone *edita, atque inibi lustrabimus eos* Adami *Characteres, quos in peregrinatione Italica viderat* Schraderus, *quosq; ex Bibliothecæ Vaticanæ Columna octava in muro ad Effigiem* Adami *exscriptos Helmstadii ediderat,* 1592: *quibus mox alia* Adamæorum Elementorum *forma ab* Hepburnæo Adami *charactere planè diversa nostris oculis subjungetur. Hæc autem talis est,*

Quoniam verò non modò in Hepburnæa Literaria Tabula, *verum etiam in* Schraderianis *Italiæ Monumentis jam allegatis nudas tantum characterum figuras intueri licet: veniendum erit ad alios Autores, qui non minus nonnulla fundamenta antiquissimarum literarum ab* Adamo *formatarum tradere conati sunt, quam nudos Characteres typis aut Cælis exprimere. Hos inter tres in primis numerantur:* Angelus Roccha à Camerino *in Bibliothecæ Apostolicæ Vaticanæ commentariô, quem concinnavit* & Romæ, 1591, *edidit:* Claudius Duretus *in Historia de Linguis Universi, quam Gallico idiomate publicavit Coloniæ* 1613; *necnon* Theseus Ambrosius ex Comitibus Albonesii I U D *in Appendice Introductionis in Chaldaicam Linguam, Syriacam, Armenicam atque decem alias Linguas, quas Papiæ in Italia evulgavit,* 1539.

Initio quidem in illud Adami Alphabetum *oculos defigemus, quod Angelus Roccha in Commentario Bibliothecæ Vaticanæ videndum proponit,* pag. 79. & *verba ejus audiemus, quæ ita habent:* Supra hujus [picti Adami] caput Characteres, sive Literæ antiquiores, nunc Hebraicæ dictæ, ejusmodi leguntur.

Hebraicum Alphabetum Antiquius.

ℸℷℲℱℽℨℶ℈ℸ℈ℂ

Ad ejusdem verò *Adami* pedes Inscriptio Latina in hanc legitur verborum formam.

Adam divinitus edoctus, primus scientiarum & *literarum inventor. Pergit* Roccha, *pag.* 80. Ratio ipsa persuadet, Adamum divinitus edoctum disciplinas, certosq; præsertim scribendi Characteres adeo necessarios aliis præmonstrâsse, sicut inscriptio docet. Hanc autem formam scribendi hôc locô positam Hebraicas inter literas antiquiorem, primumque Alphabetum fuisse CREDENDUM EST quod à dextro in sinistrum latus legitur. *Hæc* Roccha.

Porro nunc ad primum & *principium hujus* Adamæi *Alphabeti promum ac patronum pedem promovebimus. Nobis quidem nemo hactenus visus est aut cognitus, qui publicando* Literas Adamæas Theseum Ambrosium *anteverteret. Etenim Annô Christi,* 1539, *Papiæ primus evulgavit* Adami Characteres, *eosq; velut è mediis, ad quas damnati memorantur, flammis eripuit. Qua de re ipsum* Theseum *loquentem audiamus.* Sex, *inquit* Theseus in Append. *variarum Literarum,* p. 202, 203, relatis Hebraicarum Literarum generibus, operæ precium me facturum arbitratus sum, si alios haudquaquam spernendos Hebræorum Characteres, à variis non infimi nominis autoribus excerptos in hac nostra Appendice adderem. Inter libros Antonii de Fantis Tarvisini, olim Philosophi & Astrologi excellentissimi, memini me vidisse opera Razielis,

Picatricis, Bailii, Mercurii Petri, Apponis, Salomonis ac Interpretis ejus Apollonii, & aliorum multorum, ex quibus tanquam ex virenti & florido prato variarum Literarum flores & Characteres diversos collegi. Neque enim aliam ab causam tam diligenter libros illos, antequam in Vulcani potestatem a patribus nostris, in quorum manus ex testamento pervenerunt, legi; quàm ut Characteres illos, Literarum scilicet varias figuras, exscriberem. In secundo quippe Tractatu, in quo de lapidibus preciosis loquitur Raziel, reprobata illorum opinione qui dicunt viginti duas Literas, de quibus ibi loquitur, à Samuele fuisse inventas; Angelum Raphael in Libro, qui dicitur Liber ignis, illas Adæ protoplasto dedisse scriptas asseverat, & ob id filios Adami eas recusare non posse. Quarum quidem Literarum figura & nomina sunt infra scripta. *Hactenus* Theseus, *Quia vero figuris plane conveniunt* hi Angelici Characteres Adamo *traditi cum isto* Literarum Adamæarum *genere, quod suprà primô locô videndum proposuimus, quodq; nitido satis Cælô in æs incidendum, curavit* Hepburnus, *nolumus Alphabetum huc denuo transcribere, aut idem bis cum tædio Lectoris repetere, ne actum agamus.*

Veluti verò Thesei *vestigiis pressè insistit* Hepburnus *in Aurea Virga, hoc est, splendida variarum Literarum Tabula, quando easdem quas ille* Adamæarum Literarum *Figuras attulit: ita* Claudius Duretus *ne latum quidem unguem ab ejusdem* Thesei *latere discessit, nisi quòd novâ testimoniorum Symbolâ adjectâ diligentiam ejus superare conatus sit. Etenim* Primo *allegat* Ambrosium Theseum *tanquam ducem, quem imitandum sibi proposuit in divulgandis hisce* Adami Literis. *Hujus enim narrationem & auctoritatem velut scutum adversantibus objicit. Deinde hunc titulum eis prefigit*: Characteres de l' Ange Raphael, *Characteres Angeli Raphaelis.* Tertiò *plane eosdem & numero & habitu* Characteres Adamiticos, *quos* Theseus *ante seculum excudendos curavit, ob oculos ponit,* pag. 117. Quarto & ultimo *præscriptis Characteribus substruit nova fundamenta, partim petita è Cabalistarum & Ebræorum Commentariis in.* Librum Jezira, *partim ex patribus* Epiphanio & Augustino.

Primo quidem è scriptis & peruschiis Rabbinices in Librum Jezira *probare nititur, quod* patrum præceptores fuerint Angeli noti, videlicet præceptor ipsius Adami Raziel, &c. Secundo *asserit* Epiphanium *ad Panarium facere mentionem Libri, cujus titulus,* Adæ Revelatio, quando Deus immisit soporem in illum. Tertio *tradit* Augustinum *contra Faustum Manichæum meminisse* Libri Adamæi, *cujus inscriptio & argumentum fuit de* Genealogia filiorum & filiarum Adæ. Quartò *ait Librum quendam Razielis Angeli extitisse, qui hunc prætulit titulum,* Chavæ five omnium viventium Matris admirabiles & super omnes doctrinas mundi secundum evangelicam Veteris & Novi Testamenti veritatem amplectendæ Prophetiæ, conscriptæ a Raziele Adæ primi parentis Angelo ex Libro Behn, id est, Lucis purissimæ excerptæ. Quintò *denique memorat* Sanctum Thomam *librô de Ente & Essentia affirmare ab* Abele *filio*

Adami *librum fuisse compositum*, &c. Universa Dureti *Dissertatio eò collimat, ut è Libris, qui* Adamo *tanquan autori assignantur*, Literarum *Libros scribere non potuit* Adamus. *Quamobrem neutiquam se aberrâsse putat, quando* Thesei *exemplum sequntus, tale Literarum genus, quale suprà à nobis expressum est, Protaplasto Adæ tribuit. Sed ab Alphabeto* Adamæo, *ad Literas filiis* Seth *ascriptas lustrandas progrediemur.*

Alphabetum filiis Seth *sigillatim tribui non observavimus nisi ab* Angelo Roccha *in Comment. Bibliothecæ Vaticanæ* p. 8, Schradero *in Monumentis Italiæ, & autore inscriptionum, quæ visuntur Romæ in parastaticis columnis Bibl. Vaticanæ quem ducem sequnti sunt* Roccha & *Schraderus, sed dispari successu. Hic enim Literarum ordinem confundit, ipsosque Characteres rudiùs ac impolitiùs formandos curavit: Ille vero in cælebri suo Commentario, Cujus jam aliquoties neminimus, eundem plane situm & habitum Literarum filiis* Seth, *ut ipse loquitur, assignatarum exhibet, quem ipse in* Adamæo Alphabeto *videndum proposuit, & quem nos celandum suprà curavimus. Hoc* Alphabetum posteris Seth *tributum nullô aliò fundamentô fulcit* Roccha, *nisi geminîs illîs columnîs, quarum meminit* Josephus, *lib* 1. *Antiq. Jud.* Harum una, *ait Roccha*, lateritia erat, altera ænea sive marmorea: illa contra ignis Conflagrationes, hæc contra aquæ alluviones erecta, ut monumenta ipsa diutius conservarentur & permanerent. His in columnis liberales artes, & eas prefertim, quæ ad observationem siderum pertinerent, conscripserunt. *Josephus* autem ad suam usque ætatem Columnam illam marmoream in Syria durasse testatur. *Hæc* Roccha, *qui porrò addit opinandum esse, quod hòc* Alphabetum filiis Seth *præmonstratum sit ab* Adamo. Tzetzes *Chiliad*, 5. Hist. 26. Κ᾽ὰν Σῆθ ᾽εβρα☐οι λέγωσιν ᾽εφευρετι☐ω γραμμάτων quamvis *Seth* Hebræi dicant inventorem literarum: *Quo loco' ipsi parenti Setho literarum inventum tributum observat. Cæterum ab* Alphabeto filiorum Seth *ad* Literas Henochæas *descendemus.*

Henochi Literas, quoad *investigare licuit, primus publicavit* Joannes Augustinus Pantheos Venetus Sacerdos. *Is Librô, quem mirô titulô & hybridâ voce inscrisit* Voarchdumiam contra Alchimiam, & *Venetiis edidit* 1530. *Initió quidem usitatas & hodiernas* Ebræorum Literas *spectandas proponit* pag. 12. Deinde *easdem ornatiùs excusas ob oculos ponit, atq; illos Characteres fuisse asserit, quos in Monte Sinai Deus* Mosi *concesserat*, pag. 13. Tertio *Figuras literarum* Abrahæ *traditarum exhibet*, pag. 14. Quarto *denique* Henochæi Alphabeti *typum exprimit* Pag. 15.

Has Literarum Henochæarum *umbras, quibus formidolosæ suæ Voarchdumiæ arcana (mysteriô enim Ebraicarum Literarum, in primis quatuor,* רקנר *artis suæ secreta tegit) obscuravit* Pantheus, *festinus captat* Duretus pag. 127 *citati supra Libri, eásq; pro veris* Henochi Literarum *antiquitate venerabilium figuris orbi literato obtrudit. Ne verò planè tacuisse videatur, postquam hos Characteres ob oculos posuit, hæc subjungit:* Nobis, qui hôc sæculô vivimus probè innotuit extare in

Æthiopiâ Librum magnæ authoritatis & pro Canonìco habitum, qui res divinas complectitur & Enocho tanquam auctori tribuitur. *Cetera, quæ addit, planè sunt* αλλοτρια, *quare ea adscribere operæ precium haut putamus.*

Verùm *enim verò à* Pantheo & Duretho *abit Jac.* Bonaventura Hepburnus *Expressurus* Henochi characteres, & *in sua* Aurea Virga *hodiernos Characteres Ebraicos, sed elegantiusculè sculptos & punctulîs in medio instar rhomborum pulcherrimè cælatos pro* Henochæis Literis *agnoscit. Quia verò nudas saltom Literarum Figuras exhibet* Hepburnus *frustrà ab ipso rationes & diductiorem confirmationem* Alphabeti Henochæi expectaveris. Sed missis Literis Henochi, *ad* Noachi *characteres veniemus.*

Qui in colligendis ac cælandis variis Literarum generibus omnium industriam superare conatus est Bonaventura Hepburnus *in magna* & *splendida octo* & *sexaginta characterum Tabula,* Virga Aurea *dicta, hisce sequentibus figurîs sculptum exhibet*

NOACHICUM ALPHABETUM

Heic planè silent Theseus & Duretus, *audaces aliàs* Antediluvianarum Literarum *promi* & *patroni, solus* Hepburnus *loquitur; sed quô successu, mox Questione secundâ ostendemus. Neq; alibi in antiquis Monumentis* Literarum *quicquam observare hactenus potuimus, quo talis* Noachi *scriptura confirmetur, nisi cuipiam placuerit ad partes vocare* Noachi Librum, *quem Cabalistæ tradunt à* Chamo *in arca patri surreptum fuisse: De quo* Delrius *Disq. Magic.* Lib. 1. c. 5. Quest. 1. *Aut si quis velit* Noachi Testamentum, *ejusq; epistolam huc trahere quâ suprema tanti viri voluntas contineri perhibetur, quam paucis abhinc annis è ruderibus Volaterranis erutam cum aliis Etruscis Antiquitatibus* Prosper *Italus divulgavit. Atq; sic etiam lustravimus Literas* Noachom *ascriptas.*

[Editor's translation]
QUESTION I

Which Authors support the idea of Antediluvian Letters and bear witness to them, and what form do they give them?

Let us begin with the Alphabet of the first man, Adam – than which, if it is genuine, there can be no older product of human industry and skill. The

origin of this Adamitic character does not belong to today or yesterday; it
has flourished for long ages, fixing its seat in credulous minds. Most probably this first nursling of Letters, as it was supposed to be, was made
attractive by public monuments and the chisel of illustrious sculptors; thus
it obtained its hold on opinion from the glorious name of Adam and from
the very length of time in which it endured, unchallenged by severe
criticism.

We can begin with the spacious assemblage of Letters which the Scotsman Jacobus Bonaventura Hepburn, of the Order of Francis de Paola,
produced in Rome in 1616, with a 'privilege' from Pope Paul V and a
licence from his own superiors, entitling it 'The Golden Staff'. It soon
served as a public testimony to the existence of an Original Writing. Among
sixty-eight different letter-shapes, arrived at by profound study, and incised
on copper with the greatest care, was to be seen the following design:

ADAMITIC ALPHABETS

Thus we see the testimony of Hepburn regarding Adamitic letters con-
signed to monuments. So much for that. So from the bare tablet of
Adamitic characters dedicated by Hepburn to Pope Paul V, let us proceed
to consider the monuments of Italy published by Laurentius Schrader[55] of
Halberstadt in Saxony, where we may study the Adamitic Characters which
Schrader saw during his travels in Italy and which, from the eighth column
in the Vatican Library, he affixed to an effigy of Adam on the wall in 1592,
presenting to our view a greatly different version of these characters from
Hepburn's. His is like this:

Thus the bare Characters can be seen not only in Hepburn's table but in
Schrader's monuments aforesaid. Now we must come to other authors
who, equally, have tried to trace the fundamentals of the most ancient letters back to Adam and to illustrate them by pictures and engravings. We
may begin by naming three: Angelo Rocca a Camerino, in the Commentary on the Apostolic Vatican Library which he produced in Rome in 1591;
Claudius Duretus, in his *History of the Languages of the Universe*, which he
published in French in Cologne in 1613; and Theseus Ambrosius Albonen-

sis in the Appendix to his Introduction to the Chaldean, Syriac, Armenian and ten other languages which he published in Pavia in Italy in 1539.

First, we look at that Adamitic alphabet which Angelo Rocca presents in his Commentary on the Vatican Library, p. 79, with the inscription: 'Above the head [of a picture of Adam] the more ancient or Hebrew letters can equally be read.'

THE EARLIER HEBREW ALPHABET

ꓶﬡ𐎃ﬡﬡ𐎀ﬣﬡﬡﬡﬡﬡ

At Adam's feet there is a Latin inscription, which reads as follows:

Adam, instructed from Heaven, first inventor of sciences and letters. Thus Rocca, page 80. Reason itself, so this inscription avers, argues that Adam, instructed from Heaven, must have been the first to teach disciplines, and especially written characters (which are so very necessary). That the form of writing here represented is the oldest form for Hebrew letters and the earliest alphabet IS TO BE BELIEVED, because it is written from right to left. So says Rocca.

So now let us proceed to the first exponent and patron of this Adamitic Alphabet. We know of nobody who preceded Theseus Ambrosius in what he has published on Adamitic letters. For it was truly he who, in 1539 at Pavia, first made known Adamitic characters, as if snatching them from the flames to which they had supposedly been condemned. Concerning which let us listen to Theseus himself.

'I have', he says in his 'Appendix of various letters', pp. 202–3, 'considered myself as committed to establishing six kinds of Hebrew letters, if I may include various (by no means contemptible) Hebrew characters adduced by authors worthy of respect. Among the books of the late Antonius de Fantis Tarrisini, an excellent philosopher and astrologer, I remember seeing the writings of Raziel, Picatrix, Bailius, Mercurius Petrus, Appon, and Salomon, and Apollon his interpreter: indeed many more, from which, as from a verdant and flowery meadow, I collected the flowers and characters of diverse letters. It was for this reason that I diligently read these books before they were given into the hands of Vulcan[56] by our fathers who had inherited them; and I will transcribe these characters and forms of letters. In the second Tractatus, indeed, in which Raziel speaks about precious stones, rebuking those who say the twenty-two letters of which he speaks were invented by Samuel, he affirmed that the Angel Raphael, in the work known as 'The Book of Fire', gave those letters as a protoplast to Adam, and that accordingly the sons of Adam may not reject them, I give their form and names below.' So writes Theseus. These angelical characters handed down by Adam clearly correspond to the form of Adamitic letters which we spoke of earlier and which Hepburn caused to be engraved in shining copper. We will not tire the reader by transcribing them all over again.

Hepburn, in his 'Golden Staff', a splendid table of various letters, may truly be said to have been following in the footsteps of Theseus, when he included the same Adamitic forms. Likewise Claudius Duretus, who would not deviate a fingernail's breadth from Theseus, except in so far as he tried to outdo him by adding further examples. For, first of all, he invoked Theseus as a leader, declaring him a model in the dissemination of Adamitic letters and using his authority as a shield against adversaries. He gave his work the title 'Characters of the Angel Raphael' and clearly depicted the same Adamitic characters that Theseus had engraved previously, page 117. Fourthly and lastly he identified nine fundamentals, taken partly from Cabbalistic and Hebrew commentaries on the Book of Jezira and partly from the Fathers of the church Epiphanius and Augustine.

First, from the Rabbinic writings and *peruschiis* about the Book of Jezirah[57] he attempts to prove that the teachers were the well-known angels, including Adam's instructor Raziel, etc. Secondly he asserts that Epiphanius's *Ad Parasium* makes mention of the Book, the title of which was 'Adam's Revelation', dealing with the moment when God implanted *sapor* in him. Thirdly, he represents Augustine, in his *Against Faustus the Manichean*, as remembering the Adamitic books, the inscription and argument of which concerned the genealogy of the sons and daughters of Adam. Fourthly, he says that the Book of the Angel Raziel once existed and was entitled *Chavae*, or Encomium of the admirable prophecies of Chava [Eve], Mother of all living beings: about all the doctrines of the world according to the evangelical truth of the Old and New Testaments, written by Raziel, the angel of our first parent, from the Book Behn, that is to say 'Purest Rays of Light'. Fifthly, he recalls Saint Thomas saying in *de Ente et Essentia* that the Book was composed by Abel, son of Adam. etc. ... But from the Adamitic alphabet let us turn to the letters ascribed to the children of Seth.

We have not seen an Alphabet specifically ascribed to the children of Seth save by Angelo Rocca in his Commentary on the Vatican Library, p. 8; by Schrader, in his *Monuments of Italy*; and by the author of the inscriptions which are to be seen in Rome in parastatic columns in the Vatican Library, which Rocca and Schrader took the lead from, though with differing success. The latter confuses the order of letters and shapes them very crudely and roughly; the former, in his celebrated Commentary, which we have several times mentioned, exhibits it [the order] in the same style as (he says) the one he described in the Adamitic alphabet, which we reproduced above. Rocca's only basis for ascribing it to the children of Seth is the pair of columns which Josephus[58] speak of in his *Antiquities of the Jews*, Book I, one of the columns being of brick and the other of bronze or marble: the one designed against fire, the other against flood, so that these monuments should long endure. On these columns they inscribed the liberal arts and matters concerning the observation of the stars. *Josephus* affirms the marble column to have survived until his own day. Rocca relates this and moreover gives it as his opinion that this alphabet was revealed to the children of Seth by Adam. Tzetzes Chiliad,[59] v. Hist. 26. Κ'ὰν Σῆθ 'εβρα☐οι λέγωσιν 'εφευρετι☐ῶ γραμμάτων although the Hebrews called Seth the inventor of letters. Let us now descend from the Alphabet of the children of Seth to the *Enochian* letters.

The Letters of Enoch, so far as we are able to investigate them, were first published by Joannes Augustinus Pantheos, a Venetian priest, in his book which, with a wondrous and ambiguous title, he called *Voarchdumia contra Alchimiam* and published in Venice in 1530. He began by reproducing the normal and everyday Hebrew letters (page 12). Then he gave them in a more ornate form, in which, according to him, God gave them to Moses on Mount Sinai (page 13). Thirdly (page 14) he gave the shapes of the Letters of Abraham. Fourthly and lastly, he illustrated the form of the Alphabet of Enoch (page 15).

These shadows of the Letters of Enoch, in which Pantheos hid the secrets of his awesome *Voarchdumia* (he used his art to cloak four רקנר mysteries of Hebrew letters) were speedily seized on by Duretus (page 27 of his book cited above) and were brought to the attention of the literary world as the true and ancient letters of Enoch. Moreover, having displayed these characters to us, he does not hesitate to speak plainly. *It is right for us to take note, he says, that there exists in Ethiopia a Book of high authority, regarded indeed as canonical, which deals with divine things and is attributed to Enoch as author.*

It must be admitted that Jac. Bonaventura Hepburn departs from Pantheus and Duretus in the way he depicts Enochian characters; and in his *Golden Staff* he gives us ordinary everyday Hebrew characters, though most elegantly engraved, and in the midsts of beautifully-incised rhombuses, as Enochian letters. From the fact that Hepburn shows at least the bare forms of the letters, you would have expected from him (though in vain) the reasons for a more logical confirmation of the Enochian alphabet. But laying aside these Enochian letters, let us come to Noachian characters.[60]

Hepburn, whom none can outdo in collecting and engraving all the various forms of letters, as he has done in his great and splendid table of 68 characters called the *Golden Staff*, exhibits the Alphabet of Noah carved in the following shapes.

NOACHIAN ALPHABET

Here Theseus and Duretus, at other times bold exponents and champions of antediluvian letters, remain notably silent; only Hepburn speaks – but with what success, a second question will soon show. Nowhere else in ancient monuments of letters have we been able to see such a Noachian writing confirmed, unless someone should be pleased to call the 'Book of Noah' the one which, according to the Kabbalists, was stolen by Cham from his father's Ark. See Delrius,[61] *Disq. Magic. Lib*. I, c.5. *Question* 1. Or if anyone wants to cite Noah's Testament and his epistle, containing the last wishes of so great a man, which a few years ago were unearthed from the Volaterranian rubbish, with other Etruscan antiquities, by Prosper Italus. And so we have also drawn up the letters attributed to Noah.

[End of translation]

HAVING thus given the most material Arguments, and the best Authorities which I can find are brought to make good these imaginary Things, for I can look upon them as no other: I have given my Reasons why they pass for no other with me, and I leave it to the judicious Reader to consider whether they have Weight in them or no.

THE same Author puts some Stress upon the fabulous Story of the Egyptians and their early Knowledge of Letters, from the introducing of Hieroglyphical Writings by *Memnon*, of whom I have spoken already.

AFTER all these are thus considered, and their Suggestions, as far as is reasonable, duly weigh'd, I see no Reason at all to alter, or so much as doubt the *Proposition* which I have already on mature Consideration offered to discourse upon; Namely, that the first Knowledge of Letters was from the immediate Inspiration of Heaven at the publishing the Law of God from Mount *Sinai*; and that all the Neighbouring Nations, such as the *Ægyptians, Phœnicians*, &c. receiv'd the first Hints of that Knowledge which they afterwards grew so famous for, from the *Hebrews*, and had all their Knowledge and Use of Letters from them.

IT is observ'd by some Men, who are particularly critical in the literal, or constructive Translations of the Scripture, that the Words, by which *Moses* expresses the Union and Accord of the Inhabitants of the new peopled World, in the Days of *Nimrod*, in pursuing that *poor senseless* Project of building a Tower to reach up to Heaven, *&c.* are wrong translated, and that it should not be said, as in *Gen.* II. i. *The whole Earth was of one Language, and of one Speech*; But thus, *that the whole Earth*, that is, *all the People on the Earth*, were of *one Mind*, and were agreed, or of one Accord, in the Design, which follows, meaning the Project of the Tower that was to be built.

IF this Suggestion is Just, as I believe it is, it imports thus much in favour of this Proposition of mine: Namely, that having no settled Rule of Speech, or Knowledge of Letters, and no Alphabet; Custom and ordinary Usage, without any other Authority, as it does to this Day, brought them to differing Dialects, and differing Pronunciation of Speech; such as they being separated, and remote perhaps from one another, tho' not at a great Distance, yet at a Distance enough to prevent frequent Conversing together, could not easily communicate to one another: Hence they grew particular, and proper only to those Tribes, or Families that had accustom'd themselves to them, so that they might not easily and fully understand one another: But notwithstanding this, they might so far understand the general Meaning of their Speech, or by some particularly be acquainted with the other, might so interpret to each other, as to make an Agreement in the main Design: This, *I say*, however, strongly implys they had then no Knowledge of Letters, and so far tells us that the Notions *de Literatura Patriarchali*, and *Noachicum Alphabetum*, mention'd above, can have no authentick Original, nor any just Authority to suport them: This, however, as it is argued from the Opinion above named, which is only conjectural, so it may be allow'd to be a just Reply to that Conjecture.

HAVING said thus much, I leave these Learned Phantasms, *for such I think they are*, just where I found them, and so proceed to speak of the Progress in the Knowledge of Letters, after they were introduc'd, and from the just Original of Literature, which we have an Account of in the Scripture, as above.

PART IV.

HAVING thus discours'd on the Original of Letters, and fix'd, *as I think, effectually* their *Epocha*, in the Year of the World 2415, there remains to enquire, In what Manner they were made Use of in the respective Ages, after their being first given out: And by what Degrees the Writing and Printing of these Letters advanc'd to the Perfection which we see them now arriv'd to; also How, and in what Manner, and upon what Occasions the Materials for Writing and Printing, and the Instruments and Engines for the Performance of the several Parts of it were discover'd.

IN this Enquiry, we must go back to the very Beginning; for, like the Tabernacle of GOD, the Pattern was in the Mount. There the whole Art was exhibited, the Pattern set, a Specimen work'd off, and Man had nothing to do, after he was inspir'd with the Skill of Reading it, but to get Tools and imitate it. In short, to speak in the common Usage of Men, GOD himself was the first *Writing Master* in the World, and the first Work of Man was to imitate the Materials, as well as the Manner; and this was done by Degrees too, *viz.* on Stone, and by Punction, or Cutting, and Stamping, which doubtless was the first Step.

How it must be perform'd, is left to be determin'd according to the Nature of the Stone on which the Work is done. For Example, We have a Stone or blue Slate, on which, with a Piece of the same Stone, Words now are written by Excoriation, which is but a Kind of Razing the Surface in a slight Manner, and yet the Mark will remain there for many Years, if no Wet comes upon it; and if a greater Strength or Weight of the Hand were laid to the Pen, so that it might cut farther in, the Impression being stronger, would, no Question, remain also a longer Time.

IF we go farther than this, we come to *Mallet* and *Chisel*, when we cut Letters of any Depth and Length; and I have seen Letters so cut in Stone for Inscriptions, and which were to stand a very great Height from the Place of Sight, which have been very near two Foot and half long, and an

Inch and half deep. But we may reasonably suppose, that the written Law was given in two moderate Tables, or Slates, on which the Finger of GOD could write in what Manner he best pleas'd; and which he, no Question, wrote so, as that *Moses* might easily repeat them, teach the People to read them, and, by reading of those, seek for farther Knowledge in the Skill of imitating either, or both; particularly we know they were not great Stones, such as it would necessarily require to cut the Words of the Ten Commandments in, with *Hammer and Chisel*; because 'tis plain they were no bigger than *Moses* could carry, and that in one Hand, as is evident from the same Scripture.

THE Writing on those Tables, we may suppose to be such as was afterwards follow'd (I will not call it imitated,) with Excoriations or Markings by a Tool, *as above*, whether a Graving Tool, *as is not improbable*, or what other Instrument, is not very easy to know, nor very material to the Purpose. In examining the Manner of Writing, we must descend to more Particulars; it is not sufficient to say they wrote first upon Leaves and Barks of Trees, which was directed according to the several Nations in which those Writings were in Use. But I shall enter as particularly as I can into the Degrees of Improvement, as they went on.

THE *Egyptians* being so near to the *Israelites* on the one Side, as has been said, are suppos'd to be some of the first Nations that improv'd the Use of Letters, after their being communicated to them from the *Hebrews*: How long they wrote on Tables of Stone, I can find no Authority to determin; 'tis probable it continu'd some Time; as it did also among other Nations, including the Writing on Tables of Wood, as among the Gravers of Wood; cover'd with Wax, as among the *Romans*, and the like. But after that, they found a Way to supply themselves with other Things. For Example:

1. THEY wrote on the Inside of the Bark of a Tree which grew on the Side of the *Red Sea*, and in this they were soon imitated by the *Latins*, who, in their Tongue, call'd that Bark *Liber*;[62] whence Books are call'd *Libri*.

2. ON thin Boards cut out of a solid Kind of Wood, like our Walnut Tree, hard and firm, which bore the Impression of the *Stylus*, of which hereafter: And this Wood was call'd *Caudex*;[63] whence, say some, the *Latins* took Occasion to call a Book *Codex*.

3. WHERE they found not that hard Wood to write on, as in some Countries it could not be had, they used Tables, which they spread over with fine Wax, and therein wrote very easily what they had occasion to write; whence the Messenger that carry'd these Tables as Missives, were call'd *Tabellarii*; and a Letter-Carrier, or *Courier*, is still call'd

Tabellarius: But of those I may speak again, as used among the *Romans*: I am now speaking of what was in Use among the *Egyptians*.

On the Bank of the *Nile*, when running in its ordinary Course, *not as overflowing*, there grew certain sedgy Weeds, call'd *Papyri*, suppos'd to be the same with which the Cradle was made, which *Moses* was laid in when he was turn'd adrift in the River *Nile*; of those they made a kind of Stuff in the Stead of what we call Paper, to write on, in the following Manner, and from whence our Writing-Paper has since taken its Name. The Leaves of these Weeds were very thick and substantial, but soft, and easily parted into abundance of thiner Slices or Flakes; accordingly they pull'd them asunder with their Hands, spreading them in the Sun; but as fast as the Sun dry'd them, they wetted them again, by sprinkling on them some of the Water of the River, which, at the Season of gathering the Leaves, was always thick and slimy, something like melted Glew; this thicken'd the Leaves, and made them solid and firm, as they dry'd by the Heat of the Sun: These are the same mentioned Isaiah 19.7. *The Paper Reeds by the Mouth of the Brooks, shall wither, be driven away, and be no more.* My Author,[64] for this, says, That by Means of this Invention, *Ptolemy Philadelphus*[65] made up the Books which compos'd his extraordinary Library at *Alexandria*. Also the same *Ptolemy* understanding that *Attalus* King of *Pergamus*, endeavour'd to out-do him in the Magnificence of a Library, and that he began to make Collections of Books, and the Works of *Homer*, *Palamedes* and other *Greek* Authors, and to amass an infinite Number of Volumes, which he compil'd of this *Egyptian* Weed, call'd *Papyrus*; and withal, that he manag'd that in a better Manner than the *Egyptians* did; *Ptolemy*, to prevent and disappoint him, prohibited the Exportation of the said *Papyrus* out of his Dominions: And the same Author adds, that upon this Prohibition King *Attalus* invented the making of *Parchment* or *Vellum* made of the Skins of Goats and Calves, on which he taught his Officers and Clerks to write and copy the *Grecian* Poets, and other Authors, as above: These Skins, at first, were call'd *Membranæ*; from the Country which *Attalus* reign'd over, they were in other Places, call'd *Pergamenae*, and these were the last Advances that I find among the *Grecians* before the Invention of Paper.

Ptolemy however compleated his Collection for the *Alexandrian* Library, with Books written on the Leaves of the *Papyri*, as above; which however durable enough otherwise, to have continued to this Day, were not Proof against the Flames, being all destroy'd in the burning of the said Library: So that there are none to be found, at least, that I have hear'd of, in any of the most antient Collections now extant in the World.

In describing the Instruments, or Materials of Writing, by which the Knowledge and Use of Letters was propagated, We indeed shew the Excellency of the Letters themselves; for if they had not been capable of being copied, and impress'd, as above, they had been of no use to Mankind, any farther than God, the first Author, should have communicated and exhibited new Tables, and new Writings, for the Use of his Creatures; which being once read, were to be recorded as his meer Voice, and might be erected on Columns, or treasur'd up, as Records for the People to have recourse to, that the Commands of God might never be forgotten, or the Substance of them be lost to the People.

But the Letters being communicated, and not only made intelligible, but appearing to be imitable by Men, it was left to them to invent Methods of Imitation, and Instruments to work by, as their first Invention, or the art of Imitation improv'd.

Of these we meet with many Kinds; as First, a Tool, to impress the Mark, or Letter, and the Substance on which that Impression was to be made, as above; and this Tool, or Instrument, was to be stronger, or weaker, harder, or softer, as the said Substance requir'd: For Example; While they wrote on Tables of Stone, or Slate, a piece of the same Slate, or Stone, was usually made use of, to mark the Letters, as I have already observ'd; as we do to this Day in *England*, upon the ordinary blue or black Slate, which we have in great Quanties in *Cornwall* and *Devonshire*; and which they have likewise in *Germany*, and also in *Egypt*, in *Greece*, and in *Italy*.

We read of some Writings by the bare Finger; and perhaps for present reading only. There might be much of that in use among the Eastern Nations; and even for Duration also, when Persons might write on such harsh Plaister, or other Mixtures, as being soft to receive the Impression, when they wrote, grew hard afterwards (in the Weather) as Stone; many Kinds of which are yet found; and some, in particular, in *England*; of which, in *Nottingham-shire, Leicestershire*, and other Places, where they make not Walls only, but Floors of Houses of it, as also Threshing-floors, and the like.

Of these Sorts of Writings two are mentioned in Scripture; One is the Hand-writing upon the Wall at *Belshazzar*'s Feast, and the other, when our Saviour stoop'd down and wrote on the Ground, in the Case of the Woman taken in *Adultery*; but as these are both extraordinary, they only intimate, that it was not usual to write in that manner; for the Hand upon the Wall was miraculous, and 'tis probable our Saviour only stoop'd down as seeming to write, to put the *Pharisees* to a Trial, and give the guilty Part of them leave to obey their own Consciences, and make off.

When they came to write on the Barks and Rinds of Trees, and especially when they wrote on solid Tables of Wood, such as principally Box, Walnut, Ebony, *Lignum Vitæ*, and the like hard durable Substances, or Sorts

of Wood, the Instruments which they wrote with were then made either of
Bone, of Ivory, or of Iron, and afterwards of Steel; and hence it was called
Stylus: An Account of which is very accurately given, as well of its Antiquity as of its Usefulness, by the learned and ingenious Mr. *Clark* of
Pennycook[66] in *Scotland*; a Gentleman, by his Studies and Travels, furnish'd
with many Kinds of useful Learning; and who is since, by his real Merit,
advanc'd to be one of the Barons of the Exchequer in that Kingdom; to
whose Book I refer.

IT is to be observ'd withal, that during these first Ages of Literature,
Invention was continually at work, to find out some more convenient
Method of Writing, as well relating to what they wrote upon, as what they
wrote with. Tho' they knew something of Letters, they were yet sensible
that farther Improvements might be made, and that they might still
understand one another better, if they thought fit to search into the Nature
of Writing, and the Method of performing it. The *Egyptians* had long before
fill'd the World with their Manner of Writing, (*viz.*) by the Figures of
Things, and Shapes of living Creatures; these the *Greeks* call'd
Ἱερογλυφιχα᾽ and these were to give the like Sound to Words as they bore
in Speech by their usual Forms, and these, before the Use of the *Papyri*,
which I have given an Account of, were engraven, or cut in Stones from
whence *Lucan* expresses himself thus;

> — *Saxis tantum Volucresq; feræque*
> *Sculptaque servabant magicas animalia linguas.*[67]

IT was, it seems, by these Figures, that their Magicians and Sooth-sayers,
or Wise Men, as they were called, gave out their Conjurations, something
like the Oracles which followed, by which they amused the People, and
reserved a double Entendre in all they said, to preserve the Reputation of
their Skill if their Interpretations of Things failed, or their Predictions did
not come to pass. This Way of Writing, I say, continued in the World a
great while after the Use of Letters was first known; and those Figures were
for some Time also mingled with the Letters and Words which they first
learned, and so helped out one another.

IN like manner the *Greeks* and the *Latins* also used Characters, or Marks,
which they call'd *Notæ*[68] and they were, as a farther Description of them
called *Notæ Horopollinis Niliaci*; of which the Inventor, or chief Artist, at
least, liv'd in the Time of *Theodosius*: Whether this was first brought out of
Egypt, or not, as some write that the whole Body of Grammatick Learning
was, is not to my purpose now; but that the *Greeks*, and *Romans* also, made
use of these *Notæ* in their first Writings is manifest; and we have many of

them yet remaining in their Writings, the Signification of which is known and remember'd; and they were of two Kinds;

1. Meer invented Marks, such as this or that eminent Writer of that Time legitimated the Use of, as in *Tyro*[69] and *Seneca pag.* 8. where a particular Mark is made use of to signify the Word *Rempublicam*. Also, according to that same Author, another for *Eo est.*[70]

2. Initial Letters placed for whole Words were at first used in private Writing, but gradually appeared in Publick, being legitimed by Custom; such as *E. Q. R.* for *Eques Romanus*, S. P. Q. R. for *Senatus Populesque Romanus*.

ENNIUS[71] tells us, they invented, or introduc'd Eleven hundred fuch Marks as these in his Time, into use in common Writing, besides many invented by Others; as by *Tyro*, *Cicero*, *Libertus*, and the several Writers of those Times, as *Eusebius*[72] tells us; till the Number of Inventors were so many, that it would be troublesome to the Reader to repeat their Names, and till the Number of their Marks amounted to above 5000, and grew burthensom to the World. A fuller Account of this, and a sufficient Authority for what I have said of it, is included in a Speech, or Prologue rather, of *Petrus Diaconus*[73] to the Emperor *Conrad*.

> 'Nunc quis primus Notas instituerit scribamus. Vulgares notas Ennius primus mille ducentum invenit ; ad hunc scilicet usum, ut quicquid per contentionem præsentium diceretur, liberarii scriberent complures simul adstantes, divisis inter se partibus, quæs quisque verba, & quo ordine exciperet. Dehinc Tullius Tyro, Ciceronis libertus, notas præpositionum commentus eft. Post hunc Philargyrus Samius, & aliqui (lego Aquila) Mœcenatis alias addiderunt. Deinde Lucius Annæus Seneca, contractis omnibus, digesto & aucto numero, opus in quinque millia extendit.'
>
> *Vossius de Arte Grammatica*, pag. 148, line 9.

HAVING thus mentioned the Marks and Stamps used in Writing among several Persons, and in particular Countries, I come to speak of the publick Marks or Stamps used also, which were not particular to this or that Country, or Language, but that were universal, or common to all Languages in the World, and these were of several Sorts; as,

1. The Figures used in Arithmetick, which are commonly call'd Cyphers, and are the same in most of the Languages in *Europe*.

2. The Marks of Astronomers, which are also universal in all Languages; such as ♄ ♃ ♂ ☉ ♀ ☿ ☽; also the twelve Signs of the Zodiack ♈ ♉ ♊ ♋ ♌ and the rest.

3. The several Marks in Musick, directing the Measure of Notes, and the Tune, or, Consonance, and Dissonance of Sounds, which are likewise esteemed universal.

ALL these Modes of Writing are suppos'd to respect the Infant Days of Letters, before the Invention of Men carry'd those Arts on to the Perfection to which they are since arriv'd.

AFTER the Use of those *Notæ*, or Marks, which were usual in the first Ages of Letters, and which signify'd distinct Words, there were Marks impress'd in the same Age, importing whole Sentences; but those were not so frequent, because they laid too much Weight on the Memory, and young Scholars did not easily understand them; tho' it is true, it was an easier Way in one respect; because, like Figures, they were capable of being understood alike in all, or in sundry Languages: Nor was there more difficulty in making or inventing so many Marks, or *Notæ*, as above, than there has been since of inventing Words in every Language, to know them by; the Number and Variety of which is incredible, and which is a much greater load on the Memory to those who learn other Languages, than in reading their own. I say also, it was much greater than that of charging the Head with such a Number of Marks, which, as before, were never above 5000: Nay, if we may Credit *Nicholaus Trigaultius*,[74] Hist. *Sinensis*, lib. I. cap. V. he says thus, *Non pauciores Sinensibus literas esse quam voces numerantur, eas tamen ita inter se componere, ut* lxx *aut* lxxx *millia non excedant*. This indeed refers to the *Japoneses*, as well as to the other; but 'tis so that they perfectly understand one another both in Writing and Reading.

IF it be true also, as *Paciano Barcellonensi*[75] says, that at the Confusion of Languages they were, from one universal Speech or Dialect, divided into 120; or into lxxxii, as *Eusebius*'s Opinion[76] delivers it, and Abundance of other Authors; then the Variety of Writings, and the Number of Words, Stamps, Marks and Characters among them all, when the Knowledge of Letters and of Writing came to spread it self among them also, must be infinitely great.

I might proceed from this to that Part of the Art of Writing which the Learned call the ορθογραφια, that is to say, of right placing the Letters, whether separate or in Syllables, and joining them as they ought to be joyned; this we call in a more vulgar way of expression, *Spelling*, but of this hereafter.

IT would be necessary now, to mention some of the various Characters, that is to say, forms of the Letters of the Alphabet, or of the various Alphabets which are in use in the several Languages, and the manner of their Writing them: There were at first, generally speaking, three ways of Writing, and no more, I mean, that were practis'd when the Knowledge of Letters came to spread it self in the World, for at first, 'tis certain, there was but one Method, and one Language.

THE first of these, and the most antient, is from the Right-hand to the Left; and this very Thing strongly confirms what I said before, namely, That the *Israelites* were the first who had the Knowledge of Letters, seeing we find none of those Languages which would be supposed to be of Antiquity, writing any other way but in a plain Imitation of the Hebrews, reading all from the Right to the Left, except the Hieroglyphicks of the *Egyptians*, which are said originally to stand promiscuous, and to be read in the Position which they were to be found in, without Order, or without any Sequence, except as the Nature of the Creature (describ'd,) intimated to them. For Example, if a Bird was painted flying upwards, then they read from the Head of the said Bird, to the Tail of the Creature which was next above him; and so if it were a Beast, or a Fish, whether walking or Swimming and the like: This, however Custom might have made it familiar to them, was in it self very confused, and intimated in the plainest manner imaginable, that they were infinitely at a loss for a Rule to make the Marks or Figures they used more intelligible.

THUS in their manner of Accounting, of which I have made mention before, and which, as I said, was by Sticks or Reeds bundled up, it seem'd perfectly indifferent to the Person accounting, whether he reckon'd from the left to the right, or from the right Hand to the left, according to which Hand he laid out the Numbers of Reeds which he made his reckoning by.

BUT after the Hebrews had receiv'd the Knowledge of Letters from Heaven, as I have observ'd, the *Egyptians* who not only convers'd with them more intimately than any other Nation, but even among whom a great many proselyted *Egyptians* liv'd, and others that went with them as Servants, for it is not to be doubted but that the great Wonders wrought by *Moses* and *Aaron*, in the Name of God, in the *Egyptian* Court, and among the whole Nation, must make a greater Impression upon some of the People of the Country, than it did upon *Pharaoh* and his Courtiers; and that many of them were so convinc'd that the God of the *Hebrews* was the only true God, by these terrible Judgements, that they became believers, and embrac'd the Religion and the God of the *Hebrews*, and followed them, or rather went with them, into and thro' the Red Sea; as we see afterwards, the *Kenites*,[77] the Posterity of *Jethro*, *Moses* Father in Law, were found in the Camp of *Israel*, and had their Portion and Inheritance with them in the promis'd Land.

THUS the *Egyptians*, who, being proselyted as above, went with the *Israelites* into the *Wilderness*, soon with the rest learned the Knowledge of Letters at Mount *Sinai* and by the same Rule corresponding afterwards with the *Egyptian* Country communicated that Knowledge to them in the first Place; and therefore we find the *Egyptians* were the first, who following the Example of *Israel*, tho' they might corrupt the Pattern, as without doubt they did, soon had an Alphabet and Letters of their own from which afterwards the *Syriack* no doubt is derived.

THERE are, besides those, several barbarous Nations, who are said also to be very antient, and whose Writings, if themselves may be believ'd, are much more antient than in our Account the World it self is supposed to be, and these write in a perpendicular Line from the Top of the Leaf to the Bottom, or as some say, from the Bottom of the Leaf to the Top.

THESE I do not find were ever receiv'd, either in *Europe*, or in that Part of Asia which was within the Reach of the Grecian or Roman Empires, but is heard of chiefly among the *Chineses*, and *Japoneses*, who had no known Correspondence with any Part of the civiliz'd Nations, 'till within a few Ages past, when Commerce seemed to have acquainted them a little with one another, and that not much neither.

AND yet even among these *Chineses* and the *Barbarians* of the *East*, there is to be found some Affinity between the *Chaldee* Letters and theirs, so much as that we may easily perswade our selves to believe, that the one were originally but a Corruption of the other; what might occasion the Alteration of the Progression in Writing, that we cannot account for, neither is it material.

THE Subjects of the Great *Mogul*, that is to say, in that Part of the World we call more properly *India*, and several Nations of the flitting or moveable Tartars, make use of this manner of Writing, as also the Natives of *Siam*, *Pegu*,[78] and *Sumatra*; if the latter have any Writing, or Use of Letters at all, which I do not find any good Authority for.

BUT to go back to the *Israelites*, while they continued in their wandering State, and possibly had very little, if any, Correspondence with the World, the *Egyptians* excepted, *with whom I doubt not they not only corresponded, but even traffick'd for necessaries while they were in the Neighbourhood of them*; I suppose they kept the knowledge of Letters among themselves: But when they came into *Canaan*, and had an immediate, nay, a too intimate Correspondence with the *Phenicians*, that is to say, the *Canaanites*, they, in like manner learn'd from the Israelites the Knowledge of Letters.

HENCE, as I observ'd at first, the *Phenicians* so early obtain'd the Knowledge of Letters, and so mightily improv'd upon them, that *Cadmus*, a *Phenecian* Prince, travelling afterwards into *Greece*, and carrying with him, a new form'd Alphabet of his own, but drawn from the general Theory of Letters, obtain'd in his own Country from the *Hebrews*, obtain'd the Honour of being called the Inventor of all Letters in general, tho' as I have prov'd before, the Tables of Stone at Mount *Sinai*, were written by the Finger of God, some Ages before *Cadmus* was Born.

However, that we may give *Cadmus* and his *Phenicians* their Due, they certainly were the Inventors of a differing Method of writing, and forming the *Greek* Alphabet out of the Corruption of the *Hebrew*, inverting the Method; and thus the World came to Write from the left Hand to the right,[79] which is the third Method of Writing.

CADMUS, indeed, carryed but 16 Letters into Greece, the Rest were brought in a long Time after, as I have noted already, several Years after the Destruction of *Troy*. But the first and fundamental Letters of the *Greeks*, were thus brought from the *Phenicians*, and by them most certainly from the *Israelites*, who over-ran the Country of *Canaan* in so furious a Manner.

AND thus I think I have accounted for the Original of Letters, in a manner consonant to Reason and to History; nor do I meet with any Thing material that is offered against my Opinion: All that the Writers of a different Opinion have yet said against it, amounts to no more than this; that they do not think it probable, that the World was for so many Ages without so useful, and indeed so necessary an Art; and that the *Antediluvian* World, who had such a Perfection of Knowledge, as that some think we are not yet arriv'd to an equal Degree of Improvement with them to this Day, could not be suppos'd to be Ignorant to such a Degree as this.

BUT this is all begging the Question. The Patriarchs of the *Antediluvian* State, were without Question Masters of Science, and had great Discoveries made to them, or were inspir'd, let us call it what we will, with great Knowledge and Understanding; but this only proves that perhaps they might be, and 'tis possible they were, blest with the Knowledge of Letters; but it does by no means prove that they really were so, and therefore we are but still where we were, in all they can say for the Fathers of the old World.

IT is sufficient, after all, that we have an Original, *a Pattern in the Mount*, which we know was handed to *Moses* from the Finger of God, and that no History gives any Account that can be depended upon, or is more rational than this, that all the pretended Knowledge of Letters before it, is without Ground, or so much as Probability; and so far were they from having left any Remains behind them of that Knowledge, that their Posterity valued themselves infinitely upon that dull unperforming, and as we may call it, Dumb Language of *Hieroglyphicks*, and Images of Creatures, making the Brutes Speak for them, when at the same Time they knew not how to form any proper Characters for Words, or to which the Sound of Words might be appropiated.

AND if this was not the Case, how came it to pass, that whereas before this great Discovery from Heaven, they were driven to such Shifts for want of an Alphabet, and for want of the Knowledge of Letters, on the contrary as soon as the *Hebrew* was once dictated, and the Children of *Israel* were taught to write, immediately all the World follow'd the Example, and every Nation borrowing the general System, or the Idea of Writing from the *Hebrews*, began to Write, and tho' they proceeded to forming different Alphabets to themselves, as if they were for improving after that the Invention and had every one their differing way of Writing, yet the Thing it self it was apparent came all from this happy Original.

AND as the very first Thought came from hence, so did the Method of it, (*viz.*) the Prolation and joyning the Letters to form Syllables, and then rejoyning those Syllables to form Words of many Syllables, also the Manner of Writing or Impressing those Letters and Words to make them legible to others, (*viz.*) by Excoriation, or Incision, or Impression, which we come next to consider.

PART VI.

HAVING thus spoken of the Original of Letters and of the Method of Writing, it comes of Course to say something of the Materials of Writing and Printing, not as they were us'd in the Infancy of the Art only, for that has been mention'd, but as they have been used since Men came to an ordinary Skill and Improvement in the Art of Managing, Placing, Coupling and Spelling the Letters, call'd as I have said above {word missing}.

FROM the *Papyri*, a Weed growing as I have said on the Banks of the *Nile*, came the Word *Paper* in our Language, not that this was really made into Paper, such as we now use, as some think; for the Leaves were at least a Cubit or a Cubit and half in Length, and of unequal shape and Substance, and were as I have shewn, pull'd in Pieces, and several Operations about them perform'd before they were fitted for Use: But as from hence, *for ought we know*, the true Method of Paper making was deriv'd, which is it self very antient; so from hence all Compositions of any kind made to form any Thing to write upon, were, when finish'd, call'd *Paper*.

BUT let me examine then, by what Methods, and by what slow Degrees, the Knowledge and Use of Paper to write upon came into the World: From Tables of Stone, and from the Leaves and Barks of Trees, *as I have noted above*, they came to the Use of Tables of Wood, that is to say, thin Boards cut out of the Body of a Tree; these were either *Tabellae Nudae*, plain naked Boards, or Boards cover'd or polish'd over with Wax or Rosin, or such other Substance as they usually cover'd them with, in those Days. There were many Sorts of these Tables also, some very thick and coarse, upon which the Boys at the Schools usually wrote or learned their Lessons.

OTHERS they made thin and fine, and polish'd them, to be the fitter for receiving the Impression of the Stylus or Pen.

Secta nisi in tenues essemus ligna tabellas.[80]
Mart. lib. xiv.

This is fully explain'd, in that memorable Text of apocryphal Scripture, 2 Esdras, chap. xiv. ver. 24, 25, 26. *But look thou prepare thee many box-trees, and take with thee* Sarea, Dabria, Selemia, Ecanus, *and* Asiel, *these five which are ready to write swiftly; and come hither, and I shall light a candle of understanding in thine heart, which shall not be put out, till the things be performed which thou shalt begin to write. And when thou hast done, some things shalt thou publish, and some things shalt thou shew secretly to the wise: to morrow this hour shalt thou begin to write.* Ver. 42, 44. *The Highest gave understanding unto the five men, and they wrote the wonderful visions of the night that were told, which they knew not: and they sat forty days, and they wrote in the day, and at night they eat bread. In forty days they wrote two hundred and four Books.* By this it appears, there were Writers in those Days who wrote swifter, by which I understand also shorter, than others: What Books they wrote is evident from the 24th Verse, where he is bid to bring many Box-Trees with him, as well as Writers; this in the Margin of some of our Bibles, is explain'd in direct Words to be Box-Tables to write on, or Tables made of Box-Wood, which confirms also what has been said of those Tables in the former Part of this Work: What the Books were, of which two Hundred and Four, our Margin says nine Hundred and Four, could be written in forty Days by five Men, is not so easy to determine.

THERE were also small Pieces of Boards smooth'd and polish'd for Bills, or other such smaller Occasions, which did not require whole Tables, these were call'd *Codices*, and smaller yet *Codicils*, as we at this Day call a small Piece of Parchment annext to a Will; and these were call'd so because made out of the Body or Stump of a Tree; and hence from *Caudex* a Book was call'd *Codex*, and the Collection of Laws by *Theodosius, Justinian*, and others are call'd *Codes*.

The *Danes*, in Confirmation of this, call Books in their Language *Boger*, which indeed is the Original of the Word Boke or Book, and which signifies in *High Dutch*, a *Beech-Tree*, because the publick Acts were impress'd, or stamp'd, or mark'd, or written, *call it which we will*, upon Boards made of Beech and polish'd very smooth: See *Olaus Wormius*,[81] *in Fastis Danicis*, lib. I. cap. 6. These were call'd Wax'd-Tables, because the Beechen Boards were crusted over or polish'd with Wax, and to this Day our Faniering[82] Artists or Cabinet-Makers, polish over the Olive-Wood, Ebony, and Walnut-Tree, which covers and adorns their Work; I say, they polish it over with Wax, and the same may be written on very legibly and well.

NEXT to Books and Tables thus made of the Wood or Bark of Trees, the Antients came to write upon Linnen, and rather before that upon the Skins of Beasts, which we now call *Vellum* and *Parchment*; but this last was a kind of Accident, and never came into general use for the making of Books. This

Linnen was called *Linteum* from *Linum*, the Flax, of which it was made; this Linnen *Pliny*[83] tells us, was put into, or dipt in Oil, as the Cloths are which the Limner or Painter now prepares to draw a fine Picture on, *Pliny* lib. xiii. cap. xi. Of these, when they were very fine, several large Volumes of Books were made, on which the *Oracula Sibyllina* were written, *Symmachus*,[84] lib. iv. Epist. xxxiv.

ALSO the publick Leagues between Princes and States, were written in this Manner, that is to say, upon that Linnen Cloth dipt in Oil, see *Tit. Livius*[85] lib. xxxi. Also, *Constantine* caused the Laws of the Empire to be thus written; as also Epistles of private Princes one to another, *Flav. Vopiscus in Aureliano*;[86] his Words are, *Inveni Nuper in Ulpia bibliotheca, inter linteos libros epistolam D. Valeriani.*

OTHERS wrote upon a Paper made of a Substance like a Caul taken from the Bowels, or Gut, of any Beast; they were call'd *Elephantinos Libros*, which also some took to be Leaves of Ivory; but it was taken both ways; for it was a Book or Paper made of the Skin of a Beast, whether Sheep, Goat, or Calf; or of a Gut, or other thick glutinous Substance, such as the Caul was, and which being dried by the Heat of the Sun became hard and solid, and on these they frequently wrote; and such were those Manuscripts in the *Hebrew* Tongue, which *Eleazer*, the High Priest of the *Jews*, sent to *Ptolemy Philadelphus*, and which were curiously written on Parchment or Vellum, as *Josephus*[87] says expressly, *lib.* xii. *Antiq. Judaic.* And yet *Pliny* says, as I have observ'd before, which is a little strange, that the King of *Pergamos* invented Parchment to write upon, because *Ptolemy Philadelphus* prohibited the Carrying the *Papyri* out of his Dominions.

BUT to leave that, let *Josephus* answer for the Inconsistency *if there is any*; for 'tis equally strange which we read in *Varro*,[88] that the Battles of *Alexander* were written on Paper and carried to the Egyptian *Alexandria*; and this Paper was in Use long before those Times; but then it was the Paper only which was made of the Egyptian Weed *Papyrus*, that is to say, it had the name *Paper*, but was nothing of the Kind now in Use, or so much as like it.

FROM these Times, therefore, when Parchment came to be in full Use, Writing encreased and improved exceedingly; and then they soon came from the linnen Cloth, to make Paper of the Substance of the linnen Cloth, (*viz.*) the Lint or Flax itself, pressed, and bruised, and beaten fine in an Engine or Mill, and then mixed up again with Gums, and such glutinous Substance, as brought it to be a *firm Leaf* as we see at this Day. For tho' much of our Paper, in this Country, is made of the Rags of old Linnen beaten to Pumice; so the Paper also now, *that is to say the greatest Quantity of it*, is made of Flax, which is one of the first Principles in the making Linnen, and this Flax is esteemed to make better paper than that of Rags.

FROM the Paper, we come next to speak of the liquid Substance which we call Ink, and with which those, who make Use of Paper, Parchment, or linnen Cloth, write upon them; of this there has not been much Variety. The first Ink we find in Story, was made of the Blood or Juice which was found in the Fish called *Loligo*, which some call a *Calamary*, others more vulgarly the *Cuttle Fish*, and whose Blood casts a fix'd Black Colour, tingeing the Paper or Parchment with a durable Black; this is by some call'd *Niger Succus*, a Black Juice; by others the Blood of a Fish; and this was used instead of Ink, whence the *Germans* call this Creature in the old *Gothick* Language d'INKENFISCH, or in English, the *Ink-Fish*. *Pliny* tells us also of a Fish call'd the *Sepia*, whose Blood is as Black as Ink; but he does not say it will tinge or dye any Thing Black as the *Loligo* does. *Perseus* mentions this in his 3 Sat.

> *— Sepia lympha*
> *Dilutas querimur geminet quod fistula guttas.*[89]

THIS *Sepia*, or *Ink-Fish*, is found on the Coast of *Lancashire* in *England*, and formerly was more frequent there than it is now; of which the learned Dr. *Leigh*,[90] in his natural History of *Lancashire* and *Cheshire*, gives the following Account.

'The next remarkable Fish, says he, is the *Sepia*, or *Ink-Fish*, of which I have seen several upon these Shores. It has ten Horns, not much unlike those of a Snail, and with these, as with Oars, it rowes it self forward in the Water: It has two full Eyes. Its Substance seems to be a Kind of Pulp, and one Half of it is invested with a Membrane like a Leg within a Stocking; and therefore by some it is call'd the *Hose* or *Stocking-Fish*. It has only one Bone, and that upon its Back, thin, flat, and pellucid. From its Mouth descends two pellucid Ducts, which terminate in a *Vesica* which contains its Ink; by pressing this, the Ink quickly ascends, and as some Naturalists affirm, when they are in Danger of being Taken, by contracting this, they discharge such a Quantity of Ink as blackens the Water and secures them from Discovery. I have a Letter by me, written with this Ink about ten Years ago, which still continues. This Liquor was the Ink of the Ancients; hence came that Expression of the Poet, *Nigro distillans Sepia nodo.*[91] It has no remarkable Taste, and by Reason that the Whole seems to be a Kind of Pulp, it is hard to determine whether this Liquor is its *Chyle*, or perhaps the Juice of some Sea Plant which it lives upon, or else a Liquor separated from its nutritive Juices; for what else to term it. I know not, since I could not observe in it either Veins or Arteries; yet doubtless there are other Vessels adequate to those. This Fish, sometimes, the People eat; and it is observable that it will mildly Purge them like *Cassia*, or some such *Lenitive*.'

To go back from those, farther to the common People, these, as also the ordinary School-Masters and Students, made their usual common Ink of the Soot out of the Chimneys; but States Men, and Men of better Sort, used the Blood of the *Sepia* as above.

AGAIN, the Ink with which they often wrote Books, but especially the Titles and capital Letters in Books, was of another Sort, and was of a Red colour instead of Black, but this was less used than the Black. These Things they made shift with, for ought I can find in any ancient Writings, 'till they found out the proper Ingredients for Ink as we now use it. As for Printing Ink, which is a Thing by it self, and quite differing from the writeing Ink, as it was a modern Invention, and arriv'd to with, or since, the Knowledge of Printing it self, which is much more modern than the Times we are now speaking of, I leave that to be mentioned again in its Place.

BEFORE the Use of Ink, they wrote by Way of Racing,[92] or Cutting, or Scratching the Substance which they wrote upon, which I mentioned before, where I term'd it an Excoriation; and this as it was done in various Forms or Methods, so by several and very differing Instruments.

WHILE they wrote upon the Barks of Trees, and upon Tables, and especially on the wax'd or polish'd Tables, as also while they wrote on the *Tilia*,[93] they used the *Stilus*, a Pen or Instrument made first of Iron, sometimes of Bone, sometimes of Ivory; this was used I say in Writing on such hard Substances as requir'd an Incision or Cutting, and was called *Graphium*, and as afterwards the Writings on Stone or Tables of Wood required it, this *Stylus* or *Graphium* was the only Instrument. But there follow'd great Inconveniencies upon this, for the *Stylus* being made of Iron, and some of them being fork'd and having divers sharp Points, the Boys who learned to Write would often quarrel and wound one another with them, and even Men also, for they were really very dangerous Weapons.

THE Accidents which happened on this Occasion, were so many, and some of them so fatal, that the *Romans* were oblig'd to forbid the Use of them, that is to say of Iron; after which others were invented made of the Teeth of Fishes and of the Bones of Beasts, and lastly, as above, of Ivory.

As to the Authority given for the Report of Mischief done with the *Stylus*, the Persons writing with them having frequently Wounded others with them, *Plutarch* expresses it fully in *Gracchis*,[94] and among the *Romans, Martial*, and several other Writers of those Times.

> *Hàc tibi erant armata suo Graphiaria ferro.*
> *Si puero dones, non leve munus erit.*[95]
> Mart. Epig. XXI.

BUT beyond all this, *Suetonius* and *Plutarch* also in several of their Writings say, that *Casca* wounded *Caesar* in the Senate House, not with a Dagger but with a *Stylus* or Roman Pen of Iron, or perhaps of Steel.

Plut. *in Appianum.*[96]
Cassi *Brachium arreptum graphio Cæsar trajecit.*
Suetonius *in vit.* Jul. Cæs. 82.[97]

IT was a Felicity to the People of *Rome*, that these Instruments for Writing grew useless in a few Years, by the Improvement of the Age, and the better Materials they had to write upon; for in a few Years they wrote no more by Incision or Impressing, by Raceings and Excoriations, but by moist Juices tinging the Materials, and on proper smooth Substances fit to receive the Tincture, such as those I have mentioned, (*viz.*) the Blood of Fishes, and Decoctions of Soot and other Ingredients.

As the Use of Parchments, and of the *Papyri*, and of the *Tilia*, which some have mistaken for *Tilea*,[98] but was only a thin Substance, or a Kind of Skin lying between the outer Bark and the Body of a certain Tree; I say, as the Use of these came into the World, the *Stylus*, and all other Instruments which work'd by Incision or Impression were laid by, and in a little more Time became useless; and how many Kings and Emperors soever have been stab'd by the Pen, a dangerous Instrument in its kind; yet none more will ever be stabb'd by it, as an offensive Weapon, as it seems had been the Case before.

SOME think it was of this Manner of Writing, by Incision, and of the *Stylus* of Iron which *Job*[99] Speaks, Chap. xix. *Oh that my words were now written! Oh that they were printed in a Book! That they were graven with an iron pen and lead, in the rock for ever!* But I think that these were only translated according to the Author that wrote the Book; for as to the best Account we have of *Job* himself, he lived and died before the Knowledge of Letters was in the World, and the Pen-Man of his History might be allow'd to Express the Sense of the Good Man in the Manner of the Age in which he then wrote.

From this Time, the ingenious Part of the World, having found several Ways for the Writing of Books upon Materials soft and smooth, which required no Incision, the Use of these Instuments grew obsolete and fit to be forgotten; and they now serve for no more than to be remembered among the Monuments of Antiquity, as we now speak of them.

PART VII.

HAVING thus given an Account, or rather some Account, of the Writings of the Ancients, and brought them out of the Infant Days of this Art, it will not be amiss to speak a little of the general Usage of the World, from the Time that they came to the plain Use of Pen, Ink and Paper, to the Time when the Invention of the Printing Press, and the Use of Types for impressing the Letters *as Written*, was found out in the World, taking up an Interval of above 1500 Years at least; for the Writing with Pen and Ink was said to be known the latter End of the Reign of *Augustus*, tho' not in Perfection 'till some Years after; (for in St. *Luke*, we find *Zacharias*[100] calling for *a writing Table*) whereas the Art of Printing was invented in the Year 1420, by one *Lawrence Coster*[101] a Soldier of *Harlem*, who after he had found the first Font or Foundiary of Types or Letters, and had not fully put them in Use, had them stollen from him by his Servant, who carried them into *Germany*, and there claimed to be the Inventor of them, and having set up a Press, *Tully's Offices*[102] was the first Book that ever was Printed in the World. But this by the way.

ALL Intelligence, Commerce, and Correspondence in the World, was now managed by the *Pen, Ink,* and *Paper*; the Works of the Ancients were all written by their own Hands, or by the help of Clerks and Amanuenses; infinite Numbers of these People we now call copying Clerks, were employ'd to make Coppies of valuable Books; and if it be True, that there were 12000 Copies of *Virgil's Æneid*, made in *Augustus's* Days, and twice as many of *Ovid's* Metamorphosis, what innumerable numbers of Hands had been employ'd in those daily Works, and of what Labours, and what multitudes must that *Alexandrian* Library be Composed, if there really was such a Thing; for the doubt is far from being resolv'd to this Day.

THE Registers and Records of Nations must be all written in the same Manner; all the Works of the Ancients, and all the Copies[a] of those valuable Works which were in themselves innumerable, must have been made in the same manner. It would be endless to reckon them up, but let us Name a few. The Works of *Homer, Hesiod, Herodotus*, of *Livy*, of *Josephus*, of the several *Plutarchs*, of *Cicero, Julius Cæsar's* Commentaries, of the Poets, *Ovid, Tibullus, Persius, Juvenal, Lucan* and *Virgil*, with innumerable more: Among the *Hebrews*, the *Bible*, the *Talmuds*, as well the *Babylonian* as the *Jerusalem Talmud*. To what purpose should we enumerate the Particulars, ancient History is full of their Names and Works; how voluminous they are, and yet how often were they written over.[103]

IN the Exercise of so much Writing, it is no Wonder if some were very dextrous, and were as much Masters of the Pen as their Authors were of the Tongue. And as we have seen some Things most accurately done in the Art of Writing, within Five or Six hundred Years back from the present Time, there can be no Room to doubt, but that there was the like in the World many Years before that. And it must be acknowledg'd, that 'tho the Manner is much different, and there are very fine Things done with the Pen in this Age, yet that in the former Ages they greatly excell'd us. But I shall have occasion to speak of this Part again more fully in its Course.

NEXT to the Manner of Writing, and the Materials, it becomes necessary to enquire a little into the Measure of Words, which we call Prolation, the giving proper Sounds and Quantities to the Letters, either joyned together or apart.

THIS certainly came from Heaven with the Letters themselves, and the Power which inspir'd Mankind with the Knowledge of the Letters necessarily adapted them to their Sounds, and empowered those Sounds to carry with them the Signification of the Letters. Hence came the Distinction of Letters into Vowels and Consonants, which are so married together in the Art of Reading, that no Man can separate them: The Vowel like the Husband to the Wife, giving Cadence of Sound, Diction and Expression to the Consonant; and the Consonant being Capable of no Sound without the Conjunction of the Vowel to govern the Voice and make a Harmony, and is therefore call'd *Consonant* or agreeing, joyning and assisting to the Sound of the Word.

IT is something surprizing, to think how this Cadence of Sounds, and how the Joyning of Syllables in compounded Words, came to be formed in the Understandings of Men; nothing but the being satisfy'd that it was form'd above and came down from Heaven, could reconcile us to the Wonder of it.

THE writing Words, in all Languages, agreeable to the Idiom of every respective Tongue, joining them in Monosyllables, joining the Monosyllables again into compounded Words, and giving every Letter its right Place, with its Accent or Emphasis, is a surprising Thing in the Nature of it, and if fully and seriously considered, carries us beyond Nature it self, ending only in Astonishment and an unresolv'd Wonder. This is what the *Greeks* understand by the Word Ορθογραφια, and which from them we call to this Day *Orthography*.

To enter far into this Part, would be to enquire into the Grammar of every Tongue, and with *Vossius*, to write *de Arte Grammatica*, which is not my Business here; but to speak of correct Writing seems absolutely necessary, seeing if there was cxx several Languages into which the first universal Way of Speaking was divided; there are, for ought we see now, cxx thousand Ways of Speaking, (*viz.*) so many differing Idioms and Dialects of Speech which Men now make Use of in the World; some Languages, nay most Languages, being again subdivided into many differing Ways of Expression; in all which, 'tis Evident, that long living in any one Country, generally naturalizes the Speech of that Country so to our Ear, that we soon make it our own, and even forget that which was formerly our Mother Tongue.

BUT we have in *Great-Britain*, Besides the real and solid Variety of Tongues, such as the *Welch* or ancient *Britains*, the *Cornish*, the *Highland Scots* and the like; I say we have such a Variety in the Expression of our own Mother Tongue, as that in some Counties of *England* they can very ill understand one another; how the Orthographists can manage this in all Languages is not very easy to describe.

ON the other Hand, many Tongues, as the *English* we now speak for Example, having no Grammatical Syntax, no Rule for the Measures or Quantities of Words or Letters, by Consequence have no Authorities for the Usages of their Speech; but all is Assumption, legitimated only by Custom, which is Judge of the Orthography, as it is of the Propriety of Speech; and were it not that this Custom does as it were legitimate the Orthography, we should be confounded in writing many Words in the *English* Tongue, where Words bearing the same Sound, signify various Things; as particularly in the Words, *Two, Tow, Too, To, Then, Than, Bow, Bow, Bough*, and many others.

Two,   Signifying 2 in Number.

Tow,   *Flax* or *Tow*, made of *Flax*.

Too,   Too much or too long.

To,   To go to any Place, or give any Thing to a Person.

Bow,   To Bow in Compliment, or make a Bow, or to bend any straight Thing into a Curve or Arch, differing its Posture from what it was before.

Bow,   A Bow to shoot an Arrow.

Bough,   The Bough of a Tree.
Bough,   The Barking of a Dog.
Right,   The right Hand.
Right,   Just or to do Right.
Right,   Opposite to, or over against.
Wright,   A Wheel Wright, or a Ship Wright (*viz.*) a Carpenter.
Write,   To write a Letter.
Then,   Time, as *then it was so*.
Than,   A comparison (*viz.*) *better than another*.

As these are the Usages of Speech, and that no Rule is to be found for the Direction of the Speaker, other than that so it is accustom'd to be, a Stranger has nothing to trust to for the Learning these Things, or how to write them, but by the Strength of his Memory.

THE more Grammatical Languages, such as the *Latin*, the *Greek*, and other *Eastern* Languages, having establish'd Rules by which these are all regulated, the Difficulty is not so great, and they have no more to do than to place those Rules before them.

BUT, as I said, it is possible for People to forget even their own native Speech, and likewise to forget the Manner of Writing it. They tell us that the *Hebrews* who were captivated by the *Chaldeans*, and continued so Seventy Years, lost so much of the Original *Hebrew*, that except the Priests and learned Men whom they call'd Rabbies, the common People never recover'd the Use of it; and therefore the *Hebrew*, which the *Rabbies* retain'd in its Purity, is call'd, by Way of Distinction, the *Rabbinical Hebrew*; and this is taught to the Children of the *Levites* and others at their Schools, whereas the *Jews* in common used the *Chaldaic* or *Syriac* Tongues, and at last the *Greek*; and to this Day the *Rabbinical Hebrew* is no where found but in the Writings of their *Rabbies*, and in some ancient Manuscripts of their Law; and whether any of those are now extant, which if they are, must be above 2200 Year old is very hard to determine. The Orthography then of every Language, as the Tongues in Use now are governed by received Custom, is so uncertain, that nothing can instruct the Writing of those Languages, but a thorough learning and acquainting themselves with the Languages themselves, and the Customs and Usages which are allow'd in them.

IN this Difficulty we find the Writings or MSS. of divers Languages in *Europe*, not only written after a different Manner, but that the several Inhabitants spell those Languages, or several Words in them, after a different Manner from one another; and this I mean not of the unlearned Common People, for they seldom are able to spell their own Country Language, and oftentimes not to pronounce the Words of it, which is the

Reason of so many different Brogues upon their Tongues, and of so many different Dialects in one and the same Speech, and even in one and the same Country: For Example,

THE *Normans* and *Walloons* in *France*, and the *Gascoigns*, between *France* and *Spain*, the People of *Bearn*, and the People of *Bretaign*; all of them have a different Way of Speaking, and some so different from the other, or from all the Rest, as not easily to understand one another, tho' the Language is still all of it call'd *French*.

THE like it is in *Spain*, the *Biscayners* speak one Dialect, the *Castilians* another, the *Catalans* a third, and the *Navarrois* a fourth, the *Andalusians* a fifth, and yet all is call'd *Spanish*.

Even in *Italy* itself, as the *Italian* is a gross Mixture of Tongues, as well as a Corruption of the *Latin*, so what a Mixture of Dialects is there among them? The *Calabrians* speak one Kind of *Italian*, the *Genoeses* another, the *Savoyards* a third, and the *Venetians* a fourth.

NOR is this all, but the Writing of these Languages differs in itself from what it was in former Years: The Authors in *French* in the Time of *Charlemaigne*, or in *English* in *Edward* the Confessor's Time, nay, and even to the Time of *Henry* the VII are scarce to be understood now, and their Words are called *old French* and *old English*. I might give Instances of the like Changes in all the Languages in *Europe*, they being all refin'd, and render'd more polite since those Times than they were then.

WITH all these Improvements the Orthography of the Languages has also taken its share, to the bettering of the Speech, and perhaps may be like to do the same in the Ages that are to come, Speech being still capable of farther Embellishments.

IT remains then, in order to close this Discourse, that we only enter a little upon the Manner of Pen and Ink Writing, and its several Usages, Improvements, and Excellencies in the World; the Beauties of it, and the Perfection it was brought to, till it received a fatal Baulk in the still more exquisite, tho' less difficult, Art of Printing: And tho' this will not require so laborious a Search into Antiquity, nor shall I have an occasion to quote so many, or indeed any, Authors for the Enquiry; yet there will be found a certain secret Excellence in the Art of Penmanship, which will never fail to recommend it to the Ingenious part of the World, and cause the Artists in it to be valued in all Countries, and in all Ages; of which in its Place.

PART VIII.

BEING now come to the Manner of Writing, and the Use and Improvement of it as an Art, I must, according to the Method of the Learned *Vossius*, observe, that there were antiently two Sorts of Writing, *Apertus* and *Opertus*;[104] *Apertus*, or common and apparent, or *Opertus*, that is hidden and occult, or secret: I mention this to *Note*, that the latter of these, which some pretend to, as a rare or a new Discovery, as if it was born with them, and had no other Parent but in their ingenious Brain, as they would have it be thought, was yet as antient as the first Ages of Paper Writing; which I shall shew presently.

THIS occult Writing was at first used upon the Occasion of Publick Dispatches, and Business of Moment in the State only, and was called *Steganography*, being kept as a Secret among some particular Persons; and this was of two Sorts. (1) *Visible*, but written in unknown Figures or Characters; or new made Words, contrived on purpose for the Occasion. This *Steganography* we now call *Cypher*, of which all the Persons to or from whom such Writings are sent, must have the Counterpart, which in some Cases is call'd the *Key*, to write by, or read it by; This is as antient as Writing itself, and more antient than the Use of Paper. (2) The other Sort of occult or secret Writing, is *Invisible*, or unseen at first, being written with certain Liquids compounded for that Purpose, and which, tho' not to be seen at first, yet by a certain Art to be known to, and used by the Person to whom it is written, shall be made to shew itself afterwards, as plain and visible as other Writings.

OF these Kinds there were several differing Sorts, as (1) Some that could not be seen by Daylight, being written with Water distill'd from *Nitre*, and putrified or rotten *Willows*; the Words written with which, would cast a Kind of light like the Phosphorus, and were only to be read in the dark: Others could not be read unless they were held up against a Candle, or against the Stars, and then were easily seen: Others might indeed be seen

292

by Day, the Ink they were written with not requiring the Air to illuminate it; but then first it was necessary to use some other Preparation to joyn with, and fetch out to Sight, the Tinge or Colour of the first Writing, that is to say Earth, or Water, or Fire, or perhaps some of all these artfully mixt together.

SOME have written in this Manner with the milky Juice of the Herb *Tithymalus*,[105] or *Sea-Thistle*, which is also by our Simplers call'd the *Milk-Thistle*, of which *Pliny* speaks in his *Natural History*, lib. xxvi. cap. viii. Others have found the Milk of some living Creatures that would perform the same Operation; others with the Fat or Oil of Bodies of Animals; others with Urine, or with some Gums, which mixt with the Tallow or Fat of the Creatures would do the same thing: All which Kinds of Writings were not visible when plain and unmixt, the Substance of them lay on the Surface of the Paper, but were thus discover'd: *viz.* The Person who was to read them was to sprinkle some fine Dust or Sand upon them, colour'd or ting'd with black or red, and that Dust lodging upon the Writing, which was soft and glutinous, but not on the Intervals of the Paper, which were clean and dry, would thereby discover the Writing to the Eye.

OTHERS of these secret Writings were done with *Allom*, or with *Vitriol*, and these had another particular Quality, namely, that being at first perfectly conceal'd and invisible, they were to be dipt in Water, or in Wine prepared by Art for that purpose, before they could be read; and some again of these could not be read unless dipt in Water prepar'd with *Quicksilver* or *Mercury.*

FOR some of these Compositions Fire was necessary to be used to make the Letters appear, and make them legible; as when the Ink or Liquid they wrote with was made of the Juices drawn from *Lemons* or *Citrons, Onions, Cherries*, the Herb *Cyclamen*, or other acid Fruits or Plants; which tinge or contact the Surface of the Paper, and which by the help of Fire are made apparent; of all these artificial Ways of Writing, and of many other, we have a full Account, *Apud Jo. Baptistam Portam Neapolitanum*, lib. xvi. *Mag. Nat.*[106]

THE visible Writing requires no Art to describe the Subject of it; sufficient has been said already: It consists either of Letters or Marks call'd *Notæ*; of the last I have spoken already, what remains relates to the various Kinds of Letters. The Kinds which we best know are the *Hebrew*, the *Chaldee*, or *Syriack*, or *Arabick*, which differ little from one another; the *Greek*, which differs from all the rest, and the *Latin* or *European*: This *Latin* or *European*, which is best known to us, is divided in its several Characters, tho' with very little Difference in the *Alphabet*, such as the *Roman*, the *Italick*, and the *Gothick*; these (since Printing was invented) are more particularly distinguish'd, but were, even when all Things were written by the Pen, distinguish'd into the *Roman*, and the *Italian*, and the *Text-hand*, of which we shall speak again in their Places.

THERE were other Characters in former Times, in Use in this very Country, and some are still remaining, which are scarce legible to us, and yet are establish'd upon the *Roman* Alphabet, such as the *Saxon* and the *Irish*; the last is still in use among the Highlanders of *Scotland*, and the *Bible* is printed in that Character, which none but themselves can read. But it would be endless to enter here into the several Characters which have been written in *England*, and which have been written in other Countries also, which are now obsolete and almost forgotten; 'tis enough to observe that there were excellent Writers in all these Times, who wrote those Characters in a manner so fine and so exact, that no Writers can be found in our Time that can equal them, much less out-do them; and some antient Manuscripts show still the Remains of the excellent Writers of those Ages.

ESPECIALLY in the Text-writing or *Gothick*, of which some ancient Manuscripts are still to be seen, done with such Exactness, and with such exquisite Art, as nothing can come up to them (that I can meet with) in this Age; and tho' there are some very good Artists still in the World, and who are great Masters of Penmanship, especially in other Hands, *as we call them*, yet nothing excels them: There is also Writing by Engravement, performed by a Tool. This is an Incision upon brass or copper Plates, and is an Art of another Kind, and will come under our Consideration when we speak of Printing, Stamping, or Impressing, which is a Work by itself.

As we have several Kinds of Writing the same Characters in our ordinary Way, so we have a singular Way of expressing the Difference by the Word *Hand*; it is true that Writing is an Art or Operation more particularly perform'd by the Hand; but to call it by that as a Sirname, and to make the Word Hand be a Term of Art, as it is ungrammatical, so it must be confess'd 'tis without Example or Authority: The Absurdity is apparent from the following Accident in Story, which there are many living Witnesses at this Time to prove the Truth of.

'There was a famous Fellow went about this Island to shew himself for Money, who was a *German*, or rather a *Swiss* by Birth, named *Buchinger*, who not only had no Hands, but no Arms, and was born so, his Body being entirely smooth in the Places where ordinarily the Arms of Children may be said to grow; now this Man had by many Years Practice, and I suppose a very early Application, brought the Joynt of his Knees to be so supple, that, contrary to the Usage natural to our Bodies, he could turn them any way, and could as easily turn his Leg to a perpendicular Position upwards, as we all turn our Legs downwards to bear the Weight of our Bodies when we walk, at the same time preserving the ordinary Situation also for the immediate Use of his Feet, to step, walk, leap, run, or other Exercises proper for the Leg to perform.

'By this Usage of the Joynts of his Knees, he could without any Difficulty turn up his Foot, and by the help of his Toes, which were also become as tractable as Fingers, I had almost said as handy as Fingers, he would pull off his Hat, scratch or comb his Head, wash his Face, take any Thing out of his Pockets, use a Sword, (handle a Sword I was going to say) fire a Gun, nay fence and fight, and we were told he kill'd a Man with a Sword, and by what they call fair Fencing or Fighting, tho' that I do not believe; among the rest of his Performances he wrote very well, and that in several Languages, and several Characters: Now as this was perform'd with the Foot, it would be a gross Impropriety to say he wrote a very good *Foot*, and yet 'twas as absurd to say he wrote a good HAND.'

BUT Custom has legitimated this Way of Speaking in *English*, tho' it is not so express'd in any other Language, as I meet with, in the World: However I must be allow'd to follow the Usage of our Country in Speech, and after this Account given of my Thoughts about it, I can bear no Part of the blame, or be quoted as an Authority to any one else.

PART IX.

IN speaking of the Manner of Writing in a stricter Sense, I confine my self
to the *European* Writing; for of the Writing in the *Hebrew, Greek*, or *Arabick*
Tongues, there is now no Room so much as to speak, except it be to note
the miserable Degeneracy of the Writers in those Countrys; occasioned,
principally, by their Discouragements in all Science, and Arts in the Parts
of the World which are now over-run by the *Turks*. But of that, in its Place.
I say, I am now confin'd to discourse of the several Usages of the Pen in the
Christian World, and more especially in *England*, where the Art of Writing
is carried to the highest Perfection of any Part of the Globe; not the *Dutch*
excepted, tho' the *Dutch* really write very well too.

IN *England* we divide our Manner of Writing into several Hands, and
these we give several Names to, all with the Addition of the Word HAND,
as a general Term of Art; such as Text-Hand, Court-Hand, Italian-Hand,
Round-Hand, Running-Hand, and the like: Mixt with these are a Text
Italian-Hand, and the Lawyers Hand; add the Ingrossing Hand, which is,
indeed, but a kind of Text, and that, in General, is a Kind of *Gothick*, which
had its Original from the *German*, or *High Dutch* Way of Writing, who, to
this Day, print all their Books in that Character.

BEFORE I come to speak of the ordinary Writing, or the Writing the ordinary Hands used in *England*, I must mention Two Extraordinary: One is
particular to the Lawyers, and has its Usage only in the Proceedings in our
Courts of Justice, and from thence is called *Court-Hand*. As our Laws, since
the Conquest, were usually written in the *French* Tongue; some would have
it, that the Court-hand was also introduc'd by the *French*; but as we have
no Authority for saying so, and do not find that the *French*, or, indeed, any
other Nation use any such Writing, so I shall not do it the Honour of so
much Antiquity; and if the Gentlemen of the Long Robe would bear with
me for using so much Freedom with them, I should rather say it was a
Kind of Cant in Writing, such as the Gypsies and Thieves are said to use in

Speaking to amuse;[107] and tho' I do by no means compare the Gentlemen of the Law with those People I last mentioned, yet the Reason of the Thing might be just the same.

THE Lawyers, perhaps, found it necessary that their Clients should not always be too knowing in their Proceedings, and in the Particulars of the Methods they took in Solliciting; also the Law Terms, used in their Indictments and Declarations, were Things, which for sundry and various Reasons, the Lawyers were unwilling their Clients should so well understand as themselves. There may be other Reasons given also why this Hand was made use of, but who invented it at first we have no Account of.

As for Tachygraphy, or Short Writing, it has been suppos'd to be a modern Invention, and first found out by our *Sermon Writers*, a few Years since, when Writing Sermons from the Mouths of the Preachers was first in Use in *England*: But there are good Reasons to believe, that this Way of Writing was in use among the *Romans* also, and that the Speeches of their Orators, their funeral Orations, and their Pleadings at their Tribunals were often, if not always, taken in Writing from their Mouths by the Artists in this way of Writing, which was then call'd Writing by Notes or Marks, and probably this may be understood in the Scripture by what is call'd, *The Pen of a ready Writer*.[108] We have, indeed, no Remains of the Characters which they made Use of in those Times, nor do we see any such Writing as that we call *Short Hand* among the Nations round us; and those who first invented the present *Short Hand* which we now practise, doubtless are to be esteemed as Men of Merit, because they first formed it into a perfect System of Art, and placing the Vowels in a Circular, or rather a Semicircular Position about the Consonants, made the Connexion so exact, that they could not only write Short, but read what one another Wrote, which in other Short Hands could not be done.

BY this Art the Tongue has indeed been outstript by the Hand, and I have seen some who have been able to write faster than Men ordinarily speak; by which means Speeches in publick Auditories, Pleadings on Eminent Trials, Speeches at the Places of Execution, and many valuable Things which would otherwise have been lost to the World, have been preserved, even unknown to the Speakers themselves.

THIS Invention, as it is in most such Cases, has been followed with many others, pretending to improve it; but it may be said, what is not often said of any Inventors, or Inventions, (*viz.*) that the first has been the best, and that no Improver has gone beyond them or perhaps ever will.

THERE seems, indeed, to be less Occasion now for this Art than ever was in *England*, and the Occasion lessens every Day, for as to *Sermon Writing*, that is quite laid aside, (*as Sermon Hearing indeed seems also likely to be in a little more Time*) and as to Trials in extraordinary Cases, and Speeches, People have so often been reproved for Writing on such Occasions, and put out of the Courts and Places where they have attempted it, that this also seems to be left off; and as to Dying Speeches, Dying Men have been so often injured by the false and imperfect Accounts given from those that have pretended to write from their Mouths, that such People generally give (what they design to say) in Writing to the Sheriff or Officer, appointed to attend the Execution, and desire it may be made Publick; leaving Coppies with some of their Relations, in order to be sure that nothing should be added, or omitted, and so that no Wrong be done them.

THESE Things, I say, make this Art of Short Writing, or as 'tis commonly call'd writing *Short Hand*, grow out of Use in *England*, and as for *Scotland*, I scarce ever met with any that understood it there, neither in *France* nor in *Spain*.

THERE is another Art or Method of Writing which has been of very antient Usage, and tho' it is not now much in use, yet we have the Equivalent to it now, which we call a Cypher, and they are indeed the same thing that the Antients call'd *Steganography*, as above. I shall give a brief Account of this Way of Writing here, and dismiss it at once, for it has no great matter in it to make it worth while to dwell on, for any long time.

STEGANOGRAPHY is the Art of writing Secrets, so as that none but the Party, to whom they are address'd, shall be able to read or understand them, the Word it self signifying Writing that is to be cover'd or concealed: and though this Art were known amongst the Antients, yet it seems that *Trithemius*[109] was the first that set down the Rules of it, which he hath perform'd, not only in his six Books of *Polygraphy*, but more especially, in his famous Treatise of *Steganography* which has made so much Noise in the World. Now though his Design was, in part, to reveal this useful Secret, yet was he not willing to make it indifferently intelligible to all Sorts of Persons; his End being only to instruct the Learned, and the Ministers of State; and, therefore, to deter the common People from reading his Books, he pretended to a Familiarity with evil Spirits, and made use of some strange Bastard *Hebrew* Names; such as *Pamersiel, Camuel*, &c. which though he only used to illustrate the Method of this Art, yet was the good Abbot, upon this Account, suspected to be a Magician; and notwithstanding all the Endeavours that *Trithemius* used to vindicate himself, his Slanderers have endeavoured, and that with some Success, to make his *Steganography* pass in the World for a Piece full of Superstition and unlawful Magick: However there have not been wanting many learned Men who have undertaken to defend *Trithemius*, and to improve the Art he had publish'd. The most Illustrious of these Apologists was the Duke of

Lunenburgh,[110] who caused a Book on this Subject to be printed, call'd *Cryp-tography*, *i.e.* A hidden Way of Writing, in 1624. The famous *Caramuel*[111] also publish'd his *Steganography* at *Bruxels*, afterwards, at *Collen*, in 1635, which is nothing else but an Explication of *Trithemius* his *Steganography*, and of the *Clavicula* of *Solomon* the *German*: Father *Gaspar Schottus*,[112] a Jesuit, publish'd also, in 1665, his *Schola Steganographica*, wherein he defends the good Abbot; and last of all, about twenty five Years ago, one *Wolfgangus Ernestus Heidelius*[113] hath written a Commentary upon *Trithemius* his *Stega-nography*, where he sets down many new Ways of disguising one's Meaning in a Letter, by the means of Variety of Characters, with many ingenious Principles for the improving of this Art, *Vid. G. Caramuel in Cursu liberali. Baillet*[114] *Jugemens Des scavans*.

I COME next to speak of the Art of Writing as it is now practised in *Eng-land*; and here, I must confess, it is a terrible Satyr upon our Nation, to reflect how sorrily, not to say sordidly, most People, in our Country, write their own Mother-tongue, and especially how they spell it: And 'tis a little hard, that before I mention any Thing of the good Writing among us, in which our Artists, at this Time, excel most of the Nations in *Europe*, we must speak a little too of the scandalous Negligence of almost all our Peo-ple, and especially the Gentry and People out of Trade, in teaching their Children to write; Insomuch that, in some, the greater and higher the Quality of Persons be, the worse, generally speaking, they may be found to write; as if Writing, which is one of the most essential Parts of Education, was grown useless or obsolete, and out of fashion, and that it was no Scan-dal to be Ignorant of it.

I HAVE not, indeed, critically examin'd how it is in other Countries, hav-ing, however, seen the missive Letters and publick Acts of many Nations; and this I speak upon the Foot of what I have so seen of the other Kind from abroad: Namely, that many Nations write worse than the *English*, but none spell worse or so ill. I have seen some publick Writings in the *French* and in the *Spanish* Tongues very curiously written; and the *Biscayners* in *Spain* are accounted excellent Penmen: And though both these Nations, especially the *French*, have more difficult Spelling, though not more diffi-cult Pronouncing than the *English*; yet none of them that I have met with, spell their Words so ill, or are, in general, so Ignorant in the Orthography of their Speech as the *English*.

IT would be too much a Satyr upon our Education in *England* to enter into the Reason of this, or examine why our Gentry so generally, (and the Women universally) spell our Language so ill, or as it rather should be said, can not spell it at all.

BUT to come back to the Work of Writing (as now in use) it is perform'd (1.) by the Hand, Writing with the Instrument call'd a Pen, and upon Paper, or Parchment, and Vellum; or (2.) by a Graving or Carving Tool, or Instrument: This indeed follows the Pen, and performs very curious Things, by Engraving in Copper or Brass, which is afterwards made capable of Impressing the Letters on Paper by an Engine, which some call Printing, tho' perform'd after a different Manner from the ordinary Way of Printing; the Engine it is wrought with is called the *Rolling-Press*.

Now in these several Methods of Writing, the Ingenious Masters of this Art have invented several shaped Characters, or rather Methods of making the Characters by which they write; these are, as I observ'd before, ordinarily, but very improperly, call'd HANDS; from whence Men are said to write such or such a Hand: And our Writing Masters generally write over their Doors, *Here are Taught all the Hands used in* England: These several Hands are ordinarily call'd, as follows,

> *Round Hand,*
> *Italian Hand,*
> *Text Hand Small,*
> *Court Hand,*
> *Text Italian,*
> *Running Hand,*
> *Large Text,*
> *Short Hand.*

THESE, in the Printing Art, are call'd by differing Names, and those Names again multiplied according to the Size of the Letters, or Types, in which each of them are expressed, and with some particular modern Names also occasion'd by the extraordinary Performance of some modern Founders of Letters, which have made finer and more curious *Types* or Letters than what had been made before. The general Names are thus,

	Capital Roman,
	Great Primmer,
	English,
	Pica,
Roman and under	*Small Pica,*
this Denomination.	*Small Primmer,*
	Long Primmer,
	Brevier,
	Non Parreil,
	Elziver.

Italick answerable to all the several Sizes of the Roman Types above-mentioned, and bearing the Addition of their Names, as Italick Capitals, English Italick, and the like.

Gothick, among which the Roman is used in proper Names, as the Italicks are among the Roman Letters.

IN writing the several Hands, mentioned above, there is certainly requir'd different Art; and several Masters are particularly skilful, and excel in one, more than another, Way of Writing; as some excel in one Hand, some in another.

IT is needless to give Specimens here of the several Hands now in Use, and mentioned as above: The ordinary Copy-books, publish'd for the Teaching the Art of Writing, are compleat Directions in this Case; and some of them are Testimonies of the most exquisite Performances of the Masters concern'd; to which I refer.

BUT as, since the Art of Printing has been invented, the laborious part of Writing is taken off, and the Copying or Writing of Books is at an End; so neither is the Writing itself so embellish'd by Art as in former Times, nor are the Artists so innumerably many as before: But the *Printing Art* has out-run the Pen, and may pass for the greatest Improvement of its Kind in the World.

LEARNING, in particular, is infinitely beholding to it by the spreading of useful Knowledge in the World, and making the Accession to it cheap and easy: For not to speak of the Difficulty of Writing, and the Number of Hands that must be employ'd about it, 'tis most certain the Price of Books must infinitely have exceeded what it is now; and as in Trade it is a received Maxim, that Cheapness causes Consumption, so here Cheapness causing now the spreading and extending of Books, its contrary (Dearness) must have lessen'd and restrain'd it; consequently Knowledge, without it had been under greater Limitations and Restrictions, and the most useful Branches of Science, had been much more hid and conceal'd; the Knowledge of History and Geography (to launch out into no more Particulars) to how few Ears wou'd it have reach'd, and how few People wou'd have known what had been done in the World?

How little a Way wou'd the Fame of the greatest Heroe have reach'd? The Noise of a Victory would have scarce been heard farther than the Noise of the Cannon, much less could Things have continued in Time, longer than the Memory of the Persons concern'd wou'd preserve them, or that most corrupting multiplying Usage of Tradition have convey'd them; of which already we see so many fatal Effects, and by which Things of the greatest Moment done as it were but Yesterday, that is to say, within the Compass of two or three Ages, turn into Fable and Romance: Scoundrels are made Heroes, and Heroes are made Gods; for so no doubt the Deifying the first Tyrants of the World, such as *Saturn, Jupiter, Bacchus*, and *Mercury*, and *Belus* (or *Baal*) came about. Thus again the Memory of Wise Men has been handed down to Posterity, as of Monsters; and of Learned Men, as of Wizards, and afterwards as of Devils: Thus *Atlas*, said to carry the World on his Shoulders, is made a Giant carrying that load (the *Globe*) upon his Back; and *Prometheus*, a Giant, chain'd down upon Mount *Caucasus*, with a Vulture gnawing his Liver, and condemn'd to that Fate by *Jupiter* for stealing Fire from the Sun to put Life into his Man of Clay which he had made; all which was no more than this, That *Atlas* by his Wisdom and Knowledge instructed the whole World in the Knowledge of Things, and gave them just Rules for Government, whereby he might be said to bear the Weight of the World's management upon his Shoulders; and that *Prometheus* was so studious for the general Good of Mankind, that he brought Light and Life from Heaven into their Souls; and was so intent upon his Studies of the heavenly Bodies, that lying on the Ground whole Nights together upon Mount *Caucasus* (where he liv'd) the better to observe the Motions of the Stars, he contracted Diseases which eat into his Vitals, and brought him into a Consumption, preying upon his Liver, and destroy'd him. The like of *Dædalus* and *Icarus*,[115] and his making Wings to fly in the Air, which was no more than his inventing Sails for Boats and Ships to sail upon the Sea; and the like.

THESE Things have been the Effect of the Want of Letters, and of the Art of Writing; and the like wou'd be the Effect, and that notwithstanding the Knowledge of both, if the Art of Printing had not follow'd, to make what was written diffusive, by the Multitude and Cheapness of Books.

THE Effect of the Want of this is plain, in the Difficulty it has been to the World to preserve authentick Copies of the Histories of Things done in former Ages, and of Assertaining the Integrity of those Copies we have.

HOW few, and those how uncertain, are the Accounts left us of Antiquity, and how little do we know compar'd to what might have been known, of the History of the early Ages of the World? What an inestimable Loss was the burning of the Library[116] of *Ptolemy Philadelphus*, at *Alexandria*? wherein, if the whole Story be not fabulous, was 700,000 Volums, that is to say Rolls, or Tables, or Bundles of Papirij Manuscripts.

NAY such was the Fate of Things, that, if we are not misinform'd, in the Reign of good *Josiah*, there was but one Copy of God's Law[117] left in the whole World, and it was next to a Miracle, that the same Calamity, namely, the idolatrous wicked Doings of *Manasseh* his Father, had not destroy'd that one; so that, in short, if that one Copy had not been extant, the whole

Levitical Institution had been lost, and we had never known what the Laws of *Moses* were to this Day.

BUT to come nearer; How many noble Works have since that time been lost, as particularly several Books of *Livy's Roman* History are not found; and how ill are they supply'd? And how few Historians are there that record the great Actions of the Heroes of that Age? Not a Man that has given any particular Relation of the greatest Actions of *Julius Cæsar*, but his own Commentaries, which are short to a Fault; the Beginning of the greatest Battles are scarce told, but the End follows, they began to fight *so* and *so*, and then the Enemy were beaten, *&c.*

OF all the Wars of *Alexander, Quintus Curtius's* Abridgements[118] conclude the whole; the Siege of *Troy*, were it unsung by *Homer*, what shou'd we have known of it? And even now we scarce know whether it is a History, or that Ballad-Singers Fable to get a Penny.

HOW are the Books of the *Sibyls* lost, and the Histories of all the rest of the World, after the Declining of the *Roman* Empire? How imperfect is Antiquity in all those Things?

HAD Printing been in Use in the flourishing Times of *Augustus Cæsar*, when the World was full of the politest Writers; and in the Times of the other Emperors, when Learning had all possible Encouragement; how many noble Authors shou'd we have had recording the particular Histories, and some the Annals and Chronicles of those Ages, besides a *Livy* and a *Salust*, and two or three more, upon whom we are left to depend for all that we can learn of those Times?

HOW many *Virgils*, and *Juvenals*, and *Lucans*, and *Ovids*, shou'd we have seen instead of these few, in a Time when Poetry was arriv'd to so correct, and so justly admir'd a Perfection? Instead of which, how few are all the Writers of those Ages? not a Moralist among the *Greeks* but *Plutarch*, or among the *Latines* but *Seneca* and *Cicero*, and two or three more.

AGAIN, Since the Times of Christianity, How many of the Writings of the most antient Fathers have been lost? Whence is it become a Doubt among us, Whether St. *Peter* was at *Rome* or no, and who were[a] the real Successors in the Papal Chair? Can it be conceiv'd, that if Printing had been in Use, the Writings of those Times, would not have been preserv'd? Manuscripts were easily suppress'd, and once lost never recover'd; Where are the Journals of all the famous Councils and the Speeches of orthodox Heroes of the Church in the primitive Times? Among the Collections we have, how often is it said with a Note of Lamentation, *Such and such Things are lost?*

NAY to this Day, How valued, rather, how invaluable, is an antient Manuscript esteem'd; and what Rarities do we count them for preserving

History and Chronology? Much of the History and Chronology of the World, is only preserved in old Coins and Medals, Busto's and Inscriptions, Altars and Monuments, dug out of the Earth, and pickt up in the ruinous Heaps of demolish'd Towns and Castles.

BUT, in one Word, when the Writings of the Moderns have not one thousandth Part of the Weight in them, no not even the best of them, we have a Method, by which a Work once printed is scarce ever lost.

IT is true, that Books printed sometimes become scarce, and as we call it, out of Print, and sometimes are quite lost; and we think many such were lost (with respect to our *British* Affairs) in the Destruction of Abbeys and Monastries in *England* and *Scotland*, also in the first Heats of the Reformation, and perhaps in our Civil Wars; no doubt some very valuable Manuscripts were lost; and in particular those relating to Antiquity, and the first Times of Christianity in this Nation; for Example, the several Translations of the Bible, and Writings of the first Reformers were lost in the Persecutions which follow'd; we see nothing of *Wicklif*'s Writings, or any of the Fathers of the Reformation, except a few of old *Latimer*'s Sermons left among us, tho' we are assur'd they wrote and printed many Thousands; even *Tindal*'s Translation of the Bible is not to be had, except in some extraordinary Libraries.

I COULD run this Remark out into many Particulars reaching even to the holy Scriptures and the sacred Writings of the Apostles themselves, many of which, 'tis believ'd, are entirely lost in the World.

BUT to bring it down to the Case, Such is the excellency of the Art of Printing, that every Thing worth recording in the World is now so secur'd, that it may almost be said, it cannot be lost, and perhaps may never till the general Conflagration.

THE Easiness of the Performance makes the Books printed now so cheap, that the meanest and poorest People that have any Thing more than just to subsist them, may purchase Books for needful Use; so that whether Sacred or Prophane, the Knowledge of Things spreads, as far as the World is inhabited with Creatures that can read.

THIS Art of Printing was said to be found out at *Harlem* in *Holland*, but was either carry'd from thence to, or first invented at *Mentz* in *Germany*: They speak of it as something wonderful, that Printing was invented by a Man of Arms, [*Soldier*,] and Gunpowder by a Man of Letters, [*Monk*;] all that is to be said of that, is, that was a learned Soldier, and this a Chymist, or chymical Fryer, or Monk; neither of which hath any Thing wonderful in it.

IT is not to my Purpose here, to enter into a large History of the Art of Printing, or into the particular Improvements of it in the several Ages since its Invention; But the following Abridgement of both I think needful to the present Purpose, and agreeable to the Design.

IT was invented by *Lawrenzs Janzs Coster*[119] a Soldier at *Harlem*: This I find recorded in the Town Register there, in the Year 1430. The first Operation, it seems, was perform'd by Pieces of Wood, on which the Words to be impress'd were first cut with a carving Tool, and the Impression was easily made, by laying it hard on upon the Paper, just in the same manner as our Callico Printers practise at this Day; and by this Means he printed not one Letter or one Word at a time, but a Line, or Paragraph; nay at last he came so far as to print a whole Page at a stroke.

BUT finding this not to answer, except in small Things, which contain'd no more than what one of his Pieces of Wood cou'd likewise contain, he set his Invention at work, and found out a Way to cut the Mould of a Letter in Steel, and by that cast the *Type*, or Letter itself, in the same manner as is now practis'd by the Letter Founders; nor has any better Method been ever found out since, or I believe can be.

JOHN *Guttenburgh* was Comrade to this *Coster*, and having seen all his Methods, and made himself Master of the Performance, stole away his Tools, and went with them to *Mentz* in *Germany*; where having nothing to do, but to set them up and go to work, whereas *Coster* had every Thing to make over again, he (*Guttenburgh*) got to work a great while before *Coster* could be ready, and so obtain'd the Fame of being the first Inventor.

To prove this they tell us, That one *Rabbi Joseph*,[120] a Jew, in a Chronicle (of his Writing) of *Germany*, mentions a printed Book which he saw in the Year of the World 5288, that is of our reckoning 1428, as may be seen in *Scriverius*:[121] Upon the whole *Guttenburgh* carry'd the Honour of the first Inventor in *Germany*, and *Coster* in *Holland*, each Country contending for their Countryman. Both it seems agree, that *Tully*'s Offices was the first Book ever printed by this Art, printed in the Year 1465; this is said to be printed by one *John Faustus* assistant to *Guttenburgh*, as is mention'd by a N. B. in that Copy of *Tully* of the first Impression, which is now to be seen in the *Bodleian* Library in *Oxon*.

BE it which it will, *Coster*, or *Guttenburgh*, about that Time the Way of Printing began in the World, which is not full 300 Years ago; how wonderfully it is improv'd and encreas'd since that Time we are all Witnesses; it seems it came very early to be practis'd in *England*; for *Henry* VI. or *Boucher* Archbishop of *Canterbury* rather, in *Henry* VI's Time, sent over two Men to *Harlem* to learn this Art; The Men sent were *William Turner*, Master of the King's Robes, and *William Caxton*, Merchant; These managed so well that they privately prevail'd with *Fredrick Corselies*, one of *Coster*'s Workmen, to whom he had taught the Art, to come over with them to *England*, having, it seems, brib'd him with a good Sum of Money: Having succeeded thus happily, they brought him to *Oxford*, where he set up a Printing-house; and this they tell us was in the Year 1467; and there is a Treatise of *Ruffinus*[122] now to be seen, printed on a broad unshapen Octavo, in the Year 1468, about three Years after the *German* Edition of *Tully's Offices* mention'd above.

THE first Book ever printed, as *Tully* in particular, is on Vellum, but the Book of *Ruffinus* is upon Paper; for about the same Time, namely, in the Year 1417, the Making of Paper was invented, and first found out at *Bazle* in *Switzerland*, by *Anthony* and *Michael Galicion*, two *Greeks*, and this soon spread every where, the Art itself not being so difficult as that of Printing had been.

FROM *Oxford* the Printing Press came to *London, Anno* 1471, tho' *Moxon*[123] in his Art of Printing says, the first Book printed in *London* was in 1480, when also it began to be practis'd in *France, Germany*, and other remote Countries.

IN the Library at *Bennet's* College,[124] *Cambridge*, is a very antient printed Book, said to be done the most antient of any, and to be the Work of *Coster*, at *Harlem*: It is printed but on one Side of the Leaf; the Letters are plainly cut in Wood, not set and compos'd by Letters cast in Metal, as is now per-form'd; and it is wrought not with Printing-Ink, but with the ordinary Writing Ink, tho' very good; but there is no Imprimatur, so that we neither know the Time when, or the Place where it was performed.

BUT there are many Proofs for the Priority of *Coster* to *Guttenburgh*; and that in particular, that we have no Book printed by the latter before *Tully's Offices*, which were not printed till the Year 1465; whereas *Faustus*,[125] who was first a Servant to *Coster*, printed a Psalter, and another Book entitul'd, *Alexandri Doctrinale cum* Petri Hispani *Tractatibus*, dated 1442.

THIS Art was so great a Surprize to the World, at its first being pub-lish'd, that this *John Faustus* coming to *Paris*, and offering to sell some printed Testaments, or Psalters there, as if they had been Manuscripts; some of the learned Men, viewing the exact conformity of them one with another, even to a Line, a Word, a Letter, nay to a Speck; and not able to imagine which Way it was possible, and that none of their Scribes could do the like; took up *Faustus*, declar'd he was a Wizard, and a Magician, and that he dealt with the Devil, and order'd him to be prosecuted as such; thus putting him in Fear of his Life, they got the Art out of him; and this it seems is the Original of that so famous Story of Dr. *John Faustus*, or *Foster*, a *High-German* Conjurer.

ABOUT the same Time, very happily for the propagating the Invention of Printing, the Invention of Paper-making started into the World, as it were on purpose to go hand in hand with the Press; it was invented, as I have said, at *Bazil*, in the Year 1417, by *Michael* and *Anthony Galicion*, and was presently improv'd to a great Perfection.

SOME think that this Paper, made at *Basil*, was made of Flax, not of Linen Rags. The two Brothers, who contriv'd it, were *Greeks*, who fled out of their Country after *Constantinople* was besieg'd by the *Turks*: But this does not agree with the Year; it seems it was an Imitation of the Cotton Paper used in the *Levant*.

CERTAIN it is, That Cotton Paper has been of very antient Use in the *East*, there being in the *Bodleian* Library an *Arabick* Manuscript among those the University bought of Dr. *Huntingdon*, written in the four hundred and twenty seventh Year of the *Hegira*,[126] which is *Anno. Dom.* 1049, on this Paper, and some there are without Dates, which seem older.

AND as for the Linnen Rag Paper, it must be much older than 1425; for in the Archieves of the Library of the Dean and Chapter of *Canterbury*, there is an Inventory on our Paper of the Goods of *Henry Prior*, of *Christ's-Church* there; that is dated in the twentieth Year of *Edward* the Third, which is *Anno Dom.* 1346; and in the *Cotton* Library are several Writings on our Paper, as high, at least, as the fifteenth Year of *Edward* the Third.

SOME think the Rolling Press[127] was invented by *Lipsius*.[128] But there is a printed Book in the *Bodleian* Library,[129] placed *Laud*, page 138, being a *Missale secundum usum Eccles. Herbipolensis*, that is, *Wurtzburgh* in *Germany*: At the Beginning of this Book is an Instrument of *Rodulfus* the Archbishop of this Church, containing the Reason of the Publication of this *Missale*; and instead of a Seal there is annexed a Print, Engraven, of the Arms of the See, &c. very finely done (for that Time, for it was before *Durer*[a]) and on which are evident Marks of the Pressure by the Plate, with some Touches of Ink at the Edges, which they that have seen it judge to be the plain Marks of its being done, or wrought off, in a Rolling Press, and there are sufficient Reasons to prove that this Book is as antient as 1481.

THE next Form of Printing at *Harlem*, was by cutting whole Forms of Wood from Manuscripts exactly written, and without Pictures; such perhaps was the *Donatus*, which might bear Date about 1450, some say 1440; *This appears plain* (saith Mr. *Bagford*[130]) *from Copy Books which we have seen printed at* Rome, Venice, Switzerland, *and* England, *as high as* 1500.

THE third Way of Printing was with single Types made of Wood, but who invented this is not known: It was at first esteemed so great a Rarity, that the Printers carried about their Letters in Bags at their Backs, and got Money at great Mens Houses, by Printing the Names of the Family, Epitaphs, Songs, and other small Pamphlets.

THE fourth Improvement of this noble Art was the Invention of single Types made of Metal, which is owing to *Peter Scheffer*, above mentioned, first Servant, and then Son-in-Law to *Faustus*, who worked at *Mentz*; sometimes you have the Names of these two Men printed at the End of their Books, and sometimes not, sometimes with Dates as high as the Year 1457, and as low as 1490.

BUT to return to the Subject of Writing, with which I shall conclude.

HAD Writing only been the Way of Publishing in this Learned bookish Age, I believe I may venture to say, that Writing wou'd necessarily employ as many Hands as the Woollen Manufacture, and would as much have deserv'd the Name of a Manufacture; that is to say, upon a Supposition, that the Number of Books shou'd be as great, and the Itch of writing Books as strong as it is now. Of the Manner, Excellencies, and Improvement, of this excellent Art, and what it may yet be farther capable of with mathematical Rules for exact Writing; having no room to enter upon it here, I may discourse of at large hereafter in a Work by itself.[131]

EXPLANATORY NOTES

A General History of Discoveries and Improvements (1725–6)

This was originally issued in four monthly parts, each with its own title page. The first part was advertised for 12 October 1725 in the *Whitehall Evening Post* for 7–9 October. The imprint for the fourth and last part changes and reads 'London. Printed for W. MEARS, F. CLAY, and D. BROWN, without *Temple-Bar*, and sold by J. ROBERTS, at the *Oxford-Arm*s, in Warwick-Lane. Price One-Shilling.' The work was re-issued with a new title page: *The History of the Principal Discoveries and Improvements, in the Several Arts and Sciences: Particularly the Great Branches of Commerce Navigation, and Plantation, in all Parts of the known World* (London: Printed for W. Mears, F. Clay, and D. Browne, 1727 [for 1726]).

page

19   1   *What's yet discover'd ... know*: The distich is most probably by Defoe himself.

26   2   *The Learned Burnet*: Thomas Burnet (*c.* 1635–1715). In *The Theory of the Earth*, his own translation of his *Telluris Theoria Sacra*, he has a long chapter on the final conflagration ('The Burning of the World'), in which, discussing volcanoes in Italy and elsewhere, he writes: '... we must consider all the hidden invisible Materials within the veins of the Earth; Such are all Minerals or Mineral juices and concretions that are igniferous, or capable of inflammation; and these cannot easily be reckon'd up or estimated. Some of the most common are Sulphur, and all Sulphureous Bodies, and Earths impregnated with Sulphur, Bitumen and Bituminous concretions'. (Two vol. edition, London, 1719, vol. 2, pp. 89–90.)

        3   *Mount Heckela*: a volcano in Iceland.

30   4   *Canaan, not Ham*: Why Canaan should have been made to suffer for his father's offence has puzzled theologians from Chrysostom onwards and has received many different explanations. Matthew Poole, in his *Annotations upon the Holy Bible* (1683), writes: '*Quest.* Seeing Ham committed the crime, why is the curse inflicted upon his son Canaan? *Ans.* When

309

page

Canaan is mentioned, Ham is not exempted from the curse, but rather more deeply plunged into it, while he is pronounced accursed, not only in his person … but also in his posterity, which doubtless was a great aggravation of his grief … It seems therefore very probable from these words, and the Hebrew doctors and others affirm it, that Canaan did partake with his father in the sin, yea, that he was the first discoverer of his father's shame'. Defoe gives a more elaborate comic account of Canaan's part in Noah's drunkenness in *The Political History of the Devil* (1726), pp. 134–9, and a further account in *A System of Magick* (1726) pp. 13–15.

30   5 *as Mr. Milton describes it*: see *Paradise Lost*, Book 9, ll. 179–88.

6 *Babel*: In the similar disquisition on the tower of Babel in *The Political History of the Devil*, (pp. 141–2), Defoe credits Isaac Casaubon with the theory that the tower was really meant as a storehouse. (See also the account in *A System of Magick* (1727), pp. 16–18.)

31   7 *Ubi fata vocant*: whither the Fates summon.

32   8 *Sɪʀ Walter Raleigh*: Raleigh writes, in his *History of the World* (1614), Book I, chapter 8: '*First*, We are to consider that the world after the flood was not planted by imagination; neither had the children of Noah wings to fly from Shinaar to the uttermost border of Europe, Africa, and Asia, in haste'.

9 *as the Text says:* Genesis 12: 8, 'So the Lord scattered them abroad from thence upon the face of all the earth.'

34   10 *Shinaar*: often identified with Sumeria.

11 *prolation*: utterance. See note 27 on p. 326.

35   12 *Libanus, or Anti-Libanus*: Mount Lebanon, and another mountain divided from it by a valley.

36   13 *Ne plus*: *ne plus ultra,* thus far and no further.

39   14 *Periaguaes*: Burning a hollow in a tree-trunk was the method suggested by Friday, till Crusoe taught him a better one.

15 *Osyers*: willow boughs.

16 *Flags*: sedge.

17 *Primum cana salix … amnem*: Lucan, *Civil War*, Book IV, 131–3: 'osiers of hoary willows were steeped and plaited to form small boats, which, when covered with the skin of a slain ox, carried passengers and rode high over the swollen river'.

40   18 *Tarsus*: An ancient city in the fertile plain of Cilicia.

19 *Prima ratem ventis … Tyros*: Tibullus, *Elegies*, Book I, 7, l. 20: '[Why should I recount …] how Tyre, first town that learned to trust the ship to the mercy of the wind, [looks out from her towers across the vast sea-plain?]'.

41   20 *Urbs antiqua fuit … Carthago*: Virgil's *Aeneid*, Book 1, ll. 12–13: 'There was an ancient city, a Tyrian colony, named Carthage'.

page

41 21 *Cales, then call'd Gades*: the present-day Cadiz.

42 22 *South-Saying*: Defoe's alternative spelling of 'soothsaying', based on a fanciful derivation.

23 *Aruspices*: augurs or diviners.

24 *Nimrod*: A footnote to Defoe's poem *Jure Divino* (1706), Book I, p. 3 reads: '*Ninus* or *Nimrod*, call'd in Scripture, a *mighty Hunter*, was the first Man that Usurp'd Superiority of Power, and form'd Man into Governments, under his absolute Rule; all Histories agree him to be a Tyrant, and to Erect this Government against and in opposition to the Divine Power; *Vide* Sir *Walter Raleigh*. Some will have him to be the first of the Heathen Gods, and call him *Saturn*'.

43 25 *Gen.x.ult*: i.e. Genesis 10: 32.

46 26 *Fregate built Ships*: E. Keble Chatterton, in *Sailing Ships* (London, 1909), p. 232, writes: 'If ... he [the reader] will look at the stern and "counter" of the duck and swan he will easily notice the resemblance to the overhang of the early Egyptian boats. ... The ancients certainly were affected by the waterfowl in their designing of ships, and the graceful neck of the swan was a regular decoration for the stern of the later Roman ships.'

49 27 *As the shape ... these Days*: E. K. Chatterton, who notes that 'mainsail' in the Biblical text is a mistranslation for 'foresail', explains the loosening of the rudder bands thus: 'Instead of leaving the rudders to get foul of the stern cables when they had put out the four anchors, or to run the risk of being dashed to pieces by the waves, the ropes extending from the stern to the extremities of the steering oars would be hauled up so that the blades would be quite clear of the water ... Therefore, having cast off their anchors and being under way again, the rudder-ropes would necessarily be lowered'.

28 *Being afraid ... driven*: The Authorised Version reads, 'and, fearing lest they should fall into the quicksands, strake sail, and so were driven.'

29 *The Vessels were not great ... fol. 249*: Raleigh writes: 'the vessels were not great: for it was not then the manner to build shippes with decks; onely they used (as *Thucydides* saith) small shippes, made for robbing on the sea.' (*History of the World* (1614), Book II, Chapter 14.)

30 *went to Ophir for gold*: see 1 Kings 22: 48.

50 31 *round the whole coast of Africa*: Herodotus, in his *Histories*, IV, 42, writes how the Egyptian king Necos sent a fleet manned by Phoenicians to circumnavigate Africa. 'The Phoenicians took their departure from Egypt by way of the Erythraean Sea, and sailed into the southern ocean. When autumn came, they went ashore, wherever they might happen to be, and having sown a tract of land with corn, waited until the grain was fit to cut. Having reaped it, they again set sail; and thus it came to pass that two whole years went by, and it was not till the third year that they doubled the Pillars of Heracles, and made good

page

their voyage home. ... In this way was the extent of Libya first discovered.'

50   32   *as the Story says*: see Raleigh, *History of the World*, Book III, Chapter 1: '... the citizens perceiving the town unable to hold out, embarked themselves and fled into the isle of Cyprus'.

52   33   *She was seated ... Waters*: a reference to Ezekiel, 27: 4 and 28: 2, where Ezekiel prophesies the doom of the 'Prince of Tyrus', who had said in his heart, 'I am a God, I sit in the midst of the seas' and of Tyre herself, which will be 'broken in the midst of the seas'.

54   34   *Hans Towns*: towns belonging to the Hanseatic League.

        35   *Armorica the Saxon Pirates ... steer'd*: William Camden writes in *Britannia*, ed. Gibson (1692), vol. 1, p. 87: '... by the help of their nimble fly-boats, they [the Saxons] made a shift very frequently to plunder our coasts. To which allude those verses of Sidonius Apollinaris: 'Quin & Aremoricus piratam Saxona tractus/Sperabat, cui pelle salum sulcare Britannum/Ludus, & assuto glaucum mare findere lembo' ('*Panegyric* on Avitus', ll. 369–71.)

56   36   *Thule*: It is worth noting that Charles Leigh, in his *Natural History of Lancashire* (1700), Book III, p. 76, claims that 'Thule' is a Phoenician word, meaning 'darkness'.

        37   *Ratibusque impervia Thule*: Thule, impervious to keels (i.e. ships). The phrase is used by Claudian in *De tertio consulatu Honorii Augusti panegyris*, line 53.

        38   *Seneca*: A chorus in Seneca's *Medea*, ll. 364–79, says that little ships now wander at will across the oceans and that a time will come when Thule will no longer be the limit of the lands (*nec sit terris ultima Thule*).

57   39   *Ships of Burthen*: i.e. cargo ships.

        40   *Bank*: see note 112 to *A General History of Discoveries*, p. 316 below.

58   41   *our Saviour*: see Mark 6: 45–56.

60   42   *Æsculapius*: the Latin name of the Greek god of healing.

        43   *Cadmus*: Legendary founder of the city of Thebes. He was said to have taught the Boeotians the art of writing, with Phoenician letters. See note 19 to *Essay*, p. 325 below.

        44   *the story of Dædalus*: a rationalising explanation of the legend of Daedalus and Icarus, explaining their supposed flight as an allegory of sailing, was put forward by Palaephatus in his *Concerning Incredible Tales*, a treatise of uncertain date which may be a Byzantine epitome of a work belonging to the third century BC. According to Pliny the Elder in his *Naturalis Historia,* the invention of the mast and yards was ascribed to Daedalus and that of sails to Icarus.

            Defoe gives another picturesque version of this story in *A Plan of the English Commerce* (1728), in *Political and Economic Writings* (London, 2000), vol. 7, ed. John McVeagh, p. 184.

page

62 45 *Colures*: an astronomical term for the two great circles which divide the equinoctial and the ecliptic into four equal parts.

63 46 *Sues*: Suez.

64 47 *Zanguebar, Mosambique, Melinda, Monomotapa, and Natale*: i.e. Zanzibar, Mozambique, Lamu (Kenya), Monomotapa (kingdom of uncertain extent on the Zambesi), Natal (i.e. Durban, named by Vasco da Gama as 'Terra Natalis').

66 48 *Guzeratte*: Gujarat.

   49 *Din Head*: perhaps the island of Diu, at the head of the Gulf of Cambay.

   50 *Cape Comaroon*: Cape Comorin, at the southwesternmost tip of India.

   51 *Continent of Coremandell*: Coromandel, on the East coast of India between Cape Calimere and the mouth of the Kistna.

   52 *Kingdom of Golconda*: The Kutb Shahi kingdom, overthrown by Aurangzebe in 1687, included all the country from Golconda to the eastern seaboard of Orissa.

   53 *Pipley*: i.e. Pippli.

70 54 *Termegistus*: i.e. Hermes Trismegistus, equated by the ancient Greeks with the Egyptian deity Thoth; legendary author of the collection of writings known as the *Hermetic Books*.

   55 *Danaus*: see Pliny's *Natural History*, Book 7, Chapter 57, on Danaus's voyage from Egypt to Greece.

71 56 *Pillar*: Theophilus Gale, in *The Court of the Gentiles* (1669), Part I, p. 24, writes: 'Procopius, in his *Vandilicis*, makes mention of certain *pillars*, erected in *Africa*, with an *Inscription* in the *Phoenician* tongue, which he renders thus … : "We are they who fled from Joshua the son of Naue (i.e. *Nun*) the *Robber*."'

72 57 *Sir Walter Raleigh says*: see Raleigh's *History of the World*, Book III, Chapter 1.

74 58 *Hanno*: Carthaginian admiral (*fl.* 500 BC). His account of a *periplus* beyond the Pillars of Hercules, in the course of which he founded cities on the west coast of Africa, has survived in a Greek translation.

75 59 *the great Continent of America*: see Introduction, pp. 13–16.

80 60 *Prometheus … Work begun*: These lines about Prometheus also appear in *Serious Reflections … of Robinson Crusoe* (1720), p. 98, and *A Continuation of Letters written by a Turkish Spy* (1718), p. 220.

   61 *Cadmus*: Defoe discusses the legends about Cadmus inventing letters in *An Essay upon Literature*, pp. 242–4.

81 62 *from the left Hand to the right*: It does not appear that Phoenician was ever written from left to right, though the Greeks later adopted this practice.

   63 *As the Poets feign*: for instance Ovid in Book 3, Fable 2 of his *Metamorphoses*.

82 64 *Sear-cloths*: mummy cloth.

page

83   65   *Pillars or Columns of Brass … Sea of Brass*: see 1 Kings 7.

84   66   *Coloss*: i.e. Colossus.

        67   *Nebuchadnezaar's Image*: see Daniel 3: 1.

        68   *God gave him Egypt*: see Ezekiel 29: 19.

85   69   *Precepts of Noah*: In *The Political History of the Devil* (1726), pp. 177–8, Defoe writes: 'We are indeed told, that Noah left behind him certain rules and orders for the true worship of God, which were called the precepts of Noah, and remained in the world for a long time; though how written, when neither any letters, much less writing, were known in the world, is a difficulty which remains to be solved; and this makes me look upon those laws … to be a modern invention'. In *Hakluyt's Voyages* (Glasgow, 1904, VI, p. 111) Richard Wrag reports a conversation with a Banyan of Cambia who informed him that the whole religion of his people was based on seven precepts handed down from Noah; similarly, according to the Talmud there were seven laws given to Noah, binding upon Jew and Gentile alike.

86   70   *hang upon the Sea-Shore*: see the account in the *Bibliotheke historike* of Diodorus Siculus, xvii, 46, 4.

89   71   *New Spain*: the Spanish name for Mexico.

90   72   *Battle of Canna*: Hannibal inflicted a great defeat on the Romans near the village of Cannae in 216 BC.

92   73   *the Coast of Africa*: i.e. the north coast.

        74   *the Ivory is found in the Deserts*: The hero of Defoe's *Captain Singleton* (1720) describes how he and his companions come upon an enormous deposit of elephant tusks in the African desert, p. 113.

94   75   *Joshua the Robber*: see above, note 56.

97   76   *Lapis Calaminaris*: From early times brass was made by a cementation process with calamine (*lapis calaminaris*) and charcoal.

99   77   *Achan*: see Joshua 7: 21.

100   78   *Bochart, Pool*: Samuel Bochart (1599–1667), French Protestant scholar, author of *Geographica Sacra*. Matthew Poole, author of *Annotations upon the Holy Bible* (1683).

        79   *v. 7*: i.e. Ezekiel 27: 7.

102   80   *Almug*: algum, or sandalwood.

109   81   *Adramyttium*: Hadrumetum, a city in North Africa, founded by the Phoenicians.

110   82   *Galls*: A 'gall' in this sense is an excrescence on a tree, produced by insects, and used in the manufacture of dye.

        83   *Lucius Mummius*: Lucius Mummius Archaicus, consul in 146 BC.

112   84   *Justinian*: Flavius Justinian, Roman emperor at Constantinople (*c.* 482–565).

114   85   *Marquis de Lede*: In October 1720 the Marquis de Lede, a Flemish soldier of fortune in the service of Spain, led a successful expedition to recapture Ceuta from the Moors.

page

115 86 *Kingdom of Tunis*: see chapter XII *passim*.

116 87 *Guinea Grains*: the capsules of *Amomum Meleguette*, otherwise known as 'grains of paradise'.

117 88 *Richard the First ... Holy Land*: Richard I, travelling in disguise near Vienna, was captured by the Duke of Austria and handed over to the Emperor Henry VI, having to pay a ransom of 150,000 marks to obtain his freedom. Defoe was fond of this derivation for the word 'saunter' though it is not supported by the *OED*.

      89 *the last great Victory*: the taking of Belgrade: see following note.

      90 *taking of Belgrade*: The Emperor's Turkish war ended with the taking of Belgrade in August 1717.

119 91 *took the ... whole Kingdom of Tunis*: In 1535 the Holy Roman Emperor Charles V led an expedition to North Africa, capturing Tunis from the Turkish admiral Barbarossa and bestowing the kingdom on Muley Hassan and the Hospitallers. His subsequent expedition against Algiers, in 1541, was a disastrous failure, his fleet being overwhelmed by storms.

      92 *not destroying the said Canaanites*: see Joshua 17: 18.

123 93 *share this Bear-skin*: A 'bear' in stock-exchange parlance is a speculator for a fall, the term perhaps deriving from the proverb 'Selling the skin before you have caught the bear'. But Defoe here seems to mean no more than a risky undertaking.

125 94 *Ephod*: a Jewish priestly garment, without sleeves.

      95 *Atlesses*: 'Atlas' is a silk-satin.

      96 *wanting them*: i.e. lacking them.

126 97 *Habit*: dress.

      98 *Roman Virtuosi*: Defoe appears to mean something like 'men of culture'.

      99 *Juvenal often Expostulates*: see for instance *Satire* VI, ll. 259–60.

127 100 *Camblets*: The camlet or camblet was a garment of oriental origin.

      101 *Turkey Burdets*: (or burdits) a kind of cotton fabric.

      102 *Ounxes*: ounces (i.e. lynxes).

128 103 *Thrumbs*: short pieces of waste yarn.

129 104 *United States*: i.e. United Provinces.

132 105 *Common-shore*: sewer.

133 106 *Drusus Nero*: Claudius Drusus Nero, younger brother of Tiberius. He oversaw the cutting of this canal in 12 BC, during a military campaign against the Frisians.

134 107 *Marish*: marsh.

136 108 *embraceing the Christian Religion*: According to modern opinion, Christianity did not reach Britain until some time in the second century AD.

      109 *Joseph of Arimathea*: a rich follower of Jesus who petitioned Pilate for the body of Jesus after the Crucifixion and wrapped it for burial. He was

page

fabled to have come to England and founded the abbey of Glastonbury, beginning the conversion of England.

138 110 *a late Author*: the famous French scholar Pierre Daniel Huet. He wrote in *The History of the Commerce and Navigation of the Ancients* (1717) (a translation of his *Histoire de la Commerce et de la Navigation des Anciens*, 1716), p. 153, that: 'In the Year of *Rome* 259, was instituted the College of Merchants, which was also called the Mercurial College', but (p. 159) that 'While the Empire of *Rome* was in its Youth, the *Romans* finding themselves Masters of a great part of the known World, sought rather to extend their Dominions, than the Art and Exercise of Commerce'. Eratosthenes was, he says, far from deserving the reproaches given him by Strabo, who brings forward only 'very trifling Proofs', drawn from fables about Bacchus and Hercules etc., of the adventurous sea-voyages of the ancients, and 'we may certainly infer, that the Phenicians, who frequented those Seas by way of the *Red-Sea*, six or seven hundred Years before Alexander, did not lose Sight of Land in their Navigations'. He concedes, however, that by the time of Pliny the Elder the Romans were crossing the open seas to trade with the East Indies.

111 *Strabo*: Strabo, in his *Geography*, I.3.2, reproves Eratosthenes for saying that in ancient times no-one had the courage to sail on the Euxine sea, or along Libya, Syria or Cilicia. On the contrary, he says, 'the ancients will be shown to have made longer journeys, both by land and by sea, than have men of a later time, if we are to heed what tradition tell us'. Among other example he cites the voyages of the Phoenicians, 'who, a short time after the Trojan War, explored the regions beyond the Pillar of Hercules and founded cities both there and in the central parts of the Libyan sea-board'.

140 112 *Raleigh*: see his *History of the World* (1614), Book LVI, Chapter 1. Chatterton, p. 69, says: 'The theories of thirty or more banks of oars have now been pretty well dismissed'.

113 *Sesostris*: A legendary king of Egypt. According to Herodotus and Diodorus Siculus he conquered the whole world.

141 114 *Lucian*: The description of this enormous ship is to be found in Lucian's 'The Ship: or, The Wishes', in *The Works of Lucian of Samosata*, trans. H. W. Fowler & F. G. Fowler (Oxford, 1905), vol. 4, p. 35.

115 *formidable description*: Defoe may be referring to the account of Pompey's ships in Huet's *History* (see *ante*), pp. 156–7, though it is not clear why he calls it 'formidable', since Huet holds that these ships were 'chiefly serviceable for their Lightness and Agility'.

142 116 *the same Author*: presumably Huet.

117 *Alexander Magnus*: Alexander the Great.

316

page

142 118 *Bactrian Country*: Bactria was an ancient kingdom lying between the Hindu Kush and the river Oxus.

143 119 *Britain, where boisterous North Winds ... dread*: adapted by Defoe from his poem *Caledonia* (Edinburgh, 1706): see *Political and Economic Writings of Daniel Defoe*, 8 vols (London, 2000), vol. 4, ed. D. Hayton, p. 225.

144 120 *Sea Fight upon ... the River Lea*: The Danish fleet was destroyed by the Saxons in the river Lea in 895.

145 121 *Gothic Governments*: cf. Defoe's account of the 'Gothick Rules of Government' in *Jure Divino*, Book VIII.

147 122 *Scio*: now named Khios, an island off the coast from Izmir (Smyrna).

123 *Negropont*: the island of Euboea.

124 *Bajazet the Second*: The sultan Bayezid II (1447–1512) waged a successful war against the Venetians in 1499–1502.

148 125 *Anno 1457*: or rather, 1571.

149 126 *Teutonick Knights*: Defoe, in fact, later gives a lengthy historical account of them, on pp. 152–4.

151 127 *Anno 1222*: the Order was actually founded about 1191.

152 128 *Knights Templars*: a military order founded in 1118 to protect pilgrims to the Holy Land.

129 *Knights Hospitallers*: Knights of St John of Jerusalem, known also as Knights of Malta. They were founded in Jersualem *c.* 1070 for purposes similar to those of the Templars.

153 130 *Samaoides and Petzoran*: Samoyeds, a semi-nomadic people inhabiting the shores of the White Sea. By 'Petzoran' Defoe may conceivably be referring to Pechora, on the left bank of the Pechora river, which flows into the Barents Sea.

155 131 *Pot Ashes*: nowadays known as 'potash'.

132 *Train Oil*: oil obtained, by boiling, from the blubber of whales or seals.

158 133 *sell the Wooll away to Flanders*: The history of the English wool trade and the promotion of woollen manufacture by Henry VII was a favourite theme of Defoe's, and he gives similar accounts in *A General History of Trade* (1713), August issue; in *A Brief Deduction of the Original, Progress, and Immense Greatness of the British Woollen Manufacture* (1727); and in *A Plan of the English Commerce* (1728), chapter 3, though in the last he modifies his account of Henry VII, writing: '... and tho' he did once pretend to stop the Exportation of the Wool, he conniv'd at the Breach of his Order, and afterwards took off the Prohibition entirely, leaving the Success of his Undertaking, to the Industry of his People'. For a critique of Defoe's views see Peter Earle, *The World of Defoe* (1977), chapter 4.

134 *Sluice*: Sluys, a small town in Zeeland.

page

159 135 *Mr Rymer's Foedera*: the collection of treaties and other public documents published by Thomas Rymer in 1704–13.

160 136 *the Year 1338*: see the Statute of 1338, *De Lana capienda.*

161 137 *The Poor of every Nation are the same*: Defoe was fond of this trope, in various versions. It seems to derive from Dryden's 'For Priests of all Religions are the same' (*Absalom and Achitophel,* line 99).

138 *an Act pass'd in his Parliament*: i.e. the Statute of 3 Henry VII. cap. XI. It reinforces the Act of 7 Edward IV cap. III, restricting the export of wool, and says that, whereas woollen cloths 'have been, and yet daily are in great Number carried out of this Realm, unrowed and unshorn, into the Parts beyond the Sea ... whereby outlandish Nations, with the same Drapery, are set in Labour and Occupation, to their great inriching, and the poor Commons of the Crafts ... for lack of such Occupation daily fall in great Number into Idleness and Poverty, to their uttermost Destruction,' it is enacted that 'no Stranger nor Denizen carry, or make to be carried out of this Realm, any Woollen Cloths, but that they before be barbed, rowed, and shorn within the same Realm'.

164 139 *Gamaliel*: i.e. a learned and cultured man. See Acts 5: 34.

140 *Strabo and Plutarch*: Defoe seems to be getting into a muddle here. Strabo and Cicero, and Plutarch and Seneca, were roughly contemporaries; and it may be supposed that they all, to some extent, knew both Greek and Latin. The description of classical philosophy, again, takes no account of Plato and Aristotle.

141 *a late Poem*: perhaps an allusion to Dryden's remark in the Preface to *Sylvae* (1685): 'There are many who understand Greek and Latin, and yet are ignorant of their Mother Tongue'.

165 142 *the Chaldee*: more properly, Aramaic; though Chaldaean and Aramaic were closely allied.

143 HENCE *the Knowledge ... Judgment*: Defoe often returns to this theme, i.e. the over-rating of the classics as against other, often more useful, forms of knowledge. See for instance the *Review* for 16 December 1710.

166 144 *21000 Miles*: a considerable underestimate. The true rate of the earth's circulation round the sun is 1,577,280 miles a day.

145 *Copernicus this new wild Fiction ... round*: source untraced.

167 146 *Aristarchus*: the astronomer Aristarchus of Samos (born *c.* 320 BC).

147 *twenty seven Days*: The sun rotates on its own axis in roughly twenty-five and a half days, though it appears otherwise because the earth is circling the sun in the same direction.

148 *the third*: It is, of course, not strictly accurate to call the fixed angle of inclination of the earth's axis a 'motion'.

149 *Primum Mobile*: the supposed outermost sphere, added to the Ptolemaic system in the Middle Ages, and supposed to revolve round the earth

318

from east to west in 24 hours, carrying with it the (8 or 9) contained spheres.

168 150   *Tycho Brahe*: Danish astronomer (1546–1601). He attempted to reconcile the Copernican and the Ptolemaic systems.

151   *the Art of Printing*: Defoe is partly basing his account here, as in *An Essay upon Literature*, pp. 305–6, on Joseph Moxon's *Mechanick Exercises … applied to the Art of Printing*, vol. 2 (1683), but also draws on the article 'Printing' in vol. 2 of John Harris's *Lexicon Technicum* (1704), a popular technical encyclopaedia.

On the vexed question of where printing originated, it may be helpful to quote from *The Nature of the Book* (Chicago, 1998) by Adrian Johns (pp. 329–32).

> One potential orthodoxy had it that printing had been developed by a man named Johann Gutenberg, a goldsmith from the German town of Mainz. Helped by the capital of a local financier called Johann Fust, this Gutenberg was said to have perfected a process by 1455 at the latest. Then the two partners split up in acrimony. Their arguments generated a legal case, and with it a single document that happened to survive the centuries to testify to their collaboration. Fust and his son-in-law, Peter Schoeffer, then continued printing, but Gutenberg himself disappeared from the historical record…
>
> Mainz aside, probably the most significant of the many claimants was the Dutch town of Haarlem. Haarlem's rival to Gutenberg was one Laurens Janssen, better known as Coster. His story seems first to have been put forward by Adrien de Jonghe, rector and teacher of natural philosophy in the town's Latin school. Jonghe told in his patriotic history Batavia (1588) of an old man named Cornelius, who claimed to have been servant to the inventor of printing himself. Cornelius had described to Jonghe's erstwhile teacher how Coster had casually cut some letters from the bark of a beech tree and been stimulated by the stain they made in his handkerchief to make trials with reusable wooden type. Before long, he had been able to produce letters on one side of a piece of paper. Then, pasting several sheets together, Coster had proceeded to create small books. He was in operation in this way by 1440 at the latest, and probably twenty years earlier…
>
> He [Coster] has sworn his workmen to secrecy, but on Christmas Eve one of them escaped with enough knowledge and materials to set up a rival operation. … First to Amsterdam he went, and then … on to Mainz. There he set up his own workshop, announcing himself as the inventor of the new art. Mainz's

claim was thus the result of a notorious theft. And the name of this thief, Cornelius said, was Johann Faust.

The dispute between supporters of the Haarlem and of the Mainz theories continued through the seventeenth century and later, taking on an ideological character, and even now is not resolved.

168 152 *Koster*: Laurens Janszoon Coster, an innkeeper and perhaps a soldier. He is known to have been living in Haarlem 1436–83.

153 *Guttemburgh*: Johann Gutenberg (*c.* 1400–*c.* 1468). It does not seem that he was ever a servant of Coster.

154 *Ments*: Mainz.

155 *Faustus*: The popularity of the Dr Faustus story in the late sixteenth century led to his being identified with Gutenberg's associate Johann Fust. Defoe's account of him here is to be compared with the one in *An Essay upon Literature*, p. 306 and *The Political History of the Devil* (1726), pp. 378–9.

169 156 *within these two Years*: *The Life and Death of Doctor Faustus*, a farce by 'that celebrated comedian Mr Mountford,' was staged at Drury Lane during the winter of 1723–4. (See the *Post Boy* for 14–16 January 1724.)

157 *two Greeks*: according to *An Essay upon Literature*, p. 307, these were Anthony and Michael Galicion.

170 158 *EUCLID and his Elements*: Euclid's great textbook was entitled *Stoicheia* ('Elements'). During the Dark Ages his work was only known to the Arabs; it was not till the twelfth century that the Arabic version was translated into Latin.

159 *1428, or 1430*: Modern opinion would give a date later by some ten years to the earliest printing in Europe.

160 *Graving*: i.e. copper plate and steel engraving.

161 *Gunpowder*: There are in fact many references to the use of gunpowder as early as the first half of the fourteenth century.

162 *corning*: forming into grains.

171 163 *Monk, who made the Discovery*: The German monk Berthold Schwartz was traditionally credited with inventing gunpowder, in 1354; though some attributed it to Roger Bacon.

164 *Firelock*: a gun-lock in which sparks were produced to ignite the priming.

172 165 *Match*: a wick, cord, or rope of hemp, tow, cotton, etc. so prepared that when lighted it was not easily extinguished.

173 166 *Tormentarij*: *Tormentarius* (from *tormentum*, a gun) is medieval Latin for a gunner.

167 *cum multis alijs*: with many more.

174 168 *Solomon's fool*: see Proverbs 27: 22.

175 169 *Green-headed*: with the ignorance of youth.

page

176 170   *Hypecacuana*: i.e. ipecacuanha, the root of the shrub *Cephaelis ipecacuanha*, used as a purge and an emetic.

      171   *Cantharides*: name in pharmacopaeia for the dried beetle *Cantharides vesicatoria*, or Spanish fly.

      172   *the Bark*: Peruvian bark, the source of quinine.

177 173   *Sir Hugh Willoughby*: He was in 1553 appointed captain of the Bona Esperanza and captain-general of the fleet for a voyage to find a northeast passage to Cathay and India. He and his crew, parted from the rest of the fleet, attempted to winter in Lapland but perished there.

      174   *North Kyn*: North Cape.

      175   *Mr. Chancelor*: Captain Richard Chancellor of the Edward Bonaventure in the same expedition as Willoughby. He reached the White Sea and was taken to Moscow, where he was entertained by the emperor, his exploit thus leading to the founding of the Muscovy Company. An account of his voyage was printed by Richard Hakluyt.

178 176   *Verulams*: Francis Bacon was made Baron Verulam.

179 177   *Euxine Sea*: the Black Sea.

      178   *Palus Maotis*: the shallow sea of Azov, known in classical times as Lake Maeotis.

      179   *Straights of Cassa*: better known as the Straits of Kerch, joining the Sea of Azov to the Black Sea.

      180   *Taurica Chersonesus*: i.e. the Crimea.

      181   *Borysthenes*: the modern Dnieper.

180 182   *John King of Portugal*: John I (1357–1433).

      183   *John Gonzales and Tristrian Vaz*: Joao Goncalves Zarco and Tristao Vaz Teixeira. They were despatched on their expedition in 1714.

      184   *Don Henry*: Prince Henry the Navigator (1394–1460), fourth son of John I.

      185   *Anthony Nola*: Antonio de Noli (or Nola) (1419–66), Genoese navigator who made extensive explorations of the West Coast of Africa on behalf of Portugal.

      186   *Bartholomew Diaz*: Portugese navigator (*c.* 1455–1500), famous chiefly for his discovery of the Cape of Good Hope. Defoe's dates here and subsequently are evidently wrong. Diaz dicovered the Cape in 1486.

181 187   *Don Sebastian*: Sebastian (1554–78), king of Portugal. His second expedition against Morocco ended in his defeat and death at Al Kasral Kebir.

182 188   *Tammerins*: tamarinds.

183 189   *Mr. Towerson*: William Towerson made the first of his three voyages to Guinea in 1555. His journal is printed in Hakluyt.

      190   *Livery and Seisin*: Livery is the act of giving 'seisin', or possession.

185 191   *Vasco da Gama*: Portuguese navigator (1469–1524). In 1497 he was despatched with three vessels to attempt the rounding of the Cape.

page

186 192   *Lexicon Technicum*: John Harris, in his *Lexicon Technicum*, vol. 1, s.v. 'Magnet', writes: '*Sturmius* in his *Epistola Invitatoria Dat. Altorf.* 1682. Observes that the Attractive Quality of the *Magnet hath been taken notice* of beyond all History. But that it was our Countryman *Roger Bacon*, who first discovered the *Verticity* of it, or its Property of pointing towards the Pole'.

     193   *Year 1380*: Defoe presumably means 1280.

     194   *Roger Bacon*: English scientist and philosopher (*c.* 1214–92). He joined the Franciscans in 1257 and lectured for many years in Paris. He did much to advance experimental science.

     195   *an Italian of Gaeta*: not identified.

     196   *Mr. Boyl*: Defoe's account of Boyle's experiments with the magnet is taken verbatim from Harris's *Lexicon Technicum*.

189 197   *Oker*: ochre, a name given to the earthy pulverulent oxides of certain metals, such as antimony and chrome.

190 198   *Sebastian Cabot*: Genoese cartographer and explorer (1474–1557). He explored the coast of Brazil.

     199   *Variation of the Magnetism*: A compass needle points to the magnetic pole of the earth, which is not the same as the geographical one. This is known as the 'variation' of the compass, and it itself varies at different parts of the earth's surface.

192 200   *Carvels*: The carvel was a light and fast ship used by the Spanish and Portuguese.

193 201   *recovering their great Colon*y: The Portuguese recovered Brazil from the Dutch in 1661.

     202   *settled the Crown in the said House of Braganza*: In 1640 the Portuguese declared their independence of Spain and placed John, Duke of Braganza, on the throne.

195 203   *1586*: Defoe presumably means 1492.

     204   *upon the Tenters*: i.e. stretching it like cloth on tenters.

197 205   *the Congregation De propaganda fide*: the missionary society founded by Pope Gregory XV in 1622.

     206   *Lapis Contrayerva*: The *Pharmacopeia Bateana*, trans. and ed. William Salmon (London, 1694), p. 925, glosses *Lapis Contrayerva* as 'The Stone against Poyson'.

     207   *Snake Root*: the root or rhizome of several American plants, reputed to be an antidote to snake-poison.

     208   *Fustic*: the name for two kinds of wood used for dyeing yellow.

     209   *Brasiletto*: Jamaica-wood.

     210   *Teutenague*: In *Atlas Maritimus & Commercialis* (1728), p. 216, 'Tutenague' is defined as 'a Species of Tin, but soft as Lead, and blackish: not so bright as either Tin or Lead, but closer and firmer'.

     211   *Latin*: or Lateen.

page

201 212 *O'er all the liquid Mountains … Sea*: source not traced, though the phrase 'liquid mountains' was a favourite one with early eighteenth-century poets.

213 *Jaquez Velasco*: Diego de Velasquez de Cuellar (1465–*c*. 1522), Spanish explorer. He took part in Columbus's second voyage and in 1510, with a force of 300 men, took possession of Cuba for Spain.

214 *Sala*: Robert Cavelier de Lasalle (d. 1687), French explorer. Besides discovering the Ohio river, he was the first to follow the Mississipi from its upper course to its mouth.

215 *La Hontan*: Louis Armand de Lom d'Arce, Baron de Lahontan. Author of *Voyages … dans l'Amérique septentrionale* (2 vols, Amsterdam, 1705).

216 *La Barre*: not identified.

217 *Hennepin*: Louis Hennepin (b. *c.* 1640?), French missionary and explorer, author of *Voyage ou nouvelle decouverte d'un tres-grand pais dans l'Amerique* (Amsterdam, 1704).

218 *Heemskirk*: Jacob van Heemskerch (1567–1607), Dutch mariner. He served under Barents in their northern expedition and later commanded the entire United Provinces fleet.

219 *Barents*: Willem Barents (d. 1597), Dutch explorer of the northern seas.

220 *La Maire*: Jacques Joseph Le Maire, French explorer. In 1695, during his absence from France, a friend published his report on the Canary Islands and Senegal.

221 *Davis*: John Davis, English mariner (*c.* 1550–1605). He explored the arctic regions in search of a north-west passage.

222 *Smith*: John Smith (1580–1631), one of the founders of the colony of Virginia. Among his published writings is *A True Relation of Such Occurrences … of Note as hath passed in Virginia* (1608.) See also note 6 to *Essay*, p. 234.

223 *Sommers*: Sir George Somers (1554–1610), sailor, who took possession of the Bermudas for England.

202 224 *Tsalcallans*: i.e. Tlascalans.

206 225 *Neuhoff's Account of Brasil*: Jan Nieuhof, *Voyages and Travels into Brazil and the East Indies, translated from the Dutch* (1704).

207 226 *Texiera, Orelliana*: The first descent of the Amazon from the Andes to the sea was made by Francisco de Orellana (d. 1550), a Spanish explorer, in 1541, and the name 'Amazon' arises from a battle he had with a tribe of Tapuya in which the women fought alongside the men. The first ascent of the Amazon was made by Pedro Texiera, a Portuguese.

227 *Los Casas*: Bartolome de las Casas (1474–1566), known as 'the Apostle of the Indies'. He wrote an influential protest against the savage treatment of the Indians, *Brevissima Relacion de la Destruycion de las Indias* (Seville, 1552).

page
209 228 *Jesso*: the northernmost island of Japan, now known as Hokkaido.

     229 *Caisicks*: The more usual spelling is 'Caciques'.

     230 *Father Hennepin*: see above, note 217, p. 323.

     231 *De Salle*: René de la Salle (1640–87), French explorer of America.

     232 *Ferdinand Soto*: Hernandez de Soto (*c.* 1496–1542), Spanish explorer. He played a large part in the conquest of the Inca kingdom and subsequently made an abortive attempt to seize Florida, in pursuit of gold.

212 233 *black Cattle*: i.e. buffaloes.

214 234 S*ir* John *Narbrough*: Admiral (1640–88). His journal is printed in *An Account of Several Late Voyages and Discoveries to the South and North* (1694). See Introduction, p. 7.

An Essay Upon Literature (1726)

Advertised as published 'this day' in the *Post Boy* and *Evening Post* for 12–14 April 1726.

page
229 1 *Soldier ... Scholar*: see *ante*, p. 320, n. 163. The implication seems to be that Coster (see next note) was or had been a soldier, though he is also said to have been an innkeeper.

     2 *Lawrentius Costerus ... John Faustus*: see note 151 to *A General History of Discoveries*, p. 319 above.

230 3 *living records of a Thousand Years*: It was held that those who lived before the Flood lived to be a thousand and had memories in proportion.

     4 M*oses, the first Historian*: Moses was widely considered to have been the author of *Genesis*.

     5 *the first Writing*: That the Mosaic tablets were the first writing in the world is the theme of all the earlier pages of the present work. See Introduction, p. 2. Joel Reed, in an article 'Nationalism and Geoculture in Defoe's History of Writing', (*Modern Language Quarterly* 56: (1995), pp. 31–53, argues that Defoe's claim that the Mosaic tablets represent the origins of writing was an attempt to refute the deist John Toland, who found in non-European cultural history evidence that established religions were the debased descendants of an original natural religion – and indeed that Defoe's whole *Essay* is directed against Toland. But, since Toland is never mentioned in the *Essay*, this seems too speculative.

231 6 *Captain Smith*: John Smith (1580–1631), Governor of Virginia. See his *Works*, ed. Edward Arber (1884), vol. 2, pp. 397–8: 'In part of a Table booke he writ his minde to them at the Fort, what was intended, how they should follow that direction to affright the messengers, and without fayle send him such things as he writ for ... But when they came to

324

page

James towne, seeing men sally out as he had told them they would, they fled; yet in the night they came again to the same place where he had told them they should receive an answer, and such things as he had promised them: which they found accordingly, and with which they returned with no small expedition, to the wonder of them all that heard it, that he could either divine, or the paper could speake.' (Defoe mentions the story again in *Mere Nature Delineated* (1726), p. 80.)

233   7   *were in Tale*: i.e. had been counted.

234   8   *Isaiah, Ezekiel, Zephania*: see Isaiah 23, Ezekiel 27, Zephania 2.

235   9   *Achan*: see Joshua 7: 21.

   10   *built in the midst of the Sea*: see note 33 to *A General History of Discoveries*, p. 312, where this is said of Tyre.

   11   *South-sayers*: Defoe's alternative spelling of 'soothsayers', based on a fanciful derivation.

236   12   *Divisions of Notes*: The *OED* defines 'division' in music as the dividing of each of a succession of long notes into several short ones.

237   13   *Cadmus*: see note 43 to *A General History of Discoveries*, p. 312.

238   14   *the old Babel*: Jeremy Collier, in *An Appendix to the Three English Volumes in Folio of Morery*'s *Great Historical, Geographica, Genealogical and Poetical Dictionary* (1721), s.v. 'Babel', writes "Tis pretended the Ruins of this famous Tower are still to be seen about three quarters of a Mile from *Euphrates* to the East'.

   15   *Noah's drunkenness*: see note 4 to *A General History of Discoveries*, p. 309.

239   16   *young Canaan*: see note 4 to *A General History of Discoveries*, p. 309.

240   17   *Raleigh*: see Raleigh's *History of the World* (1614), Book 1, Chapter 6.

242   18   *The Year of the World 2515*: According to the standard chronology of Archbishop Ussher the world was created in 4004 BC.

   19   CADMUS: Pliny, in his *Natural History*, Book VII, 56, writes: 'I am of the opinion that the Assyrians have always had writing, but others, e.g. Gellius, hold that it was invented in Egypt by Mercury. while others think it was discovered in Syria: both schools of thought believe that Cadmus imported an alphabet of 16 letters into Greece from Phoenicia and that to these Palamedes at the time of the Trojan war added ... four characters, ... and after him Simonides the lyric poet added another four.'

243   20   *which the Israelites shou'd have destroy'd*: see Joshua 17: 18.

244   21   *Prometheus*: see *post*, note 23, p. 326, and compare the more elaborate rationalising account of Prometheus in *A General History of Discoveries*, pp. 79–80.

   22   *St. Augustine*: Augustine, in Book XVIII, Chapter 8 of *The City of God*, writes: 'In the aforesaid king's time [that of the Assyrian king Saphrus] Prometheus (as some hold) lived, who was said to make men of earth, because he taught them wisdom so excellently well.' He goes on to

page

speak of Atlas, Prometheus's brother, in a similar Euhemeristic vein, saying that he is said to have been a great astronomer, 'whence the fable arose of his supporting heaven upon his shoulders; yet there is a huge mountain of that name, whose height may seem to an ignorant eye to hold up the heavens'.

244 23 *Theophrastus*: The Greek writer Theophrastus (*c.* 370–*c.* 287 BC) explained the fire that Prometheus was supposed to have stolen from heaven on man's behalf as symbolising philosophy. (Pauly, *Realencyclopaedie der classischen Altertumswissenschaft*, s.v. 'Prometheus'.)

245 24 *Dr. Goodwin*: Thomas Godwyn (or Godwin) writes in his *Moses and Aaron. Civil and Ecclesiastical Rites, used by the Ancient Hebrews* (London, 1625), p. 304: 'Some say *Cadmus* brought the use of letters into *Greece*; others say, *Palamedes*: some say *Rhadamantus* brought them into *Assyria*: *Memnon* into *Egypt*: *Hercules* into *Phrygia*: and *Carmenta* into *Latinum*. Likewise some say the *Phenicians* had *first* the knowledge and use of letters. ... Others say the *Ethiopians*: others the *Assyrians*. But upon better grounds, it is thought, that *Moses first taught the use of letters to the Jewes*, and that the *Phenicians* learned then from the *Jewes*, and the *Grecians* from the *Phenicians*.'

25 *Palamedes*: son of Nauplius, king of Euboea, a figure in the post-Homeric legends about the Trojan war. He came to be regarded as the inventor of the alphabet and of weights and measures. The grammarian Marius Servius (early 5th century AD), in his commentary on the *Aeneid*, Book 2, asserts that it was Palamedes who introduced letters into Greece.

26 *Memnon*; According to Greek myth, Memnon was the beautiful son of Tithonus and Eos (Dawn). He is usually identified with the king of the Ethiopians, who fought on the Trojan side in the Trojan war and was killed by Achilles, but immortalised. Defoe, however, evidently regards these as two separate figures.

27 *Prolation*: Defoe's use of the word 'prolation' (utterance) is somewhat idiosyncratic.

246 28 *Sir Walter Raleigh observes*: Raleigh's *History of the World* (1614), exact reference untraced.

247 29 *Raleigh's Account*: see Raleigh's *History the World* (1614), Book 1, Chapter 7, 5.

248 30 *Josephus*: Flavius Josephus, Jewish historian (AD 37 – after 93).

249 31 *him that invented musical Instruments*: Jubal. See Genesis 4: 21.

250 32 *The word Mazzaroth*: see Job 38: 32.

251 33 *Lud. Vives*: Juan Luis Vives (1492–1540), Spanish scholar. His commentary on St Augustine's *City of God* was first published in 1522 in an edition of that work. Defoe's source-reference, probably taken from Theophilus Gale, is correct.

page

251 34 *Dr. Gale*: see Theophilus Gale, *The Court of the Gentiles; or, a discourse touching the original of human literature, both philologic and philosophic, from the Scriptures and Jewish Churches.* (1669–77), Part I, p. 67.

35 *THEUTCH*: In the *Phaedrus* Socrates recounts the legend of Theuth (or Thoth) telling the king of Egypt of his new invention, writing, and being begged by the king to suppress it, as liable to destroy memory.

36 *Monsieur Du Pin*: Louis Ellies Dupin, French ecclesiastical historian. In his *Dissertation préliminaire ou prologomenes sur la Bible* (Paris, 1699), vol. 1, p. 426, he writes [my translation]: 'The most common opinion among the Pagans as to the origin of Letters is that the Phoenicians were the inventor of them, and that Cadmus brought the discovery to Greece. Eupolemus makes Moses their inventor, and his view is approved by Eusebius in the ninth Book of his *Evangelical Preparation*, chapter 4, and by Isidore of Seville. It is nevertheless certain that the art of writing is more ancient than Moses, and he himself mentions things written before his day. Suidas believes that Abraham is the first author of Letters, as well as of the Hebrew tongue; but he also is mistaken: for the Assyrians or Chaldeans among whom he lived had their own language, which Abraham spoke, and it seems they also had an alphabet.' Dupin also compiled the *Nouvelle bibliothèque des auteurs ecclésiastiques*, 58 vols (Paris, 1686–1704), a voluminous edition of the writings of the Fathers (referred to by Defoe on p. 253 under the Latin title *Biblioteca Patrum*).

252 37 *Trismegistus*: Hermes Trismegistus (identified by the ancient Greeks with the Egyptian deity Thoth), the legendary author of the collection of writings known as the Hermetic Books.

253 38 *Pæmander ... Asclepius*: dialogues belonging to the *Corpus Hermeticum* (see previous note). A Latin translation of the *Asclepius* was preserved among the works of Apuleius.

39 *(a) By St. Clement in lib. i Aromat*: 'Aromat' is probably in error for *Stromateis*, a work by St Clement of Alexandria in which he attempted to show that the Jewish scriptures were older than any writings of the Greeks.

40 *Tract de 5 Hæres ... Dei*: Augustine wrote a tract *De Heraesibus Quodvult Deum* in 428. Book 8, Chapter 23 of his *City of God* quotes from the dispute between Asclepius and Trismegistus about the power of God.

41 *Cyril of Alexandria*: St Cyril, Patriarch of Alexandria (d. 444). He wrote an *Apology against Julian the Apostate*.

42 *St. Justin*: St. Justin Martyr (*c.* 100–*c.* 165), early Christian apologist.

43 *Lanctantius*: Lactantius, Christian convert and apologist (*c.* 240–*c.* 320), appointed by the Emperor as tutor to his son. His *Divinae Institutiones* (304–11) sought to commend the truth of Christianity to men of letters.

page

254 44 *Hepburn*: James Hepburn (1573–1620), a Scottish linguist, joined the Order of St Francis of Paola, taking the name in religion of 'Bonaventura'. He travelled widely and was credited with being able to speak to the people of every nation in their own tongue. He was for six years keeper of the oriental books and manuscripts in the Vatican library. A large print, known as 'The Golden Virgin' designed by him and engraved in Rome in 1616 depicts the Madonna and beneath her seven columns, in which, in Latin and Hebrew, he explains his design of praising the Virgin in seventy-two languages.

255 45 *Enoch*: A Book of Enoch, probably written between 200 BC and 64 BC, circulated in the early church and was often quoted by the Fathers, though by the time of the Renaissance it had disappeared, not being rediscovered till the eighteenth century. It was from the pillars described there that Abraham supposedly learned astronomy and the sciences.

      46 *Mr. Pool*: Matthew Poole, author of *Annotations upon the Holy Bible*. Defoe is referring to a continuation of Poole's work '*by certain judicious and learned divines*', published in 1696.

256 47 *Josephus*: slightly adapted from *The Works of Flavius Josephus, translated into English by Sir Roger L'Estrange* (1702), chapter 3 (not 2), page 6.

257 48 *the learned Burnet*: Thomas Burnet, in *The Theory of the Earth* (1684), Book I, chapter 6, p. 68, gives the first announcement of his theory in the following words: '*Moses* saith, the *great Abysse* was broken open at the Deluge. Let us then suppose that at a time appointed by Divine Providence, and from causes made ready to do that great execution upon a sinful World, that this *Abysse* was open'd, or that the frame of the Earth brake and fell down into the *Great Abysse*'.

      49 *name the Rivers*: see Genesis 2: 11–14.

258 50 *the learn'd Bugi*: 'Bugi' is in error for 'Bang': see Introduction, p. 13.

      51 *Angelus Roccha*: Angelo Rocca (1545–1620), Italian scholar. He was put in charge of Vatican publishing by Pope Sixtus V in 1585 and later became Bishop of Tagaste. The Latin in Defoe's note means: 'In his commentary in the Apostolic Library of the Vatican which he published in Rome in the year 1591'.

      52 *Claudius Durretius*: Claude Duret, author of a history of languages entitled *Tresor de l'histoire des langues de cet univers, contenant les origines, beautés, perfections, décadences, mutations, changements, conversions et ruines des langues Hebraiques, Chananéenne, Samaritaine, Chaldaiques*, etc. (Cologne, 1613).

      53 *Theseus Ambrosius*: Theseus Ambrosius Albonensis, author of *Introduction in Chaldaicam linguam, Syriacam, atque Armenicam, et decem alias linguas. Characterum differentium alphabeta … Mystica et cabalistica quam plurima scitu digna*. [Introduction to the Chaldean, Syrian and Armenian lan-

guages. Alphabet of the different characters. ... The mystic and cabbalistic knowledge most worthy to be known.] (Papiae, 1539.)

258 54 *Hepburnus*: see note 44, p. 328.

264 55 *Laurentius Schrader*: author of *Monumentorum Italiae, quae hoc nostro sae-culo et a Christianis posita sunt, libri quatuor* (Halberstadt, 1592).

265 56 *into the hands of Vulcan*: i.e. burnt.

266 57 *Book of Jezira*: the *Sefer Yetsira*, a mystical work, probably belonging to the 3rd century AD, which later became one of the central texts of the Kabbalah.

267 58 *Josephus*: see *ante*, note 47, p. 328.

59 *Tzetzes Chiliad*: Joannes Tzetzes was a Byzantine grammarian who flourished at Constantinople in the 13th century AD. His verse *Book of Histories*, usually known as *Chiliades* because its first editor arbitrarily divided it into books of 1000 lines, is a literary, historical, theological and antiquarian miscellany.

60 *Noachian characteres:* cf. Defoe's *The Political History of the Devil* (1726), p. 161, where he says that he considers the *alphabetum Noachi* to be a 'modern invention'.

268 61 *Delrius Disq. Magic.*: The *Disquisitionum magicarum libri sex* of Martinus Antonius del Rio (3 vols, Louvain, 1599/1600).

271 62 *Liber*: cf. Sir John Clerk's *De stylis veterum* (see below, note 66). 'Igitur Isidorus, lib. 6. orig. cap. 14. *Liber est, interior tunica corticis, quae ligno adhaerat, in qua antiqui scribebant.* ... unde & *liber* dicitur in quo scribimus.' [Therefore Isidorus writes in Book 6, chapter 14: 'Liber is the inner coating of tree-bark, with which the ancients used to write. ... hence the name 'liber' [book] for what we write in.']

63 *Caudex*: '*Codex*' or '*caudex*' is Latin for the trunk of a tree.

272 64 *My Author*: Defoe may be referring to Sir John Clerk (see note 66 below), though he is not quoting from him verbatim.

65 *Ptolemy Philadelphus*: Egyptian monarch, born 308 BC.

274 66 *Mr. Clark of Pennycook*: Sir John Clerk of Penicuik, son-in-law to the Duke of Queensberry and a friend of Defoe's. (See Paula R. Backscheider, *Defoe: His Life* (1989), pp. 208–9.) He was the author of a treatise on the stylus and on writing materials generally, *Dissertatio de stylis veterum, et diversis chartarum generibus.* It seems to have been first published in 1731, thus Defoe was presumably reading it in manuscript.

67 *Saxis tantum Volucresq ... linguas*: 'These Phoenicians first made bold, if report speak true, to record speech in rude characters for future ages, before Egypt had learned to fasten together the reeds of her river, and when only the figures of birds, beasts, and other animals, carved in stone, preserved the utterances of her wise men.' Lucan, *Pharsalia*, Book III, lines 222 *et seq.*

page

274   68   *Notae*: Defoe's discussion of the use of *Notae* or 'marks' (i.e. symbols and abbreviations) among the ancients, is based closely on *Aristarchus sive De Arte Grammatica Libri Septem* by Vossius (the Dutch classical scholar G.J. Voss, 1577–1649), a work first published in 1635.

275   69   *Tyro*: Tullius Tyro was the 'libertus' or freed man of Cicero. (A few lines later, Defoe has mistaken the word 'libertus' for a proper name.) The *Encyclopaedia Britannica*, 11th edn, explains: 'According to Suetonius the first introduction of shorthand signs or *notae* was due to Ennius; but more generally Cicero's freedman M. Tullius Tyro is regarded as the author of these symbols, which commonly bear the title of *Notae Tironianae*. The Tironian notes belonged to a system which was actually tachygraphic; that is, each word was represented by a character, alphabetic in origin, but having an ideographic value.'

        70   *Eo est*: Defoe has misread Vossius, who writes (Book I, p. 140): 'At apud Tyronem et Senecam pro eo videas ~~~', ('And in Tyro and Seneca you will find the symbol ~~~ for it [i.e. for *Senatus Populusque Romanus*]').

        71   *ENNIUS*: Quintus Ennius (239–169 BC), Latin epic poet.

        72   *Eusebius*: Eusebius Pamphili, Greek theologian (*c.* 260–*c.* 340 AD), author of an *Ecclesiastical History*.

        73   *Petrus Diaconus*: 'Now let us set down who first instituted *Notae*. Ennius was the first to introduce common 'Notes', of which he invented twelve hundred; his purpose being, clearly, that whatever might be said during a discussion could be written down by a group of scribes working together, dividing the words between them and putting them in the right order. Hence Tullius Tyro, Cicero's 'freed man', devised 'notes' for prepositions. After this, Philargyrus Samius and Aquila and other freedmen of Maecenas added further Notes. Eventually Lucius Annaeus Seneca extended them to five thousand.' There are one or two minor errors in Defoe's transcription: 'mille ducentum' for 'mille & centum', 'liberarii' for 'librarii', and 'quaes' for 'quot'. The full text of Petrus Diaconus's 'proloquium' to Conrad I on the subject of 'Notae', from which Defoe is quoting, is to be found in the *Grammaticae Latina* of Helias Putschius (Hanover, 1605), pp. 1579–1638. Petrus explains that Rudolf, the imperial Chancellor, has urged him to restore the 'Book of Notes', which has become almost incomprehensible and to dedicate the work to the Emperor. (The latter (*c.* 990–1039) is normally known as Conrad II but chose to refer to himself as Conrad I since he was the first Conrad to be elected Emperor.)

276   74   *Nicholaus Trigaultius*: Nicolas Trigault (or Trigaultius), author of *De Christiana expeditione apud Sinas* (1615), an account of Jesuit activity in China.

page
276   75   *Paciano Barcellonensi*: Paciano Barcilonensis, in his *Epistle* 2, says that, according to Epiphanius and Augustine, after the confusion of tongues at Babel there were 72 different languages in the world – a figure derived from the number of the descendants of Noah mentioned in the genealogies of the tenth chapter of Genesis.

       76   *Eusebius's Opinion*: 'lxxxii', as we see from Chapter 41 of Vossius, is a slip for 'lxxii'.

277   77   *Kenites*: an obscure Semitic clan which belonged to the south of Palestine. The name is possibly connected with 'Cain'.

278   78   *Pegu*: a place in the south of modern Burma, once the centre of a considerable kingdom.

279   79   *from the left Hand to the right*: see *A General History of Discoveries*, p. 81, where Defoe similarly asserts that Cadmus's alphabet was intended to be written from left to right.

281   80   *Secta nisi ... tabellas*: Martial's couplet (*Epigrams*, Book XIV, 3) runs: 'Secta nisi essemus ligna tabellas,/Essemus Libyci nobile dentus onus'. (If we had not been cut into thin tablets, we should be the noble burden of a Libyan tusk.)

282   81   *Olaus Wormius*: Olao Worm (Olaus Wormius) writes in *Fasto Danici* (1643 edn), p. 23: 'Ac primo quidem patriis notis, Runicis videlicet, sive in fagis, unde etiamnum apud nos Libri *Boger* dicuntur'. [And truly in traditional Notae or in Runes, or in beechwood, for which reason books are among us still called *Boger*.]

       82   *Faniering*: possibly veneering.

283   83   *Pliny*: see Pliny's *Natural History*, Book 13, Chapter 21.

       84   *Symmachus*: Vossius, in his Chapter 38, quotes the fourth-century author Quintus Symmachus, *Epistles*, Book IV, 34: 'Monitus Cumanos lintea texta sumserunt'. (The prophecies of the Cumaean sibyl can be read in linen books.)

       85   *Tit. Livius*: Vossius quotes Livy: 'Foedera publica sic exarabant' ('They wrote their public treaties in this fashion'). Much of the information on pp. 282–4 of Defoe's text is taken from Chapter 38 of Vossius.

       86   *Flav. Vopiscus in Aureliano*: the Life of Aurelian, one of the several lives of Roman emperors supposedly contributed by Flavius Vopiscus to the *Augustan History*, a work compiled in the 4th century AD. It reads: *Inveni nuper in Ulpia bibliotheca, inter lineos libros, epistolam D. Valeriani* (I recently discovered in the Ulpian Library, among linen books, the letter of D. Valerianus).

       87   *Josephus*: In L'Estrange's *Josephus* (see *ante*, note 47, p. 328), p. 323, we read that the agents of the Jewish high-priest Elazar brought to King Ptolemy of Egypt 'Certain *Manuscripts of the Jewish Laws* Written upon *Parchment* in Golden Letters ... the leaves were so artifically put together, that there was no Discerning where One Skin joyn'd to another'.

page

283   88   *Varro*: see Pliny, *Natural History*, XIII, 11: '... hanc Alexandri Magni victoria reperatum auctor est M. Varro, condita in Aegyto Alexandria'. (M. Varro writes that this [i.e. paper] was discovered with the victory of Alexander, when Alexandria was founded in Egypt.)

284   89   *Sepia lympha ... guttas*: 'When water is poured in, the blackness disappears, and the tube sprinkles the diluted stuff in blots upon the paper'. (Persius, *Satires*, III, lines 13–14.)

        90   *Dr. Leigh*: Charles Leigh, *The Natural History of Lancashire, Cheshire, and the Peak, in Derbyshire* (1700), Part 1, pp. 132–3.

        91   *Nigro distillans Sepia nodo*: Sepia exuding a circle of black.

285   92   *Racing*: To 'race' (a variant of 'raze') here means to cut or tear.

        93   *Tilia*: the inner bark of the lime-tree.

        94   *Gracchis*: In Plutarch's *Life* of Caius Gracchus we read that on the day when Opimius, as consul, was proceeding to abrogate laws passed by Gracchus, there was a scuffle between their followers, and Quintus Antyllius told Gracchus's friend Fulvius to get out of his way. 'Upon this he was presently killed with the strong stiles which are commonly used in writing'. (*The Dryden Plutarch*, revised by Arthur Hugh Clough, 1910, vol. 3, p. 154.)

        95   *Hac tibi erant ... erit*: Martial, *Epigrams,* Book XIV, epigram 21: 'These stylus-cases furnished with their own steel styluses are for you. If you give one of them to your boy, it will be no trifling present'.

286   96   *Plut. in Appianum*: Defoe has misread Vossius, who writes *Sic Cascae, ut apud Plutarchum est & Appianum*, i.e. Thus Casca's, as it is in Plutarch and Appian.

        97   *Cassi Brachium ... Jul. Cæs. 82*: 'Caesar grasped Cassius's [properly Casca's] arm and ran it through with his stylus'. (Suetonius, in 'Julius Caesar' in his *The Twelve Caesars*.)

        98   *Tilea*: It is not clear what Defoe is meaning by 'tilea'.

        99   *Job*: see Job 19: 23–4.

287 100   *Zacharias*: see Luke 1: 63.

      101   *Lawrence Coster*: see *ante*, above, note 115, p. 316.

      102   *Tully's Offices*: Cicero's *De Officiis*. Moxon, in his *Mechanick Exercises* (see *post*, note 119), says: 'The Book which is commonly reputed to have been first Printed, is *Tullies Offices*, ... which in the close of it is said to be printed at *Mentz*, in the year of our Lord 1465 (so says that Copy in the *Bodleyan* Library) or 1466 (so that in the Library of *Corpus Christi*).' There was also an undated edition of this work by the Cologne printer Ulric Zell, roughly at the same time.

288 103   *written over*: i.e. copied again.

292 104   *Apertus and Opertus*: Vossius (chapter 40) says: *Tertia superest divisio ex scribendi modis; quatenus unus est apertus ac vulgaris, alter opertus sive occultus.* ('There is also a third division among methods of writing: of which

one is open and for all to see, and the other is concealed or occult.') This and the two following pages in Defoe's text are closely based on Chapter 40 of Vossius.

293 105 *Tithymalus*: Pliny, in Book 26, chapter 39 of his *Natural History,* writes: The tithymalos is called by our people the 'milk plant' and by some persons the 'goat lettuce'. They say, that if characters are traced upon the body with the milky juice of this plant, and powdered with ashes, when dry, the letters will be perfectly visible, an expedient which has been adopted before now by intriguers, for the purpose of communicating with their mistresses, in preference to a correspondence by letter'. (*The Natural History of Pliny*, ed. J. Bostock & H. T. Riley, 6 vols. (London, 1855), vol. 5, p. 177.)

106 *Apud Jo. Baptistam ... Mag. Nat*: Chapter XII, pp. 62–4, of the *Magiae naturalis sive de miraculis rerum naturalium libri* (Naples, 1589), by Giovanni Baptista Porta (first published in a shorter version in 1558) is devoted to various kinds of invisible writing.

297 107 *amuse*: i.e. deceive.

108 *The Pen of a ready Writer*: Psalms 45: 1.

298 109 *Trithemius*: Johann Trithemius (1462–1516), German historian and divine, abbot of Spanheim. He was the author of *Polygraphia* (1518) and of *Steganographia: hoc est Ars per occultam scripturam animi sui voluntatem absentibus aperiendi certa* (posthumously printed in Frankfurt, 1606). His *Steganographia*, the first systematic work on cyphering, was suspected of necromancy but found a number of defenders. It was highly esteemed by John Dee, who interested Queen Elizabeth in it.

299 110 *Duke of Lunenburgh*: Augustus, duke of Brunswick-Luneburg (1579–1666) wrote, under the pseudonym Gustave Selenus, a defence of Trithemius entitled *Cryptomenityces et planissima stenographia a Jos. Trithemio magice et aenigmatice conscriptae enodatio traditur* (Luneburg, 1624).

111 *Caramuel*: Juan Caramuel Lobkowitz (1606–82), author of *Steganographie nec non Claviculae Salomonis germani Trithemii ... genuina, facilis dilucidoque declaratio* (Cologne, 1635).

112 Gaspar Schottus: Gaspar Schott (1608–1666), Jesuit, author of *Schola steganographia* (Nuremberg, 1665).

113 *Wolfgangus Ernestus Heidelius*: Wolfgang Ernest Heidel (*fl.* 1676–1721), author of *J. Trithemii ... Steganographia ... vindicata* (Nuremberg, 1721).

114 *Baillet*: Adrien Baillet gives an account of Trithemius's defenders in his *Jugements des scavans sur les principaux ouvrages des auteurs*, 4 vols (Paris, 1685–6), vol. 3, p. 24.

302 115 *Dædalus and Icarus*: see note 44 to *A General History of Discoveries*, p. 312.

116 *burning of the Library*: The Alexandrian library was burnt in 47 BC.

page

302 117 *one Copy of God's law*: The story of the finding of the copy is related in 2 Kings, 22.

303 118 *Quintus Curtius's Abridgement*s: Quintus Curtius Rufus wrote in the first century AD a history of Alexander the Great in ten books, of which the first two are lost.

305 119 *Coster*: The passage about Coster and Gutenberg is adapted from Joseph Moxon's *Mechanick Exercises … Applied to the Art of Printing*, vol. 2 (1683), p. 4, as are Defoe's next five paragraphs, in places verbatim. For further details on the origins of printing see note 151 to *A General History of Discoveries*, p. 319.

      120 *Rabbi Joseph*: Joseph b. Meir ha-Kohen, author of *Dibre ha-Yamin le-Malke Zarfat w.Otoman* (1554).

      121 *Scriverius*: Peter Schrijver (1576–1660), Dutch classical scholar and historian.

306 122 *Ruffinus*: Tyrannius Rufinus, of Aquileia. He produced, *c.* 1473, a Latin translation of the *Ecclesiastical History* of Eusebius, adding two books to it.

      123 *Moxon*: Moxon writes, p. 10: '… we have scarce any copies of Books there Printed remaining (that I have ever seen) earlier than the year 1480'.

      124 *Bennet's College*: This was for some time an alternative name for Corpus Christi College.

      125 *Faustus*: There is a more elaborate version of this story about Faustus in *A General History of Discoveries*, pp. 168–9.

307 126 *Hegira*: The era beginning with the flight of Mohammed from Mecca to Medina in 622 AD.

      127 *Rolling Press*: A copper-plate printer's press in which the plate passes in a bed under a revolving cylinder. It was invented in 1545.

      128 *Lipsius*: Justus Lipsius (1547–1606), Belgian classical scholar.

      129 *printed Book in the Bodleian Library*: Mr. Geoffrey Groom of the Bodleian Library writes that the Wurzburg Missal referred to by Defoe is still in the Bodleian, now shelf-marked *Auct. 1 Q 1. 7*. 'The volume had come into the Library with the Laud manuscripts in the 1630s and had been treated as a manuscript, having at one stage been shelfmarked *MS.Laud D.138* (*not*, page 138), before becoming *MS.Laud misc. 301*, and then *Auct 1 Q 1.7*.' This copy in fact lacks the first ten leaves.

      130 *Mr. Bagford*: John Bagford (1650–1715), compiler of the *Bagford Ballads* and of some *Proposals for printing an Historical Account … of Typography* (1707).

308 132 *a Work by itself*: It does not appear that Defoe ever wrote such a work.

TEXTUAL NOTES

The textual policy for *Writings on Travel, Discovery and History by Daniel Defoe* is described in the General Editors' Preface printed in Volume 1, pp. 3–4. Bibliographical details of each work will be found in P. N. Furbank and W. R. Owens, *A Critical Bibliography of Daniel Defoe* (London: Pickering & Chatto, 1998), referred to as 'F&O' below. The numbers in the left-hand column refer to the Pickering & Chatto page numbers.

A General History of Discoveries and Improvements (1725–6)

The copy-text is the first edition, issued in four parts between October 1725 and May 1726 but paginated continuously (F&O, 225(P)).

60a   V] IV
85a   was not] was

An Essay upon Literature (1726)

The copy-text is the first edition of 1726 (F&O 227), the only one published. For the convenience of readers, I have provided my own translation of the long Latin quotation from Thomas Bang (pp. 263–8).

251a   Augustine's] Augustus's
252a   xxiv] xiv
255a   1656] 1576
287a   Copies] Copiers
303a   and who were] and who, and who were
307a   *Durer*] *Purer*

INDEX

Writings by Defoe appear directly under title; works by others appear under author's name. 'DD' indicates Defoe.

Spellings of proper names are generally modernised, with cross-references where needed.

Index prepared by Douglas Matthews.